Art and Copyright Law

This book tackles the lack of synchronicity between art and copyright law, proposing practical and interdisciplinary tools through which to navigate this conflict.

In the past decades, high profile lawsuits have been filed against artists accused of plagiarism, including Jeff Koons, Barbara Kruger and Andy Warhol. This book demonstrates how these cases are at odds with contemporary artistic reality, in which the use of antecedent visual forms is common practice. Focusing on the dichotomies of "original/copy" and of "old/new", this work addresses this phenomenon from both theoretical and legal perspectives. Using Swiss copyright law as the main case study, the book comparatively assesses other international legal frameworks. Through understanding the origins of the conflict between art and copyright, the book highlights solutions to handle copyright cases with a new methodological approach.

The book will be of interest to researchers in the field of art and copyright law, intellectual property and art.

Giulia Walter is a lawyer based in Zurich, Switzerland. She studied law at the universities of Lucerne, Geneva and Vienna and obtained a PhD at the University of Zurich. Specializing in art law and intellectual property law, she strives to adopt an interdisciplinary approach bridging between the disciplines of law, (legal) sociology and art theory. In her work, she has, in particular, engaged with Niklas Luhmann's systems theory, which allows an accurate description of the interactions of different autonomous social systems (such as art and law) by preserving their differences and analyzing their reciprocal expectations.

Intellectual Property, Theory, Culture
Series Editor: Johanna Gibson, Herchel Smith Professor of Intellectual Property Law, Queen Mary University of London, UK

This series presents theoretical and cultural examinations of intellectual property laws, developments, and policy. Volumes in the series may be identified by their innovative and critical analyses and their original contributions to international debate. Interdisciplinary in approach, the series will be of interest to intellectual property experts and stakeholders, policy advisors, and NGOs, as well as students and researchers in the very critical areas of intellectual property law, anthropology, and cultural studies.

Also in the series:

Patenting Lives
Life Patents, Culture and Development
Edited by Johanna Gibson
ISBN 978-0-7546-7104-6

Disrupting Copyright
How Disruptive Innovations and Social Norms are Challenging IP Law
Margery Hilko
ISBN 978-0-367-35497-8

Art and Copyright Law
An Interdisciplinary Study on Interpictoriality
Giulia Walter
ISBN 978-1-032-97448-4

https://www.routledge.com/Intellectual-Property-Theory-Culture/book-series/IPTC

Art and Copyright Law

An Interdisciplinary Study on Interpictoriality

Giulia Walter

Routledge
Taylor & Francis Group
LONDON AND NEW YORK

First published 2025
by Routledge
4 Park Square, Milton Park, Abingdon, Oxon OX14 4RN

and by Routledge
605 Third Avenue, New York, NY 10158

Routledge is an imprint of the Taylor & Francis Group, an informa business

Published with the support of the Swiss National Science Foundation

British Library Cataloguing-in-Publication Data
A catalogue record for this book is available from the British Library

ISBN: 978-1-032-97448-4 (hbk)
ISBN: 978-1-032-98412-4 (pbk)
ISBN: 978-1-003-59850-3 (ebk)

DOI: 10.4324/9781003598503

Typeset in Times New Roman
by Deanta Global Publishing Services, Chennai, India

Per Elsa

Contents

Acknowledgments

The project of this thesis has brewed slowly during my law studies. Its kick-start, as often happens in life, was pure coincidence and a venture.

I was lucky to find, at the University of Zurich, in general, and at the Chair of Legal Sociology of Prof. Dr. Christoph B. Graber, in particular, a great academic home. Prof. Graber has been a great supervisor and mentor. He accompanied my endeavor with his kind and enthusiastic ways and offered the best possible conditions in which to write serenely. His own doctoral thesis "*Zwischen Geist und Geld. Interferenzen von Kunst und Wirtschaft aus rechtlicher Sicht*" (Baden-Baden 1994) opened my eyes on the importance of an interdisciplinary approach in legal research. Our project "*Art irritates Law, Law irritates Art*", initiated together with Prof. Roger Fayet, was an everlasting source of inspiration. For all the above, his scientific guidance, humanity and trust, I am deeply grateful. I also thank Prof. Dr. Dan Wielsch. His "*Zugangsregeln*" (Tübingen 2008) has been pivotal to this research. I have learned immensely from how he has been able to link systems theory with technical legal knowledge. Naturally, I was beyond happy when he accepted to prepare the second review of this thesis.

Crossing the finish line of this doctoral thesis would have been impossible without the presence of the following people in my life.

I thank Asst. Prof. Filippo Contarini, PhD (University of Lausanne) for the countless hours spent talking about systems theory. His infectious passion for scientific research has been a beacon, and with him, I felt less alone. I am also grateful for our side projects (which came to light in the form of articles and conferences). These filled my tanks up at critical moments, giving me the energy to continue with renewed motivation.

My dear brother and friends have been a wonderful network of encouragement, distraction and joy all along. I am sure you know who you are, but I will make sure to tell you how grateful I am to have you in my life.

Lastly, I thank my parents for teaching me a *way of being in the world*, yet trusting me to choose my own path as well as for the unconditional support they have always given me.

Zurich, September 2024

Abbreviations

AG	Advocate General at the CJEU
AJP	Aktuelle Juristische Praxis
Art.	article
AVMSD	Directive 2010/13/EU of the European Parliament and of the Council of 10 March 2010 on the coordination of certain provisions laid down by law, regulation or administrative action in Member States concerning the provision of audio-visual media services (Audiovisual Media Services Directive)
BBl	Bundesblatt (Federal Gazette)
BJM	Basler Juristische Mitteilungen
c.	consideration
CC	Swiss Civil Code of 10 December 1907, SR 210
cf.	confront
Ch.	chapter
Cir.	Circuit
CJEU	Court of Justice of the European Union
CopA	Federal Act on Copyright and Related Rights of 9 October 1992, SR 231.1
cit.	cited as
CMO	Copyright Management Organization
Const.	Federal Constitution of the Swiss Confederation of 18 April 1999, SR 101
CoRo	Commentaire Romand
DE-CopA	German Copyright Act
DFC	Decision of the Swiss Federal Supreme Court
DSM-Directive	Directive (EU) 2019/790 of the European Parliament and of the Council of 17 April 2019 on Copyright and Related Rights in the Digital Single Market and amending Directives 96/9/EC and 2001/29/EC
ECHR	European Convention on Human Rights
ECommHR	European Commission of Human Rights
ECtHR	European Court of Human Rights
Ed.	edition

ed./eds.	edited by
e.g.	*exempli gratia*
et seq./et seqq.	and the following (page(s), paragraph(s), etc.)
EU	European Union
fn.	footnote
Found.	Foundation
F.Supp.2d	Federal Supplement, 2nd series
GFCC	German Federal Constitutional Court
GFCJ	German Federal Court of Justice
GRUR	Gewerblicher Rechtsschutz und Urheberrecht
GRUR Int.	Gewerblicher Rechtsschutz und Urheberrecht
International	
GRUR-RR	Gewerblicher Rechtsschutz und Urheberrecht (Rechtsprechung-Report)
GRUR-RS	Gewerblicher Rechtsschutz und Urheberrecht (Rechtsprechung-Sammlung)
i.e.	*id est*
Inc.	Incorporated Company
Infosoc-Directive	Directive 2001/29/EC of the European Parliament and of the Council of 22 May 2001 on the harmonization of certain aspects of copyright and related rights in the information society
IP	Intellectual Property
JdT	Journal des Tribunaux
LDA	Loi sur le droit d'auteur
let.	letter
Ltd.	Limited
N	Marginal No.
oCopA	Out of force Swiss Copyright Act
oDE-CopA	Out of force German Copyright Act
JdT	Journal des Tribunaux
p./pp.	page/pages
para.	paragraph(s)
PatA	Federal Act on Patents for Inventions of 25 June 1954, SR 232.14
PraxKomm	Praxiskommentar
s.	see
SCC	Swiss Criminal Code of 21 December 1937, SR 311.0
SDNY	Southern District of New York
SFAC	Swiss Federal Administrative Court
SFSC	Swiss Federal Supreme Court
SHK	Stämpflis Handkommentar
SIWR	Schweizerisches Immaterialgüter- und Wettbewerbsrecht
SMI	Schweizerische Mitteilungen über Immaterialgüterrecht

SR	Systematische Sammlung des Bundesrechts (Classified Compilation of Federal Legislation)
TRIPS	Agreement on Trade-Related Aspects of Intellectual Property Rights
UCLA	University of California, Los Angeles
UK	United Kingdom
US	
U.S.C.	United States of America
United States Code	
VIP	Very Important People
Vol.	volume
vs.	*versus*
WCT	WIPO Copyright Treaty
WIPO	World Intellectual Property Organization
WPPT	WIPO Performances and Phonograms Treaty
ZHdK	Zürcher Hochschule der Künste (Zurich University of the Arts)
ZUM	Zeitschrift für Urheber- und Medienrecht

Materials

- Brief of Amici Curiae Law Professors in Support of Appellees and Affirmance of February 28, 2020, in the United States Court of Appeals for the Second Circuit, The Andy Warhol Foundation for The Visual Arts, Inc. vs. Lynn Goldsmith, Lynn Goldsmith, Ltd., (cit. Amicus Brief, p. …)
- Botschaft zu einem Bundesgesetz über das Urheberrecht und verwandte Schutzrechte (Urheberrechtsgesetz, URG), zu einem Bundesgesetz über den Schutz von Topographien von integrierten Schaltungen (Topographiengesetz, ToG) sowie zu einem Bundesbeschluss über verschiedene völkerrechtliche Verträge auf dem Gebiete des Urheberrechts und der verwandten Schutzrechte vom 19. Juni 1989 (cit. Federal Gazette of June 19, 1989 (BBl 1989 III 477), p. …)
- Botschaft zur Änderung des Urheberrechtsgesetzes sowie zur Genehmigung zweier Abkommen der Weltorganisation für geistiges Eigentum und zu deren Umsetzung vom 22. November 2017 (cit. Federal Gazette of November 22, 2017 (BBl 2018 591), p. …)
- Gesetzentwurf der Bundesregierung – Entwurf eines Gesetzes zur Anpassung des Urheberrechts an die Erfordernisse des digitalen Binnenmarktes vom 31. Mai 2021, Bundesgesetzblatt Jahrgang 2021 Teil I Nr. 27, Drucksache 19/27426, ausgegeben zu Bonn am 4. Juni 2021 (cit. Explanatory Memorandum 19/27426, p. …)
- Beschlussempfehlung und Bericht des Ausschusses für Recht und Verbraucherschutz (6. Ausschuss), Drucksache 19/29894 vom 19. Mai 2021 (cit. Recommendation and Report 19/29894, p. …)
- Report on the implementation of Directive 2001/29/EC of the European Parliament and of the Council of 22 May 2001 on the harmonization of certain aspects of copyright and related rights in the information society, June 24, 2015 (2014/2256(INI)), Committee on Legal Affairs, Rapporteur Julia Reda (today Felix Reda) (cit. Report on the implementation of Directive 2001/29/EC of the European Parliament and of the Council of 22 May 2001 on the harmonization of certain aspects of copyright and related rights in the information society, June 24, 2015)

Introduction

> "You absolutely cannot discuss copyright with lawyers because it's a complete impasse and won't even come close to a discourse or dialogue. If you start talking to them about why copyright is no longer viable, they close the conversation. Copyright is not copyright anymore, but more about how this world is functioning."
>
> Elaine Sturtevant, Interview by Hans Ulrich Obrist (2008)

I.I Defining the problem*

In the last decades, lawsuits involving visual artists accused of plagiarism made headlines in the newspapers of the Western world. Jeff Koons, Barbara Kruger, Richard Prince and Andy Warhol were sued in the United States, some of them more than once. Jeff Koons was also sued in France, along with Peter Klasen and others.[1] Artists Luc Tuymans and Samson Kambalu were accused of copyright infringement in Belgium.[2] The latter and John Baldessari were sued in Italy. All these suits have one thing in common: Artists accused of copying copyrighted material without permission. Based on very different argumentations, the courts charged with the decision achieved mixed verdicts, sometimes favoring the first authors and copyright holders, sometimes the downstream artists who had copied from them.**

In Switzerland, too, there have been a couple of such cases. In 1992, for example, when Mike Bidlo was showing his works in an exhibition titled "Not Léger" at the Bruno Bischofberger gallery in Zurich, ProLitteris – the copyright collecting organization for visual artists in Switzerland – sued him. The works exposed were all slightly modified copies of famous works by Fernand Léger, but they had been signed by Mike Bidlo with his own name. According to the gallery's account of the

* This book is based on my PhD thesis, submitted to the University of Zurich in December 2023. Literature and jurisprudence have been considered until September 27, 2023. Punctual updates (including some new literature) were made between September and December 2024.

** Throughout the text, we use pronouns of different genders. Unless resulting otherwise from the context, we intend all genders to be included in each case.

1 Cf. Millet, p. 115–123.

2 Cf. the documentary movie of the trial, available at: <https://www.youtube.com/watch?v=XvtbwTb-Scvw> (all websites last visited on November 4, 2023).

DOI: 10.4324/9781003598503-1

events, "the exhibition was closed by the district attorney's office in Zurich, pending investigation. The catalogues, invitation cards and posters were destroyed by the director of ProLitteris in the presence of Bischofberger".[3]

Whereas ProLitteris insisted that Bidlo's artworks constituted an unlawful reproduction of Léger's originals, exponents of the art world, such as curators and art historians Bice Curiger and Willy Rotzler, wrote in defense of both Bidlo and Bischofberger. They, thus, explained that the technique of copying was not only an old habit of artists, but also that it had been cultivated by Fernand Léger himself.[4] Bidlo's artworks had to be inserted in the postmodern strand of artmaking that challenged art's constraint to always produce *new* and had, therefore, to be considered independent enough to be free utilizations under copyright law.[5] The following decision of the Zurich Court of Appeals is not public, but the matter is discussed by several copyright lawyers when they address the issue of appropriation art under Swiss copyright law in their writings.[6]

In another lesser known case, happening in 2006, the "Emma Kunz Zentrum", charged with the administration of Kunz's copyrights after her death, sued artist Thomas Hirschhorn for the reproduction of 34 works by Emma Kunz and the inclusion thereof in one of his artworks called *Spatial Front 2005* (2005). The Zentrum also sued Hirschhorn's gallerist Barbara Gladstone in New York, who had offered the artwork for sale. Whereas, according to the plaintiff, Emma Kunz's works had not been changed enough to be a free utilization, Hirschhorn insisted that he had merely quoted her, thereby not infringing copyright. Moreover, the work consisted of 2,000 visual elements, among which only a few of them were copies of Emma Kunz's works. Moreover, according to Hirschhorn, these would "enter into a dialogue with Emma Kunz's artworks". In the end, the parties settled out of court, so we do not know how a hypothetical court would have handled the question.[7]

Because most copyright infringements are prosecutable only on complaint, the alleged plagiarisms only become such when the use is challenged before a court.[8] The risks artists face in these cases are multiple and defined by copyright legislation and litigation. For example, their ongoing or planned exhibition can be ceased lest danger of copyright infringement, the artworks deemed to be infringing can be confiscated or removed from museum and/or gallery spaces and the publication, distribution and sale of the catalogues and of the visitors' guides containing

3 A record of the events is available at the gallery's website (<https://www.brunobischofberger.com/bidlo-bio>).

4 The two art experts may have referred to Léger's *La Joconde aux clés* (1930).

5 Glaus/Studer, p. 34.

6 Cf. Egloff, Von der "freien Benutzung", p. 409; Glaus/Studer, p. 34; Schmidt-Gabain, p. 132.

7 Cf. a short account of the events by Franziska Nyffeler, Hirschhorn-Emma Kunz, November 27, 2006 (<https://franziskanyffeler.net/hirschhorn-emma-kunz/>).

8 Griffiths, p. 347, reminds that "nobody is obliged to sue"; more on this topic in Chapter 8, I.I; Bung/Gruber/Kühn, p. 12.

reproductions of the works can be forbidden.[9] Moreover, the involved artists and gallerists could face pecuniary penalties, fines and other correlated legal expenses (such as the fees for hiring a lawyer in a copyright proceeding).

But copyright law seems to have a societal dimension that goes beyond practical litigation. For example, an exhibition of Cornelia Sollfrank's works was planned at plug.in, an independent art space in Basel, that has since closed, was cancelled by the organizers because of their fears of copyright infringement. As the artist underlines in her doctoral thesis, no legal action had been initiated at that point. The self-censorship on the part of the gallery was rather "an act of *anticipatory obedience*".[10] In other cases, artists reflect on copyright legislation in their own artworks, thus making copyright itself a sort of artistic medium. Copyright law seems, thus, to exert effects that are independent from the outcome of a court process. We will contextualize and discuss these cases later in this work.[11]

The legal situation just described is at odds with the contemporary artistic reality, in which the use of, or reference to, antecedent visual forms is very common.[12] Strategies for copying are taught in art schools,[13] appropriation artists have received prizes for their works,[14] and, in recent years, many personal and collective exhibitions have been organized all over the world to showcase the ways by which artworks thematize their past, making copious use of visual references to previous artworks.[15]

It seems that the central question "when is a copy a replica, and under what circumstances does it become an original?"[16] is answered very differently – and starting from radically different criteria – depending on whether one asks the question

9 Cf. the judge reading out the demands of the plaintiff in <https://www.youtube.com/watch?v=XvtbwTbScvw> (at 1.56'14"); Millet, p. 115.

10 Sollfrank, Performing the Paradoxes, p. 258 (emphasis added).

11 See Chapter 6, I.

12 Buskirk, Creative Intent, p. 235.

13 Stalder, p. 46; Shore, p. 69 et seqq.; Adler, The Future of Art, p. 571; in the exhibition "Ja, wir kopieren! Strategien der Nachahmung in der Kunst seit 1970", shown at the Kunstmuseum in Solothurn during Summer 2023, it was explained how many art professors at the F+F School of Art and Design in Zurich taught their students different strategies to copy to create new art.

14 Christian Marclay and Elaine Sturtevant received prizes at the Venice Biennale in 2011, cf. <https://www.artforum.com/news/christoph-schlingensief-and-christian-marclay-awarded-golden-lions-at-the-venice-biennale-28419>.

15 We recall the following, but there are more: *Von Bildern. Strategien der Aneignung* at the Kunstmuseum Basel in 2015–2016; *Why Pictures Now* a personal retrospective of the work of Louise Lawler at the MoMa in 2017; *Riffs & Relations: African American Artists and the European Modernist Tradition* at the Phillips Collection in Washington DC in 2020; *Copy and Paste: Repetitions in Japanese Imagery* at the MK&G in Hamburg in 2020; *Mixing It Up: Painting Today* at the Hayward Gallery in London in 2021; *Déjà-Vu: Die Kunst der Wiederholung von Dürer bis Youtube* at the Kunsthalle in Karlsruhe in 2021; *Give and Take. Images upon Images* in 2022 at the Hamburger Kunsthalle; the personal of Christian Marclay in 2023 at the Centre Pompidou and many more.

16 Buskirk, The Contingent Object, p. 72.

in the art or in the legal system.[17] Focusing on the dichotomies of "original" and "copy" (a material difference) and of "old" and "new" (a temporal difference), this book addresses the exposed phenomenon from both an art theoretical as well as a legal perspective. The aim is to understand the origins of this apparent lack of synchronization between art and copyright law and measure its extent.[18]

To do so, our reflection starts within art history. In the first part, we shed light on the object of scrutiny of this work – defined as the "interpictorial original copy" – by inserting it in the context of an ever-evolving art system understood as autopoietic.[19] The question that we will answer in this part is how it happened that a copy of a previous artwork can, today, be considered as original. By drawing a parallel between WALTER BENJAMIN's notion of auratic original and copyright law, the interpictorial original copy is, from the start, framed as an impossible object. This insight will allow us to better understand copyright law's ways of functioning and to describe its contradictions as epiphenomena of this initially encountered blind spot.

In the following part, focusing on the protection of facts of art under copyright law, we analyze how copyright constitutes its object of protection: The work. We then turn our gaze back to copyright and, by increasing the level of observation, we provide a description of copyright law as an "oscillating structure". This operation will also allow us to understand why, in the described structure, interpictorial original copies are likely not bestowed with copyright protection, notwithstanding their status as artworks in their system of reference.

In the third part, we proceed to analyze what we call copyright law's "regime for interpictoriality", i.e., all those normative spaces – such as copyright exceptions – in which copyright law accommodates uses of previous works for the creation of new works and artifacts. Toward the end of this part, we increase the level of observation again and provide a description of copyright's ambiguous relationship with art in light of the obtained results. As will be shown, copyright law's potential of declaring a *new* artwork as infringing, despite its societal function to foster innovation and creativity, makes the relation between art and law problematic.[20] This situation, which has already been described as the "paradox of intellectual property",[21] not only arises in the context of interpictoriality in visual art but also with other new forms of creativity, such as remixes, covers, mashups and music sampling;

17 The same piece of information constitutes a communication with radically different meanings and effects, depending on the system of reference cf. BARALDI/CORSI/ESPOSITO, p. 117; R/HOLGER, p. 20; cf. also DREIER, p. 208 and LUHMANN, Law as a Social System, p. 111.

18 DREIER, p. 208 f., at fn. 30.

19 More in Chapter 1, I.

20 Copyright law may foster innovation, but it is not neutral toward what this innovation entails. When innovation constitutes copyright infringement, a dilemma starts, cf. THAMPAPILLAI, p. 109; CARRIER, p. 914, exposing the example of the Napster decision (*A&M Records, Inc. vs. Napster, Inc.*, 239 F.3d 1004 (2001)) and how this stifled innovation.

21 Cf. SOLLFRANK, p. 327; similarly, DRAHOS, p. 26.

with internet means of communication, such as memes, GIFs and so-called fan art and fan fiction; as well as with technological innovations.

The encountered paradox will constitute the analytical point of departure for the fourth part. Here, we will expose the doctrinal and judicial reactions to said situation of impasse and describe them as a form of legal self-critique, in which fundamental rights and other general principles and interests are called upon to correct the results of a private law that is perceived as dissatisfying.[22] This part ends with a methodological critique and an outlook to the last part of the work.

In the last part, we ask what copyright law can do for interpictorial original copies. We sketch out ways for copyright law to recognize the difference between original work and interpictorial use and propose a new model of copyright that is more cognitively open to how knowledge and innovation is produced in other systems of society.

II.I A couple of words on method

II.II Managing complexities with an external perspective on law

In the introduction, we have explained that the aim of this book is to study the relation between copyright law and art. The phenomenon of artworks being declared illegal on grounds of copyright law is taken as the case study, as it is a particularly vivid case of a tense interaction happening at the intersection of copyright law and contemporary art. The object of analysis, the relation between art and law, involves two fields of society, each with different knowledge, methods, specific terminology and experts.[23] For this reason, this work profusely draws from historical and theoretical art sources as well as classically juridical sources.

To be able to handle the complexities of these two fields of knowledge, however, we will constantly enter and exit them – thereby changing *level of observation* multiple times over the course of the reasoning. For example, the question will not only be "*what* is a copyrighted work?", but also "*how* is the concept of work constructed in and by copyright law?".[24] To exit a field cannot mean to exit society completely and adopt a higher, somehow omniscient perspective. Rather, it necessarily means entering another one, with which it becomes possible to see something else in that field that may have remained invisible (second order observation).

While the methodology of legal practice and doctrine is focused on the law itself and, thus, tends to address situations normatively as problems to be categorized (subsumed) and solved, a legal-sociological approach makes it possible to treat such situations simply as phenomena to observe and analyze. The advantages of adopting such perspective on law reside in the possibility to accurately describe and handle the interdisciplinary complexities of the factual context in which the

22 WIELSCH, Grundrechte, p. 120.

23 ZIEGERT, p. 31.

24 Cf. LUHMANN, Law as a Social System, p. 451; in this sense, the work will sometimes take the form of a qualitative meta-analysis.

observed phenomenon – and the laws addressing it – are situated.[25] This second order observation, i.e., the possibility to observe *how* it is observed by another observer,[26] will be provided by the sociological instruments of systems theory as conceived by Niklas Luhmann (1927–1998†).

II.III Why systems theory

Starting from the very first, i.e., the epistemic premise according to which society is composed by functionally differentiated autopoietic systems, this theory is entirely built on *distinctions*. These distinctions are understood as being made by an observer that is always situated and operating within a system.[27] To emerge, systems have historically differentiated themselves thanks to the building of self-reference and of operative closure. Self-reference, however, is itself built on the unity of the difference system/environment and, thus, of its *re-entry* within itself on the side of the system.[28] Explanations deriving from a principle (which, in the system of law, could be that of justice, equality or a norm identified as hierarchically higher) are, thus, substituted with explanations deriving from distinctions, understood as observations operated within and by the system of reference using them.[29]

The methodological advantages of a systems theoretical approach reside, first, in the consistency of its use of terms and concepts. From this characteristic arises a versatility of the theory to describe even apparently different situations as similar (e.g., as functional equivalents) or find analogue strategies of "paradox unfolding" at different stages of a system's operativity. For example, by retaining the difference "system/environment", we observe that, to the law system, art is part of the "environment", and, from the perspective of the art system, the same is true for law. Their interactions (which we described before as "tense"), can be described, in turn, with theoretical tools such as the "irritation" or the "structural coupling".[30] Another advantage is the very accurate description of its object, i.e., the entire society,[31] that the theory enables.[32] Such description, based on a *differentiating* rather than an ontological approach, treats existing descriptions as self-descriptions of an autopoietic and, thus, operatively closed system. With this approach, the question whether something *is* loses importance behind questions such as *why it is, how it is*.[33]

25 Graber, Copyright, p. 125 et seq.; cf. also Camenisch, p. 30.
26 Luhmann, Wissenschaft, p. 113.
27 Luhmann, Soziale Systeme, p 30.
28 This spatial–physical description of systems should not raise the expectation that systems are physical entities. Systems are merely the difference they themselves set from the environment, Fuchs Peter, p. 99.
29 Luhmann, Law as a Social System, p. 66; Teubner, Selbstsubversive Gerechtigkeit, p. 16 et seq.
30 Amstutz, Der zweite Text, p. 382; Luhmann, Law as a Social System, p. 459, describes structural couplings as the "channeling of irritations".
31 Luhmann, Soziale Systeme, p. 9.
32 Siri/Möller, p. 208 and 210.
33 Luhmann, Law as a Social System, p. 60; Luhmann, Art as a Social System, p. 244.

The consequence of this approach is that, in this work, we do not ask what is identical to something else but how the observer is observing when she identifies something as identical to something else.[34] Specifically, how does copyright arrive at the result of calling something a copy of something else. Such perspective on the object also realizes the task of declaring the normal as improbable and, thus, of highlighting the contingency of its emergence.[35]

Another consequence of conceiving art as an autopoietic system of society[36] is that what counts as art is a question strictly left to the art system to determine.[37] All other societal systems (that is, law too) are put in the position of second order observers, limited to register what the art system itself calls art and to draw their own conclusions based on this "fact".[38] To determine whether something is considered art, we are simply going to observe what is said and written about it in its system of reference. In particular, we will avoid answering this question *normatively* but, rather, start from the assumption that what art considers art *is* art and refrain from asking whether it *should be* considered art.[39]

Notwithstanding the externality of the just described perspective, this work remains, ultimately, a juridical one. A difficulty of the systems theoretical approach is to be able to shift from an external, sociological description to the normative sphere. A sociological theory of law is not bound to respect the norms, practices and assumptions of its object. It is both freer to capture its objects as well as incapable of enforcing a direct change in the system of law.[40] Its value resides, thus, in opening new insights on tried and tested knowledge, shedding light on latencies and blind spots and creating room for potential irritation.[41]

For the legal situation to change, it does not suffice to describe facts with art theoretical or sociological instruments. Rather, to advance a change, the observed situation must be translated into a problem that concerns law itself and the means to repair it must be law's own.[42]

II.IV On comparative analysis

Again and again, this book adopts a comparative approach led by the question of how the phenomenon of interpictoriality is handled in other copyright systems of

34 LUHMANN, Identität, p. 21.
35 LUHMANN, Soziale Systeme, p. 162.
36 LUHMANN, Law as a Social System, p. 59, explains that a sociological theory "would only be an adequate theory if it described the system as a system that describes itself".
37 LUHMANN, Ausdifferenzierung Kunst, p. 139, asks provocatively "Who else?"; cf. also LUHMANN, Challenge, p. 53 et seq.
38 LUHMANN, Art as a Social System, p. 244.
39 Cf. ADLER, Against Moral Rights, p. 266; cf., at length, Chapter 1, I, for a discussion of how the art system defines "art" also through the question: "What is art?".
40 Cf. LUHMANN, Law as a Social System, p. 60 and 70.
41 LUHMANN, Soziale Systeme, p. 280.
42 LUHMANN, Law as a Social System, p. 60 and 258.

the Western world.[43] Different legal systems are compared in this book for mainly two reasons.

The first is that modern law must be intended as the law of a world society (*Weltgesellschaft*).[44] On the one hand, there are. in copyright law. international conventions that – thanks to instruments such as national treatment and minimum standards – harmonize and interconnect different national copyright systems to each other. On the other hand, even if courts commissioned to decide on copyright cases that operate locally or nationally, they are inserted in a dynamic of networking that makes their operations potentially connectable to other local operations.[45] As a subsystem of society, modern art, too, must be understood as an art-of-the-world (*Weltkunst*).[46] Artists are inter- and transnational players (insofar as they produce, expose and sell abroad or as their artworks are received and commented on by critics around the globe) and recurring "big events" in the artworld (such as the Venice Biennale, the documenta in Kassel or Athens or the Art Basel franchise) are, by definition, international.[47] If, with systems theory as a *theory of society*, we aspire to adopt a global consideration of societal phenomena that facilitates the building of interdisciplinary links between law and society, it is a comparative approach that best serves this purpose.[48]

The second reason we compare different copyright systems on how they handle the artistic phenomenon of interpictoriality purely concerns the legal method and the strategic search for the best solution to an individuated problem. For example, it has been advanced by copyright scholars in civil law countries that the fair use solution is better because it is inherently more flexible.[49] One of our aims is, therefore, to test such claims and, in the affirmative case, sketch out ways to implement "best copyright practices" in the Swiss national copyright system.[50]

The comparative approach is inhabited by various dangers, mostly caused by the encounter with the observed legal system's foreignness and otherness. Overwhelmed by the magnitude and the difference of the other, the automatic reaction of the observer could be one of suppression and absorption, i.e., to wrongfully conclude that the compared systems bear many more similarities than they actually do. This projection of the observer's certitudes onto a foreign legal system could

43 In a functionalist comparative analysis, different copyright systems are compared based on how they deal with the same societal phenomenon ("the segment of life"), i.e., here, interpictorial art. The existence of interpictorial art is, thus, our comparison's *tertium comparationis*, cf. BOGDAN, p. 46 et seqq. and BAER, p. 739.

44 ZIEGERT, p. 45; cf. also TEUBNER/FISCHER-LESCANO, p. 23; GRABER, Using Human Rights, p. 97.

45 ZIEGERT, p. 43; for example, the decision of the Tribunale di Milano of July 13, 2011 (Giacometti Variations) on the case involving Baldessari's alleged plagiarism of Giacometti's statues and the decision of the Cour d'appel de Paris of December 17, 2019 (*Bauret vs. Koons*) mention and briefly discuss the fair use doctrine valid in the US.

46 LUHMANN, Weltkunst, pp. 7 et seqq.; GRABER, Archaic Cultural Expressions, p. 160.

47 BOHN, Gegenwarten, p. 64 et seqq.

48 ZIEGERT, p. 38.

49 See Chapter 5, II.III and IV.

50 Cf. BOGDAN, p. 65.

also bear the risk of invisibilizing the experience of their own legal system's contingency, revealed by the confrontation with the other system's functional equivalents and different self-descriptions. Instead, crucial differences must be exposed and held in mind when confronting legal systems.[51]

The copyright legal system of Switzerland, a civil law country, is traditionally conceived as a *droit d'auteur*-system as opposed to common law's *copyright* system.[52] Such different nomenclature suggests the existence of different philosophical foundations.[53] In civil law countries, the origins of a subjective right of authors in their work are thought to be anchored in natural law.[54] The focus is on the author's natural entitlement to his work, which is seen as both his property as well as an extension of his soul and personality. This has had practical consequences in the development of the body of law that we call today the law of copyright (in Switzerland: *Urheberrecht*, *droit d'auteur* and *diritto d'autore*). In civil law countries, an artifact may be considered a work if it bears the mark of originality, which is traditionally conceived as the expression of the author's personality (and, more recently, the proof of the author's creative choices reflected in his work[55]). For the same reason, civil law countries are traditionally the stronghold of moral rights – a strain of personality rights of the author arising from the creation of a work (although Switzerland may be considered atypical in this sense).[56]

On the other hand, common law countries' copyright laws are justified by logics of investment protection and founded on utilitarian principles of maximization of the societal benefit.[57] The exclusive rights of the author in his work are traditionally conceived less as property and more as a monopoly,[58] i.e., as always relative to a common, bigger good. The consequences of this different view have been, for example, that common law countries did not know – until recently – the institute of moral rights of the author in his work and that the emergence of a work was traditionally explained with the "sweat of the brow" doctrine, a theoretical construction that looked for the evidence of labor (time, money, energy) rather than for proof of creativity.[59]

Another fundamental difference between compared copyright systems concerns the judicial system and the power courts have in the respective countries.[60] Whereas the United States (US), Germany and France (as the compared countries of choice) all have Constitutional Courts, the highest court in Switzerland – the

51 Baer, p. 739; Bogdan, p. 85.
52 Cf. Ginsburg, Copyright, p. 487; for simplicity, she refers only to "copyright". This thesis does the same.
53 Kleinemenke, p. 31 et seqq.; Ginsburg, Copyright, p. 487.
54 Strowel, p. 289 and p. 294 et seqq.
55 See Chapter 2, I.
56 Cf. Rigamonti, Deconstructing, p. 392.
57 Kleinemenke, p. 47.
58 Strowel, p. 289.
59 Sherman, Appropriating, p. 35.
60 Baer, p. 740.

Swiss Federal Supreme Court (SFSC) – does not have such power.[61] By force of Art. 190 of the Federal Constitution of the Swiss Confederation ("Const."), "the Federal Supreme Court and the other judicial authorities apply the federal acts and international law". This rule aims at more than the self-evident binding nature of the law in a constitutional state. It means that federal laws must always be complied with, regardless of their legal assessment. Swiss judges are, therefore, prohibited from refusing to apply or correcting federal laws on the grounds of unconstitutionality.[62] Many of the differences with the German system, encountered in Chapter 5, must, therefore, be explained in this way.

As BOGDAN explains, similarities and differences between legal systems are two sides of the same coin. The individuation of differences or, on the contrary, of similarities, is often caused within the observer, who can operate only on one side of the coin.[63] Although, as described, the compared copyright systems are different in many ways; many authors tend to treat these differences as isolated phenomena of a much more extensive, core similarity.[64] Other authors have, instead, focused on the recent convergence of the civil and common law copyright systems by way of globalization and international conventions. For example, the US has adopted moral rights and abandoned the sweat of the brow doctrine,[65] whereas civil law countries, with the adoption of the three-step test and its economic proportionality assessment in its second and third step, have come a step closer to seeing copyright as relative to context and economic exploitation of the work.[66]

A thorough in-depth-analysis of similarities and differences between the handled copyright systems and an investigation of their underlying economic, social and political reasons exceed the scope of this inquiry.[67] What we are interested in is, apart from potentially useful peculiarities of different copyright systems, the individuation of common macro-characteristics relative to the copyright treatment of the artistic operation of copying that are observable in the contemporary art world. As will be shown, the interpictorial original copy is an unsolved problem of both civil and common law copyright systems. For this reason, this work tends to put the accent on similarities rather than differences. Although given the above, we are conscient of the fact that this might be an approximation; however, we think that this perspective will best serve the purpose of this work.

61 BAER, p. 740; MOSIMANN, Kultur Kunst Recht, N 140 *ad* § 4.

62 LOOSER, N 5 *ad* Art. 190; DFC 138 II 440 (*Law firm*), p. 444.

63 BOGDAN, p. 55.

64 Cf., among others, GINSBURG, Copyright, p. 487 et seq., explains that it is more a matter of *different emphasis* than of proper difference; RIGAMONTI, Deconstructing, p. 381 et seqq. and 399 et seqq., by focusing on moral rights and dividing "rules from concepts", he shows that the difference is more a matter of self-description and philosophical foundation of the system than a real difference in the rules adopted; GEIGER, Reconceptualizing, p. 122, underlines how, even in the civil law tradition, copyright has been conceived as a "socially rooted right" under the concept of *Sozialbindung des Urheberrechts* (i.e., social function of copyright).

65 GERVAIS, Feist, p. 949 et seqq.

66 GERVAIS, How Intellectual Property, p. 15.

67 Cf. in detail BOGDAN, p. 57 et seqq.

Part I

The interpictorial original copy

> (...) What happens when a new work of art is created is something that happens simultaneously to all the works of art which preceded it. The existing monuments form an ideal order among themselves, which is modified by the introduction of a new work of art (...), and this is conformity between the old and the new.
>
> T.S. Eliot, Tradition and the Individual Talent (1919)

DOI: 10.4324/9781003598503-2

1 An art historical *novum*

I.I Introduction

Creation *ex nihilo* does not exist.[1] To revisit existing forms in a new creation and, thus, to form analogies and correspondences between artworks is a common practice in all artistic disciplines.[2] Such practice is so common that it characterizes art itself, without being something separate from it.[3] It is on this background, for example, that ABY WARBURG (1866–1929), historian of art and culture, conducted the research that he is mostly known for: His unfinished project "Bilderatlas Mnemosyne". In it, with the help of photographic reproductions of artworks, excerpts from newspapers and advertising placed on black tables, WARBURG retraced what he called the migration and recurrence of visual themes, symbolical forms and patterns across time and cultures, from antiquity to the Renaissance and beyond to contemporary culture.[4]

Sourcing from art history and copying certain things is, thus, a technique, among others, for creating art.[5] For the better part of history, however, artists subtly blended existing imagery into new compositions and designs of their own. The borrowed motifs that appear in Renaissance and baroque art are assimilated into the subsequent work so that the classical models used as the basis for academic training became integral to the artist's own formal vocabulary.[6]

1 FISCHER, Sampling, p. 94; on the "myth" of originality, LUHMANN, Darum Liebe, p. 62, wrote: "nobody can ever live without copying. When someone believes to be original, it only means that she is copying the idea of being original" (translation is mine).

2 DERRIDA, Grammatologie, p. 297; ZUSCHLAG, p. 205; DÖHL, Mashup, p. 11 et seq.

3 BEYER, Interpikturalität, p. 27, explained: "if all aspects of the culture use this new operation [of appropriation, pastiche, quotation], then the mode itself cannot articulate a specific reflection upon that culture". In systems theoretical terms, that would "make no difference" anymore; cf. also LETHEM, p. 61, who wrote: "it becomes apparent that appropriation, mimicry, quotation, allusion, and sublimated collaboration consist of a kind of *sine qua non* of the creative act, cutting across all forms and genres in the realm of cultural production"; cf. also DÖHL/WÖHRER, p. 4 and SHAFRIR, p. 214.

4 Cf. BEYER, Interpikturalität, p. 59; VERWOERT, p. 144; RÖSCH, p. 97.

5 BUSKIRK, The Contingent Object, p. 97; even for Kant, genius and imitation are intimately related, and imitation plays an important role even in works of great originality, cf. GREANEY, p. 649.

6 BUSKIRK, The Contingent Object, p. 88.

DOI: 10.4324/9781003598503-3

Yet, in the second half of the twentieth century, something changed. Rather than camouflaging the borrowed elements in the global composition of the new artwork, artists boldly began to embed sources and leave them unaltered in their finished artworks.[7] Although the copied portion was left almost intact in the final artwork, it became an integral part of the work, helping distinguish it from earlier traditions in a layering of quotation and reference.[8]

An example of these two different modes of building referentiality is provided by art historian and critic DOUGLAS CRIMP. In the first mode, the artists referenced a previous style, carefully selecting it from the history of art and re-actualizing it in their present.[9] It is the case of Robert Mapplethorpe's portrait, nude and still life photography, in which he displays "the stylistics of pre-war studio photography".[10] Even if historical references are present in the works of Mapplethorpe, they are organically blended in the final oeuvre so that we have the impression that this is formally new, original. In the second mode, characteristic, for example, of the artistic practice of Sherrie Levine, the artist copied the whole thing.[11] Levine famously re-photographed whole pictures (it is the case of Edward Weston's portrait of his son, which she re-photographed entirely, or of the even more known re-photographs of Walker Evans's portraits) so that her artworks appear fragmentized (are they even Levine's?). Since the 1980s, this development has been generally called "appropriation art".[12]

II.I Two characteristics of the system of art

According to NIKLAS LUHMANN, society is a system made up of subsystems, which are made up of communication,[13] itself the smallest unit of society. Each subsystem has constituted itself in view of its specific function, over which it has complete exclusivity in the system of society.[14] Both law and art are functional subsystems (other such subsystems are, e.g., religion, science, politics, economy, education). This means, first, that only art (or law, respectively) can decide what art (or law) is in society but also that only art can assert itself as art in society.[15]

The systems as described by LUHMANN are autopoietic, meaning that they constitute and re-constitute themselves continuously out of their own communication.[16] New elements in the system are the result of the system's past operations and

7 LIPMAN/MARSHALL, p. 7.
8 BUSKIRK, The Contingent Object, p. 88.
9 CRIMP, Appropriating, p. 128.
10 CRIMP, Appropriating, p. 128 et seq.
11 CRIMP, Appropriating, p. 128 et seq.
12 BANTLEON, p. 305 et seq.; BUSS/GRAW/KRÜMMEL, p. 2.
13 Society is nothing but communication; LUHMANN, The Work of Art, p. 191.
14 LUHMANN, The Self-Reproduction, p. 228.
15 BOHN, Gegenwarten, p. 76 et seq.; see also HALSALL, p. 68 and 73 and LUHMANN, Art as a Social System, p. 244.
16 LUHMANN, The Work of Art, p. 191: "The systems produce the elements, of which they consist, by means of the elements of which they consist".

become themselves the condition for future operations.[17] In this way, communication incites more communication, with the result that a certain discourse, and not another one – which will eventually be forgotten – will develop. The operativity of a functionally differentiated subsystem of society could be ensured only with the introduction of "operative closure", which presupposes some degree of recursivity. The system must have the possibility of recognizing its operations as its own, i.e., it must have a memory.[18] This does not mean that the system remembers everything but, rather, that *the system sees itself as the result of its own past.*[19]

It is precisely in relation to this past that the autopoietic art system is best understood. Indeed, a first characteristic of the art system is its recursive operating, with which the system constantly re-*actualizes its past* by making it the theme of new artworks. Outside systems theory, this way of working was described with the concept of interpictoriality, which we will introduce below. A second characteristic of the art system's operating is the tendency, observable since modernity, to define as art only the new and then, since the early avant-gardes, as a constant *overcoming of the past* in an always renewed subversive stance with respect to its previously set boundaries.[20] As we will see later, these two partially mutually contradicting characteristics are fundamental to make sense of the *novum* previously described and to inscribe it in the history of art.

II.II Interpictoriality

In the art system, communication is made of artworks and of what is communicated, i.e., said and written, about them.[21] In an autopoietic system, artworks must appear as knowing their own past and as being built upon it (second-order observation).[22] *Singularia*, that is, works that are too different from the rest, cannot be attributed to the system, i.e., be observed as art.[23] To signal their belonging to the system, artworks cite, copy, reject, renew and ironize or, in other words, thematize,

17 Baraldi/Corsi/Esposito, p. 37.

18 Art & Language, p. 21.

19 Luhmann, Ausdifferenzierung Kunst, p. 145.

20 Bohn, Gegenwarten, p. 65; Habermas, p. 4.

21 Graber, Zwischen Geist und Geld, p. 95; cf. also Koller, p. 48 et seq., who differentiates between the "memory function" and the "oscillator function" of the art system. The first being the characteristic of the system of seeing itself as the result of its own past. The latter opens instead a window of possibilities in the future.

22 Baraldi/Corsi/Esposito, p. 27; this is done with a mix of the right doses of historical reference to an artistic style and the own readiness to surprise, see Luhmann, Art as a Social System, p. 146 et seqq. and 332; Halsall, p. 117 et seq. and this thesis at Chapter 1, I.II.

23 Luhmann, Art as a Social System, p. 338; cf. also Krauss, p. 62, "the priorness and repetition of pictures is necessary to the singularity of the picturesque, because for the beholder singularity depends on being recognized as such".

by means of a similar visual language (be it style, motifs, composition, subject, etc.) other artworks in themselves.[24]

The fact that new artworks thematize old artworks is a way the system has found for building and maintaining its self-referentiality. This, however, happens to various degrees: Traces of other artworks and other art historical references might be evident at times and, at others, be implicit, realized by the artist unconsciously at the moment of creation.[25] Sometimes, the references appear only at the intersection of the artwork with its presentation in critical or interpretive contexts, where it is read in relation to and, therefore, becomes part of the history of art.[26] The functioning mode of art historical research is precisely the comparison of artworks, the creation of relations between these and the respective artists and their styles in an open and ever-expanding network of influences and references.[27] An example thereof is art historian Beate Soentgen's take on Adreas Gursky's *Untitled IV* (1997):

> The way in which Gursky uses the [horizontal] bands seems to activate the expressive pictorial structure the Abstract Expressionists already borrowed from Romanticism, as much as it does the explicitly expressionless order of Minimalist or Conceptualist pictures...we cannot be sure whether the expression stems from the represented things or from the representation.[28]

Scholars in art history and theory have referred to image-to-image relations with a huge variety of terms. During our research, we came across the following: Imitation, plagiarism, copy, variation, paraphrase, translation,[29] inversion,[30] citation, pastiche,[31] reception, allusion, homage, fake[32] and parody,[33] but many more are possible.[34] These terms are sometimes positively (such as homage, or translation) or negatively (fake, plagiarism) connotated, in the broad as much as in the

24 Luhmann, Art as a Social System, p. 52 et seq.; Art & Language, p. 21; Leach, p. 133; Luhmann, Ausdifferenzierung Kunst, p. 143.
25 Cf. Mosimann, Kultur Kunst Recht, N 124 *ad* § 1; on this, paradigmatic is an introductory affirmation by Leo Steinberg that "all art is *infested* by other art" in Lipman/Marshall, p. 9 (emphasis added).
26 Buskirk, The Contingent Object, p. 105; Luhmann, Art as a Social System, p. 131; Isekenmeier, In Richtung, p. 13; Bantleon, p. 305 et seq.
27 Luhmann, Die Welt, p. 305; Graw/Kleefeld/Rottmann, p. 6; cf. also Döhl, Pastichebegriff p. 27; Ribettes, p. 159; Gamer, p. 31; Clair, p. 26, "You could even say that an artwork only exists through the (re)reading it is done thereof" (translation is mine).
28 Soentgen, p. 55.
29 Cf. e.g. Keuper, p. 1 et seqq.
30 Cf. Greaney, p. 650, defines "inversion" as a subversive kind of imitation that allows for dialogue and originality.
31 Pastiche was defined by Jameson, p. 114, as a "parody that has lost its sense of humor".
32 Römer, p. 5.
33 See Rose, Pictorial Irony, p. 1, who treats parodies as a special case of (comic) interpictoriality.
34 Cf. Carlut, p. 13; Bantleon, p. 305 lists different practices: "referencing, emulating, paraphrasing, borrowing, reusing, reworking, acquiring, copying, duplicating, reproducing, replicating, confiscating, purloining, plagiarizing or even stealing".

legal contexts. Moreover, they tend to only refer to a very specific phenomenon and, thus, can be easily used improperly.

With the concept of interpictoriality (interpicturality, intericonicity, intervisuality, intertextuality of images are all possible synonyms[35]), a tentative suggestion was made to overcome this problem, i.e., to build an overall term capable to suppress positive or negative connotations.[36] The term "interpictoriality" was coined after the term "intertextuality", which has its origins in the late 1960s.[37] With it, interpictoriality shares common foundational and methodical characteristics.[38] In art theory and art history, interpictoriality designates the relations between images as well as the modes of their transformations. It relates to art's characteristic of aggregating antecedent forms into new artworks and building up on them in a sort of dialogue between artists and artworks of different times and spaces.[39]

The development of the concept of interpictoriality was not only motivated by the necessity to work with a more neutral terminology. Interpictoriality is also a particular way *to look* at art and at art history, one that puts the focus on the evident phenomenon of recurrence of forms in art in a methodologically more pointed way.[40] As a *method*, then, interpictoriality overcomes research premises such as the imperative of originality and redirects the analysis away from genetic questions of origin, influence, source, tradition and borrowing, toward communicative-semiotic questions of how sense is constructed through the relations between images.[41]

Through the lens of interpictoriality, each new artwork can be seen as being in conversation with all artworks that have come before it.[42] When examined in this way, art history appears a lot less linearly and much more like a system that recursively returns to itself – not in the sense that history repeats itself (*how would that be possible?*), but in that art history becomes a valid subject of new artworks.[43] In this sense, the concept of originality, which entails the claim of the artwork to be first and unique, outside of time and history, must also be relativized to the point of contingency: Ultimately, it is just a way among others to look at art.[44]

35 Isekenmeier, Einführung, p. 7; Gamer, p. 18 et seq.

36 von Rosen, p. 209; Gamer, p. 12 and 20.

37 von Rosen, p. 209; Ribettes, p. 171.

38 von Rosen, p. 208 et seq.

39 Beyer, Interpikturalität, p. 60; Ribettes, p. 171; Isekenmeier, In Richtung, p. 39.

40 von Rosen, p. 209

41 von Rosen, p. 209.

42 Feireiss, p. 16; Ribettes, p. 164.

43 Rose, Parody, p. 56; Jameson, p. 115 et seq.; as for example in Peter Weibel's *Inszenierte Kunstgeschichte* (1988) (or: "Mise-en-scène of art history"), exhibited at the Österreichisches Museum für angewandte Kunst in Vienna (discussed by Römer, p. 180 et seqq.); cf. on this also Hutcheon, p. 55.

44 Cf. Saunders, p. 99.

II.III An artwork is an artwork is an artwork[45]

Sherrie Levine: "I kept them because I didn't think of them as art. They were in a box with a bunch of odds and ends. I was lucky to recover them".

Martha Buskirk: It's interesting that the shoes were in this very tenuous state "between being art and not being art".[46]

In this excerpt from a longer interview, artist Sherrie Levine and art critic Martha Buskirk are talking about Sherrie Levine's ready-made artwork *2 Shoes* (1992), constituted by a simple pair of brown lace-up shoes for children. It is interesting to underline the uncertainty (even of the artwork's author) about the status of the shoes as "art". The women seem to reflect – and even to appreciate – their flickering between the state as art and as non-art.[47] When does this oscillation stop? How is it decided that something is art?

As previously exposed, systems theory is founded on differences, not on identity: It is, therefore, anti-ontological.[48] It follows that art is not defined in material terms, as a sum of objects or practices, or in philosophical terms but, rather, in terms of a *difference* from something else.[49] The unity of art, i.e., its being what it is, is, thus, conceived as a paradoxical unity of a difference between the system and its environment.[50] The question what modern art *is* redirects straight back to the observer, who is the one making the difference.[51] In society, the art system has the prerogative on the phenomenon of art. The attention is, thus, put onto the system as a whole and on the various processes it generates internally.[52] Central is the process of *communication for further communication*.[53] This is also the reason why systems theory puts what is communicated about artworks in the center of its understanding of the functioning of art.[54]

45 A variation from Gertrude Stein's famous line "A rose is a rose is a rose", from the poem "Sacred Emily" (1913). With this title, we want to underline the importance of the system's recursivity for defining and always redefining its own boundaries.

46 Buskirk, Interviews, p. 100; on Marcel Duchamp's Fountain (1917) and on sociological thoughts of why it became an artwork, see Edelman, De l'urinoir, p. 88.

47 Cf. Kucsko, p. 325, who asks: "Can an object change its nature, > be an everyday object, > become an artwork, > again become an everyday object, > again become an artwork? And what does this mean for copyright protection?" (translation is mine).

48 Kost, p. 131; Halsall, p. 57 and 68; observation, which seems like a single operation, is actually composed by two different, yet simultaneous steps: In a first step, the system distinguishes itself from the rest that is not itself; in a second step, the system indicates the system side of the distinction between itself and the environment.

49 Halsall, p. 68; Luhmann, Irritationen, p. 60.

50 Baraldi/Corsi/Esposito, p. 167; Luhmann, Art as a Social System, p. 204.

51 Luhmann, Irritationen, p. 99.

52 Zijlmans, p. 12.

53 In the endless unfolding of communications after communications, no finality or necessity can be detected. All is accounted on contingency: Luhmann, The Self-Reproduction, p. 228; Zijlmans, p. 7.

54 Luhmann, Law as a Social System, p. 44 and 53; Luhmann, The Work of Art, p. 194, the work of art can be considered as a compact communication or as a program for innumerable communica-

It is not a coincidence that precisely during Romanticism, in the historically first-ever autopoietic art system, art criticism was thought to work as a "medium of reflection" (WALTER BENJAMIN) for art[55] and to complete the artwork by creating a "multidimensional continuum" to it.[56] It is, then, that the critical observation of artworks became uncoupled from the rationales of religious canon and started being driven by irrational criteria, such as "good taste" and "genius".[57] The resulting insecurity could only be absorbed by an already autopoietic art system capable of working with indeterminacy without being held accountable for it by other systems, for example, religion.[58] The central question – "what is art?" – began, thus, to be answered by the system and is the main evidence of the existence of an autopoiesis of the art system, free at last, since the eighteenth century, to provide the answer according to its own standards.[59]

The coupling between artworks and the communication about them continued in such a way that the abstract question of what art was came to influence artworks, which during the twentieth century started pushing the limits of the definition of art in always new and unexplored territories.[60] For example, artworks stopped representing something and started referring only to the process of making art, thereby closing the system on a reflection about itself. Representation was reduced until the point it was completely negated, with techniques such as the mobilization of the found object, the random form, the reference to non-artistic forms[61] and more.[62]

tions about the work of art; cf. also GRABER, Zwischen Geist und Geld, p. 95; ZIJLMANS, p. 12. To expose the huge importance of communication about artworks and artists in the art system, we can cite the example of fictional artist "Hank Herron" (discussed by CROW, p. 11 et seqq., SCHAAR, p. 892, HALSALL, p. 214 and RÖMER, p. 19): In the early 1970s, art critic Carol Duncan wrote a couple articles about Hank Herron's alleged practice of replicating Frank Stella's artworks and signed them in the name of a fictional art critic called Cheryl Bernstein. Whereas neither Hank Herron nor Cheryl Bernstein ever existed; they came to "life" through the *de facto* inclusion of Herron in the art discourse. The result was that the two characters had a tangible (and, thus, real?) resonance, both during the time they were believed to exist and even after they were discovered to be an invention of Duncan. In 1973, Gregory Battcock included a paper by Cheryl Bernstein (a.k.a. Carol Duncan) in a collection of essays called *Idea Art: A Critical Anthology* and edited by him, which according to HALSALL, p. 214, ensured the subsequent existence of Herron/Bernstein in the art system.

55 LUHMANN, Art as a Social System, p. 53; LUHMANN, Ausdifferenzierung Kunstsystem, p. 329.

56 BOHN, Autonomien p. 42; cf. also LIPPARD, p. x, who states that she understood herself, even as an art critic, as a "writer-collaborator" of artists.

57 Cf. on the categories of "genius" and "taste" in the aesthetic judgment cf. GUMBRECHT, Prose, p. 156.

58 LUHMANN, Ausdifferenzierung Kunst, p. 138; LUHMANN, Medium, p. 106, explains how this has not always been the case. Before the functional differentiation of the art system, demonstrating the ability to follow a set of formal rules (i.e., copying from a model) was enough for the result to be seen as art, whereas not following these rules would have assured the rejection of the result.

59 LUHMANN, Art as a Social System, p. 271.

60 LUHMANN, Art as a Social System, p. 44; HABERMAS, p. 5; MAGERSKI, p. 100; BOHN, Gegenwarten, p. 66; MORTIER, p. 9, calls this the "terrorism of novelty"; FISCHER, Sampling, p. 79; FUCHS CHRISTINE, p. 52.

61 BOHN, Autonomien, p. 46.

62 FISCHER, Sampling, p. 79; LUHMANN, The Work of Art, p. 193.

Artists even started to make it very unlikely for their artworks to be seen as such, for example by writing unreadable texts, or in so-called happenings, in which the artistic performance itself was dissimulated and the casual passer-by had to discover it.[63] Eventually, with some forms of conceptual art, the artist's statement became even more important than the actual realization of the artwork.[64]

For LUHMANN, these constant calls into question of the system's own boundaries are all attestations of self-referentiality and autonomy.[65] Only an autonomous art system could reproduce itself even at its very edge and go even further, i.e., reintegrate the very negation of art – a *transgression* of its boundaries – back in the system.[66] The art system functions, transforming the *unlikeliness of the artwork's emergence* as art into the *likeliness of its preservation*.[67] For an artwork to succeed, it must be unlikely in the moment of creation, even appear as not art. The brown shoes (the everyday object) became *2 Shoes* (the artwork) through their *ex post* inclusion in the art system. Obviously, their artistic quality does not reside intrinsically in their objecthood. Rather, it is precisely their extremely unlikely quality as art that made them successfully cross this improbability into a plausibility.[68]

Around the 1960s, as artists began to use the strategy of copying to produce new artworks, they were similarly doing something that was, at the time, unlikely to succeed if judged to the standards of what had come just before. In the following section, we expose how even the previously described *novum* is best understood as a transgression of the boundaries previously set in the art system. To do so, we briefly retrace the history of the dichotomy original and copy and of how they came to be one the conceptual opposite of the other.

III.I The "original copy"

III.II A brief history of copies and the original

For the better part of the history of art, the concept of "copy" signaled a positive concept denoting abundance.[69] In a culture dedicated to permanence and stability, i.e., not yet functionally differentiated, *novitas* was synonym of deviation and was,

63 LUHMANN, Art as a Social System, p. 293.

64 BOHN, Autonomien, p. 42; LAWSON, p. 145; cf. LIPPARD, p. xix, explicitly calling conceptual art as "non-art", "not-art" and "anti-art"; ICKOWICZ, p. 23, with further references, signals, in this respect, "the risk of reducing contemporary art to a regression and negation without end".

65 LUHMANN, The Work of Art, p. 193; for others, instead, they signal a process of deconstruction, see FUCHS CHRISTINE, p. 54.

66 LUHMANN, Art as a Social System, p. 293; cf. also ART & LANGUAGE, p. 21; FISCHER, Sampling, p. 79; MAGERSKI, p. 104 et seq., explains that by doing so, "art risks its own end" (translation is mine); BOHN, Gegenwarten, p. 76.

67 LUHMANN, Art as a Social System, p. 214, asks with an open question: "How is it possible that the improbability of emergence continually transforms itself into the probability of preservation?"; cf. also FUCHS CHRISTINE, p. 133.

68 LUHMANN, Art as a Social System, p. 126 and 297.

69 FISCHER, Sampling, p. 34 et seq.; LUHMANN, Ausdifferenzierung Kunstsystem, p. 342 et seq.; LATOUR/LOWE, p. 178; RIBETTES, p. 160; GOPNIK, p. 22.

thus, observed with mistrust.[70] Only around the second half of the seventeenth century did the expectation start to develop that artworks be new and that only in this way they would be appreciated.[71]

The enhanced interest of society in the "new" and in the "original" by simultaneous disappearance of the preference for the aesthetics of the *mimesis* or the "old" and the "traditional" can be explained, first, with the invention of the book press. This made the first technical reproduction possible as well as increasingly easier and quicker.[72] The advent of the book press entirely changed society.[73] Because new books were published in improved quality and contained fewer mistakes, they started to be preferred to the old ones.[74] As ESPOSITO notes, the main practical application of the book press was found in the daily production of papers containing, indeed, news.[75] This caused, on one side, the "new", which used to be seen suspiciously as a deviation and an exception to the rules,[76] to suddenly be recognized and to have a structuring power for further communication. In other words, the stability that was once based on the perpetuation of tradition was newly based on the constant of variation. Because continuous destabilization was expected, it stopped destabilizing.[77] On the other side, the book press changed the connotation of the copy, which, as something by definition is equal to its past, started to signal the already known, the used up and, thus, the uninteresting.[78] The disgrace of the copy as an *independent* artistic category, however, developed parallel to the emergence and subsequent expansion, starting in the seventeenth century, of an art market reaching beyond the circumscribed reality of patronage and local exchanges.[79] In this increasingly international art market, transactions were often far-reaching and were, thus, carried out by a series of intermediaries.

Copies had, until then, been its own category of artworks, traded on a thriving side art market of lower priced and extremely sought-after pieces.[80] If ill-intentioned, the intermediaries of the art market could, for lack of scrutiny along the

70 MORTIER, p. 10 et seq.; HAUG, p. 3 et seq., explaining that Christian tradition was hostile to novelties and that every aspiration to innovate was seen with suspicion. So, when innovations were made, they were presented as traditions. See also LUHMANN, Ausdifferenzierung Kunstsystem, p. 342 et seq.; LUHMANN, Irritationen, p. 58 and 65 et seq.; LUHMANN, Medium, p. 106, explains that when art was not functionally differentiated and copying from a model was still the rule, artworks did evolve in time but at a slower pace that allowed for a model to be recognized and groups of artists and artworks to be formed around it. We could say that because the new was presented as being old, the re-entry of the difference old/new happened on the side of the old.

71 LUHMANN, Die Welt, p. 304 et seq.; MORTIER, p. 9, speaks of "one of the deepest mutations of aesthetic values in the history of Western civilization" (translation is mine).

72 PEUKERT, Drei Entstehungsbedingungen, p. 131; cf. also ESPOSITO, Unberechenbarkeit, p. 37.

73 LUHMANN, Irritationen, p. 64

74 LUHMANN, Ausdifferenzierung Kunstsystem, p. 343.

75 ESPOSITO, Altes, p. 136.

76 LUHMANN, Irritationen, p. 65.

77 ESPOSITO, Altes, p. 137.

78 FISCHER, Sampling, p. 34 et seq.; LUHMANN, Art as a Social System, p. 200.

79 LUHMANN, Ausdifferenzierung Kunstsystem, p. 324; GOPNIK, p. 22.

80 HELSTOSKY, p. 813 et seqq.

resale chain, sell a copy at a higher price by fraudulently claiming that it was the original and simulating a different provenance. Even if not created for deceitful purposes, a copy could suddenly mutate into a forgery "after it had passed through several hands and was purchased in a dealer's shop, provided that the dealer knew that the object was a copy yet sold it at a price worthy of a Renaissance original".[81] The copy was, thus, inhabited by a suspicious duality, as it could be sold as the copy it was or as an original, which would have *de facto* transformed it into a forgery.[82]

In this respect, the vicissitudes involving Italian sculptor Giovanni Bastianini (1830–1868) are paradigmatic. In 1863, Bastianini realized, on commission, a bust in the style of the Italian Renaissance. In 1864, when the bust was sold by the commissioner to an art dealer, it was advertised not as a modern copy or as a genuine antique but, rather, as "that which [t]he [buyer] saw and examined".[83] When the bust was sold again to the French state, it had already lost its status as a remake of an Italian Renaissance bust, as it ended up in the Louvre, exposed alongside the work of the likes of Michelangelo and Benvenuto Cellini and, thus, held for a Renaissance original.[84] It is interesting that, as the events unfolded and the provenance of the bust was revealed, French experts initially denied the possibility of its modern provenance and vehemently insisted on its originality. Only in the face of overwhelming evidence to the contrary did they rephrase and define the bust "as a deception, an imitation, but *not as art*".[85] Once uncovered as a copy, the artwork could not be autonomous art anymore but, rather, at most, the proof of the mimetic virtuosity of the author.[86]

Because the similar looking artwork was plagued by the risk that it could possibly be (or potentially become) a fake, the original artwork was constructed as its positively connotated semantical opposite.[87] Given the presence of copies that could become forgeries on the art market if misused, only the original artwork signaled scarcity and could, thus, guarantee quality and value. These were symbolized by a higher price.[88] The concept of original, consequently, changed meaning from an aesthetical point of view. From a simple designation of provenience and

81 Helstosky, p. 818.

82 Luhmann, Ausdifferenzierung Kunst, p. 138; Luhmann, Ausdifferenzierung Kunstsystems, p. 324; Moskowitz, p. 173; cf. also McClean, p. 320; Ribettes, p. 161.

83 Helstosky, p. 800.

84 Helstosky, p. 800.

85 Helstosky, p. 823 (emphasis added); Moskowitz, p. 173 et seqq., critically exposing the scholarly discussions that painted Bastianini as a forger.

86 Natale, p. 52.

87 Ribettes, p. 161; Mortier, p. 10, 197 and 202, writing that neither original, nor copy, are inherently "positively" connotated and that everything is the fruit of accent, insistence, taste and habit. At p. 200, he writes that originality is a confused and ambiguous notion that becomes clear only as the conceptual opposite of the slavish imitation and of the copy.

88 Luhmann, Irritationen, p. 71; Luhmann, Ausdifferenzierung Kunstsystem, p. 324.

source,[89] original started meaning "an artifact without precedence"[90] that brings to the fore new forms in its respective present rather than simply repeating and validating its past.[91] New did not mean "another one, another copy" anymore but, rather, positively and materially divergent, surprising and, most of all, unique.[92] In such a panorama that emphasized so much personal invention, the copy could not but be rejected: To repeat something that was conceived having a unique existence could only mean to have an entirely devalued conception of art.[93]

III.III Walter Benjamin's "The Work of Art in the Age of Its Technological Reproduction"

The original character of an oeuvre was so conceived, in material terms, as residing in the traces of the brush, in the very form of the artwork, in an indivisible unity of concept and execution.[94] To tell a copy from an original, art historians based their judgments on a direct, qualitative examination of the piece to establish whether it was transmitting "aesthetical emotions", which copies were constructed as naturally devoid of.[95] The formal novelty original artworks could bring about became the decisive criterion to tell good art from bad art, thus driving its development throughout the modern era.[96]

WALTER BENJAMIN's famous essay, "The Work of Art in the Age of Its Technological Reproducibility", written in 1935, must be situated on this art historical background. In it, BENJAMIN discussed the "original" in the light of what it identifies as its opposite, i.e., the "reproduction". BENJAMIN delineated the dichotomy by speaking of the unique existence of the work of art and by observing, on the contrary, how the increasingly easy mechanical reproduction could never take the place of an original:

> In even the most perfect reproduction, one thing is lacking: the here and now of the work of art – its unique existence in a particular place. It is this unique existence – and nothing else – that bears the mark of the history to which the work has been subject.[97]

According to BENJAMIN, the original emerges from the author's personality through a creative and organic process. By contrast, the reproduction forcibly arises from the original work by means of a technical or mechanical process. For this reason,

89 LATOUR/LOWE, p. 178.
90 LUHMANN, Irritationen, p. 64; LUHMANN, Ausdifferenzierung Kunstsystem, p. 343 et seq.; MORTIER, p. 31.
91 BOHN, Gegenwarten, p. 65.
92 LUHMANN, Die Welt, p. 304 et seq.; BOHN, Gegenwarten, p. 75.
93 RIBETTES, p. 163; LUHMANN, Individuum, p. 222.
94 CLAIR, p. 16.
95 NATALE, p. 49 et seqq.; ERNST, p. 501; RIBETTES, p. 159.
96 CLAIR, p. 40.
97 BENJAMIN, p. 21.

it cannot be an artwork.[98] BENJAMIN built his whole argument around the central dichotomy of "original/reproduction". According to it, with the advent of technical reproduction, the "aura" of the original artwork has been lost and art, together with its perception, has changed forever.[99] As he argued, only the uniqueness, the *hic et nunc*, of the work of art, which links the object to its own history and makes it appear as the same over time, makes the auratic experience possible.[100] On the contrary, reproductions cannot conceal their lack of authenticity, or in BENJAMIN's terms:

> The whole sphere of authenticity eludes technological – and of course not only technological – reproduction.[101]

Shortly after BENJAMIN's death in 1940, the emergence of postmodern artworks demonstrated how BENJAMIN's conclusion was deeply rooted in modernist preconceptions. The history of art taught that the concept of the "original" could only emerge from the existence of multiple similar exemplars, from which the supposedly original could stand out.[102] The aura was, therefore, not a characteristic emanating intrinsically from the original but was, rather, constructed through the opposition of the supposedly original to other inferior reproductions.[103] Ironically, the very possibility of technical reproduction, which BENJAMIN identified as the cause for the loss of aura, had been one of the historical conditions for the emergence of the unique and authentic original as an aesthetical concept.[104]

III.IV The meta-originality of the postmodern copy

At the dawn of the 1960s, what has afterward been referred to as "postmodern art" began to critically reflect on the premises of artmaking that had been uncontested for two centuries. Principles such as originality, intention, expression,[105] authorship, competence and property[106] were classified as modernist and were, therefore, challenged at the very level of artworks.[107] Whereas the aesthetic principle of

98 BENJAMIN, p. 29 et seq.; TEILMANN-LOCK, p. 50 et seq.
99 LATOUR/ HENNION, p. 92.
100 BENJAMIN, p. 21.
101 BENJAMIN, p. 21; for an analysis on the concept of authenticity in BENJAMIN's essay see ZELLER, pp. 70-85.
102 BAECKER, p. 58, speaks about the "copy as the underlying condition of the original"; BUSKIRK, The Contingent Object, p. 72.
103 RÖMER, p. 70.
104 MENOCAL, p. 293.
105 CROW, p. 12; ZUSCHLAG, p. 208.
106 KRUGER, p. 90.
107 RÖMER, p. 100 et seqq.; GELSHORN, p. 219; MAGERSKI, p. 113, writes that the destruction of the art institution happened in the artwork itself; ESPOSITO, Altes, p. 138; LUHMANN, Ausdifferenzierung Kunstsystem, p. 348; MORTIER, p. 203 explains this phenomenon also by stating that because the "new" had stopped surprising, new ways had to be found to always bring about the effect of novelty.

originality had enforced an invention, conceived as a new form in every artwork and, thus, each time a material change,[108] copying meant not to transform what was there, not to augment reality in any way. Rather than being without precedence, the *raison d'être* of the copy was precisely to look like something that had already been made. As a reaction to what had happened until then in the history of art, postmodernism became the "style of mixing styles".[109] Repetition, the decontextualization of historical references and the grasping in new artworks of old forms became the strategies of choice to *make a difference* from the modernist predecessors.[110]

Yet postmodernist art is plagued by a paradoxical position.[111] Exactly as the early twentieth century modern art movements described themselves as a series of abrupt ruptures with the past, postmodern art, too, sees itself as in rupture with the modernist past (hence the prefix "post").[112] Even appropriation art, often classified as the most radical form of repetition, is – when read as a gesture of breaking with tradition, or to say it with Crow, of "recycl[ing] old forms, but only to do away with old attitudes"[113] – reiterating the programmatic modernist intention of wanting to be different from its past. Despite its own will, it, thus, conforms to the modernist stance[114] insofar as the preference for the old over the new is interpreted as a rule-breaking gesture; it creates something that is radically and unavoidably new. The denial of the new through the repetition of an old form becomes, thus, *new* itself, exactly as the denial of originality through the reproduction, at the level of the artwork's form of previously existing forms, becomes itself *original*.[115] In other words, the copy is, here, original because it is a copy.[116]

III.V The original copy as "re-entry"

In systems theoretical terms, the postmodern copy can be described with two different "re-entries", a concept that describes the otherness of the same.[117] In a re-entry, the form of the difference re-enters in what the difference itself differentiates

108 Bohn, Autonomien, p. 55; Lijster, p. 10.
109 Luhmann, Art as a Social System, p. 210.
110 Luhmann, Art as a Social System, p. 127; Magerski, p. 105; Buskirk, The Contingent Object, p. 91; in the words of Ullrich, Rituale, p. 139, "these old-new images are documents of a liberation that occurs when artists portray works of the art history just as curiously and unbiasedly as a piece of landscape, a still life, or a person" (translation is mine); cf. also McClean, p. 318.
111 For example, Hutcheon, p. 14 et seq., explains that postmodernism paradoxically manages to re-legitimize culture as it subverts it.
112 Cf., for example, Krauss, p. 66; Barron, Claims of Art, p. 395.
113 Crow, p. 20.
114 Ullrich, "Gurskyesque", p. 110.
115 Athanassopoulos, p. 286; Ullrich, Rituale, p. 233 et seq.; Römer, p. 121; Hildebrand-Schat, p. 220.
116 Talking about the work of Andy Warhol in her dissenting opinion to *Andy Warhol Found. for the Visual Arts, Inc. vs. Goldsmith*, 598 US ___ (2023), p. 4, Justice Elena Kagan expressed herself as follows: "his appropriations and his originality were *flipsides* of each other" (emphasis added).
117 Baraldi/Corsi/Esposito, p. 195.

(i.e., designates, observes).[118] Time would be necessary to see the re-entry as such (the fact that the same difference is used twice). In the operations of systems, however, the two passages happen simultaneously and are, thus, invisibilized.[119]

First, the postmodern artwork showcasing an art historical reference is making the "old" available as "new". The new of postmodern art is the new use of the old, that is, the re-entry, on the side of the new, of the difference old/new in itself.[120] In this sense, to distinguish it from the previous groundbreaking artistic movements, MARKUS BRÜDERLIN proposed to describe postmodern art as the "avant-garde of the old" and BORIS GROYS as the "repetition of the new".[121]

Similarly, notwithstanding the rejection of the modernist concept of originality, which was founded on the effect of surprise and deviance a new form could provoke,[122] the repetition of an existing form did not make the surprise effect disappear. Rather, when an art historical reference is found in a new artwork, the effect of surprise that was previously caused by formal novelty (i.e., by the evident crossing of the unmarked space to a new, marked space[123]) is newly caused by the decontextualization itself, i.e., by the sudden realization of having arbitrarily and unexpectedly accessed the supply of historical forms.[124] This also means that the difference between a copy and an original is no longer located in a *material* difference of the original from the copy, but it has been replaced with a temporal difference instead.[125] The *identical* copy strips the original of its entitlement to unicity by diluting the aesthetic-ontological categories that have kept them apart.[126] The new original is, thereby, a dematerialized artwork, meaning that the transmission of its intentions does not depend anymore, or not primarily, on visual qualities (material aspects such as uniqueness, permanence and decorative attractiveness are deemphasized)[127] but simply on its assertion that it is, indeed, new and not of yesterday.[128] In this sense, it became possible for a copy, i.e., for a reproduction of an artwork previously existing, to be a full artwork, another original.[129] Again, with

118 LUHMANN, Law as a Social System, p. 105 et seq.; at p. 204, LUHMANN defines a re-entry as "incalculable".
119 LUHMANN, Identität, p. 18.
120 LUHMANN, Challenge, p. 54 et seq.; LUHMANN, Weltkunst, p. 31; RIBETTES, p. 159.
121 GELSHORN, p. 219 and 233. Both descriptions contain a paradoxical, indeterminate moment: How can the old be vanguardist? Does the new not disappear when repeated? For this reason, they relate well to the just described re-entry of the difference old/new in itself.
122 ESPOSITO, Predicting Innovation, p. 238; LUHMANN, The Work of Art, p. 196; LUHMANN, Weltkunst, p. 32; HUBER/LUHMANN, p. 129.
123 LUHMANN, Art as a Social System, p. 29 et seqq.
124 LUHMANN, Art as a Social System, p. 127 and 262.
125 LUHMANN, Die Welt, p. 261.
126 ERNST, p. 502.
127 Cf. LIPPARD, p. vii et seqq. and 5; ICKOWICZ, p. 23 et seq.
128 LUHMANN, Die Welt, p. 261.
129 ERNST, p. 508 et seq.; cf. also LATOUR/LOWE, p. 183; MILLET, p. 120 et seq.

the concept of re-entry, the postmodern copy can, thus, be described as the difference original/copy re-entering itself on the side of the original.[130]

Because the way postmodern artists made new art that continued to irritate, provoke and expose society to the contingency of its own categories, it was in line with the ways of operating of the art system described above: On one side, the interpictoriality and, on the other, the transgression.[131] What had initially been conceived as the overcoming, or even negation, of the principles that were governing art (and its definition) has been *reabsorbed* by the art system as a new artistic practice.[132] For artists who may have wanted to problematize the notion of authorship, this meant that they became themselves authors.[133] For their copies, even if they were the complete and intentional reversal of the criteria that were valid during the preceding modernist period,[134] this meant that they became original artworks themselves.[135] Paradoxically, their critique to the *status quo* in the art system, with which they wanted to distance themselves from the past and make things different, could only be grasped and interpreted as such if these artworks themselves were to be reabsorbed as artworks by the art system.[136]

IV.I Interim conclusions: The "interpictorial original copy" in the blind spot of modernism

Our analysis has highlighted two important characteristics of the art system. First, that it can be observed as a system operating recursively by creating (visual) references to its own past. New artworks refer to old ones, forming a complicated network of visual cross-references and hints at each other. In this *modus* of observing art, the concept of originality becomes an historically contingent construct, while the focus is put on the interpictorial characteristics of the system. Second, we identified the tendency of the art system to describe itself, starting with the avant-garde, as a series of radical acts of overcoming its own past. In the moment of emergence, it is extremely unlikely that the work is perceived as art. Paradoxically, it is this unlikeliness that eventually makes works into proper *art*works. In this interpictorial network marked by radical historical shifts that is visual art, we could individuate a *novum*, the artifact that, precisely by showcasing its interpictoriality explicitly

130 Cf. Thalmair, Exhibition Format, p. 30; Buskirk, The Contingent Object, p. 58 et seqq.

131 Cf. above at Chapter 1, I.II; Art & Language, p. 21.

132 Römer, p. 187; cf. also Thalmair, Copying, p. 348.

133 Andreas Beyer, Aneignung ist ein Prinzip der Kunst an sich, June 15, 2016 (<https://www.unibas.ch/de/Aktuell/News/Uni-Research/Aneignung-ist-ein-Prinzip-der-Kunst-an-sich.html>); McClean, p. 319.

134 Ullrich, Rituale, p. 139, just some years before (e.g., during the period of the avant-gardes), to do so would have been seen as "a betrayal of the autonomy of art" (translation is mine).

135 Cf. Bauer, p. 36.

136 We, again, touch upon the problem of the transformation from the unlikeliness of the emergence to the likeliness of its preservation, cf. above at Chapter 1, I.II and Luhmann, Art as a Social System, p. 214.

instead of dissimulating it (the "re-entry"), becomes a work of art. We call this artwork an "interpictorial original copy".

Benjamin had developed a theory according to which the aura of the original was lost through its technical multiplication. Because he died in 1940, he could not see or describe what emerged shortly after, i.e., that some among these multiples could reinstate, through their improbable status as "new artworks negating the category of novelty", a paradoxical unicity.[137] Though Benjamin anticipated the advent of what has been later called the "culture of the copy", [138,139] he had not seen – because it simply was not there yet – how this culture advanced the emergence of another difference, by which, in some cases, a reproduction could be deemed other than "a weak counterfeit of the original" but an authentic (auratic?) artwork itself.[140] Enter postmodernism; the aura "starts hesitating, it cannot make up its mind about where it should settle".[141]

The existence of the "original copy" exposed the contingency of the modernist narrative by which reproductions could not be autonomous artworks.[142] Whereas today, reproductions of other artworks can be considered autonomous artworks – think of, for example, Sherrie Levine's *After Walker Evans* (1981) – in the modernist eyes of the past, this would not have been possible.

In systems theoretical terms, such an impossible position is defined as a blind spot. Every observation must use a distinction to be able to observe the world. The blind spot is the point from which the observation starts, and it is located where the boundary is drawn that separates the two sides of the distinction used to observe.[143] The result for operations of having a blind spot is that they are blind to their own operating, "for they cannot observe themselves without coming up against the paradox of the unity of the different".[144] The blind spot of an operation can only be seen with a subsequent operation based on another distinguishing indication, i.e., by observing other observers observing, thus discovering what they cannot see.[145] Despite their paradox, observations remain operative thanks to the facticity of their execution, which hides the paradox.[146]

When retaining Benjamin's main difference original/reproduction to observe art, the existence of the original copy, i.e., of an interpictorial artwork showcasing a

137 Zumthor, p. 146.

138 Leach, p. 129, uses (or copies!) the term coined by Hillel Schwartz in his book *The Culture of the Copy*, New York 1996; cf. also Ortland, Bildregime, p. 270; cf. also Fleck, p. 92 et seq.

139 Benjamin, p. 23.

140 That the ideas of aura and authenticity are interconnected is considered a scientifically established fact, cf. Zeller, p. 71.

141 Latour/Lowe, p. 185 (translation is mine); on the fact that the "original copy" changed the very definition of art, cf. also Fleck, p. 92 et seq. and Hutcheon, p. 33.

142 Cf. Wenzel, p. 218 et seq.; Blunck, p. 18 and 26; Zuschlag, p. 216.

143 Luhmann, Theory of Society I, p. 110, 258

144 Luhmann, Theory of Society I, p. 326.

145 Luhmann, Theory of Society II, p. 177; Luhmann, Decision Making, p. 90 et seq.; Lüdemann, p. 64; Luhmann, Identität, p. 26.

146 Luhmann, Decision Making, p. 91.

previous artwork and handled as new and original, is made invisible by the impossibility of classifying it as belonging to one or the other side.[147] If the operation uses the difference original/reproduction to observe an original copy, it will only be able to describe it as a reproduction – something that the original copy definitely is – but not simultaneously as an original, as in that distinction, the original is marked as the other side of the reproduction, i.e., as all that a reproduction will never be. In this sense, the interpictorial original copy becomes a sort of impossible and yet existing object.

In the following chapters, we will locate the interpictorial original copy within copyright law and analyze the normative statements associated to it.

147 The conceptual counterpart on the side of the original would be the confusion existing between "originalité et original au sens matériel", in which the latter would actually be just another copy of the original, cf. Ickowicz, p. 173; cf. also Römer, p. 123, in which he speaks about the work of Richard Prince, based on copies of the "original template, which was itself already a copy" (translation is mine).

Part II

The work or "the original"

"What is this curious unity that we designate as work?" Michel Foucault, What is an Author?

(1967)

DOI: 10.4324/9781003598503-4

2 The fundamentals of the work

I.I The historic evolution of copyright law

Dating back to its origins, copyright law has operated principally by regulating the right to copy artifacts of human ingenuity. Actions for copyright infringement have ever since been brought following a suspicion of copying and have been successful only after a sufficient substantiation of this claim.[1] Yet what has counted as copying has considerably varied in the history of copyright law.

Under the printing paradigm of copyright law, which derived from the historical system of privileges,[2] the most fundamental dichotomy was that between authorized and unauthorized copies. Being the immaterial and abstract concept of work yet to be invented, there was still no difference between the copy, understood as one among other specimens of a book, and the copy, understood as the original exemplar from which multiples are derived.[3] In the understanding of the Statute of Anne of 1710, considered by many the first copyright act,[4] the object of protection of copyright law was the concrete copy of a book. Infringement was thought in terms of the action of using specific technologies by which one could make copies (in particular re-printing, engraving and casting).[5] The aim of copyright law was not to curb imitation, per se, but to prohibit the unauthorized multiplication and distribution of samples that would constitute direct competitors on the market.[6] For this reason, because no exemplars had been made from the original copy, abridgements and translations of existing books were not considered infringing.[7] Similarly, the right to produce engravings was attached to the ownership of the physical plates for printing.[8] A rightsholder could only protect himself against the unsanctioned copying of that same book. It was, thus, forbidden to repeat *the act*

1 Balganesh, Normativity, p. 205; Towse, p. 11.
2 Teilmann-Lock, p. 42; Rigamonti, Geistiges Eigentum, p. 28 et seqq.
3 Teilmann-Lock, p. 27.
4 Teilmann-Lock, p. 1.
5 Teilmann-Lock, p. 28.
6 Teilmann-Lock, p. 105; Ortland, Bildregime, p. 277 speaks of the initial copyright as a market regulator for engravings.
7 Teilmann-Lock, p. 29 et seq.
8 Teilmann-Lock, p. 36.

DOI: 10.4324/9781003598503-5

of copying (in German: *Nachdruckverbot*"[9]) that had already been performed by the authorized person. Unauthorized copies were seen as having counterfeited not a "concept of work", but the much concreter authorized samples. These differed from the unauthorized copy only insofar as they were, indeed, authorized.

Copyright law considerably expanded in scope between the end of the eighteenth and the beginning of the nineteenth centuries.[10] The change initiated in the field of visual art, where the narrow bond of visual artworks to their physical embodiment made the protection of the printing paradigm of copyright law insufficient and, thus, unsatisfying for artists.[11] Reproducing a design is not an act forcibly deriving mechanically from the design itself, i.e., the engraving.[12] "Copy" was not to be interpreted in its everyday sense anymore, that is, as it had been derived from the book printing industry.[13] Rather, a copy could also be an artifact showcasing only an approximate likeness,[14] that which "comes so near to the original as to give to every person seeing it the idea created by the original".[15] Accordingly, the 1735 Engravers' Act (a predecessor of copyright for the visual arts in the UK) already defined an infringing copy as a reproduction "in the whole or in part, by varying, adding to, or diminishing from the main design" and, thus, identifying the object of protection not in the physical engraving but, rather, in its design.[16] Copyright lawyers increasingly used the term "reproduction" for defining the infringing copy until they became, as they are today, synonyms.[17]

The theoretical and historical framework around artistic artifacts at that time introduced into the overall conceptual framework of copyright law the valuable distinction between a *unique* original ("the work") and the *multiple* copies ("the work exemplars"). Under the original-copy paradigm of copyright law, how a concrete copy was produced is irrelevant because the object of protection has become conceptually independent from its carrier.[18] The assessment of whether there is an infringing copy has shifted from the question of how the supposed copy was realized to what it looks like and, therefore, to a "more modern assessment of the *degrees of nearness, or similarity*".[19]

9 Rigamonti, Geistiges Eigentum, p. 28 et seqq.
10 Teilmann-Lock, p. 27.
11 Teilmann-Lock, p. 121.
12 Ortland, Bildregime, p. 277.
13 Teilmann-Lock, p. 117.
14 Teilmann-Lock, p. 121; Griffiths, Copyright's Imperfect Republic, p. 342.
15 Teilmann-Lock, p. 42 et seq.
16 Teilmann-Lock, p. 36.
17 Teilmann-Lock, p. 108 and 116 et seqq.; cf. also Rigamonti, Geistiges Eigentum, p. 32 et seq., however, mainly reasoning on the emergence of the concept of "intellectual property" (*geistiges Eigentum*) for tracking the occurred change.
18 Rigamonti, Benjamin, p. 92, fn. 5; Griffiths, p. 342.
19 Teilmann-Lock, p. 44 (emphasis added).

II.I The difference between "work" and "work exemplar"

When copyright started defining the act of copying as a reproduction, i.e., the creation of a similarity between the original and its copy, it became possible to conceptualize the original work as something different than merely the first material copy from which more copies could be lawfully derived. Today, copyright law is regulated around the leading difference between the original work (in German: *Werk*) and the copy in the sense of an embodied exemplar of that work (in German: *Werkexemplar* or *Vervielfältigungsstück*).[20]

In this difference, the work designates the object of protection of copyright:[21] An immaterial creation of the mind, malleable and dynamic enough to accommodate, to a certain extent, technical and artistical novelties.[22]

In this modern understanding, the material embodiments of a work only constitute secondary concretizations of the abstract-immaterial work and signal, at most, its presence within them.[23] Even though, as often happens with artworks of the visual arts, only one unique exemplar exists, which means that the work concretely coincides with its unique physical embodiment, the latter is just another exemplar, while the work remains ubiquitous and conceptually detached from its physical embodiments.[24] This becomes clear when more than one exemplar exists, as the work exists simultaneously in all exemplars without being identifiable with just one among them.[25]

The difference between work and work exemplar also means that the work, ubiquitous as it is, can be embodied – lawfully or unlawfully – in an exemplar created by a person that is not the author of the work. Today, copying means to reproduce a protected work elsewhere, irrespectively of the means used and potentially in any form.[26] Provided that the photograph she has taken *is* indeed a copyrighted work, a photographer can protect herself against the copying of the therein depicted forms in a painting, in an illustration, even in a movie. All discussions have, thus, left the question of the belonging of such artifacts to a specific domain (be it music, photography, visual art and so on) and have relocated on the concept

20 Rigamonti, Benjamin, p. 93.

21 Sherman, What Is A Copyright Work, p. 102. In this sense, the role played by the work in copyright law is like that of the concept of invention in patent law. Exactly as the invention, the work is an abstract and general concept that condenses the doctrine and provides for a common denominator able to operate with a great range of different intellectual outputs, cf. Mersch, p. 68 and 105.

22 Sherman, What Is A Copyright Work, p. 107; Teilmann-Lock, p. 6; Peukert, A Critique, p. 33 et seq.

23 Peukert, A Critique, p. 101; Peukert, Drei Entstehungsbedingungen, p. 128; Teilmann-Lock, p. 120; Griffiths, p. 343.

24 Teilmann-Lock, p. 121.

25 Dreier, p. 207; such difference is thematized in Art. 16 para. 3 CopA, which states that the assignment of the ownership of a copy of a work (in our terminology, to avoid confusion, of an exemplar) does not include the right to exploit the copyrights tied to it, even in the case of an original work. Purchasing a work exemplar, even if it is the original and unique exemplar, does not mean receiving copyright ownership of the therein embodied work cf. Rigamonti, Benjamin, p. 93.

26 Teilmann-Lock, p. 6.

of work itself and on whether its criteria are fulfilled.[27] How the work is defined, therefore, becomes of pivotal importance because, as a sort of unit of measure of copyright, it defines copyright protection as well as limits its scope.[28]

III.I The element of originality in the definition of work

To become a work, an artifact must display a sufficient level of "originality", uniqueness in Germany (*Eigentümlichkeit*),[29] individual character or just individuality, in Switzerland.[30] Indeed, most court discussions on copyright eligibility revolve around this criterion,[31] which alone carries the burden of accommodating the opposing interests underlying copyright law.[32]

The definition of originality incurred an important shift of paradigm at the end of the twentieth century. This shift can be traced back to developments that happened in the environment of the law system that were registered by copyright lawyers that influenced the doctrinal discussions happening around the definition of the work.

Authors were thought to have complete authority over their oeuvre, which was seen as originating from their very "selves" and, thus, sharing their own peculiar characteristics.[33] The author could not *choose* to do something original, or as CARL SPITTELER (1845–1924) wrote: "no conscientious writer ever strives for originality. If he has an important personality, he will of his own accord turn out to be more original than he and his readers would like".[34] What is created by this author-genius is, thus, by definition, inimitable.[35] For the courts, the concept of "originality" corresponded to the necessity of a personal imprinting of the author in his oeuvre.[36]

27 MÜLLER, p. 250.
28 HUG, Switzerland, p. 257.
29 PLUMPE, p. 196.
30 However, the CopA of 1922, in force until 1993, required the work to be an "original creation" (Art. 1 para. 2 oCopA), cf. DESSEMONTET, Intellectual Property, p. 39.
31 CHERPILLOD, L'objet, p. 117, fn. 24. Instead, the criterion of individuality proved to be the most difficult to determine in practice, see: CHERPILLOD, SHK CopA, N 2 *ad* Art. 2; STUDER, p. 9.
32 REHBINDER/HAAS/UHLIG, OFK CopA, N 5 *ad* Art. 2 CopA; similarly, SHERMAN, Appropriating, p. 34.
33 KRAUSS, p. 56, writes that "the condition of his own singularity [would have] guarantee[d] the originality of what he makes".
34 As quoted in MORTIER, p. 203 (translation is mine). At p. 208, MORTIER writes about the "delirium of the individual", who thought of himself as unique and capable to remake the art world according to a personal aesthetic.
35 PEUKERT, Drei Entstehungsbedingungen, p. 136; cf. also LUHMANN, Individuum, p. 222; and JAMESON, p. 114: "the great modernisms were predicated on the invention of a personal, private style, as unmistakable as your fingerprint, as incomparable as your own body. But this means that the modernist aesthetic is in some way organically linked to the conception of a unique self ... which can be expected to generate its own unique vision of the world and to forge its own unique, unmistakable style".
36 CHERPILLOD, L'objet, p. 116 et seq.; see also: GRABER, Zwischen Geist und Geld, p. 107; TROLLER, Bedeutung, p. 272, writes that "the question whether and how the personality of the author is recognizable in the work was never asked". Indeed, even back when originality was understood as "having origin in the author", the question of the "recognizability of the author in the work" was

The decade following the year 1960, however, was marked by an art system increasingly going through a general depersonalization of the artmaking process.[37] Two texts, in particular, catalyzed the theoretical critique toward the role of the author as it had been previously conceived since the Romantic era.[38] In "The Death of the Author", a text written in 1967, ROLAND BARTHES announced, with manifesto-like momentum, the demise of the author's myth as it was conceived by classical literature criticism (but the same could have been written about the whole field of art history). Paradigmatic in this sense is the conclusion to its essay, in which he declared that "the birth of the reader must be ransomed by the death of the Author".[39] In his 1969 lecture "What Is an Author?", MICHEL FOUCAULT closely analyzed the author's role in the discourses of art and literature, concluding that the author is nothing but a function and that, as such, he is subject to variations in space, culture, and time. Far from being the idealized romantic figure of the tormented genius or the sole source of originality acting upon the impetus of a transcendent inspiration, FOUCAULT argued, the author is a mere discursive element of organization and classification – an "index of reality".[40] As such, he might be constructed as being a constant level of value, a field of conceptual coherence, a sign of stylistic unity and a figure at the crossroads of historical events.[41]

The art world reflected the undermining of the idiosyncratic author by making traces of the author's hand disappear from the artmaking process. The definition of original artwork formulated in Vienna in 1960 at the Third International Congress of Artists – "[a print] for which the artist made the original plate, cut the wood block, worked on the stone or any other material" – was quickly surpassed:[42] Duchamp and others displayed everyday objects as artworks. Robert Rauschenberg produced artworks in two identical exemplars to undermine the belief that spontaneity and improvisation could not be simulated.[43] Andy Warhol produced artworks

asked only once, i.e., in DFC 110 IV 102 E. 1 (*Zierpuppen*). In the decision, the Court wrote: "the judge should be able to recognize by looking at the work, that this stems from one person and from this person only"; for the UK cf. KEARNS, p. 84.

37 CHERPILLOD, L'objet, p. 116; so too in other countries, GERVAIS, Originalité(s), p. 390 et seqq.; GROYS, p. 125; WALRAVENS, p. 27.

38 WOODMANSEE, p. 280.

39 BARTHES.

40 FOUCAULT, p. 213.

41 FOUCAULT, p. 214.

42 BUSKIRK, The Contingent Object, p. 73, adds that "[this] definition, with its attempt to retain some version of the artist's hand, was established at the very moment when it was destined for obsolescence"; we see here the important category of the artist's "hand", also discussed by ICKOWICZ, p. 163 et seqq.

43 GELSHORN, p. 139 et seq., talks about Robert Rauschenberg's *Factum I* and *Factum II* (both 1957); RÖMER, p. 72, explains how, until then, the brushstroke had been considered by the "fanatics of the original" as a not reproducible expression of the artist and of originality.

in series,[44] often delegating the artwork's material realization.[45] And many others started imitating gestures and forms "originally" made by others.[46] Of the canonical author remained the signature, the process of "selection or designation" and, thus, the function of attributing things to people.[47]

These changes were received in the copyright literature,[48] which started framing authorship as the problem of how to construct the causality between author and work now that the author's hand had retroceded behind other factors and was not as materially self-evident as it had been in the past.[49] This coincided with the fragmentation and loss of stability of the criteria for the definition of a copyrighted work.[50] The requirements shifted from a "subjective" paradigm – focused on how the personality of the author appeared in the artifact – to a more "objective" one – to be looked for in the work itself.[51]

The described shift made originality what we know today. Diametrically opposite to what SPITTELER had believed, the author is not a genius from whose personality works inexplicably arise anymore but is now, rather, a "form-giver",[52] whose *choices* between alternatives of arrangement as reflected in the artifact are

44 BUSKIRK, The Contingent Object, p. 74, underlining the increasing importance of "techniques of mechanical reproduction"; GELSHORN, p. 140, makes the example of Andy Warhol, who, in his words, "wanted to be a machine". At p. 149, she quotes Warhol himself, who declared "that he could do 4'000 [artworks] in a day. And they'd be all masterpieces because they'd be all the same painting".

45 JONES, p. 200 and 422, when asked about the meaning of his work, Warhol answered: "Why don't you ask my assistant Gerry Malanga some questions? He did a lot of my paintings"; BUSKIRK, The Contingent Object, p. 74, explains the remarkable feature of Warhol's enterprise, consisting of "subcontracting" and the delegation "not only of production, but even of decision-making".

46 GELSHORN, p. 142, explains how imitative processes make every spontaneity disappear and every individual gesture become a formula; ironically, LEVINE, p. 126 even appropriated parts of Barthes' text, see also GAMER, p. 63;

47 BUSKIRK, The Contingent Object, p. 74; BUSKIRK, Interviews, p. 106; cf. also GRABER, Zwischen Geist und Geld, p. 96 et seqq. for a systems theoretical analysis of the process of creation of an artwork and the insertion thereof in the context of twentieth century poststructuralist theories.

48 Cf. MCCLEAN, p. 317; GRABER, Zwischen Geist und Geld, p. 107; ADLER, The Future of Art, p. 593, "the romantic concept of a single, all-knowing artist who controls meaning was always a distortion".

49 SAUNDERS, p. 100.

50 CHERPILLOD, L'objet, p. 116 et seq.; GRABER, Zwischen Geist und Geld, p. 107; MÜLLER, p. 238; KUMMER, Werk, p. 25; KUMMER, Werkbegriff, p. 126 et seq.; and FUCHS CHRISTINE, p. 54; for the UK, similarly, KEARNS, p. 84

51 CHERPILLOD, SHK CopA, N 18 and 21 *ad* Art. 2; DESSEMONTET, CoRo CopA, N 14 *ad* Art. 2. Also presented this way by KUMMER, Werk, p. 30; CHERPILLOD, L'objet, p. 117 and 132, explains "objective" in the sense that the distinctive characters that make up a work are visible in the work itself and not in the personality of the author. "Subjective" stands for the search of the link between work and author. Cf. also WALRAVENS, p. 150, for France.

52 This, explains LUHMANN, Weltkunst, p. 30 and LUHMANN, Ausdifferenzierung Kusntsystem, p. 345, because the inexplicable emergence of new must be attributed to someone. The attribution of "new" is, thus, personalized up to the point of the "cult of the genius"; cf. also PEUKERT, Drei Entstehungsbedingungen, p. 134 et seq., who explains how, before the late Middle Age, when things started to change, it would have been impossible to attribute the emergence of the "new" to someone: The sole creator was God.

central to determine appropriability.[53] The author cannot be looked for in the work anymore; rather, it is the forms of the work that, if original, signal the presence of an author to the law.[54]

This reification of the work becomes the conditions for the establishment of copyright's subject-object relationship that is at the basis of author's rights. The work is reattributed to the author as an object of his exclusive rights in a second moment, after it has been verified that the artifact at stake is, indeed, a work.[55] Only those who created a work become authors,[56] and only those who are authors enjoy rights over their works' use and are, therefore, able to regulate the access to their works.[57]

Even if she must now be guessed behind the forms of the work she produces, the author has not moved an inch:[58] The equation between work and author's personality is still very present in the concept of moral rights, which manifest into a strong (and enforceable) intimate bond of authors to their works.[59] Similarly, we visit exhibitions prominently titled with the artists' names (even those who, inspired by Barthes, had tried to disrupt their own centrality).[60] Moreover, the control over

53 Cherpillod, L'objet, p. 133 et seq.; Cherpillod, SHK CopA, N 27 *ad* Art. 2; the criterion of the author's choices seems to be common to many other definitions of originality, cf. Gervais, Originalité(s), p. 391 et seqq., for example, in France, the Netherlands, Belgium, the European Union, and even the United States. For Germany, see Müller, p. 232; for France, see Walravens, p. 149, exposing the jurisprudence on the criterion of "choix arbitraire".

54 Ickowicz, p. 30.

55 Wielsch, Relationales Urheberrecht, p. 64; cf. also Barron, Claims of Art, p. 379; Sherman, Appropriating, p. 46; cf. also Berger, p. 12, who writes that the author as "subject" is protected only indirectly.

56 For this reason, it is argued that the attention given to the "author" in copyright history is disproportionate compared to the largely unexplored notion of the work, cf. Bellido, p. 128; Barron, Claims of Art, p. 369; Peukert, Drei Entstehungsbedingungen, p. 127.

57 Egloff, CopA Commentary, N 2 *ad* Vorbemerkungen Art. 9–15 CopA; Cueni, p. 658; Vischer, Urheberrecht, p. 253, affirms: "either the whole protection, or nothing; *tertium non datur*" (translation is mine); the *tertium*, however, might be, in some cases, the protection against unfair competition under the UWG.

58 As Saunders, p. 101 et seq., explains, "only if the subject is identified with the free and self-reflexive cogito can post-structuralism look post-subjective" and "the post-structuralist strategy is no less subject-centered than the Romantic historicism it purports to displace"; interestingly, indeed, in an interview made by Robert Rosenblum, Mike Bidlo (one of the biggest appropriationists) stated: "I think everyone brings their own signature and personality into their work, even if they're making replicas", p. 193.

59 That a connection between individual character and moral rights still exists despite the change of paradigm in the definition of work is demonstrated by the scholarly opinions according to which moral rights should not apply to non-individual works (Art. 2 para. 3bis CopA). For example, it has been argued that non-individual works have a lower connection to the personality of their authors and, thus, a lower one to moral rights automatically, see Egloff, CopA Commentary, N 38 *ad* Art. 2; Barrelet/Egloff, CopA Commentary, N 20 *ad* Art. 11; agreeing Oertli, p. 604; for Adler, Against Moral Rights, p. 265 and 269 et seqq., moral rights embody an obsolete conception of art; cf. also Rigamonti, Deconstructing, p. 359.

60 Ironically, Michel Foucault (and, thus, his name!) is arguably one of the most quoted authors in academia, and Andy Warhol, with permanently traveling exhibitions, pop art-themed gadgets and

the circulation of a work is still regulated by the "form" of authorship and the rights related to it.[61] In a German case in which at stake was the unsanctioned use of Disney's characters Donald Duck and Mickey Mouse, this aspect became very clear. The defendant had argued that because the plaintiff had not decided to sue the painter Roy Lichtenstein for his previous use of the same Disney figures,[62] he had concluded that the figures must have been freely usable. The German Federal Court of Justice (GFCJ) clarified that

> even though the plaintiff could have sued Lichtenstein for his use and that if she did, the use could have probably been considered a copyright infringement, the fact that she omitted to do so does not authorize third parties to infringe the rights of the plaintiff.

The fact that the plaintiff did not sue other previous artists for their unsanctioned uses of the same work "does not allow to conclude that she will not proceed against other parties".[63] In other words, copyright law does not "protect the world" from copies[64] but, rather, authors and other rightsholders, i.e., subjects who wish to keep control over their creative outputs.[65]

The following analysis does not inquire on the psychological motives behind authors' decisions to sue or not to sue in case they suspect a possible infringement of their copyright. Rather, it focuses on the understanding of the requirement of "originality" imposed by copyright law on artworks as the very precondition to every entitlement an author may be able to assert in the form of the artwork.

---

a prolific foundation, has acquired a truly larger-than-life dimension. The paradoxicality of it all is underlined by CROW, p. 26, who commented that despite these attempts at depersonalizing the oeuvre, behind Warhol's paintings was a decidedly original author: Him. This is also a re-entry.

61 BERGER, p. 12 et seq.; COOMBE, p. 8; SAUNDERS, p. 102.

62 The painting discussed here is probably *Look Mickey* (1961).

63 GFCJ of March 26, 1971 (*Disney-Parodie*), GRUR 1971, p. 588 et seqq. (translation is mine).

64 This finding shall be relativized. In Chapter 6, I.I, we show how copyright law also has a societal dimension that exerts effects beyond sole litigation. An example is the cancellation of Cornelia Sollfrank's exhibition in Basel in an act of "anticipatory obedience", even if the rightsholders had filed no complaint.

65 PEUKERT, Two Cultures, p. 398.

3 Three axes of copyright protection

I.I Introduction

In the following pages, the aim is to deconstruct the definition and then re-create an order that will shed a different light on tried and tested knowledge on the concept of "work". To do so, the various statements found in literature and case law will be grouped on three axes:

- The first axis concerns the question of *what* is looked for when trying to individuate originality (I);
- The second axis defines, instead, *how much* originality is needed to ultimately bestow protection (II);
- On the third and last axis is located the question about *where* in the artifact at stake the originality shall be found (III).

Functioning as the coordinates of copyright and interacting with each other in always different but deeply intertwined ways,[1] these three axes define the scope of protection of copyright law.

II.I What is the individual character?

The first axis defining the scope of protection gathers the answers to the question: What is eligible for copyright? With an added degree of abstractedness, the question can be paraphrased into: What form do things have to take to be seen as works in copyright law? When dealing with the requirement of individual character, it seems that even courts defer an ultimate definition, resorting, instead, to additional, similar criteria.[2] There is no such thing as "the Work" but, rather, a series

1 For example, as recognized by Vischer, Neue Tendenzen, p. 286, the opening of copyright toward the protection of ideas would forcibly weaken its individuation based on the principle of statistical uniqueness (cf. at Chapter 3, IV.I).

2 Mijatovic, Werk, p. 436; Züllig, p. 294; Sherman, Appropriating, p. 34, refers to originality as that "something special" that enables copyright law to label a work original and that is "very difficult, if not impossible", to determine; Metzger, p. 27, states "there is only original in plural form, but no more originality".

DOI: 10.4324/9781003598503-6

of different definitions and concurring ways to determine it.[3] Such is demonstrated by the multiple paraphrases that one can encounter: Originality,[4] uniqueness, singularity, novelty,[5] surprise,[6] peculiarity, creativity[7] and aesthetics.[8] But also by the many definitions *ex negativo*:[9] The banal, the simple, the obvious, the artisanal, the already known and the usual are not individual.[10]

As the Western aesthetic is one of transformation, the realm of creation is that of "the more", at most of "the less", but surely not that of the "nothing".[11] This more (or this less) could be a matter of selection,[12] of re-presentation.[13] As an example, let us think of the action of taking a picture. When taking the camera and looking into the viewfinder, the objective selects something out of reality; we do not see everything anymore but a smaller portion of what our peripheral vision allows us to see. A layer of meaning is added in the picture (when observed from a second-order perspective): Someone decided to select that something, to take it out of the flow

3 EGLOFF, CopA Commentary, N 11 *ad* Art. 2; SOMMER/GORDON, p. 287 et seqq.

4 The most popular synonym, cf. MIJATOVIC, Werk, p. 435, who quotes DFC 125 III 328 (*Niederhauser*), DFC 113 II 190 (*Le Corbusier*), DFC 110 IV 102 (*Zierpuppen*), DFC 106 II 71 (*Kasperlifguren*), DFC 100 II 167 (*Späti Laden*). On whether the concepts of originality and individuality are equivalent, cf. RENOLD/MOSIMANN, Kultur Kunst Recht, N 65 *ad* § 1, who assert a narrow relatedness of the criteria of originality and individuality; KUMMER, Werk, p. 35 and 38, argued instead that individuality is easier to reach compared to originality; TROLLER, Immaterialgüterrecht, p. 362; TROLLER, Bedeutung, p. 271, pleaded, instead, for the contrary opinion, according to which individuality stands for an "enhanced originality". To us, it seems that, today, the use of "originality" seems to only endorse the discourse on the individual character, without qualitatively adding anything to it, cf. similarly SENN, Innovation, p. 77.

5 EGLOFF, CopA Commentary, N 13 *ad* Art. 2; STUTZ, p. 11. With regard to novelty, individuality requires intellectual creations to not only be "new" in the terms of an intellectual creation but also, and to a sufficient degree, *distant* from the previously known so that it can be established that not just anybody could have come up with the same form, cf. EGLOFF, CopA Commentary, N 11 *ad* Art. 2; SFSC 4C_120/2002 of August 19, 2002 (*Hobby Kalender*), sic! 2003, p. 28 et seqq.; DFC 110 IV 102 (*Zierpuppen*).

6 Decision of the Cantonal Court of St. Gallen of June 19, 2002 (*Mummenschanz*), sic! 2003, p. 116 et seqq., p. 119.

7 DE WERRA/BENHAMOU, Kultur Kunst Recht, N 15 *ad* § 7.

8 SOMMER/GORDON, p. 288.

9 MERSCH, p. 104, the concept of invention, too, has been mostly described negatively.

10 DFC 105 II 297 (*Montre "Monsieur Pierre")*; DFC 134 III 166 (*Arzneimittelkompendium*), DFC 130 III 714 (*Meili*).

11 The "author" returns; etymologically, "author" derives from Latin *augere*, meaning "to augment". The author is someone who "augments", who acts on nature and changes it, cf. EDELMAN, The Law's Eye, p. 86; PEUKERT, A Critique, p. 29; BUCCAFUSCO, p. 378; SHORE, p. 34; RIBETTES, p. 158; in an historical perspective, see HAUG, p. 9; LUHMANN, Die Welt, p. 305.

12 LUHMANN, Weltkunst, p. 8; PHILIPPOPOULOS-MIHALOPOULOS, p. 25; LUHMANN, Art as a Social System, p. 263.

13 EDELMAN, The Law's Eye, p. 86, writes that nature is indeterminate and only receives its determination from art. So, "land" becomes a "landscape" only on condition of a pre-existing aesthetic notion thereof; KRAUSS, p. 59, writes how nature is constituted in relation to its "capability of being formed into pictures".

of reality,[14] and bring it out of its "disinterested detachment" (HEGEL).[15] Afterward, one can choose to add another form, to make another difference:[16] A special effect through a filter or postproduction, a different color or a shape, a light conveying a particular meaning or some dramatic contrast. One can choose to distort the subject, to make it different from how it would otherwise emerge from reality, e.g., by adding or removing elements from it. These actions could contribute to making the artifact stand out as a work, i.e., to bestow individuality on the "disinterested and detached vastity nature is".[17]

If not a matter of selection out of reality, it can be a matter of creating something anew, perhaps an abstract subject, one that does not look like anything. Because no one creates *ex nihilo*, in a vacuum of reality, the raw matter for such operation is always drawn, consciously or unconsciously, from one's life experiences,[18] from what abstract painter TERRY WINTERS called a "database of forms",[19] and ANDRÉ MALRAUX the "*musée imaginaire*".[20] Be it a visual reminiscence from one's own past, a lecture of art history, a flashback from a museum visit, or a Google image search, every creative process starts somewhere in the middle of society.[21] These confused – at times genuinely forgotten – inputs are later remixed, kneaded, put together or separated, modified in such a way until the result appears satisfying to the author and identifiable to the art critic or historian as artwork.

From the point of view of law, the inert matter starting from which artists create their visual artworks has the same status as language: "everyone speaks, but *only the author creates his style*".[22] In this respect, some authors bring into focus the interdependence between the history of copyright and a certain aesthetic of autonomy advanced in the art system at the same time.[23] Not every selection from nature's inertia, change to the already existing, creation from or distortion of reality amounts to a copyrightable work. Rather, copyright law decides, among all things created, what is a work and what is not.[24] To inquire when and in what copyright sees a work means to produce a topology of under what circumstances copyright law reconciles the notion of "nature belonging to everyone" (*res communis*) with

14 BERGER, p. 18; Richard Prince, quoted by RÖMER, p. 123, speaks of the camera as of a pair of "electronic scissors".

15 EDELMAN, The Law's Eye, p. 83; cf. also PLUMPE, p. 196; cf. also GROYS, p. 126.

16 LUHMANN, Art as a Social System, p. 29 et seqq.; GRABER, Zwischen Geist und Geld, p. 97.

17 EDELMAN, The Law's Eye, p. 79.

18 BOHN, Autonomien, p. 41; LETHEM, p. 68, writes: "all ideas are second-hand, consciously and unconsciously drawn from a million outside sources"; cf. also MIJATOVIC, Kreativität, p. 91; HAUG, p. 8 et seq.; SHORE, p. 127 and MOSIMANN, Kultur Kunst Recht, N 124 *ad* §1.

19 As abstract painter Terry Winters declared in <https://www.youtube.com/watch?v=rq9ooNpGBB8&feature=youtu.be> (at 2'05").

20 ANDRÉ MALRAUX, Le musée imaginaire, Paris 1965; cf. LUHMANN, Weltkunst, p. 15.

21 Cf. CRAIG, Copyright, p. 230.

22 EDELMAN, The Law's Eye, p. 83 (emphasis added).

23 WIELSCH, Zugangsregeln, p. 45; PLUMPE, p. 183; SHERMAN, Appropriating, p. 35.

24 REHBINDER/HAAS/UHLIG, OFK CopA, N 5 *ad* Art. 2 CopA; WIELSCH, Relationales Urheberrecht, p. 92, reminds to always think about "the other side of the distinction".

the fact that, if certain conditions are realized, things may become the object of the exclusive, subjective right of an author.[25]

II.II "Novelty" as the lowest common denominator of the individual character

The idea of promoting "the new" through the causal attribution thereof to the author is embedded within all regimes of intellectual property protection, including copyright law.[26] Whereas in the Swiss Federal Act on Patents for Inventions ("PatA"), the "novelty" of the invention is explicitly required by law (Art. 7 PatA); in copyright law, it merely represents one of the elements composing the complex notion of originality (even though it is sometimes elevated as a sort of full synonym thereof[27]).[28]

In copyright law, the new is not only a temporal difference (i.e., the other side of "old").[29] The new of copyright law is, rather, a material difference, i.e., it is "everything that does not already exist",[30] and, therefore, concerns the material relation between analogous (*gleichartig*) and novel (*neuartig*).[31] Because the novelty of the artifact is a difference that the artifact's existence states with respect to what preceded it, it can be obtained not only by addition of elements but also by their subtraction.[32] This difference (or this sum of differences) is the starting point to establish whether there is matter that can be called a work of copyright law.

This idea of the new becomes clear when the SFSC mentions "existing forms" to argue for the presence (or the absence) of an individual character.[33] According to the court, the mere combination and modification of existing forms must be judged as a mere artisanal performance and, thus, be denied an individual character.[34] So, for example, the SFSC denied copyright protection to the chair model LC 1, designed by Le Corbusier, because of the previous existence of two similar

25 Edelman, The Law's Eye, p. 79; similarly, Bung/Gruber/Kühn, p. 11.

26 Ohly, p. 280 et seq.; Senn, Innovation, p. 73 et seqq.; Peukert, Drei Entstehungsbedingungen, p. 134; Peukert, A Critique, p. 29; on the relationship between the law and innovations, cf. Camenisch, p. 38 et seqq.

27 In Switzerland among others, Egloff, Commentary CopA, N 13 *ad* Art. 2; Stutz, p. 11; SFSC 4C_120/2002 of August 19, 2002 (*Hobby Kalender*), sic! 2003, p. 28 et seqq.; DFC 110 IV 102 (*Zierpuppen*).

28 Senn, Innovation, p. 77 et seq.; Fischer, Sampling, p. 42, similarly in German copyright law, novelty is verified by means of the criterion of the "*Schöpfungshöhe*".

29 Cf. Hoffmann-Riem, p. 24.

30 Reinhart, p. 235.

31 Hoffmann-Riem, p. 24; Haug, p. 8; Ortmann, p. 174; Bohn, Gegenwarten, p. 75 reports Reinhart Koselleck's axiom for uniqueness, defined as the fact that "every event produces more and simultaneously less than what was contained in its past, hence its surprising novelty" (translation is mine).

32 That "*less is more*" is demonstrated also in DFC 143 III 373 (*Max Bill*), c. 2.8.3. and c. 2.8.5., in which the SFSC stated that the individual character must not be denied because "a further reduction of forms would not be possible"; rather, the essential minimalism of the stool justified its protection.

33 Senn, Zweckänderung, p. 213.

34 In DFC 100 II 167 (*Späti Laden*), DFC 106 II 71 (*Kasperlifiguren*), DFC 110 IV 102 (*Zierpuppen*), DFC 117 II 466 (*Sekundarschulanlage*), SFSC 4C_86/2000 of June 13, 2000 (*Vaca lechera*), sic!

models (the so-called Wassily chair, designed by Marcel Breuer, and the colonial chair by Ole Wanscher) whose overall impression highlighted the similarity existing between them rather than the tiny differences.[35] In another decision, the court held that "intellectual creations that are new but so close to the already known that others could also create the same form, do not have an individual character".[36]

If the artifact at stake features already known lines and shapes, its individual character must be denied, even if these are arranged differently or are slightly modified: This is the conclusion to which the SFSC came in DFC 105 II 297 (*Montre "Monsieur Pierre"*), when it argued that, even if the attaching system of the watch could *not* be mistaken for that of another watch, it did not distinguish itself enough to be more than a mere variation of previously known shapes.[37] In the "*Vaca lechera*" decision as well, the SFSC found that a logo depicting a cow on a mountain had no individual character because it was too close to other representations of cows and its color, posture and morphology were not different.[38] Similarly, the SFSC stated that individuality depends on the relationship between what has been invented by the author and what instead was borrowed from the public domain (*Gemeingut*).[39] Other times, the SFSC held that only configurations that do not exclusively contain elements from the public domain can be deemed individual.[40]

The comparison between the artifact at stake and the already known shapes (*Formenschatz*) is a question of fact (*Tatfrage*) that should be proven by the parties in the proceeding.[41] For example, the defendant could bring documents proving that similar artifacts existed previously. This would speak against the protectability of the artifact at stake, which would then be seen as a mere variation of existing forms. However, as Senn argues, the question of novelty compared to already

2001, p. 729 et seqq.; SFSC 4C_120/2002 of August 19, 2002 (*Hobby Kalender*), sic! 2003, p. 28 et seqq., c. 4 and DFC 142 III 387 (*Terrasse*), c. 3.2.

35 DFC 113 II 190 (*Le Corbusier*), c. II.1; such outcome was later confirmed in SFSC 4A_78/2011 of May 2, 2011 (*Le Corbusier 2*), c. 2.4.

36 DFC 110 IV 102 (*Zierpuppen*), c. 2 (translation is mine); here, we recognize also the element of the causal attribution of the new to its first and sole creator. If "the new" could be created by others as well, then this attribution to only one person would not be justifiable.

37 DFC 105 II 297, E. 3 (*Montre "Monsieur Pierre"*).

38 SFSC 4C_86/2000 of June 13, 2000 (*Vaca lechera*), sic! 2001, p. 729 et seqq.; in another decision (SFSC 4C_448/1997 of August 15, 1998 (*Clown*), sic! 1999, p. 198 et seqq.), however, the SFSC affirmed the individuality of a drawing of a clown doing a somersault. Although both clown and cow drawings were judged similar to commonly known representations of the respective object, the posture of the clown was decisive for the work to be judged individual (even if, upon a closer look to the drawing, the clown seems sitting rather than doing a somersault).

39 This specific wording only in DFC 110 IV 102 (*Zierpuppen*).

40 DFC 113 II 190 (*Le Corbusier*), DFC 113 II 306 (*Psychologie Dissertation*), DFC 117 II 466 (*Sekundarschulanlage*), DFC 125 III 328 (*Niederhauser*), SFSC 4C_448/1997 of August 15, 1998 (*Clown*), sic! 1999, p. 198 et seqq.; SFSC 4C_120/2002 of August 19, 2002 (*Hobby Kalender*), sic! 2003, p. 28 et seqq.; cf. also Zurich Court of Appeal of July 7, 2009 (*Love*), sic! 2010, p. 889 et seqq., c. 1.3.

41 Senn, Zweckänderung, p. 214; cf. Commercial Court of Aargau of January 5, 2015 (*Totenkopf-Tattoo*), sic! 2015, p. 449 et seqq., p. 451.

existing forms is apparently treated by courts as a question of law (*Rechtsfrage*). If the court concludes that an artifact is individual because it stands out against the previously known shapes, it is often unclear according to which method this outcome is reached and, for example, whether the court has been provided with evidence as to the contrary and has engaged itself with this documentation.[42]

II.III The theory of statistical uniqueness

The theory of statistical uniqueness (*statistische Einmaligkeit*) was formulated by MAX KUMMER in his 1968 seminal work *Das urheberrechtlich schützbare Werk*.[43] According to the theory, a work is only individual if it is unique.[44] To determine this uniqueness, the theory is based on a two-step comparison. In the first step, the work is compared to what already exists (called by HILTY the *Fundus*[45]) to establish its relative novelty, i.e., the difference it manages to establish in comparison to its past considered in a given moment.[46] In the second step, the theory futurizes the notion of novelty; the work is compared to what could hypothetically be created but has not yet been created in order to establish the distance from what already exists.[47] The second step, thus, assesses the "statistical" probability of a similar creation, bestowing a copyright only on creations deemed improbable to arise.[48]

In the conception of the SFSC, the second step means that no individual character is present if there is a high probability that the same, or essentially the same, artifact would have resulted from the same task.[49] In this sense, the statistical uniqueness proposes an enhanced version of novelty. Not only must the work be new – different – with respect to what already exists in the present but also to future hypothetical artifacts. This surplus of novelty, to be ascertained in the present but realizable only in a "future present", is clearly speculative: An image of the future that we have today, when this future does not yet exist and is only a possible projection. How the "present future" will actually look when it occurs is clearly not discernible.[50]

42 SENN, Zweckänderung, p. 214.

43 DESSEMONTET, CoRo CopA, N 14 *ad* Art. 2; TROLLER, Bedeutung, p. 270; VISCHER, Neue Tendenzen, p. 281 et seq.; the theories of KUMMER were also received beyond Switzerland. In Germany, for example, cf. LOEWENHEIM/LEISTNER, DE-CopA Commentary, N 44 *ad* § 2.

44 KUMMER, Werk, p. 30.

45 HILTY, Urheberrecht, N 159.

46 KUMMER, Werk, p. 30; cf. also SENN, Zweckänderung, p. 213.

47 HILTY, Urheberrecht, N 158; REHBINDER/HAAS/UHLIG, OFK CopA, N 9 *ad* Art. 2.

48 CHERPILLOD, SHK CopA, N 23 *ad* Art. 2.

49 DFC 134 III 166 (*Arzneimittelkompendium*), c. 2.3.1; DFC 142 III 387 (*Terrasse*), c. 3.1; cf. also Commercial Court of Zurich of January 25, 2022 (*Hotelrevue*), c. 4; REHBINDER/HAAS/UHLIG, OFK CopA, N 9 *ad* Art. 2.

50 Cf. on this ELENA ESPOSITO, Open Future, November 23, 2015 (available at: <https://futureswewant.net/esposito-open-future/>).

II.III.I The reception of the statistical uniqueness

The SFSC or other lower cantonal courts have never strictly applied the statistical uniqueness.[51] Despite this fact, the theory is said to have incisively influenced courts' argumentations and the copyright doctrine in general,[52] bringing more objectivity and legal certainty in the determination of the individual character.[53]

The theory was criticized for its inherent bias toward declaring individual more complex works, as these, even if they are composed of trivial elements, naturally augment their statistical improbability inasmuch as they augment the difference from other artifacts "by addition".[54] KUMMER saw no contradiction in that. For him, the judgment of copyright should not be about the quality of the creation but merely about its statistical diversity.[55] Only in this way could a neutral-objective test be created.[56] For this reason, however, the test was criticized for detaching copyright law from its object – the reality of art and culture and the promotion thereof – and for creating a, perhaps, objective, yet meaningless and empty copyright protection.[57]

The theory was further criticized for not being as objective as it claimed to be. Due to the *de facto* lack of statistical information about existing works and of a comparable measure of the degree of their similarity, the assessment of statistical uniqueness still had to function based on the judge's discretion in establishing what was new enough to be considered unique.[58] Moreover, KUMMER never proposed a method to really measure the statistical probability of the creation of a similar artwork. Our impression is, thus, that the theory did not really provide more objectivity but limited itself to substitute the subjective element of the personal imprinting of the author in the work with the abstract element of futurized-statistical novelty. Despite much praise about the theory's alleged merit of providing more objectivity, the theory of statistical uniqueness, too, contains an element of incalculability and indeterminacy that is concealed behind its self-description as "statistical".

51 Cf. for example DFC 134 III 166 (*Arzneimittelkompendium*), c. 2.3.1., DFC 130 III 714 (*Meili*), c. 2.3., DFC 130 III 168 (*Marley*), c. 4.5.; Zurich Court of Appeal of July 7, 2009 (*Love*), sic! 2010, p. 889 et seqq., c. 1.1, in which the court explicitly held that the statistical uniqueness alone cannot be decisive.

52 TROLLER, Bedeutung, p. 266.

53 MACCIACCHINI, Doppelschöpfung, p. 353; TROLLER, Bedeutung, p. 269 and 276.

54 CHERPILLOD, SHK CopA, N 28 *ad* Art. 2.

55 CHERPILLOD, SHK CopA, N 30 *ad* Art. 2.

56 MACCIACCHINI, Doppelschöpfung, p. 353; CHERPILLOD, SHK CopA, N 30 *ad* Art. 2

57 DESSEMONTET, Intellectual Property, p. 40.

58 CHERPILLOD, L'objet, p. 135; CHERPILLOD, SHK CopA, N 25 *ad* Art. 2; very well put in a decision of the Zurich Court of Appeal of June 30, 1983 (*Managertyp*), SMI 1985, p. 221 et seq., p. 223 et seq.: "On one side it is completely impossible, even in the era of computers, to determine whether a similar artifact already exists. Even more so, such a comparison is not possible for works that will at best only be created in the future.... What the "normal observer" regards as a "tangible" difference is again a question of evaluation.... Therefore, even if the criterion of statistical uniqueness is applied, it depends on a certain subjective feeling of the judge" (translation is mine).

II.III.II The theory in its art historical context

KUMMER understood that art was not about the originality of the author. He saw that art wanted newly to realize a breakout in all possible styles, an exceeding of fantasy in the unexplored and the yet unthought.[59] The theory's explicit purposes were, thus, to move forward from the previous requirement of author-bound originality, consider the developments in the art world and encompass those depersonalized new artworks that "declared art the artless".[60] The individual character determined with the theory of statistical uniqueness made it possible, according to KUMMER, to avoid importing external, aesthetical values within the law of copyright. By facilitating the assessment of the individual character based on formal aspects, such as the novelty of the form and the probability of a similar creation, the theory would prevent the consideration of qualitative aspects, avoiding lawyers becoming censors for the visual arts.[61]

If we put the theory of statistical uniqueness in its (art) historical context, however, we discover many commonalities. The contemporary artistic environment was dominated by the aesthetic doctrine of modern formalism, especially as conceived by CLEMENT GREENBERG (its most influential exponent). According to GREENBERG, art was to be evaluated only in terms of the strictly visual characteristics of the works that comprised it, thus transcending all notions of subject-matter and context.[62] All that counted was what happened within the medium-specific limitations of painting, such as "the flat surface, the shape of the support, the properties of pigment".[63] His views on art were also inextricable from the attributes of the pure optical space, and this was understood by him as the space of painting alone – the only place where pure form and composition could be performed.[64] In a similar fashion, the statistical uniqueness puts the artifact, conceived of as an independent entity, in the center. How the artifact looks and the forms it displays are decisive elements for evaluating its eligibility for copyright.

KUMMER did consider the discrepancy that could arise between copyright protection established with his theory and the judgments of the artistic world. Most notably, the result achieved under his presentation theory (cf. above at Chapter 3, II.VI) may have collided with an interpretation of the individual character as the expression of statistical uniqueness. In other words, not all that is identified

59 As reported by GRABER, Zwischen Geist und Geld, p. 106; cf. also HABERMAS, p. 5, describing the avant-garde as "invading unknown territory, exposing itself to the dangers of sudden, shocking encounters, *conquering an as yet unoccupied future*. The avant-garde must find a direction in a landscape into which no one seems to have yet ventured" (emphasis added); cf. on this characteristic of art in Chapter 1, II.III.

60 KUMMER, Werk, p. 2 et seq., 29, p. 75 et seqq.; DESSEMONTET, CoRo CopA, N 11 *ad* Art. 2; DFC 130 III 168 (*Marley*), c. 4.2.

61 KUMMER, Werk, p. 24, 37, 73; cf. also GRABER, Zwischen Geist und Geld, p. 106; CHERPILLOD, SHK CopA, N 30 *ad* Art. 2.

62 BARRON, Claims of Art, p. 391.

63 As quoted in BARRON, Claims of Art, p. 390.

64 BARRON, Claims of Art, p. 389

by the presentation theory as art would be rewarded with copyright protection.[65] According to KUMMER, however, lawyers should only be concerned with the law and not ask themselves whether something *is* or *is not* art.[66]

Yet, although admittedly neutral and freed from qualitative judgments, his own theory inevitably favors determinate artistic practices and styles while disfavoring others. While preaching absolute objectivity and detachment from any aesthetical value, the theory is soaked in the aesthetics of its *air du temps*.[67] Under the regime of statistical uniqueness, all those postmodernist artworks that programmatically "exploit[ed] the space occupied by everything that [GREENBERG'S] analysis negated"[68] among them, our interpictorial original copies could either not achieve protection or only with difficulty.

II.IV The incalculable element in the determination of copyright eligibility

Novelty alone, i.e., the verifiable creation of difference, is not enough to establish copyright eligibility. While it may be the *conditio sine qua non* for copyright protection, the equation does not function the other way round – a new artifact constitutes the basic condition for considering it a potential fact of copyright – if the artifact is *only* new, however, it will probably be denied protection.[69] The objective and verifiable requirement that the artifact be new is, thus, completed by other elements that shall establish that it is also more than just that, i.e., sufficiently distant from what already exists, sufficiently artistic, creative, surprising, improbable and so on.[70] This is also visible in the theory of statistical uniqueness; if the first step is supposed to simply ascertain whether an artifact is new, the second step opens the door to considerations of a more abstract order. Because what will be created in the future is unknown, the surplus of novelty that is required for individuality (the "futurized novelty") is speculative and contains an incalculable moment.

Originality being built on the elements of pure novelty and another of a more speculative, subjective order is the case not only in Switzerland but also elsewhere. In the United States, for example, where protection under copyright law exists only in "original works of authorship" when "fixed in a tangible medium of expression" (17 U.S.C. § 102(a) of the Copyright Act), the concept of originality underwent a paradigm shift in 1991. From the "sweat of the brow" doctrine that used to reward

65 TROLLER, Bedeutung, p. 274.

66 KUMMER, Werkbegriff, p. 126 et seq.

67 Cf. ORTLAND/SCHMÜCKER, p. 1768.

68 BARRON, Claims of Art, p. 395.

69 CRAIG, Copyright, p. 105, writes "the fundamental characteristic, or *sine qua non*, of originality is that the work originates from the author; it must be independently produced and not copied. The debate about appropriate formulations of the originality doctrine is concerned only with the question: '*what else?*'".

70 HILTY, Urheberrecht, N 164; REHBINDER/HAAS/UHLIG, OFK CopA, N 8 *ad* Art. 2; THOUVENIN, Irrtum, p. 70 et seq.; already REINHART, p. 235: "individuality is what does not already exist and what surprises, shocks" (translation is mine).

industriousness on the part of the author, the Supreme Court advanced the "modicum of creativity" standard in *Feist Publication Inc. vs. Rural Telephone Service Co.*[71] The requirement of originality was, thus, concretized as the necessity for the work to be independently created by the author but also to possess at least some minimal degree of creativity.[72] This means, first, that the work cannot be a copy of another work or material, i.e., that it must be new. Creativity, on the contrary, must be found in the choices and decisions made by the author and manifesting in the work. Any reliance on skill, training, knowledge and judgment of the author that cannot be discerned from the form of work itself, cannot be considered as creative.[73] A similar situation occurred in the European Union (EU), where the decision *Infopaq International A/S v Danske Dagblades Forening* harmonized the originality standard. The CJEU now considers that the Directive 2001/29/EC (Infosoc-Directive) only protects original subject matter in the sense that it qualifies as the author's own intellectual creation by displaying the author's creative abilities and his or her free and creative choices.[74] Similar to the US standard, the CJEU requires the artifact not only to be new but also to have a "creative aspect".[75]

Both factual and legal considerations underlie the determination of the individual character. Because the determination of the individual character in the Swiss CopA is then presented, as other originality requirements elsewhere, as a question of law,[76] it does not surprise that, when observed from a second-order perspective, a moment of pure self-reference and, thus, of indeterminacy can be diagnosed.

II.IV.I Photography: "The problematic child of copyright"

The search for "more" than just novelty becomes evident in the category of photography. While it is unlikely that two perfectly equal pictures exist, with the consequence that all pictures will have to be considered new, their originality is notoriously uneasy to assess.

Historically, courts have had a hard time bestowing copyright to the category of photography. Seen as a merely mechanical process in which the individual could not assert his "personal touch", a common tactic has been to aestheticize the results to make them fit into traditional pictorial definitions and then, as a consequence,

71 Balganesh, Causing Copyright, p. 36 et seq.

72 *Feist Publications, Inc., vs. Rural Telephone Service Co.*, 499 US 340 (1991), p. 345.

73 Balganesh, Causing Copyright, p. 38.

74 Snijders/Deursen, p. 1178, quoting CJEU of July 16, 2009 - C-5/08 (*Infopaq International vs. Danske Dagblades Forening*) and CJEU of December 11, 2011 - C-145/10 (*Eva-Maria Painer vs. Standard VerlagsGmbH et al.*); cf. also Bullinger, PraxKomm DE-CopA, N 14 *ad* § 2.

75 Rosati, Why originality, p. 597; according to Stokes, p. 41 et seq., this raised the bar for copyright protection in the UK. Before the Infopaq decision, UK courts had simply required that the work not be copied from another work and that it employed "sufficient skill, judgement and/or labour".

76 Senn, Zweckänderung, p. 214; Craig, Reconstructing, p. 215; on the difference between norms and facts s. Luhmann, Law as a Social System, p. 113.

into the property rationales of copyright law.[77] Examples of this aestheticizing attitude of courts are manifold. In the French copyright infringement case *Bauret vs. Koons*, for example, the Paris Court of Appeal indulged in a lengthy description of the *Enfants* picture taken by Jean-François Bauret in 1970, which later served as a basis for Jeff Koons's sculpture *Naked* (1988). The court held that *Enfants* constituted a new concept of nude, raw and devoid of any sexual connotation, which, as such, revealed the personality of the author. The particular use of light was meant to confer some "sculptural character" to the photograph, and the overall composition (including the pose of the bodies and the hands) added a "geometric" dimension to the work. According to the court, the latter served to dispel any idea that the pose of the children would be spontaneous. Rather, they had been directed by the photographer to assume a certain pose and expression.[78]

In Italy, the Tribunale di Roma held that a famous picture of anti-mafia judges Falcone and Borsellino was not characterized by "particular creativity", as it did not showcase a peculiar "choice of pose, lights, cut, and background". The court did not see the intention of the photographer of achieving "a pictorial and creative objective with innovative and artistic value" based on a "unique and unrepeatable project, in which the author synthetizes his vision of the subject". It, therefore, denied copyright protection.[79]

Even the SFSC, in a rare excess of zeal, described photography as the "problematic child of copyright law" in a decision in which at stake was a concert picture of the singer Bob Marley.[80]

II.IV.II The "Meili" and "Marley" decisions

A comparison between the SFSC's decisions DFC 130 III 168 (*Marley*) and DFC 130 III 714 (*Meili*) can serve as a good example of how the judges concretize the search for, while simultaneously constructing, the required "more".[81] In both decisions, the SFSC had to determine the copyright eligibility of a snapshot. In the first, "Marley", the snapshot was a portrait of singer Bob Marley taken at a concert by Max Messerli. In the second one, taken by Gisela Blau, the portrait was of whistleblower Christoph Meili holding the bank documents he had become famous for disclosing.

77 Ickowicz, p. 38 et seq.; Senn, Fotografie, p. 140 et seq.; Tushnet, Thousand Words, p. 714, writes: "In order to find that photographs are copyrightable, courts had to *identify photographers as authors*…by emphasizing particular choices made by photographers, especially timing, angles" (emphasis added); Teilmann-Lock, p. 103; Kearns, p. 69, testifying for the UK, the USA and France; Plumpe, p. 178; the somewhat difficult position of photography as art is underlined in the art historical research, too, cf. Brunet, p. xiii: "art without art, hence art for all".

78 Cour d'appel de Paris of December 17, 2019 (*Bauret vs. Koons*).

79 Tribunale di Roma of September 12, 2019 (*Falcone and Borsellino*).

80 DFC 130 III 168 (*Marley*), c. 4.5. (Sorgenkind des Urheberrechts).

81 Sherman, Appropriating, p. 35.

Despite the many common features of the two cases (both were portraits, both were decided in 2003, both involved the application of Art. 2 para. 1 CopA), the court arrived at two opposite outcomes: "Meili" was denied copyright protection, while "Marley" was bestowed with one. It is precisely this aspect, the difference in outcome despite the many commonalities of the case and a very similar judicial argumentation, that makes the comparison interesting.

In both decisions, the court listed the relevant criteria to impart an individual character to a photographic work; the choice of the subject; the cut of the picture; the moment of the shot; the use of a particular objective, filters, of a special film; and the play with contrast and exposure.[82] Then, it clarified that the mere *use* of photo-technical instruments would not be enough to achieve individuality, as decisive is the visual aspect of the achieved result.[83] By explaining further that not the portrayed event or thing but, rather, the configuration of the image itself (*Gestaltung*) must be "statistically unique",[84] the SFSC transposed the debate over their individuality on the aesthetic realm, making it *incalculable*.[85] While it can be verified, with some archive research, whether a picture is objectively new (i.e., whether it is not a copy), to verify whether it is "uniquely configurated" requires an aesthetic judgment more than anything else. Indeed, it is on this point that the two decisions differ.

As they were not copies of already existing pictures, both "Meili" and "Marley" were objectively new. The configurative aspects required for the individuality of a photograph were judged individual in the "Marley" snapshot, but they were considered non-individual in the "Meili" snapshot. So "Marley" is described as "appealing and interesting", a result given by the "facial expression and attitude" of the pictured singer, "whose flying dreads resembled a sculpture" and "among

82 DFC 130 III 714 (*Meili*), c. 2.1; DFC 130 III 168 (*Marley*), c. 4.5; similar criteria were judged decisive by the CJEU of December 11, 2011 - C-145/10 (*Eva-Maria Painer vs. Standard VerlagsGmbH et al.*). At para. 91, the CJEU held that "the photographer can choose the background, the subject's pose and the lighting. When taking a portrait, he can choose the framing, the angle of view and the atmosphere created. Finally, when selecting the snapshot, the photographer may choose from a variety of developing techniques the one he wishes to adopt or, where appropriate, use computer software. *By making those various choices, the author of a portrait photograph can stamp the work created with his 'personal touch'*" (emphasis added); and by US Courts, cf. Amicus Brief, p. 11, which reports that originality in a photograph can lie in "posing the subjects, lighting, angle, selection of film and camera, evoking the desired expression, and almost any other variant involved".

83 DFC 130 III 714 (*Meili*), c. 2.1; DFC 130 III 168 (*Marley*), c. 5.1.

84 DFC 130 III 168 (*Marley*), c. 4.5.; DFC 130 III 714 (*Meili*), c. 2.3; later confirmed in DFC 134 III 166 (*Arzneimittelkompendium*), c. 2.3.1, in which the court explained that "it is the multiplicity of the personal decisions of the author, the surprising and unusual combinations that make up the individuality of the work"; GORDON/SOMMER, p. 297; REHBINDER/HAAS/UHLIG, OFK CopA, N 9 *ad* Art. 2.

85 Or, in other words, it did not present its method to establish individuality as based on facts (e.g., on the fact of the existence – or not – of a similar picture) but, rather, handled it as a question of law. The problem is that often existing pictures (or artifacts in general) are not exact copies but only present a series of similarities. Therefore, in the determination of individuality flow facts as well as legal indeterminate considerations. It is then difficult to understand what reasons underlie a decision.

which a special effect particularly resulted by the shade of one, projected on the singer's face".[86] The "Meili" picture, instead, is associated to attributes such as "banal" and "obvious".[87]

II.IV.III Analysis of the decisions and what they tell us about the individual character

In the rightful assumption that aestheticizing was the way to go for substantiating the individual character of the picture, MOSIMANN and HOSTETTLER argued that Gisela Blau *did* make creative choices and suggested that she wanted to make "Meili" appear as a Moses holding the 10 Commandments.[88] In the picture, one could also see Christoph Meili staged as a convicted felon in a prison's mugshot, perhaps to underline the polarization caused by his disclosure of classified documents. In this way, we would be arguing for the presence of something that the SFSC might not have seen in the picture. Even more revealing, however, is to put the argumentation of the SFSC under another type of scrutiny.

Here, we are not interested in arguing that the "Meili" picture deserved protection and that the court made a mistake in not recognizing that Blau's picture was original. Rather, we turn our gaze back to copyright law and observe it observing the picture, asking what it sees. Let us make a hypothesis, that the judges' reproachment of the banality in Blau's photograph, which resulted in her picture not being protectable, had been *an intentional aesthetical choice*. What if Blau wanted us, when looking at Meili's portrait, to see nothing more than a normal citizen – hair uncombed, rumpled pullover – who became a hero by pure coincidence? Perhaps, what we think is a sincere rendering of his *persona* is, in fact, such a crafty and subtle representation to appear imperceptible – after all, pictures do this all the time.[89]

We do not know whether Blau's picture was effectively staged and, thus, mendacious, as we suggested in our working hypothesis, or if it was simply hastily taken. Yet we may ask whether copyright law would be able, in absolute terms, to see *the refusal to aestheticize* – a strategy that is so common in today's artistic practice[90] – *as an aesthetical choice itself.* The "Meili" picture had to be not just new but also something "more" to be deemed a photographic work. Whereas in Bob Marley's picture the court saw an expressive portrait, with the criteria of cut, light, contrast and so on fulfilled, they did not see them sufficiently deployed in "Meili". The SFSC judged it as less formed – a factual account of the world. So, even if Marley's snapshot was probably less planned than Meili's, it managed to convey

86 DFC 130 III 168 (*Marley*), c. 5.2.

87 DFC 130 III 714 (*Meili*), c. 2.

88 MOSIMANN/HOSTETTLER, p. 126

89 HUTCHEON, p. 88, 117; GROYS, p. 128 et seqq., with further references to seminal texts (e.g., Siegfried Kracauer and Roland Barthes).

90 And yet this is a known strategy of contemporary artists, cf. SENN, Fotografie, p. 153; cf. BOHN, Autonomien, p. 45; cf. also the statement of artist Jill Magid "*What is considered banal or cliché might be hiding something*" (at <https://www.jillmagid.com/info/statements>).

the impression that the photographer behind it took certain creative choices, making him effectively an "author" under copyright law. Or to say it as Tushnet did, because "copyright protects only expression", the "transparency" of Meili's snapshot, its "privileged access to truth", was a burden to its protection.[91] Gisela Blau's mistake, if we may call it so, was that by wanting her picture to resemble reality as much as possible, it ended being confused for such.

II.V Measuring the artistic worth, or the judge as art critic

A common self-description of copyright law is that it is aesthetically neutral and capable of judging eligibility for protection by transcending the artistic and qualitative aspects of the artifact.[92] The quality of something as either artistic or not should not be relevant in the assessment of the individual character. The doctrine agrees that the wording of Art. 2 para. 1 CopA, reading "works are *literary and artistic* intellectual creations", does not have any delimitative function.[93] Nonetheless, it seems that this categorization into artistic and non-artistic works, avoided at a previous stage, returns in a slightly different form in the courts' quest for the individual character.[94]

A very common way to assess the eligibility for copyright is based on the direct assessment of the "artistic" worth of the work, which is seen as signaling that the artifact has individual character. For example, in DFC 105 II 297 (*Montre "Monsieur Pierre"*), DFC 106 II 71 (*Kasperlifiguren*) and DFC 110 IV 102 (*Zierpuppen*), the SFSC stated that the objects that were respectively at stake (in the order: A watch, porcelain dolls and marionettes) could have been considered eligible for copyright only if they were elevated to the rank of artworks.[95] In all these three decisions, the court seemingly wanted to control whether the artifacts reached the threshold of artwork. Because the artifacts were not artworks of the visual art according to Art. 2 para. 2 let. c CopA, the term "artwork" was used as a general judgment of value.[96] In all three, the artwork quality – and, therefore, the respective individual character – was ultimately denied.

In other cases, the SFSC focused its argumentation on unspecified aesthetical requirements. In DFC 100 II 167 (*Späti Laden*), the configuration of the interior design had to "meet aesthetical requirements" to be eligible for copyright.[97] In DFC

91 Tushnet, Thousand Words, p. 711.

92 Cf. for example, the decision of the Civil Court of Canton Basel-City of January 24, 1995 (*Postkarte*), BJM 1995, p. 248 et seqq., p. 250, "it is not the judge's task to judge the aesthetic value of pictures" (translation is mine).

93 Cherpillod, SHK CopA, N 10 *ad* Art. 2.

94 Wild, Urheberrechtsschutz, p. 90, is in favor of the search for the "artistic" in copyright cases, something he identifies as an elementary condition for copyright protection; cf. also Senn, Fotografie, p. 137 et seqq.; Kearns, p. 72, makes a similar argument for English copyright law.

95 DFC 105 II 297 (*Montre "Monsieur Pierre"*), c. 3; DFC 106 II 71 (*Kasperlifiguren*), p. 73 c. 2; DFC 110 IV 102 (*Zierpuppen*), p. 106 c. 3.

96 Similarly in Kearns, p. 80.

97 DFC 100 II 167 (*Späti Laden*), c. 7.

143 III 373 (*Max Bill*), the "artistical configuration" of the stool had to indisputably exceed the requirements of the design protection to be eligible for copyright.[98]

In other decisions, the judges of the SFSC did not consider the aesthetical worth as a threshold to reach but paid particular attention to the appearance of the artifact at stake, describing it at length and with accurately selected words, as is done with the formal analysis of artworks. In DFC 113 II 190 (*Le Corbusier*), for example, the court identified "aesthetical and objectively satisfying forms" in the seating furniture designed by Le Corbusier.[99] The court also said that the furniture gave an "artistical impression", due to the interaction of many elements and their layout, among which the use of curved steel tubes surely played a special role.[100] In DFC 117 II 466 (*Sekundarschulanlage*), the SFSC stated that the originality of the work resided in the harmonious disposition of the structure, in the interplay between window surfaces and construction elements and in the clear arrangement of the interiors. Secondarily, the court considered the succeeded incorporation of the edifice in the environment and in the previously existing structure.[101] Again, in DFC 143 III 373 (*Max Bill*), the considerations of the court contain statements of general aesthetical order, such as: "classical shapes sometimes distinguish themselves precisely because the elegance of their configuration with minimal elements is impressive" but also statements accurately describing the bar stool designed by Max Bill. For example, the court admired how its different parts were arranged in an "optimal angle" and then attached to the "well-proportioned seating area".[102] More recently, in a decision in which a grill shaped in the form of a ring (called *Feuerring* in German) was at stake, the court stated that the unbiased observer would not, at first sight, recognize in the object a grill but, rather, an artistic object that would reveal itself as being a grill only on closer inspection. The "artistry" of the grill made the court conclude on the presence of the individual character.[103]

The most accurate examination of an artifact's configuration, however, is contained in a 2009 decision of the Zurich Court of appeals concerning Robert Indiana's artwork *Love* and a producer of wristwatches that ProLitteris accused of copying Indiana's work in the dial of one of its models. To assess whether the producer of wristwatches had infringed Indiana's rights, the Court of Appeals first considered whether *Love* constituted a copyrighted work. In doing so, the judges gave a veritable translation of what they were seeing in words:

98 DFC 143 III 373 (*Max Bill*), c. 2.2.

99 DFC 113 II 190 (*Le Corbusier*), p. 198 c. I.2.

100 DFC 113 II 190 (*Le Corbusier*), p. 198 c. I.2.

101 DFC 117 II 466 (*Sekundarschulanlage*), p. 469 c. 2.

102 DFC 143 III 373 (*Max Bill*), c. 2.8.3 (translation is mine); a recent case of the Cour d'appel Paris, September 27, 2023 (*Cuny vs. Rampazzi*), is even more articulate in this respect. The court held that "the combination of a rounded structure in the shape of an asymmetrical harp", the "*airy and sensual appearance* due to the rounded shape", the fact that it "alternately resembles *an amphora, a moving seaweed, loose legs or a plunging, dynamic fish due to its asymmetry*" and "the embodiment of both *movement and serenity*" are all elements characterizing the originality of the "Lyre" lamp, designed by Philippe Cuny (translation is mine; emphasis added).

103 SFSC 4A_472/2021 of June 17, 2022 (*Feuerring unpublished*), c. 6.1.2.

> The word is arranged in capital letters on two lines of two letters each; the L and the O appear on the top line, and the V and the E appear on the bottom line. While the letters L, V, and E are at right angles, the O runs diagonally from bottom left to top right at a 45% angle. The hyphenation of the word follows the German rules, but without a hyphen. There is no spacing between the letters within each line or between the top and bottom lines of letters; the respective letters and serifs merge with each other at their edges. According to the arrangement of the letters, the image or the outer outline of the sculpture is rectangular. In the two-dimensional images, the letters each extend to the edge of the image, sometimes even appearing slightly "cut" and completely filling the entire surface. By taking up the entire surface of the picture and fusing the letters together, a space-filling division and segmentation of the entire picture surface is created. At the same time, the letters appear as surface elements and the spaces in between also acquire an independent formal meaning as structuring elements. As an example of this, reference can be made to the form of an arrow pointing downward, which is created by the seamless vertical merging of the letters L and V. The area-structuring effect of the letters also appears as a surface element. Such effect is further emphasized in the three-color images by the different colors chosen for the spaces in between. By using the entire surface of the image and by avoiding any other element of representation, the viewer's gaze is automatically focused on the word "love" and its meaning.[104]

In all decisions containing these lengthy descriptions of the artifact at stake, the individuality was ultimately affirmed. Perhaps engaging in such a detailed and attentive formal analysis of the work influences the final judgment, making it lean toward the recognition of an individual character. Or perhaps, stroked by the overall aesthetical effect of the artifact at stake and determined to award copyright protection, judges try to justify themselves with a literal description of what they see. Either way, subjective rationales entering the judicial decision – according to the majoritarian opinion – should be avoided.[105]

104 Zurich Court of Appeal of July 7, 2009 (*Love*), sic! 2010, p. 889 et seqq., p. 890, E. 1.2 (translation is mine).

105 As Cherpillod, SHK CopA, N 21 *ad* Art. 2, explains, "the current jurisprudence of the SFSC follows an objective concept of individuality, according to which the configuration of the work must stand out from the ordinary and therefore cannot amount to a routine achievement". He then continues: "the jurisprudence leaves the judge a certain discretion to decide what is that detaches itself from the ordinary. This shall not mean that the judge can express a value judgment of the aesthetical qualities of the work" (translation is mine); cf. also Egloff, CopA Commentary, N 13 *ad* Art. 2.

II.VI The presentation theory as a method to establish individuality

KUMMER not only formulated the theory of statistical uniqueness but also another one,[106] known as the "presentation theory", which has been less fortunate in its scholarly reception. Though this theory was not understood as an instrument to assess the individual character but, rather, as a way to individuate artistic "facts of copyright",[107] it was often *mis*interpreted in this way and consequently rejected.[108]

A hint at the presentation theory was, nonetheless, made in the already mentioned 2009 decision of the Zurich Court of appeals concerning Robert Indiana's artwork *Love*. When assessing the eligibility for copyright of Robert Indiana's *Love*, the court of appeals stated, among other considerations on this matter, that "in the field of minimal art it can suffice that not the object itself, but *the modality of its presentation*, is the expression of the individual character".[109] By affirming that the modality of the presentation of the artwork – and, therefore, not the artwork itself – can be the proof of individual character, the court clearly referenced the presentation theory (even if not naming it explicitly). Because the *Love* decision is the only one ever taken on the individual character of a work of the visual art in Switzerland, we do not know whether this jurisprudence – and the subtle reference to the presentation theory – will be upheld by other courts and, in particular, by the SFSC.

The cantonal Court of Zurich ultimately came to the verdict that *Love* was, indeed, a work of copyright. What stands out of this decision is how elements of the public domain – the word "love" as well as the font used, called "Clarendon"[110] – were transformed into protectable components of a work of the visual art. The presentation theory is only one among the many aspects considered by the court. As seen, the argumentation goes on to analyze the artwork's configuration in detail,[111] and, in some passages, the court seems to underline that its judgment on the eligibility for copyright of *Love* is the subsumption from an agglomerate of aspects rather than from one, decisive element: "the individuality is reinforced by the inclined O and the diagonal effect caused…, but the creative achievement is not

106 Discussed in Chapter 3, II.VI.

107 KUMMER, Werk, p. 76, though, in some passages, vaguely suggesting the contrary, cf. also KUMMER, Werk, p. 80; in KUMMER, Rechtsprechung 1980, p. 202 speaking of the theory as one of the possible elements of a definition of "work" and regretting the fact that copyright lawyers, by rejecting the presentation theory, "so stubbornly close their minds to the facts that they claim to regulate" (translation is mine); MACCIACCHINI, Irrtum, p. 31.

108 Cf. VON BÜREN, p. 388 et seq.; STUDER, p. 9, rejects it by arguing that it would introduce a foreign body – extrapolating copyright eligibility from the context of the artwork rather than from the artwork itself – in the structure of copyright law; TROLLER, Bedeutung, p. 265; WILD, Soziologischer Werkbegriff, p. 65; SOMMER/GORDON, p. 293.

109 Zurich Court of Appeal of July 7, 2009 (*Love*), sic! 2010, p. 889 et seqq., c.1.1 (translation is mine, emphasis added).

110 As also admitted by the Court, cf. Zurich Court of Appeal of July 7, 2009 (*Love*), sic! 2010, p. 889 et seqq., c. 1.3.

111 See Chapter 3, II.VI.

reducible to only that".[112] Ultimately, it is not possible to reconduct the verdict into one or other statement – something that mirrors the complex existence of a work of art – impossible to reduce to a unitary lecture.[113]

II.VII Change of perspective: The return of the excluded rationales

Invisibilized by the use of other seemingly unitary concepts such as "non-banal", "surprising" and "non-artisanal",[114] our analysis of jurisprudence and doctrine on the axis of *what* the individual character is has shown that the answers are, in essence, an interplay of two different aspects.[115] On one side, the notion of individual character is *quantitative* and constructed as objective (I). On the other side, the research for the individual character becomes, if not openly, at least secretly *qualitative* as we identify the "return" of previously excluded rationales of aesthetical order (II).

(I) As they establish the novelty of the artifact at best with technical, almost statistical-mathematical methods by looking at how many differences it creates compared to its past, the arguments on this side tend, in their self-description, toward the highest possible objectivity.[116]

Clearly located on this side of the axis is KUMMER's theory of statistical uniqueness, with which he aimed, as explained, to develop a neutral test able to overcome the old author's personality-related concept of originality and assess copyright eligibility by excluding every judgment of aesthetical order on the work. Also objective in nature are all ponderings on the novelty of the artifact.[117] Where courts consider whether the artifact at stake is new compared to what had previously been done, they do an operation of subtraction by comparing what was there before to what has just been created, and they establish whether a residual difference remains that could potentially qualify for copyright protection.

112 Just two lines below, the court considers the contrasted colors chosen and repeats that "the individuality and creativity of the work does not only reside in there", s. Zurich Court of Appeal of July 7, 2009 (*Love*), sic! 2010 p. 889 et seqq., c. 1.3.

113 Cf. GRABER, Zwischen Geist und Geld, p. 91 et seq.

114 The requirement of non-banality signals both novelty (something "banal" is something already known) as well as the *quality* of something that does not bore; "surprising" is only something that goes against the expectations (i.e., new) and is, therefore, capable to exert an effect of surprise; "artisanal" is something done well (*a regola d'arte*) by someone skilled, but who does not exceed the rules and is, therefore, not a "genius".

115 Already TROLLER, Bedeutung, p. 273, had recognized the "plurivalent meanings of individuality" and opposed KUMMER's objective notion of individuality (as statistical uniqueness) to ULMER's artistic-subjective notion; this same duality is also recognized by VON BÜREN, p. 386 and by REINHART, p. 238. For the debates in Germany, see MÜLLER, p. 233, fn. 272.

116 GRABER, Zwischen Geist und Geld, p. 106, calls this a "formal work definition"; THOUVENIN, Irrtum, p. 70 et seq.; cf. also COHEN, p. 1162; BARRON, Claims of Art, p. 397; cf. in France WALRAVENS, p. 422, for discussion between the criteria of novelty and originality.

117 See Chapter 3, II.V.

On this side of the axis, a sort of "cultural and aesthetical agnosticism" is preached for the determination of copyright eligibility. Aesthetic considerations play no role in discerning eligible from non-eligible artifacts for copyright protection, and the judge shall absolutely abstain from pronouncing himself on the aesthetical worth of the object at stake or the artistic merits of the author to avoid becoming an art critic.[118] This stance on the individual character clearly embodies a very common self-description of copyright law, according to which aesthetics and the related subjective preferences of judges shall have absolutely no role in the judgment, and of law, more in general, according to which arguing objectively, with verifiable and non-confutable exactitude is possible and desirable.[119]

We observe, here, a very self-referential law, which is either not interested in the adherence between law and life, or it just assumes that, as if in an equation, in which individuality is assessed "objectively", the obtained result will naturally indicate the presence of art.[120] It may be asked whether such a stance is viable and not simply unthoroughly reflected upon, for, as argued above and demonstrated for the case of the theory of statistical uniqueness, even a copyright law that declares itself not concerned with aesthetics "necessarily draw[s] on certain ideas of artistic production, authorship, creativity, and individuality".[121]

(II) On the other side, the opposite equation becomes true. Individual is only the artistic, and not the other way round. Led by incalculable subjective-aesthetical rationales, the standard for the individual character is, here, thought to complete the objective metric of novelty with considerations capable of filling the individual character with "life".[122]

We can further differentiate. The aesthetical appearance of the artifact may either be assessed directly by a "judge-improvised-art-critic" and considered as a factor that contributes to the establishment of individuality (1),[123] or the artistic quality is imported into the decision from the environment of law and considered as evidence for, or as an element of, the presence of individual character (2).[124]

118 TROLLER, Bedeutung, p. 276; REHBINDER, N 34; SHERMAN, Appropriating, p. 40.

119 TROLLER, Bedeutung, p. 276; ORTLAND, Aesthetics, p. 231; BARRON, Claims of Art, p. 397; MCCLEAN, p. 338 et seq.; DOUZINAS, p. 26; LUHMANN, Law as a Social System, p. 117.

120 So already VISCHER, Urheberrecht p. 251; KEARNS, p. 63, the problem is that "the original is broader than the artistic". We could add that the artistic is broader than the individual: Between the two concepts, there is no identity.

121 ORTLAND/SCHMÜCKER, p. 1768.

122 THOUVENIN, Irrtum, p. 71; DOUZINAS, p. 26: "But while the law explicitly sets itself apart from aesthetics and judgements of taste, the process of legal judgement introduces back again into the domain of law those elements law needs to keep away"; KEARNS, p. 71.

123 KEARNS, p. 66.

124 So already VISCHER, Urheberrecht, p. 251, quoting from a study by Joseph Kohler (1849–†1919), and EDELMAN, De l'urinoir, p. 88, who reports that the Tribunal de grande instance de Tarascon, deciding on the matter of Pinoncelly urinating in Duchamp's "Fountain", based its decision on whether "Fountain" was art or not on referencing what was valid at that time in the art world, i.e., that "'Fountain' could constitute art even if there was no creative act at all" (translation is mine).

(1) We have seen how, in many decisions, the judges confronted themselves with the artifact at stake from a close distance, i.e., they described it profusely with a jargon drawn from the sphere of aesthetics (in the decisions we have read, we have seen attributes such as "classical", "elegant", "minimal"). In other cases, the quality as artwork was judged as a threshold to reach for the artifact to be bestowed with copyright protection. In all these cases, we see that the considerations of a "judge-improvised-art-critic" play a role in the ponderation of arguments, ultimately, establishing whether the artifact at stake is enough of an (art) work to be bestowed with copyright. Problematic, in this first case, is the fact that the aesthetics of the work at stake are assessed by a judge, i.e., a lawyer who does not have formal training in art and who will, therefore, tend to oversimplify things, enhancing some aspects of the work while overshadowing other ones that may be important for an accurate appreciation of the artifact at stake.[125]

(2) In other cases in which the judgment clearly takes the "artistic worth" of the object into account, it is not the judge's voice expressing an opinion. Rather, by means of the judge, an external opinion, coming *prima facie* from somewhere else but not from the law, is sought, i.e., given legal recognition. A clear example thereof is the so-called presentation theory (in detail above at Chapter 3, II.VI) that declares individual an artifact that the circumstances present as an artwork. Despite having been almost univocally rejected by scholarship, the theory was mentioned in the decision concerning the artwork *Love* by Robert Indiana, in which the court stated that not the object itself but the way it is presented could be a proof of individual character.[126] Other such ways to import external rationales into the legal argumentation have been, e.g., to substantiate for an individual character with the fact that the work received positive reactions of the public, as was done in the decision "Mummenschanz" of the cantonal court in Saint Gallen;[127] to argue that the work has become a timeless classic, such as in DFC 113 II 190 (*Le Corbusier*);[128] that it has been exposed in museums (also in "*Love*")[129] or awarded with prizes, as mentioned in "Watch Flemming".[130] Not surprisingly, however, the consideration of these aspects in the quest for determining individuality was criticized for their "metajuridical" quality.[131]

125 Ortland, Bildregime, p. 286 et seq., underlines that judging images in the context of copyright law presupposes a considerable visual competence; moreover, judges often determine copyrightability on the basis of poor black and white reproductions of the artwork, which, in an art historical context, would be unthinkable, cf. also Millet, p. 121.

126 Zurich Court of Appeal of July 7, 2009 (*Love*), sic! 2010 p. 889 et seqq., p. 889.

127 Decision of the Cantonal Court of St. Gallen of June 19, 2002 (*Mummenschanz*), sic! 2003, p. 116 et seqq.

128 Mentioned in DFC 113 II 190, p. 200 (*Le Corbusier*).

129 Mentioned in the opening of the decision of Zurich Court of Appeal of July 7, 2009 (*Love*), sic! 2010, p. 889 et seqq.

130 Mentioned in a decision of the Lucerne Court of Appeal of June 24, 1998 (*Watch Flemming I*), sic! 1998, p. 567 et seqq.

131 Cherpillod, SHK CopA, N 33 *ad* Art. 2; Wild, Soziologischer Werkbegriff, p. 63, notes that the name "Le Corbusier" is mentioned 20 times in in DFC 113 II 190 (*Le Corbusier*), a possible sign that the name of the designer was not completely unimportant to the judges.

These imported judgments may be described with what in systems theoretical terms is known as an "external reference". With an external reference, a system finds its environment worth considering not only as a realm of facts from which to derive conclusions (subsumption) but also with regard to the standards that are found there. In this case, selected elements from the environment of the system become information, i.e., *differences that make a difference* in the system that is using them for its own operations.[132] Even if it could appear as if a legal system referencing an external standard was a system losing autonomy, it must be clarified that the operation always remains an internal operation of the system.[133] The legal system is, thus, not truly outsourcing its judgment; rather, it will find an internal legitimization, a legally founded argument to make the external reference to aesthetical standards characterize the legal system itself.[134]

III.I How much individual character?

We have already exposed that *what* is understood as individual cannot coincide with "the nothing" but must realize "the more", i.e., a material difference from the past. The second axis we could identify by analyzing the relevant jurisprudence and doctrine concerns the question: "How much individual character must the object at stake showcase in order to be eligible for copyright?", or formulated differently, "How many differences from the past must the artifact advance in order to be considered individual and be granted protection?".[135] While the individual character remains the same,[136] the question of the "how much" calibrates the required degree of individual character from a quantitative perspective, i.e., the threshold to obtain protection.[137]

Even if it is not always explicitly presented in this way, in the background of such discussions are a series of preoccupations about the best possible way by which copyright law can fulfill its function in society, i.e., encourage the progress of the arts,[138] foster the overall qualitative advancement of society[139] while, thereby,

132 LUHMANN, Law as a Social System, p. 112 and 317; LUHMANN, Irritationen, p. 62.

133 LUHMANN, Law as a Social System, p. 106.

134 LUHMANN, Law as a Social System, p. 97 and 106.

135 Already HILTY, Urheberrecht, N 164; in Germany see BULLINGER, PraxKomm DE-CopA, N 23 et seqq. *ad* § 2 treated this question separately; cf. also SENN, Zweckänderung, p. 212.

136 DFC 148 III 305 (*Feuerring*), c. 5.3; SENN, Zweckänderung, p. 212.

137 In Germany, such debate is summed up under the key word *Gestaltungshöhe* and whether this is enough "high" to obtain protection, cf. BULLINGER, PraxKomm DE-CopA, N 23 et seqq. *ad* § 2; similarly, in the art historical context, MORTIER, p. 11, states: "Originality is also a question of degree. Sometimes it must be radical, as far removed as possible from any model or antecedent; other times, it is reduced to a difference, a deviation" (translation is mine).

138 BARRON, Claims of Art, p. 369.

139 NETANEL, Copyright's Paradox, p. 3; GEIGER, Die Schranken, p. 145; TOWSE, p. 198; on the close relationship of public cultural promotion and copyright, see LENSKI, p. 141 et seqq., especially p. 153 et seqq., cf. also GRABER, Kulturverfassung, p. 658.

justifying its own existence.[140] To realize this function, copyright law provides an *ex post* individual reward and, by doing so, attempts to incentivize the *ex ante* production of creative expression for the benefit of society.[141] How to concretely calibrate copyright protection, thus, becomes of central importance.[142]

While there seems to be broad agreement on the purpose of copyright law in theory, the debates concern how to best realize it in practice:[143] Creativity shall both be promoted through the *free* access to cultural goods as well as through the *restricted* access in order for the creators to internalize use rights and, thus, stimulate the production of more culturally valuable goods.[144] Each variation on the "how much", i.e., the threshold to obtain protection, is strictly correlated to an increase (or a decrease) in the difficulty to reach it: A high threshold for the individual character would create a copyright that is very difficult to obtain and, thus, exclude many artifacts from its scope, whereas a low threshold would not allow artifacts to be excluded from protection but would also establish too many monopolies which would end up being excessively loose and therefore meaningless.[145] Developments in the technological, cultural and artistic fields require an adjustment to this found balance.

Not surprisingly, this balancing between the reach of exclusive rights and its negative side – the public domain – was called the "dilemma" of copyright law".[146] In the following, we expose the ways by which Swiss copyright law concretely addresses this dilemma.

140 Craig, Copyright, p. 105.

141 Balganesh, Foreseeability, p. 1574; Towse, p. 10; this explanation is especially common in common law countries. In civil law "*droit d'auteur*" systems, utilitarian rationales are intertwined with humanistic ones that put the focus on the author's personality and, thus, on rights such as the integrity of the work, attribution, disclosure and, in some cases, withdrawal. Such difference, historically important especially regarding the "philosophical" foundation of the two copyright systems, is now downplayed by many authors, cf. Towse, p. 20; for Switzerland see Hilty, Urheberrecht, N 88 et seqq.

142 Wielsch, Zugangsregeln, p. 17; Geiger, Die Schranken, p. 143.

143 Balganesh, Foreseeability, p. 1579.

144 Wielsch, Relationales Urheberrecht, p. 67.

145 Bullinger, PraxKomm DE-CopA, N 24 *ad* § 2; Ladeur/Vesting, p. 131; cf. Ramello, p. 132, "the structure of minimal copyright was designed to grant individual incentives through private appropriability, but without significantly impacting on the public dimension connected with the sharing process", as the small coin has an accordingly low protection scope.

146 Kummer, Werk, p. 168; in similar terms also Ladeur/Vesting, p. 131; Mijatovic, Kreativität, p. 237; Wielsch, Relationales Urheberrecht, p. 68; this "dilemma" is not only negotiated at the level of the definition of the protection scope but is also addressed at the level of copyright exceptions. In a seminal and much-cited article about fair use, Judge Leval, p. 1108, wrote that copyright "is intended to motivate the creative activity of authors by the provision of a special reward...the monopoly created by copyright thus rewards the individual author in order to benefit the public". At the same time, though "excessively broad protection *would stifle, rather than advance, the [law's] objective...[thus] strangl[ing] the creative process*" (emphasis added).

III.II The statistical uniqueness

The theory of statistical uniqueness states that, to be protected, an artifact must be different, unique.[147] Even though it was described as providing a perfectly balanced measure between a too rigid and a too lax threshold to determine copyright eligibility,[148] the formula of the statistical uniqueness does not give any practical indication on how much an artifact must effectively be different (with respect to the already existing) and how decisively it must distance itself from the past in order to be seen as individual with respect to future hypothetical creations.

KUMMER, too, seems to have asked himself the same question, as he explained that not every "arbitrarily small" variation, one that can be only seen through a magnifying glass, can be called individual.[149] Rather, in order to be seen as unique, the new work must showcase variations from the already existing that the "normal observer" can detect with his physiological optics.[150] The individuality of the artifact must appear "obvious" to the observer,[151] but the dimension of this obviousness is not fixed: Millimetric variations are not obvious in a suprematist painting by Kasimir Malevich, but they become obvious in the field of cartography.[152] Ultimately, he explained, there is no absolute measure for the required "obviousness". Individuality depends on the work's nature: "who observes a city plan, reads in millimeters; who observes a painting, in centimeters; who observes a picture of a mammoth in the style of pop art, in decimeters; and who observes an airplane hangar, in meters".[153] The determination of individuality shall, therefore, be directed by an always different degree of fineness that matches the type of work to be considered.[154]

As already explained, the SFSC understands the statistical uniqueness as referring to the overall configuration of the work. In DFC 134 III 166 (*Arzneimittelkompendium*), the court explained that an artifact (in that case, a medicinal compendium and, thus, a linguistic work according to Art. 2 para. 1 CopA) might even be statistically unique "strictly speaking", but if it merely contains a banal combination of everyday expressions or if its form is predetermined by an inherent logic, then it shall not be considered individual.[155] The court, thus, suggested that the threshold for protection shall be set somewhere higher than where the mere creation of something that is purely statistically unique would already be.

147 KUMMER, Werk, p. 67.
148 KUMMER, Werk, p. 168; MACCIACCHINI, Konflikt, p. 167.
149 KUMMER, Werk, p. 67.
150 KUMMER, Werk, p. 67.
151 KUMMER, Werk, p. 70 uses the word "*handgreiflich*", which can also be translated as "palpable", "evident" or "apparent".
152 KUMMER, Werk, p. 70.
153 KUMMER, Werk, p. 70 (translation is mine).
154 KUMMER, Werk, p. 70.
155 DFC 134 III 166 (*Arzneimittelkompendium*), c. 2.3.1, cf. also Commercial Court of Zurich of January 25, 2022 (*Hotelrevue*), c. 4.

III.III The rule of the leeway

A constant jurisprudence of the SFSC established what we may call the "rule of the leeway" (in German: *Gestaltungsspielraum*).[156] The rule proposes a concrete method to try and solve the previously described dilemma of how to determine the standard with which to judge whether the artifact at stake is individual.

According to the rule, the individual character shall be judged in view of the leeway that was available to the author in the moment of the conception and realization of the work, as only within this free framework is a creative achievement possible.[157] The circumstances susceptible to influence the dimensions of the leeway are the type of work and its purpose, i.e., whether the artifact fulfills a practical purpose and, thus, whether its realization is submitted to constraints to the creative freedom.[158] If the technical constraints imposed by the type of work or its purpose are such that no leeway is left, protection cannot be granted.[159] In all cases (therefore, a rule), a copyright can be granted only if the creative leeway has not been under-utilized given the circumstances of the single case.[160]

III.III.I The (mis)interpretation of the rule

Scholars have long interpreted this jurisprudence as reducing the degree of individuality, depending on the available leeway and, thus, the category the artifact belongs to. So, for example, De Werra and Benhamou wrote that the required degree of individuality is not always the same and that it must be weighed differently according to the circumstances of the single case, influencing the degree of the creative freedom (*liberté creative*) that the author disposed of.[161] Having understood it similarly, many authors have criticized this reduction to the criterion

156 The "rule" is mentioned in DFC 100 II 167 (*Späti Laden*); DFC 106 II 71 (*Kasperlifiguren*); DFC 113 II 190 (*Le Corbusier*); DFC 117 II 466 (*Sekundarschulanlage*); Cantonal Court of Vaud of March 2, 1993 (*Zeitungsartikel*), JdT 1996 I, p. 242 et seqq.; DFC 125 III 328 (*Niederhauser*); SFSC 4C_448/1997 of August 15, 1998 (*Clown*), sic! 1999, p. 198 et seqq., c. 4; SFSC 4C_86/2000 of June 13, 2000 (*Vaca lechera*), sic! 2001, p. 729 et seqq.; SFSC 4C_120/2002 of August 19, 2002 (*Hobby Kalender*), sic! 2003, p. 28 et seqq., c. 2; DFC 130 III 168 et seqq., c. 4.1, (*Marley*); DFC 130 III 714, c. 2.3 (*Meili*); DFC 143 III 373 (*Max Bill*); DFC 148 III 305 (*Feuerring*), c. 5.1. DFC 148 III 305 (*Feuerring*), c. 5.3.

157 DFC 148 III 305 (*Feuerring*), c. 5.3; very similar in the jurisprudence of the CJEU and of the GFCJ, cf. Bullinger, PraxKomm DE-CopA, N 14 *ad* § 2.

158 De Werra/Benhamou, Kultur Kunst Recht, N 9 *ad* § 7; Lüthi, p. 67, notes how a shape can be configurated differently not only in creative but also technical ways. It follows that if there are several technical possibilities, these have to be considered not as restricting but, rather, as widening the leeway.

159 DFC 148 III 305 (*Feuerring*), c. 5.1; SFSC 4A_472/2021 of June 17, 2022 (*Feuerring unpublished*), c. 6.3.2; DFC 113 II 190 (*Le Corbusier*), p. 197 c. ii.2a; similarly in the USA, cf. Kearns, p. 64: American copyright law protects the "useful" arts. A predominance of utility in the artwork can preclude copyrightability; Buccafusco, p. 377, stating that "there must be freedom to choose".

160 Cf. DFC 130 III 714 (*Meili*), c. 2.3., in which the court stated that the creative leeway had not been fully utilized ("*ausgenutzt*").

161 de Werra/Benhamou, Kultur Kunst Recht, N 9 *ad* § 7.

of individuality to the circumstances.[162] SENN argued that the "rounding down" of the individuality criterion is problematic because it must still be about *art*works.[163] According to him, it is not the *degree* of individuality that should be adjusted to the category of work but, rather, the same individuality that should be ascertained with the help of different criteria, specifically tailored to the category to which the work belongs.[164] The reduced degree of individuality according to the leeway was also criticized by HILTY, who argued that the fact that a lack of leeway justifies a lower degree of individuality makes the individuality criterion itself a farce: If the leeway is so narrow that a creative activity is virtually impossible, then copyright protection should simply not be bestowed.[165] Moreover, he added, a differentiation of the requirements for protection is stated nowhere in the law.[166]

Such diffused belief is based on a (legitimate) misinterpretation attributable to a series of unfortunate formulations, mostly expressed in decisions of the SFSC taken in the field of architecture (Art. 2 para. 2 let. e CopA) and applied art (Art. 2 para. 2 let. f CopA). For example, the court assumed that because buildings have a practical purpose and architects incur many technical constraints, the available leeway for the individual configuration of works of architecture is small.[167] As a consequence, according to the judges, the CopA does not require the architect to provide a "distinctively original work characterized by absolute novelty" but, rather, conforms with a "slender degree of independent activity" and with an "only partial novelty".[168] To mark this distinction, the judges even coined the concepts of "*originalité marquee*" and "*originalité simple*".[169] In another, more recent decision, the SFSC had to decide whether an architectural project was too similar to a previous one and, therefore, infringing. On the matter, the court held that the second architect provided sufficient substantial modifications of the original plan, the individuality of which was weak (*faible*).[170] These last decisions suggest the validity, also in Switzerland where it has not been theorized much, of the so-called small coin (in German: *kleine Münze*), i.e., the lowest possible threshold for copyright eligibility, with which an accordingly small scope of protection is granted.[171]

In other decisions, the court held that the smaller the leeway, the easier individuality should be recognized,[172] while it repeatedly argued for "proportionally high

162 Cf. for example THOUVENIN, Irrtum, p. 61 et seqq.; EGLOFF, CopA Commentary, N 13 *ad* Art. 2.

163 SENN, Individualität, p. 524.

164 SENN, Fotografie, p. 148 et seq.; another opinion DESSEMONTET, Le droit d'auteur, Rn. 181.

165 HILTY, Hobby Kalender, p. 29 et seq.

166 HILTY, Urheberrecht, N 164.

167 DFC 100 II 167 (*Späti Laden*), DFC 117 II 466 (*Sekundarschulanlage*), DFC 125 III 328 (*Niederhauser*).

168 DFC 142 III 387 (*Terrasse*), c. 3.1.

169 DFC 100 II 167 (*Späti Laden*); criticized by VON BÜREN, p. 387.

170 DFC 125 III 328 (*Niederhauser*), p. 333 c. 4.

171 Cf. REHBINDER/HAAS/UHLIG, OFK CopA, N 20 *ad* Art. 2; GEIGER, Flexibilising Copyright, p. 186, translates it as "small coin"; this is also known in the US under the name "thin copyright", cf. BALGANESH, Normativity, p. 223.

172 DFC 125 III 328, E. 4b (*Niederhauser*); recently quoted in DFC 148 III 305 (*Feuerring*), c. 5.1.

requirements" for the individual character of works of applied art.[173] Moreover, with a formula that has been later called the "rule of the doubt",[174] in case of incertitude about their individual character, it shall be decided by the presence of a mere artisanal model (in German: *handwerklich*, in French *industriel*) and, thus, *against* protection.[175] This approach has been justified with the argument that, given the large number of possible forms for designing seating furniture, it cannot be claimed that their shape is dictated only by their purpose and, thus, that a large leeway exists for what concerns their configuration.[176]

In another field of copyright law, the category of literary, scientific and other linguistic works (Art. 2 para. 1 let. a CopA), the Commercial Court of Canton Zurich recently established that the requirements for the individual character in are "generally very low".[177] In an older decision, the SFSC had considered that a journalistic news report had individual character because of the low leeway the journalist disposed of. Because the article was about events that could have been reported by everyone else as well, the journalist had clear limits with regard to its individual configuration.[178] In the already discussed DFC 130 III 714 (*Meili*), however, the court held that Gisela Blau did not use the leeway she disposed of and, therefore, produced something that could not be protected.[179] The fact that, just like the journalist who writes an article with the purpose of objectively informing the public,[180] a press photographer may have wanted to achieve a precise result when taking her photograph, was not taken into account. Gisela Blau even insisted on the journalistic achievement of having been at "the right time in the right place, having recognized the historical meaning of the occurrence of January 8, 1997 and having documented it with a photograph".[181] This, however, was later judged a processual mistake by commentators.[182]

173 DFC 148 III 305 (*Feuerring*), c. 5.1; similarly did the GFCJ, see: Hilgert, p. 15; another opinion Buydens, p. 276.
174 DFC 148 III 305 (*Feuerring*), c. 5.2.
175 SFSC 4A_78/2011 of May 2, 2011 (*Le Corbusier 2*), c. 2.3.; DFC 143 III 373 (*Max Bill*), c. 2.6.1.; DFC 148 III 305 (*Feuerring*), c. 5.1.
176 Cherpillod, SHK CopA, N 19 *ad* Art. 2; DFC 113 II 190 (*Le Corbusier*), c. I.2, in which the court even stressed this statement with a highly uncommon statement: "seriously, this cannot be said, even for modern furniture" and DFC 143 III 373 (*Max Bill*).
177 Commercial Court of Zurich of January 25, 2022 (*Hotelrevue*), c. 4.
178 Decision of the Cantonal Court of Vaud of March 2, 1993 (*Zeitungsartikel*), JdT 1996 I 242 et seqq.
179 DFC 130 III 714 (*Meili*), c. 2.3; in the field of photography (Art. 2 para. 2 let. g CopA), the required individuality was described as "slightly over the average", De Werra/Benhamou, Kultur Kunst Recht, N 12 *ad* § 7 and as "not to be set too high".
180 Decision of the Cantonal Court of Vaud of March 2, 1993 (*Zeitungsartikel*), JdT 1996 I 242 et seqq.
181 DFC 130 III 714 (*Meili*), c. 2.2.
182 Mosimann/Hostettler, p. 126.

III.III.II The decision Feuerring and the right interpretation of the rule

In the decision *Feuerring*, which concerned a grill in the form of a big, metal bowl, the SFSC seized the opportunity to clarify its previous jurisprudence and confute the misbelief that the requirements for individual character change according to the work category. The judges explicitly held that the requirements for protection are always the same for every category of work. What changes is only the available room within which the author can take free and creative choices (the "leeway"). This is smaller when the artifact serves a practical purpose. Because the individual, artistic form can only arise from the portion of the artifact that is not already predetermined by the purpose of use, the requirement of individuality becomes harder to fulfill if the presence of a purpose dictates part of the final form of the artifact. Only in this sense shall the criterion of the individual character be understood as being relative to each work category. The individual character itself, however, remains the same across different types of works.[183]

By shifting the judge's power of appreciation from the question of the individual character itself to the question of how big the leeway was and whether this was sufficiently used or not, the rule gives the impression of a concrete guidance on whether and when to allocate a copyright. Notwithstanding the "rule of the leeway", however, the question regarding how the threshold for protection should be determined remains unsolved. Individuality shall be judged with respect to the available leeway, but the formula does not reveal anything about the required *degree* of individuality. Rather, as THOUVENIN stated, the "elegant" formula allows the question to be "circumnavigated", introducing another factor of indeterminacy in the establishment thereof.[184]

III.IV The style of artworks

Works of art (Art. 2 para. 2 let. c CopA) are bi- or tridimensional aesthetic presentations that do not serve any practical purpose.[185] According to the just exposed rule of the leeway, because no practical purpose imposes constraints on their creation, the freedom to configure artworks is virtually infinite.[186] Consequently, one could reasonably expect that, among the many categories of works handled so far, the individual character of artworks must be the most pervasive and total.

As the Zurich Court of Appeals explained in the "*Love*" decision, however, the leeway may be reduced not only in case of technical constraints but also in

183 DFC 148 III 305 (*Feuerring*), c. 5.3; already THOUVENIN, Irrtum, p. 68 and 73; cf. also SENN, Zweckänderung, p. 212.

184 THOUVENIN, Irrtum, p. 63.

185 DFC 148 III 305 (*Feuerring*), c. 5.3; VON BÜREN/MEER, SIWR II/1, p. 101 and SOMMER/GORDON, p. 292; see also the decision of the GFCJ of November 13, 2013 (*Geburtstagszug*), GRUR 2014, p. 175 et seqq., p. 176 at para. 16 "works of the purpose-free visual art" and LUHMANN, Art as a Social System, p. 44 and 153.

186 Also in Zurich Court of Appeal of July 7, 2009 (*Love*), sic! 2010, p. 889 et seqq., c. 1.3.

the case of stylistic constraints.[187] Treating it on par with a technical constraint, the Zurich Court held that the nature of some works – among them, works of the minimal, contemporary art (such as Robert Indiana's) – can sometimes leave little room for personal choices of the author with regard to their configuration.[188] That not only the purpose of the artifact but also the style followed by the author *may restrict the possibilities* of configuration was similarly stated in DFC 113 II 190 (*Le Corbusier*), in which the SFSC held that existing style trends restrict the possibilities of configuration of works.[189]

III.IV.I Style as a self-organizing element of artworks

Understood as the relation, visible in the artwork, of form (of the artwork) and context (what surrounds the artwork),[190] style ensures the reproduction of the system with every new artwork.[191] If, on one side, the artwork's style grants recognizability and a dose of consistency, it simultaneously does not harm the predicate according to which each output shall remain unpredictable.[192] Under the regime of style, an artwork can assert its own necessity,[193] so that, ultimately, artistic styles also limit the autonomy of the artist in conceiving his artworks.[194]

Around 1750, when copying became negatively connotated and originality began being researched with and in every new artwork, the functional equivalent to copying from a model – a matter of perpetuation of the autopoiesis of art – became the belonging to a style.[195] Through the construction and succession of artistic styles, the process of recursivity and relative repetitiveness became historicized,

187 Cf. Luhmann, Law as a Social System, p. 327: Rules and valid reasons are normally treated as unity; they can be dissociated if a new problem or a social change in values sufficiently irritates the legal system.

188 Zurich Court of Appeal of July 7, 2009 (*Love*), sic! 2010, p. 889 et seqq., c. 1.1.

189 DFC 113 II 190 (Le *Corbusier*), p. 197; cf. also Gervais, Originalité(s), p. 390 ; Buydens, p. 276.

190 Luhmann, The Work of Art, p. 197; Derrida, Genre, p. 61 et seqq.; Leach, p. 131, compares "styles" to "swarm behaviors", i.e., behaviors of replication and copying.

191 Luhmann, Art as a Social System, p. 209, "reproducing art within the artwork".

192 Gumbrecht, Über den Stil, p. 289 et seqq.; Luhmann, Art as a Social System, p. 122; p. 130 et seq.; see also: Focillon, p. 1, "the oeuvre is an attempt towards uniqueness...and at the same time it belongs to a system of complex relations" (translation is mine); Luhmann, Weltkunst, p. 28, explains that both style and unicity can be observed in an artwork; Mijatovic, Kreativität, p. 92, describes this as a paradox: "how can something be different and at the same time similar?" (translation is mine).

193 Luhmann, The Work of Art, p. 205.

194 Luhmann, The Work of Art, p. 197; Derrida, Genre, p. 56, is here paradigmatic. In essence, a rhetoric exercise, it sketches out the unseizable dictates of artistic genres: "without claiming to lay down the law or to make this an act of law, I merely would have summoned up...the sense of a practice"; cf. also Graber, Zwischen Geist und Geld, p. 99, who describes the creation of an artwork as the result of the interplay between first- and second-order observation and concludes that "One cannot speak of a dominance of the author over the work" (translation is mine).

195 Luhmann, Art as a Social System, p. 208 et seq.; Magerski, p. 108; Luhmann, The Work of Art, p. 196 et seqq.; see also above Chapter 1, I.

and each style received a sort of decay time.[196] Today, the recognizability of a style in an artwork governs the communication within the art system[197] and organizes the contribution of each artwork to the system. At the level of the artworks' observation (second order), style allows for artworks to be described, analyzed and criticized.[198]

III.IV.II Artistic styles and copyright law

The indispensable function of artistic styles absolved within the art system seems to be recognized by copyright law. Artistic styles are considered as being in the public domain, meaning that they cannot be monopolized by the exclusive right of someone and can be reproduced freely.[199]

An example is provided by a decision of the GFCJ about a forged watercolor in the style of Emil Nolde. This painting, which also depicted his typical landscape motifs, did not constitute a copyright infringement because it was not a copy of an existing painting by Nolde.[200] More recently, the Higher Regional Court of Hamburg noted, while concretizing the copyright concept of "pastiche" according to the new § 51a DE-CopA in the "*Metall auf Metall*" case, that because styles are already not protected by copyright, the exception of pastiche shall cover "more" than just stylistic borrowings.[201]

What the decisions "*Le Corbusier*" and "*Love*" suggest, moreover, is the readiness of courts to treat the artistic style as a necessity and, therefore, as a restriction to one's leeway in the moment of creation. The assessment of the individual character is, thus, not only adapted to constraints dictated by purpose and technicity but also by artistic styles and, thus, by considerations of aesthetical order (as in an "external reference").[202] So, even if the Zurich Court recognized that both the word "love" and the used font (Clarendon) are in the public domain, an aspect that would

196 LUHMANN, Art as a Social System, p. 130 et seq.; cf. BOHN, Autonomien, p. 61; MAGERSKI, p. 108.

197 DERRIDA, Genre, p. 64, expressed it this way: "Can one identify a work of art, of whatever sort…, if it does not bear the mark of a genre, if it does not signal or mention it or make it remarkable in any way?"; LEACH, p. 130, makes the example of architecture, for which the same "rule" applies: If an architecture student designs a building in form of a pineapple, the professor is likely to question his student's ability. If the student were to design a building vaguely similar to buildings designed by famous architects, it is likely that the design will be deemed acceptable.

198 LUHMANN, The Work of Art, p. 197 et seqq.

199 Cf. WALRAVENS, p. 41.

200 GFCJ of June 8, 1989 (*Emil Nolde*), NJW 1990, p. 1986 et seqq., at para. 1988, cf. also JAYME, p. 34 et seq.

201 Higher Regional Court of Hamburg of April 28, 2021 (*Metall auf Metall III*), GRUR 2022, p. 1217 et seqq., p. 1222 at para. 77; the same logic was advanced by the German legislature in its explanatory memorandum to the 2021 amendment of the DE-CopA, s. Explanatory Memorandum 19/27426, p. 90 and 91.

202 A similar idea is proposed by BUYDENS, p. 276, for the field of applied art, in which the designer has to respect "trends of style".

speak against their protectability, it ultimately concluded that the artwork of the minimal art fulfilled the definition of work at Art. 2 para. 1 CopA.[203]

The autopoietic development of art depends on the possibility of the emulation of styles in subsequent artworks. Coincidentally, artistic styles are kept free from copyright monopolization. If someone is to commit a copyright infringement, it is required that he borrows more than a known style. Artworks that build interpictorial references only by emulating an existing style (but not also the specific forms of an existing artwork) can continue to playfully test improbable connections without worrying about the possibility of infringing copyright. It is the case, for example, of the artwork *Portrait of V.I. Lenin with Cap, in the Style of Jackson Pollock III*, realized by the duo Art & Language in 1980, which mixed elements of Soviet and US American history to hint at the Cold War with irony and a critical eye.

Peter Weibel's long titled artwork *Jackson Pollock converges in 1952 with Donald Judd's galvanized iron crates of 1967, which hide under Andy Warhol's OMO boxes of 1964* (1988), is another example of an artwork that mixes styles and ideas of three authors in total.[204]

Painting, photographing or sculpting in someone else's style will, thus, not infringe copyright – only copying an actual artwork will.[205] Copyright also seems to recognize that a style might constitute a set of immaterial constraints that artists comply to when conceiving and realizing their artworks. It, thus, takes them into account when determining the leeway available to the artist at the moment of creation and, consequently, the individual character.

III.IV.III The stylistic necessities of contemporary art

A question regarding the protectability of many contemporary artworks is to what extent courts would be ready to adapt the threshold of individuality to recognize the stylistic necessities of postmodernism and, thereby, adopted techniques, such as the general "deskilling", i.e., the intentional absence of discernable craft or skill in the realization of artworks and the relocation of the artistic achievement on intellectual operations and even copying, as in the case of interpictorial original copies.[206]

Both copying and other techniques of deskilled artmaking could result in the lack of a discernable individual character. At the same time, this should be weighed against the background of the artist's style – i.e., the necessity of the artwork to present itself as it does. Some copyright lawyers seem to recognize that the artists'

203 Zurich Court of Appeal of July 7, 2009 (*Love*), sic! 2010, p. 889 et seqq., c. 1.3.

204 Cf. Römer, p. 196.

205 Egloff, Commentary CopA, N 25 *ad* Art. 2; Mijatovic, Kreativität, p. 92; Cherpillod, Liberté, p. 357.

206 Deskilling can take many forms. Also, copying could be observed through the lens of deskilling: Römer, p. 88, makes the example of Sherrie Levine, whose photographs "irritate" because they refuse to assert a "creative act"; cf. also Roberts, p. 77, who writes that appropriation art has been commonly described "as getting the hand out of art and putting the brain in".

technical skills have become less important than the conceptual ability to place images in different settings and, thereby, change their meaning.[207]

A decision of the Tribunal de Paris in a proceeding for the recognition of co-authorship involving wax sculptor Daniel Druet and artist Maurizio Cattelan also goes in this direction.[208] According to the judges, an author is not only the person who materially realizes the artwork, something Druet had been hired to do, but also who gives precise directives. Moreover, the court gave importance to the *mise en scène* of the sculptures, considering that these, too, were an integral part of the work. For example, in the case of *La Nona Ora* (1999), the court considered that these directives only emanated from Maurizio Cattelan:

> Daniel Druet was in no way in a position...to take the slightest part in the choices relating to the scenic setting of the said sculptures (choice of building and size of rooms housing the sculptures, direction of view, lighting, even destruction of a window or parquet floor to make the staging more realistic and striking) or to the content of the possible message to be conveyed through this staging.[209]

The question is whether it is possible to enforce a change within the existing copyright framework or if the proposals to include new conceptual art forms will be forcibly relegated to the margins of copyright law, leaving copyright's criteria unaltered. For example, as reported by MÜLLER, German copyright scholars proposed in the 1960s to bestow the conceptual artist only with a related right, not with a full copyright, in order to accommodate the artworks' need for protection with their lack of originality.[210] In his doctoral thesis on "antiart and copyright law", GERHARD RAU also individuated in the requirement of originality the main burden to the protection of newer art forms. For this reason, he proposed to bestow copyright protection independently from the fulfillment of individuality or any other level of originality. In this way, every artwork ever created would achieve copyright protection. Only that would free the judgment from the arbitrariness of the decision and overcome the discrepancy existing between legal and artistic evaluations.[211]

In trying to achieve a protection for contemporary artworks, these lawyers have advanced the complete elimination or circumvention of the requirement of originality. They have, thus, underlined how the obstacle to the protection of these artworks lies precisely there but also how difficult it is to imagine a copyright

207 LANDES, p. 2.

208 Tribunal de Paris of July 8, 2022 (*Druet vs. Cattelan*); Druet had sued Cattelan for co-authorship of eight wax sculptures he had realized on the latter's commission.

209 EMMANUELLE JARDONNET, La justice donne raison à Maurizio Cattelan contre Daniel Druet, July 8, 2022, (<https://www.lemonde.fr/culture/article/2022/07/08/la-justice-donne-raison-a-maurizio-cattelan-face-a-daniel-druet_6134012_3246.html>) (translation is mine).

210 MÜLLER, p. 241. Related rights are notoriously bestowed for a particular achievement ("*Leistung*") or performance rather than for the creation of an original work.

211 RAU, p. 41 et seq.; cf. also FUCHS CHRISTINE, p. 134.

protection in which the requirement of originality is different. By relegating contemporary art to the margins of copyright legislation, these authors are also accepting a sort of "gatekeeping function" with respect to the core of copyright.

III.V The non-original photograph

Due to its partially mechanical-automatic component, photography has always been considered the "problematic child" of copyright law. Putting it on par with other creative outputs, courts have often aestheticized photographs and looked for a proof of creative choices in their configuration.[212]

In the United States, due to an extremely low threshold for protection, photographs are treated as original works of authorship in the majority of litigated copyright cases,[213] i.e., already when they are autonomously created and are not copied.[214] Because under the "modicum of creativity" standard, "even a slight amount suffice[s]" for the threshold to be reached, and "[t]he vast majority of works make the grade quite easily".[215] Other countries, such as Italy, Spain, Germany and Austria, have resolved the dilemma of unoriginal photographs by relegating their protection to the domain of neighboring rights.[216] These countries, thus, grant unoriginal photographs a copyright *sui generis*, that is conceptually separated from the "real" copyright insofar as it is not concerned with the problem of originality. Tradeoff to this right is the smaller scope of protection and a shorter duration.

In Switzerland, where "a high originality criterion has been kept for photographs to avoid the copyright protection of mechanical renderings of reality",[217] the legislature introduced in April 2020 a new form of protection for non-individual photographs (Art. 2 para. 3bis CopA) after lobbyists from professional photographers' groups had lamented the lack of protection for their work for years.[218] The new provision, existing in this form only in Switzerland,[219] considers photographic depictions and depictions of three-dimensional objects produced by a process similar to

212 See in Chapter 3, II.IV.I.

213 Subotnik, p. 1493.

214 Subotnik, p. 1494 and 1511, quoting a decision of the Southern District Court of New York in which it was established that "unless a photograph replicates another work with total or near-total fidelity, it will be at least somewhat original in the rendition".

215 *Feist Publications, Inc., vs. Rural Telephone Service Co.*, 499 US 340 (1991), p. 345.

216 Rigamonti/Bernasconi, p. 329.

217 Hug, Switzerland, p. 259 at fn. 15; this approach resulted in a number of judicial decisions in which courts have denied protection to photographs: The already mentioned DFC 130 III 714 (*Meili*) is the most notable example. Other examples are the decision of the Aargau Commercial Court of August 29, 2012 (*Nicolas Hayek*), sic! 2013, p. 344 et seqq., p. 347, in which the protection was denied to one of the two pictures at stake and the decision of Canton Basel-City Court of Appeal of May 20, 2016 (*Panoramabild*), sic! 2016, p. 594 et seqq., which denied protection to a panorama photograph of the Basel Minster.

218 Rehbinder/Haas/Uhlig, OFK CopA, N 34 *ad* Art. 2; see the archive of the working group for photography protection at the website <http://fotografie-urheberrecht.com/index.html>.

219 Rehbinder/Haas/Uhlig, OFK CopA, N 45 *ad* Art. 2.

that of photography as works, even if they do not have individual character. It is, thus, the first provision that abandoned the requirement of individuality as an element of the definition of a copyrightable work.[220]

Although the protection as an individual photographic work (Art. 2 para. 2 let. g CopA) continues to be more attractive because of a longer term of protection and, as argued by many authors, a generally larger protection scope,[221] this provision was rejected unanimously. When this norm was introduced, Swiss copyright lawyers reacted calling it a "foreign body" in the structure of copyright. Others described it as a "system breach" and as "alien to the system".[222]

With their observations, these authors discursively re-established the pre-existing barrier between individual works – the only ones traditionally admitted within copyright law – and other non-individual artifacts, which have always been excluded. Again, copyright lawyers have accepted a sort of gatekeeping role by trying to maintain the standards of copyright law sufficiently "high".

III.VI Change of perspective: The dilemma of copyright

Copyright lawyers tend to describe copyright protection as a neutral award, granted regardless of merit and value.[223] Not every creation, however, even if objectively new, is awarded copyright protection: This signals a need for copyright lawyers to negotiate a threshold, the overcoming of which will bestow protection. So, doctrine and courts refuse protection to artifacts that are judged too banal or artisanal or to belong to the "everyday experience", i.e., not surprising enough to be awarded with copyright.[224]

In theoretical discussions, the stance according to which copyright cannot be awarded to a creation is seldom explicit: Scholars will rarely admit that something is not protected because the level of creativity is too low.[225] Yet protection of non-original photographs is relegated to the margins of copyright law in most countries,[226] and protection schemes that are too liberal get rejected by doctrine because of the perceived risk of copyright law protecting the worthless. Such happened, for example, to KUMMER's presentation theory, to the new provision of Art. 2 para. 3bis CopA, and happens regularly to the attempts of lowering of the

220 EGLOFF, CopA Commentary, N 35 *ad* Art. 2; EGLOFF, Neues, p. 275.

221 Not only is the duration of protection considerably longer for photographic works, as many authors argue, their scope of protection is also larger, cf. WALTER, p. 380 and REHBINDER/HAAS/UHLIG, OFK CopA, N 40 et seqq. *ad* Art. 2 with further references.

222 MOSIMANN/HOSTETTLER, p. 129; for an overview cf. WALTER, 378.

223 HILTY, Urheberrecht, N 165; cf. also BULLINGER, PraxKomm DE-CopA, N 24 *ad* § 2; KEARNS, p. 64.

224 DFC 113 II 190 (*Le Corbusier*), p. 197; DFC 143 III 373 (*Max Bill*), c. 2.1; DFC 148 III 305 (*Feuerring*), c. 5.1.

225 Cf., however, the discussions on the rejection of the small coin by part of the literature in SCHLÜTER, p. 49.

226 Cf. Chapter 3, III.V.

requirements for protection.[227] Other recognizable hints at this "copyright-preserving" attitude are visible in the need to make copyright more difficult to attain than other types of intellectual property protection that have a more marked market orientation, i.e., the protection of designs.[228] The discussions surrounding the protection of the "small coin" also typically triggers the need to differentiate industrial property protection (unfair competition law) from intellectual property protection (copyright law), the latter protecting only "above-average" achievements.[229] We have called this the "gatekeeping function" of copyright lawyers and courts, i.e., the will to keep copyright protection exclusive, an award to above-average creative efforts.

The risk of protecting the worthless with a too-low threshold meets, on the other side of the coin, the risk of advancing a too-exclusive stance by means of a too-high threshold. If realized, both risks would disable the purpose of copyright, i.e., that of protecting only what needs protection to realize the societal goal of copyright.[230] The problem seems to be that there is no objective way to elaborate the perfect threshold for copyright protectability that also signals what is *worth* protecting because of its cultural or societal value.

The production of scholarship in this field is endless as well as seemingly able to provide the most disparate conclusions:[231] While an economic approach to copyright law will tend to regard copyright as essentially good for providing incentives to authors (and, thus, all expansions of the scope of exclusive rights as even better),[232] legal cultural studies will come to the opposite conclusion, observing how a too-broad copyright prevents follow-on innovation to arise (and, thus pleading for limited rights on intellectual outputs).[233] Copyright law must "walk in darkness" and test the alternatives, guided only by its own self-evidence that a higher threshold makes it naturally more difficult to obtain protection, thereby expanding the public domain. Conversely, a lower threshold makes protection easier to obtain but restricts access to culture and inflates the scope of what this protection entails.[234]

The reality shows that there is always a discrepancy between what is deemed having value in the art world and the criteria copyright law has for ascertaining

227 E.g., the criticism expressed toward the presentation theory gathered by VON BÜREN, p. 389; the criticism expressed toward the lowering of the required individuality expressed by HILTY, Urheberrecht, N 164.; the unanimous criticism expressed toward Art. 2 para. 3bis CopA and its categorization as a foreign body in the structure of copyright law, cf. WALTER, p. 377 et seqq.; cf. also KEARNS, p. 84 et seq.; SENN, Individualität, p. 524; HILTY, Hobby Kalender, p. 29 et seq.

228 DFC 148 III 305 (*Feuerring*), c. 5.3 (translation is mine).

229 SCHLÜTER, p. 49.

230 Cf. MÜLLER, p. 235; Art. 2 para. 3bis CopA was conceived precisely for this reason, cf. REHBINDER/HAAS/UHLIG, OFK CopA, N 41 *ad* Art. 2.

231 Cf. ORTLAND, Aesthetics, p. 228.

232 BARRON, Copyright Infringement, p. 98; PEUKERT, Irrtum, p. 40 and 49.

233 Cf. BARRON, Copyright Infringement, p. 94; BALGANESH, Foreseeability, p. 1579; CRAIG, Copyright, p. 11 et seqq., 26.

234 BULLINGER, PraxKomm DE-CopA, N 24 *ad* § 2.

this value and bestowing protection accordingly. To name one example, Marcel Duchamp's "Fountain" (1917), elected the "most influential piece of modern art" in a survey conducted by the Turner Prize sponsors,[235] would still be judged uncopyrightable. Lowering the threshold for attaining protection is perhaps an insufficient strategy to discern what deserves protection and distinguish it from what is, instead, worthless in other spheres of society. Because it would still not recognize the most influential artwork as an original work worthy of copyright protection, it seems that the individual character is inherently inadequate to absolve the task.[236]

IV.I Where is the individual character?

The third axis concerns the question "Where is individuality?" and the attempts of copyright law at stipulating the site upon which the individual character must be located.[237] Since the copyright amendment of 1989, it is unequivocal that the individual character must arise from the work itself and from this only, i.e., neither from the personality of the author, nor from the context of the work.[238] To decide whether the artifact is a work, courts shall consider its overall impression (*Gesamteindruck*), i.e., the interplay of all configurative choices with each other.[239] This forbids courts to conduct a "tessellated examination" of the object, i.e., to divide it into parts that might – when observed independently from the rest – be considered non-individual.[240]

Even though not explicitly anchored in the Swiss CopA,[241] it is undisputed in international copyright literature (and the Swiss make no exception) that only

235 Charlotte Higgins, Work of art that inspired a movement...a urinal, December 2, 2014 (<https://www.theguardian.com/uk/2004/dec/02/arts.artsnews1>).

236 Fuchs Christine, p. 129, 135 and 138.

237 Sherman, Appropriating, p. 37.

238 Federal Gazette of June 19, 1989 (BBl 1989 III 477), p. 521; DFC 143 III 373 (*Max Bill*); DFC 130 III 168 (*Marley*); Egloff; CopA Commentary, N 13 *ad* Art. 2; Cherpillod, SHK CopA, N 18 *ad* Art. 2; Fuchs Christine, Avantgarde, p. 139.

239 Rehbinder/Haas/Uhlig, OFK CopA, N 7 *ad* Art. 2; Züllig, p. 294; Haas, p. 48 at fn. 141; Decision of the Lucerne Court of Appeal of February 5, 2003 (*Knoblauchpresse*), sic! 2003, p. 731 et seqq., p. 739 et seq.; Decision of the Cantonal Court of St. Gallen of June 19, 2002 (*Mummenschanz*), sic! 2003, p. 116 et seqq., p. 119.

240 DFC 143 III 373 (*Max Bill*), c. 2.4; cf. Handle, p. 164; the "overall impression" given by an artifact, judged decisive for deciding the question of eligibility for copyright, might also encompass elements that are non-individual. These elements should not, in principle, be considered; cf. DFC 136 III 225 (*Guide Orange*), c. 4.2, in which the court explained that neither the type of binding nor the paper participated to the individual character of the artifact at stake. Tushnet, Thousand Words, p. 718, affirms that "there is a sort of magic by which unprotectable parts together become protected".

241 See, however, international copyright law, i.e., Art. 2 para. 1 of the Berne Convention (implicitly), Art. 9 para. 2 TRIPS, and Art. 2 WCT as: "Copyright protection shall extend to expressions and not to ideas", or in the French Code de la Propriété Intellectuelle, at L. 112-1: "les dispositions du present code protègent les droit des auteurs sur toutes les oeuvres de l'esprit, quels qu'en soient… la forme d'expression", cf. Walravens, p. 33.

expression is protectable, while the underlying idea shall remain free.[242] The dichotomy expression/idea is classically used as one of the junctures in which the scope of protection, including the need to maintain things in the public domain, is mediated.[243] The unclarity crystallizes around the question of what consideration, if at all, shall be given to the invisible dimension of the artifact in the determination of the scope of protection of the work; in other words: "How far from the surface of the material object is copyright law willing to extend the owner's rights?"[244] In the copyright literature, this problem is often referred to as the opposition of form and content, another dichotomy that is stated nowhere in the CopA.[245]

IV.II A brief delineation of the concepts of idea, expression, content and form

To understand what we mean, we first need to briefly delineate the two oppositions of concepts "idea/expression" and "content/form". Neither on the meaning of the four concepts, nor on the respective oppositions is there general and full agreement in the copyright literature.[246] Rather, at times, we find form conceptually opposed to idea (as "idea/form").[247] At others, scholars further divide form in internal and external form.[248] Often, content and idea are used as synonyms.[249] An accurate reconstruction of the theoretical debates over the differences between idea, form, expression and content exceeds the scope and the purpose of the present work. We will, thus, limit ourselves to briefly shed light on the four concepts as they are commonly defined in Swiss law, and then propose an understanding of the four concepts based on which we will continue our analysis.

As mentioned, common in copyright is the notion according to which only expression is protected, while ideas shall remain free. Copyright protection extends to the expressed idea, an idea made perceptible, while leaving intact (that is, in

242 Cf. Ickowicz, p. 280 et seq., who reports that in a case in 1987 handled before the Tribunal de Paris, Christo was denied copyright protection. He had claimed that the wrapping of trees on the occasion of an action by an advertising agency was an infringement of his copyright, but the court argued that the idea of wrapping things was not protectable. On the contrary, the reproductions of his wrapping of a concrete building, for example the Pont-Neuf in Paris (which he packed in 1985), was protected by the Appeal Court in Paris.

243 Hugenholtz, p. 278; Walravens, p. 32 et seqq.; Stokes, p. 164, fn. 172: "[I]t is a cliché of copyright law that copyright does not protect ideas: it protects the expression of ideas. But the utility of the cliché depends on how ideas are defined".

244 Sherman, What is a Copyright Work, p. 103 et seq., so too Commercial Court of Zurich of January 25, 2022 (*Hotelrevue*), c. 6.

245 So too the Commercial Court of Zurich of January 25, 2022 (*Hotelrevue*), c. 6.

246 Handle, p. 17; Karnow, p. 118.

247 Cherpillod, L'objet, p. 24 et seqq., individuates in the work of Josef Kohler (1849–1919), the origin of the distinction between form and idea; the opposition form and idea is found in Vischer, Urheberrecht, p. 256; Cherpillod, L'objet, p. 136.

248 Kummer, Werk, p. 10, individuates in the work of Josef Kohler (1849–1919) the origin of the concept of "inner form". Both Kummer, Werk, p. 11 and Cherpillod, L'objet, p. 29 et seqq. dismiss this concept.

249 Handle, p. 59.

the public domain) what has not emerged and is, therefore, unascertainable. For its part, the SFSC formulated that "the idea is only protected once it is dressed in perceptible form",[250] suggesting at once that "the perceptible form" might be a synonym of the accomplished expression and that the idea might reside within the form and be an inherent part of it. KUMMER called all that is "not yet expressed" the "non-form", suggesting that expression realizes form.[251]

For the purposes of the following analysis, we can settle for the following understanding: The idea (or the "non-form", in KUMMER's terminology) is all that precedes the potential work and, as such, is still unexpressed, relatively abstract and fluctuating. The expression is the moment of the concretization of the idea, which ultimately realizes a form, i.e., all that has arisen to the surface has become perceptible and sensible in a work. Accordingly, the content of a work would encompass all the invisible, the non-fully visible and the intelligible parts of the work, i.e., much of what the idea once was before being expressed.[252] In our understanding, the concepts of idea and expression are, therefore, "abandoned" by the overcoming of the realized work, which shall then be described with the dichotomy of form and content.[253]

IV.III The linearity of copyright protection

An unformed idea, or KUMMER's "non-form", does not fulfill the work definition (yet), even if, mentally, it is concretized up to a point that it could be explained or shown in detail any minute. That, at most, is only a work *in potentia*: It has the power to become a work in the moment of actual creation (in the German legal jargon, the action of creating is a *Realakt*),[254] which will make it "a fact of copyright".[255]

Once the idea is expressed in a perceptible form, it is the latter that constitutes the imperative reference point for building up a judgment on copyright eligibility.[256] As opposed to content, considered as being too fluctuating and abstract for the legal assessment,[257] the form is deemed to be the only part of a work that, in addition to being conveniently perceptible, is also stable and, thus, objectively verifiable.[258] The perceptible form, conveyed by the material support "carrying" the work,

250 DFC 116 II 351 (*Medium*), p. 354 (translation is mine).

251 KUMMER, Werk, p. 8 and 20, the "Nichtform".

252 Cf. in this sense ICKOWICZ, p. 290 et seqq. and then at 307 speaking of the "intelligibility" of oeuvres.

253 Cf. the explanations given by ICKOWICZ, p. 287 et seq., who speaks about "conception" (for the not-yet-expressed-idea) and "realization" for the perceptible form, capable of giving rise to a sensible experience.

254 DFC 116 II 351 (*Medium*), p. 354 c. 2

255 CHERPILLOD, L'objet, p. 136, however, states that "originality can reside in the entire creation, in the ideas as much as in the formal elements" (translation is mine).

256 FISCHER VERONIKA, p. 265; DESSEMONTET, SIWR II/1, p. 218; MIJATOVIC, Kreativität, p. 53.

257 COHEN, p. 1170; SHERMAN, Appropriating, p. 39; cf. also SAID, p. 335 et seqq.

258 ICKOWICZ, p. 273; cf. PEUKERT, Drei Entstehungsbedingungen, p. 137 et seq., cf. CRAIG, Copyright, p. 19; SHERMAN, Appropriating, p. 37; BARRON, Claims of Art, p. 370, argues that the perception of "stability" of the artistic object is a modernist bias, later confuted by postmodernist thought.

is, thus, the focal point helping determine the work's scope of protection,[259] even if the object of protection – the immaterial work – "transcends" the sole form.[260] As expressed by REINHART, "the work as such is not perceptible by the human being; rather, the work is perceived by means of an agent", which is the physical realization of the work.[261] For this reason, protection reaches beyond the identical reproduction of the artifact's form and encompasses, up to a certain point, even related and similar-looking forms.[262]

Even though the focal point of copyright is on the form, a wide consensus exists on the fact that pure form does not exist and that a work is a holistic and complex mixture of form and content. Consequently, copyright lawyers and courts conceive copyright to be not only the protection of form.[263] At least to the extent the content coalesces in the form and is undiscernible from it,[264] it is protected together with the form as part of the work.[265] As the Commercial Court of the Canton of Zurich explained, the central question regarding the protection of content is its degree of concretization, i.e., whether it is sufficiently *formed*.[266] This formulation makes us wonder whether courts have the instruments to actually discern content and treat it separately from form at all.

When deciding on the copyright eligibility of an artifact, moreover, courts will never spontaneously ascertain the work's content after they have deliberated on the work's form. Copyright's criterions are tailored to look for the individual character within the surface of the artifact, i.e., its expressed form. In this sense, to the

259 ICKOWICZ, p. 275.

260 CHERPILLOD, L'objet, p. 115; KARNOW, p. 120; for ICKOWICZ, p. 277, such conceptualization is "paradoxical"; COHEN, p. 1172, on the focus of copyright on the unprotectability of ideas, argues that "disputes about copyright scope become disputes about identifying those expressions that should be treated 'like' ideas".

261 REINHART, p. 234 (translation is mine).

262 BULLINGER, PraxKomm DE-CopA, N 33 *ad* § 2; see below at Chapter 4.

263 Commercial Court of Zurich of January 25, 2022 (*Hotelrevue*), c. 6; KUMMER, Werk, p. 21, quotes DFC 88 IV 123 (*Lehrbuch*), c. 1 to substantiate his statement; CHERPILLOD, Le droit d'auteur, p. 14, quotes the same decision but asserts the opposite, i.e., that the SFSC established that only form is protected. In the decision, which concerned the eligibility for copyright of a textbook, is stated: "the content of a work is not per se free and copyright protection [is] not only forms protection" (translation is mine). This statement is preceded by an exemplary list of elements that, according to our understanding of the notion of form and content, are part of the work's form (e.g., planning, choice and gathering of the material as well as its arrangement and structuring).

264 Cf. on this FOCILLON, p. 1, "Finally (to temporarily respect the terms of an apparent opposition) [the artwork] is matter and spirit, form and content".

265 DESSEMONTET, SIWR II/1, p. 218: Often, content and form cannot be divided because they coalesce in the work; REHBINDER, N 31 and PAHUD, p. 116 et seqq.; MIJATOVIC, Kreativität, p. 55; KUMMER, Werk, p. 8 and 20, says "that only the form is copyrightable is only true if it means that only the expressed thought – not the idea – is protected. To divide between form and content, instead, is misleading"; similarly, SHERMAN, Appropriating, p. 38, states that idea and expression are "inextricably interwoven"; on the jurisprudence side of things, see DFC 101 II 102 (*Annabelle*), c. 2b; Commercial Court of Zurich of January 25, 2022 (*Hotelrevue*), c. 6.

266 Commercial Court of Zurich of January 25, 2022 (*Hotelrevue*), c. 6.

shallow eye of copyright law, all art is "retinal art":[267] "*une organization de signes, en vue de produire un effet esthétique*".[268] If the form of an artifact is not individual, the artifact will not qualify for protection, irrespective of its content. If, on the contrary, the form is individual, there is no banal content that can stop the work from being eligible for a copyright.

IV.IV Change of perspective: The non-linear artwork

The analysis of the dichotomies "idea/expression" and "form/content" has shown that copyright law individuates the presence of a work preponderantly, if not exclusively, in the form of the artifact. Even if copyright lawyers admit that form without content does not exist, it does not consider the content of a work independently from its form, nor has it the instruments to do such at the level of the ascertainment of the individual character. On the contrary, even the courts' affirmations regarding the protectability of content are always mediated by the inquiry as to whether this content is sufficiently concretized into a form.

The four concepts idea, expression, form and content are, thus, organized by copyright law on a presupposed linearity.[269] First, the author has an idea. Second, he *expresses* this idea in a form that best carries this idea. Once expressed, the idea becomes the work's content, which, as the Commercial Court of Zurich paradigmatically expressed in a recent decision, "forms the form of the work".[270] Different authors with different ideas will, thus, naturally and inevitably produce different expressions and different looking works. Only a new idea, according to the assumed linearity, will produce a new form that will eventually be copyrightable.[271] If reversed, this assumption means that similar forms will forcibly be presupposed as inhabited by similar contents and, thus, be, from a copyright perspective, the same work.[272]

With this notion of artwork, copyright law remains attached to a very traditional aesthetic canon that is now long surpassed.[273] The emergence of conceptual art brought about what Lucy R. Lippard called the "dematerialization of the art object".[274] Because conceptual artists declared in their working program the centrality of the idea and the subsidiarity, even irrelevance, of the execution,[275] sometimes the point of reference for a copyright law that looks for protectability in the

267 Ickowicz, p. 275.
268 Cf. Walravens, p. 50.
269 Sherman, Appropriating, p. 38.
270 Commercial Court of Zurich of January 25, 2022 (*Hotelrevue*), c. 6.
271 E.g., Schack, N 359; Mijatovic, Kreativität, p. 99.
272 We can refer here to conceptual artist Sol Lewitt's words, see Lewitt, p. 79: "The idea becomes a machine that makes the art". For him, however, "execution [wa]s a perfunctory affair".
273 Ickowicz, p. 275.
274 Lippard, p. vii; cf. also Kost, p. 127, who writes "in Conceptual Art this concentration on our physical experience and our confrontation with form, material, and surface begins to dissolve".
275 Cf. Luhmann, Art as a Social System, p. 5; Stokes, p. 163 et seq.

expressed form is missing altogether. The contemporary artwork is not forcibly a reified object anymore. If it does have a material "corpus", it is often not so central for its interpretation. Moreover, the existence of artworks today is often a dynamic one: Time, duration, transformation and process (of production) are all integral elements of the work of art since the 1960s.[276]

In this respect, many authors have lamented the insufficiency of copyright protection vis-à-vis the artistic developments of the twentieth century. Even the apparently comprehensive protection of the work's content within the work's form is, thus, insufficient for this type of art.[277] Many copyright scholars have pleaded for a more extensive protection, one that goes beyond the sole surface and counts the artifacts' intelligible components.[278] An open question remains as to whether copyright law can contribute something to this type of art, i.e., if this type of art would benefit from being protected by copyright law in the first place. Copyright lawyers tend to assume that this is the case.[279] How concretely such a copyright would work, however, is not clear.

Interpictorial original copies have an even more fundamental problem with copyright law as not only do they risk not being protected – as other conceptual art forms do – but also risk infringing someone else's copyright. By focusing upon the meaning of the work at the expense of its visual appearance, these original copies invert the linearity normatively required by copyright law. Indeed, original copies perform a reversal of such linearity, in which the expression is the same and the idea is different.[280] Of the use of an old form as a new artwork, the transformation of a copy into an original (the previously described re-entry) copyright law can only see the repetition of a copyrighted work, therefore, omitting to see all that has fundamentally changed about the artwork in the process. In this precise context, this explains why appropriation artworks are not eligible for copyright, as a lawyer affirmed that the "mere idea of copying is not copyrightable",[281] confirming how copyright law is short-sighted in this respect.[282]

When it is done in an artistic context to create a new artwork, copying is never an end in itself.[283] Only if copyright law works, as it does within the framework of its own linearity, will an original copy appear only as a mere copy. By focusing on the form of the artwork only, however, copyright fails to see that *everything else around it has changed*. In the face of these evident changes, we can even conclude

276 Ickowicz, p. 24.

277 Another burden for the protection of conceptual art, however, only in the USA, is the requirement of "fixation", regulated at § 102 US Copyright Act, see Kucsko, p. 329.

278 Vischer, Neue Tendenzen, p. 285, writing about conceptual art and Vischer, Urheberrecht, p. 256; cf. also Kucsko, p. 329 et seq.; Fuchs Christine, p. 139; Ickowicz, p. 287 et seqq.

279 Affirmatively Fuchs Christine, p. 130; Ickowicz, p. 279 et seqq., presenting two instances in which Christo, earning mainly from photographic reproductions of his public installations, turned himself to copyright law.

280 Sherman, Appropriating, p. 39.

281 Hilgert, p. 26.

282 Cf. Stokes, p. 160; Sherman, Appropriating, p. 39.

283 Ickowicz, p. 32.

that the two works are the same only if the observer adopts the visible form as the sole distinction with which it sees the world.[284]

V.I Interim conclusions

V.II Looking back at copyright law

Starting from the rather simple legal definition anchored at Art. 2 para. 1 CopA, we have seen how the central concept of copyright's scope of protection – the work – emerges and evolves gradually as doctrine and jurisprudence elaborate ways to bring it to life. In the process, the already abstract requirement of the individual character has been related to a complex mix of *other* abstract requirements. Novelty, creativity, originality and improbability seem all to participate to the sketching out of the individual character without ever being fully synonymous to it.[285] Notwithstanding the fact that the work is one abstract and general concept, its doctrinal and judicial concretization does not allow for the identification of one unique principle, from which all the rest is derived.

By dividing the various statements on what constitutes a "work" on three different axes – *what, how much* and *where* – we have obtained an atypical systematization of the legal material. This has revealed a different way to conceptualize the object of protection of copyright, at ease with its ontological instability and not trying to force it into a *fixed* definition.[286] It does not surprise that the definition of a work cannot be located by means of inductive analysis[287] but, rather, is recursively constructed by scholars and courts at every single concretization of the written provisions.[288] The answers to whether an artifact qualifies for copyright protection or whether it is considered to be a (partial) reproduction of another already existing work do not result from an ontological definition of "the work" but, rather, from the activity of comparing different concrete artifacts and the ongoing judicial evaluation thereof.[289]

284 Luhmann, Identität, p. 21, reminds how something is identical always only in the eyes of the observer, who uses a difference with which something can appear as identical.

285 The continuous deferring of meaning can be theoretically described with Derrida's concept of *différance*, i.e., the simultaneous convergence of temporality – contained in defer – and of space – contained in differentiate that reveals the polysemy underlying copyright's opposition of terms: Derrida, Margins, p. 3 and 7; cf. also Teubner, Umgang mit Rechtsparadoxien, p. 37.

286 Cf. Peukert, A Critique, p. 34 and 133; Sherman, What Is a Copyright Work, p. 119; cf. also Dreier, p. 195 et seq.; Craig, Reconstructing, p. 222.

287 Sherman, Appropriating, p. 40 et seq.; Peukert, A Critique, p. 33.

288 The norm is not created until it is applied, Luhmann, Law as a Social System, p. 354; Luhmann, Menschenrechte, p. 229; cf. also Ladeur/Vesting, p. 124 et seq.

289 Peukert, A Critique, p. 34.

V.III The two sides of the work definition

We have seen that the individual character must arise from the work itself, conceived as a material artifact, of which the external appearance, within the spatial boundaries its form occupies, is decisive.[290] Aspects regarding the content of the work and the context of its presentation are neglected to the point that judges will only consider the content of a work as a "content-within-a-form" and will require from content that it is sufficiently formed. So, the required novelty is ascertained by looking for a difference, a visual distinction the artifact must create with respect to its past. Existing forms, or their recombination, will not produce a work. Under the statistical uniqueness, the work must assert itself as different from what already exists and even from what may arise in the future. In this sense, copyright law is "retinal" in that only those aspects that can be impressed on the judge's retina can and will be considered.[291] The work as the object of protection of copyright law is, thus, defined with criteria that prevalently focus on formal aspects of an artifact.

Yet the work of copyright law is not only this. While the main focal point, as described, is set on formal novelty, these rationales are completed by considerations of another order. This "other" of copyright protection is characterized by the return of more abstract and even subjective rationales. Previously excluded aesthetic aspects may be (re)considered in the judgment, and the judge could recur to external references (such as the consideration of the artistic style or the presentation theory) to assess them. Here, copyright law demonstrates a cognitive openness toward its environment. Concerned with the discrepancy that might arise between copyright protection and art, lawyers may develop ways to adhere copyright protection to the *realia* proposed by the artistic and cultural world.[292] So, for example, the presentation theory, which delegates the judgment to the practices valid in the art world, was formulated precisely by KUMMER, who had otherwise conceived a perfectly impermeable copyright law, freed at last from considerations of the aesthetic order. Similarly, lawyers lament the lack of protectability of newer art forms, such as conceptual art, and plead for a broader search of originality that encompasses aspects of the work that have remained invisible in its final form.

These two argumentative positions are not an "either/or"; rather, they are conjured alternatively and simultaneously in one sole opinion and in one sole court argumentation. Let us take, once again, the decision of the Zurich Court of Appeals regarding Robert Indiana's work *Love* as example. On deciding *what* is valid as the individual character, we note how the court proceeded in one direction just before adding, a couple lines below, a piece of substantiation that, when closely analyzed, rebuts what had just been stated. The court affirmed: "the criterion of statistical uniqueness can be applied for deciding on the matter of the work's

290 ICKOWICZ, p. 33, 275; FUCHS CHRISTINE, p. 138 et seq.; FISCHER VERONIKA, p. 265; DESSEMONTET, SIWR II/1, p. 218; REINHART, p. 234.

291 ICKOWICZ, p. 275.

292 ICKOWICZ, p. 59; MILLET, p. 115 et seq.

individual character",[293] then relativizes by stating that "this criterion alone cannot be decisive".[294] By proceeding with the lecture, we understand that the statistical uniqueness is just cursorily mentioned in the judgment but not really considered in the decision's argumentation. The court then mentioned the presentation theory as a possible, alternative way to establish the individual character and proceeded to a close analysis of the work's visible configuration (paying much attention to how exactly the word "love" is written, the position of the "O" and so on).[295] We may, thus, ask why the court mentioned the statistical uniqueness if it was to return to what this theory would like to exclude in the first place: An external reference to the art system by means of the presentation theory or the close consideration of the artifact's aesthetic aspects.

Similar fluctuations in the argumentative line can also be found in DFC 130 III 168 (*Marley*). In this decision, the SFSC argued for the individual character by resorting to a "light" version of the statistical uniqueness (it did not apply it fully, i.e., in two separate comparative steps but, rather, focused on a series of criteria that should signal when uniqueness is "attained" in the configuration of a photograph). When concretely addressing the snapshot at stake, however, the court ultimately argued with aesthetic-subjective reasons, describing the picture with formulations such as "appealing and interesting", or "reminiscent of a sculpture".[296]

When confronting decisions taken by different instances on the same subject, these changes become even more evident. For example, when the SFSC overturned the decision of the lower instance in DFC 143 III 373 (*Max Bill*), it did it by explaining that even though similar stools may have already been designed in the past (and one even in the same period of Max Bill's stool at stake), this aspect was not important. For Switzerland's highest court, decisive in that case was the "artistical impression" given by the artifact. Rather mysteriously, the SFSC did not mention the criterion of statistical uniqueness and plainly dismissed the fact that the lower instance may have tried to do precisely that by arguing that because other similar stools existed, Max Bill's could not be considered individual.[297]

V.IV An oscillating copyright

With such a perspective on the law,[298] the judicial decision does not appear, as it otherwise would to an observer internal to the system, as a rhetorical way to

293 Zurich Court of Appeal of July 7, 2009 (*Love*), sic! 2010, p. 889 et seqq., c. 1.1, discussed in Chapter 3, II.V.

294 Zurich Court of Appeal of July 7, 2009 (*Love*), sic! 2010, p. 889 et seqq., c. 1.1, discussed in Chapter 3, I.5. and 6.

295 Zurich Court of Appeal of July 7, 2009 (*Love*), sic! 2010, p. 889 et seqq., c. 1.2 and 1.3, discussed in Chapter 3, II.V.

296 DFC 130 III 168 (*Meili*), c. 5.2., discussed in Chapter 3, II.IV.II.

297 DFC 143 III 373 (*Max Bill*), discussed in Chapter 3, II.V.

298 Such observation is not founded on the research for one principle. It does not try to preserve the unity of the system but is, rather, comfortable with differences, cf. LUHMANN, Law as a Social

help the best motives prevail over the worst[299] but, rather, as a text that *oscillates* between pieces of argumentation that are, seen from this perspective, logically incompatible.[300] As GUMBRECHT wrote, an oscillation is characterized by the fact that "at any given moment…, one can only occupy *one of the two sides* in the field"[301] and that "from one moment to the next, the absolute freedom to change positions exists, and it is *impossible to forget the other pole and even to resist its attraction*".[302] For copyright protection, this means that the moment one tries to describe the work with just one abstract requirement ("a principle"), the need arises for the description to be completed with something else: An aspect that the chosen word or method seemed not to be able to convey or sufficiently encompass.[303]

So, the first step in the theory of statistical uniqueness is completed by a second that concretizes the necessity of a "distance". For lack of foreseeability into the future, this futurized novelty cannot be concretized by abstracting and subjectivizing the stakes. Similarly, in judicial decisions, considerations of objective novelty are kneaded with a close analysis of the artifact's configuration and occasional slips into aesthetical judgments. Moreover, the minute a court seems to consider the content of a work, it reminds of the fact that it is only possible to do so if such is sufficiently formed. Lastly, all elucubrations on the definition of the scope and threshold of copyright protection resolve in what was described as a "dilemma", that is, in the oscillating figure *par excellence*.

In this model, the two sides of the oscillation define the logically incompatible extremes of what is acceptable as juridical argumentation. By tuning with each other in always different ways, these sides define and construct "the work". This picture of copyright law explains why the outcome of a judicial decision is always open and reveals why it is uneasy to predict when, and based on which piece of argumentation, the law might recognize some artifacts as works or, on the contrary, state that something is not protected.[304] If juridical argumentations (and communication, in general) did not oscillate, all would stop in favor of the recognition of a certain rationality, a consent, a truth. In the absence of alternatives, of movement, decisions would not be needed.[305] Instead, once a side is marked by a distinction,

System, p. 66; only an observation of second order reveals the paradoxes, cf. TEUBNER, Umgang mit Rechtsparadoxien, p. 33.

299 LUHMANN, Law as a Social System, p. 352.

300 LUHMANN, Law as a Social System, p. 308, reminds us that even good argumentations might contain logical mistakes; cf. also TEUBNER, Umgang mit Rechtsparadoxien, p. 33.

301 GUMBRECHT, Broad Present, p. 73 (emphasis added).

302 GUMBRECHT, Broad Present, p. 73 (emphasis added).

303 ESPOSITO, Paradoxien, p. 36 et seq., writes: "the reference to one of both values forcibly implies the reference to the other" (translation is mine).

304 SHERMAN, What Is a Copyright Work, p. 119, generally about the legal system cf. LUHMANN, The Self-Reproduction, p. 233.

305 Before the final decision is effectively taken, however, it is impossible and undesirable to focus on one side only, cf. LUHMANN, Law as a Social System, p. 350 et seq.; FISCHER-LESCANO/CHRISTENSEN, p. 224.

one can (must!) always consider the other, unmarked side.[306] In the end, the decision defines an either/or: The juridical argumentations of courts oscillate between the two sides only until the very last moment, in which they freeze in the final verdict of the judge.[307] The oscillation characterizing the whole legal system, however, restarts just after, as the decision will be received and quoted, for confirmation or rejection, by lawyers, scholars and other courts.[308]

306 LUHMANN, Ausdifferenzierung der Kunst, p. 147.

307 LUHMANN, Law as a Social System, p. 348 and p. 460; the periphery of the law system, instead, can continue to oscillate, as only courts are in charge of dealing with the system's paradox, cf. LUHMANN, Law as a Social System, p. 33 and 302 et seqq.; cf. TUSHNET, Thousand Words, p. 709, describing the handling of images made by US courts with an oscillation, too – that between "opacity" and "transparency".

308 Because "the ultimate reasons are always penultimate reasons" and the system will restart oscillating just after the decision, LUHMANN, Law as a Social System, p. 356; TEUBNER, Umgang mit Rechtsparadoxien, p. 28.

4 The work's scope of protection

I.I The mark of individuality

In a somewhat circular fashion, the work's scope of protection is defined by the extent of the work itself; defined as an original (or individual) achievement, the work starts and ends where the "mark of individuality" disappears.[1]

This means that there is no identity between the artifact and the work of copyright law, as the former is produced in another sphere of society, i.e., art in the case of visual artworks. Even smaller parts of an artifact recognized as a work are protectable as works on their own insofar as they are intellectual creations with an individual character (Art. 2 para. 4 CopA).[2] This so-called element protection (*Elementenschutz*) applies to intermediate stages of works (unfinished works) as well as to portions of works.[3] In this sense, the work as individual intellectual

1 Reinhart, p. 235; Goldstein, p. 1181; for Germany, see: Dreier/Jehle, p. 229; the landmark decision of the CJEU of July 16, 2009 - C-5/08 (*Infopaq International vs. Danske Dagblades Forening*) contains a similar reasoning. Infopaq was a media monitoring and analysis business, that collected and summed up news from selected Danish newspapers. The quarrel concerned whether this activity, which resulted each time in an extract of 11 words, constituted infringement of the right of reproduction of the authors represented a professional association of Danish daily newspaper publishers. At para. 30 of the decision, the CJEU established that copyright protection only covers "works". Parts of a work are treated as works, provided they contain elements which are the expression of the intellectual creation of the author and are, thus, eligible for copyright (see para. 39 of the decision). As Stokes, p. 49, says, a copyright need not be extensive if it is the author's *own intellectual creation*.

2 Para. 4 repeats the content of Art. 2 para. 1 CopA. We can refer to what has been written for the individual character until now, see Chapter 3; cf. also Egloff, CopA Commentary, N 40 *ad* Art. 2; decision of the Zurich Court of Appeal of May 24, 2012 (*Tunnels d'Arrissoules*), sic! 2013, p. 445 et seqq., p. 446; Hilgert, p. 13. An exception is the notion of "work obtainable commercially" at Art. 19 para. 3 let. a CopA. Here, as "work" is not considered the work of Art. 2 para. 1 CopA but, rather, the exemplar as it circulates and is sold, see DFC 140 III 616 (*ETH Dokumentenlieferdienst*), c. 3.6.3. In DFC 133 III 473 (*Pressespiegel*), c. 3.1, as work exemplar was considered the entire journal or newspaper, and not individual articles, even if they likely qualified as works when considered individually.

3 Decision of the Zurich Court of Appeal of January 24, 2013 (*Bildungssoftware*), sic! 2013, p. 697 et seqq., c. ii.5.2; insofar as the (portion of the) artifact amounts to an intellectual creation with individual character, it is irrelevant if it was intended by the author as an independent whole or as a part of something bigger, and even if it is finished or unfinished, see Egloff, CopA Commentary, N 39 *ad* Art. 2.

DOI: 10.4324/9781003598503-7

creation is the smallest protectable unit of copyright protection.[4] Notwithstanding the fact that the work, as defined at Art. 2 para. 1 CopA, shall be judged in its "overall impression", i.e., without dissecting it into parts, the subelements of a work might qualify as protectable works.[5]

From a copyright perspective, an artwork is, thus, not treated as a conceptual unity but, rather, as an aggregate of protected and unprotected parts, a potential multitude of tinier (art)works in a bigger artwork. The practical consequence of this insight is that the scope of protection of copyrighted works extends not only externally, i.e., against creations that build up on the totality of an artwork and add new elements to it, but also internally. If an artist borrows only a portion from a bigger artwork, i.e., realizes what could be called a partial copy (*Teilkopie*), she is not fully safe from claims of copyright infringement.[6] Provided that the copied portion is individual even when considered independently from the rest of the artwork, the same rules apply for this portion as they do for the whole work.

II.I The "distance doctrine"

To decide the question of how far a copyright protected work reaches in concrete cases, copyright law uses the method of the so-called distance doctrine (*Abstandslehre*; in Germany, a very similar method is called *Verblassenstheorie*, i.e., fading theory). The doctrine is used to determine the type of use of a previous copyrighted work in a newer artifact and address related normative questions, e.g., whether the use required prior consent of the author of the previous work and, in the affirmative case and if the consent was missing, what rights of the author are touched upon (if the author's right to produce copies of her work, e.g., or the right to change the work).[7]

If we are to deconstruct the word "distance" to understand what it means exactly, we can use the concept of "sequential innovation" as the interplay of the concepts of sequence and relative novelty.[8] A sequence is commonly referred to as a repetition of things of the same – or similar – type. It suggests the relative motion of a repetition (in time or space) but also the stillness of its elements' invariability, of the fact that all can be traced back to the same element the sequence is made of. In other words, a sequence is, thus, a line of multiple immobility; as such, it describes what remains unvaried and is, thus, recognizable in downstream artifacts based on one initial work. Innovation, for its part, stands for variation and discontinuity.[9] As we have seen in the previous chapter, copyright law associates novelty to the

4 SHERMAN, What is a Copyright Work, p. 119.
5 SHERMAN, What is a Copyright Work, p. 117.
6 DREIER/JEHLE, p. 229; SHERMAN, What is a Copyright Work, p. 116.
7 Decision of the Aargau Court of Appeal of July 31, 1990 (*Swissbase*), SMI 1991, p. 80 et seqq., p. 84.
8 Originally deriving from the domain of patent law, it was implanted in copyright law by HAAS, p. 23 et seqq. and 33 et seqq., to describe those "works of literature and art that use chronologically previous works".
9 LUHMANN, The Work of Art, p. 195; ORTMANN, p. 174 et seqq.

formally new, i.e., to the creation of a sensible difference. As the distance doctrine defines how far the work extends, here too, novelty stands for the perceptible creation of something more. The distance the doctrine refers to is, therefore, a "spatial" separation of the newer creation from the previous work on which the former is based. The attribution of a specific use to a category is based on a comparison between the overall impressions of the old and the new artifacts.[10] Decisive is only the degree of visual discrepancy or conformity between them.[11] In the case of a computer program, for example, the court limited itself to count the elements of the first work that were still there in the second. Other aspects, such as qualitative and contextual observation, are barely considered.[12]

Because the boundaries between the abovementioned categories are blurry and one is just the continuation of the other, in practice, it is difficult to attribute a specific category.[13] Court decisions on the matter are deemed to be highly unpredictable and plagued by two subjective moments.[14] First, judges must decide how to weigh the individuality of the template's elements (i.e., if they are highly original or, rather, a "small coin"). On the basis of the evaluation of the borrowed elements' individuality, the judges must second determine whether the implemented changes were enough for the artifact to exit the work's protection scope.[15]

As it was, for example, recognized in a case of interior design, if an architect receives a copyright for a "not sensationally" creative project, his work will only be protected within the scope of the individual "surplus" created by him, not for the non-individual rest.[16] Similarly, when deciding whether an architectural project was too similar to a previous one, the SFSC held that not only had the second architect provided sufficient substantial modifications of the original plan but also that the individuality of the former was weak (*faible*) and, thus, follow-up innovation would be relatively easy to establish.[17] In this way, judges re-balance the fact that sometimes copyright protection is bestowed for a small creative output with an accordingly small protection scope, while a high degree of individuality protects

10 Already Reinhart, p. 234 et seqq., even before the distance doctrine, had put emphasis on the comparison; Wild, künstlerische Darbietung, p. 100; Mijatovic, Kreativität, p. 99; Haas, p. 48; cf. also Federal Gazette of June 19, 1989 (BBl 1989 III 477), p. 524; for German law cf. Blume Huttenlauch, p. 112 and Schack, N 342.

11 Haas, p. 48; Decision of the Aargau Court of Appeal of July 31, 1990 (*Swissbase*), SMI 1991, p. 80 et seqq., p. 84; see also Commercial Court of Aargau of January 5, 2015 (*Totenkopf-Tattoo*), sic! 2015, p. 449 et seqq., p. 453.

12 Hilty, Bildungssoftware, p. 707, criticizes the current method and argues that only with a qualitative and contextual observation of the work would the distance doctrine make sense.

13 Reinhart, p. 234 et seqq.

14 In Switzerland cf. Schmidt-Gabain, p. 132; de Werra/Benhamou, Kultur Kunst Recht, N 21 *ad* § 7; Haas, p. 24; in Germany, where the same approach is followed: Schack, N 342; Maassen, p. 213; Ortland, Aesthetics, p. 230.

15 Maassen, p. 213; Rehbinder/Haas/Uhlig, OFK CopA, N 2 *ad* Art. 3.

16 DFC 100 II 167 (*Späti Laden*).

17 DFC 125 III 328 (*Niederhauser*), p. 333 c. 4.

against imitation and all sorts of modifications, a "small coin" will only protect against slavish imitation.[18]

As seen before with the definition of work, not every small change to an existing artifact or work will be held as innovative under copyright. Rather, a qualified degree of novelty is needed to declare something as innovative. The more the individual traits of the source material *fade* into the downstream work, the more the use will be considered to be outside the scope of protection of the work (therefore, as mentioned, the distance doctrine is also called "fading theory").[19] If a sufficient visual similarity is attested, the doctrine conceives the chronological second as a variation of an archetype-work, fixed at the point where a particular combination of forms deemed to be individual is considered having arisen for the first time.[20]

The distance doctrine shall guide the subsumption of the artifact under one of three different types (or degrees) of use of a previous work in one's new artifact: The minor alteration (*Umgestaltung*), the derivative work (*Werk zweiter Hand* or *Bearbeitung*) and the free utilization (*freie Benutzung* or *Neugestaltung*).

III.I Types of uses of a work

III.II The minor alteration

First in the "line" of spatial distance from the work, we find minor alterations (*Umgestaltung*). Minor alterations are described as a mere quantitative, uncreative change to the original work.[21] Expressed with the words of HAAS, i.e., with the previously explained concept of sequential innovation, minor alterations are merely sequential creations that do not amount to an innovation, as they do not showcase the creativity level and the distance from previous works required.[22] Because minor alterations build on a previous work by only slightly changing it, they do not add

18 REHBINDER/HAAS/UHLIG, OFK CopA, N 10 and 14 *ad* Art. 2; JAYME, p. 34; HUG, Bob Marley, p. 57 et seqq., at fn. 43, states that "the lower the individuality, the smaller the copyright scope of protection"; DFC 125 III 328 (*Niederhauser*), p. 333 c. 4, in which the SFSC admitted the protectability of an architectural work, even if it extensively relied on previous plans made by another architect. The fact that the work traits (in particular the flat rooftop and the division into three building groups according to the architectural plans) completely took second place behind the defendant's own creation, and the fact that these elements were "weakly individual" were decisive to recognize an individual character; cf. also DFC 136 III 225 (*Guide Orange*), c. 4.2 *in fine*; for Germany, see HILGERT, p. 15; BULLINGER, PraxKomm DE-CopA, N 36 *ad* § 2; MÜLLER, p. 235; in the US, BALGANESH, Normativity, p. 221 et seqq., explains how a so-called "thin copyright" will only protect against a "super-substantial similarity".

19 Cf. SUTTERER, p. 135; according to SCHULZE, Gedanken, p. 505, the "Verblassensformel" dates back to Eugen Ulmer (1903–†1988).

20 TERZIDIS, p. 60; in art theory and history, cf. VERWOERT, p. 146; ISEKENMEIER, In Richtung, p. 21, "iconographic analysis tends to take the historical precedent as the source" and is, therefore, responsible for the "predominance of intentionalism in art history".

21 REHBINDER/HAAS/UHLIG, OFK CopA, N 2 *ad* Art. 3.

22 HAAS, p. 26.

any new formal element that could be considered individual, and they, thus, fall into the scope of protection of the work.[23]

Minor alterations are subsumed under Art. 10 para. 2 let. a CopA, which covers the right of reproduction of the author, i.e., the right of realizing copies of the work (in German *Vervielfältigungsstücke*). As copies in the sense of *Vervielfältigungen* count not only as identical replicas of the original but also, as best expressed by the GFCJ,

> under the reproduction right of the author fall even those alterations that are distant to the original to a wider extent but that do not dispose of an own creative expressiveness and that, for this reason, notwithstanding the alterations that may have been carried out, find themselves in the protection scope of the original.[24]

Because even the right to alter the work is an exclusive right of the author (Art. 11 Abs. 1 let. a CopA),[25] minor changes could also amount to an infringement of this other right.

Examples of minor alterations are cuts, photocopies and copies, even when the work is miniaturized or enlarged.[26] A notable example of an artist realizing miniatures of other works is Richard Pettibone, who created smaller versions of famous works by Andy Warhol, Ed Ruscha and Roy Lichtenstein. Seen as one of the predecessors of the 1980s appropriation art movement, he offered an "inventive, often humorous critique of 20th century art".[27] An example, if it was still protected by copyright, could be the addition of a moustache to the Mona Lisa in Duchamp's *L.H.O.O.Q.* (1919).[28]

Given how the work is defined and its abstract and malleable nature, its protection scope is entered even if the same set of forms is materialized in a different medium, whatever its nature (so, for example, if a painting is made of photograph, as in the photorealist works of Peter Nagel,[29] or if a photograph is taken of a painting, as in the works of Louise Lawler, is often the case).[30] An example of the practice of changing the medium is Silke Wagner's series *Coverworks (New works)*

23 Hilgert, p. 27, makes a difference between Appropriation Art "in the narrow sense" and Appropriation Art "in the broad sense". To the former category belong artistic copies that do not change the work they are based upon. To the latter category belong artworks that add elements to the original work or change what was previously there. This categorization – it goes without saying – only makes sense from a legal point of view, where such difference is given a normative value. It does not have a parallel in art theory.

24 GFCJ of May 16, 2013 (*Beuys-Aktion*), GRUR 2014 p. 65 et seqq., p. 70 at para. 36 (translation is mine), also quoted in: Dreier, p. 206. The same is held by Barrelet/Egloff, CopA Commentary, Art. 10 N 16.

25 Rehbinder/Haas/Uhlig, OFK CopA, N 2 *ad* Art. 3.

26 Wild, künstlerische Darbietung, p. 101.

27 Cf. <http://www.artnet.com/artists/richard-pettibone/>.

28 Barrelet/Egloff, CopA Commentary, N 16 *ad* Art. 10.

29 Cf. Maassen, p. 192.

30 Barrelet/Egloff, CopA Commentary, N 16 *ad* Art. 10.

(2010). With these, she appropriated works of well-known female artists and changed the technique of realization, e.g., a painting by Georgia O'Keeffe became a sculpture; Nancy Graves's sculpture *Byrd* (1983) became a neon installation.[31]

Many interpictorial original copies could be qualified as minor alterations and fall under the reproduction right of the author because, according to the law, they have not sufficiently changed their template. While copyright law focuses upon the material embellishment, that is, the physical change introduced to the object, the distinguishing feature of an original copy lies not in its physical or material nature but in the meaning that is given to the image embodied in the context of another artwork.

III.II.I A special case: "The monopolization of reality"

The reality of photography shows that a photographer can take a picture that is barely distinguishable from another one that has already been taken.[32] Here, similarity is not created by involving the previous work in the process (e.g., by photocopying or photographing the previous work). Rather, similarity is created indirectly, by "doing the same thing another time". Whether the second picture represents an enforceable invasion of the copyright protection scope of the first picture depends on many variables. First, of which, is on whether the first picture is judged to have an individual character (Art. 2 para. 2 let. g CopA) or not (Art. 2 para 3bis CopA).

Motifs cannot be monopolized,[33] but the question is what in a picture qualifies as "motif" – an objective portraiture of a given reality – and what, instead, as "individual configuration" thereof.[34] In a decision of the Appeal Court of Canton Basel-City, in which at stake was a panorama picture of the city, taken from above, the judges explained:

> the area of the photograph at stake cannot be monopolized; this motif is chosen and pictured since a long time…the cut of the picture and the proportions are not original or individual; the photograph presents an image that everyone – especially with the technical auxiliary means available today – could accomplish, at least in a very similar way.[35]

In this case, the fact that a similar picture could have easily been taken again was a burden for bestowing copyright protection: The picture was not sufficiently "new" or statistically unique for the pictured motif to be monopolized.

The second variable regards how the copyright flowing from the new Art. 2 para. 3bis CopA will be calibrated. Given the quantity of pictures that are taken

31 Cf. <https://www.oldenburger-kunstverein.de/ausstellung/silke-wagner/>.
32 Teilmann-Lock, p. 103.
33 Maassen, Plagiat, p. 206.
34 Cf. on this the two decisions "*Marley*" and "*Meili*" in Chapter 3, II.IV.II.
35 Canton Basel-City Court of Appeal of May 20, 2016 (*Panoramabild*), sic! 2016, p. 594 et seqq., c. 2.3 (translation is mine).

every day and given that all photographic depictions of three-dimensional objects are automatically protected, an exclusive and comprehensive right on non-individual pictures would rapidly cause a "monopolization of reality". Even if it goes against the systematics and the wording of the law, the reproduction right flowing from Art. 2 para. 3bis CopA may have to be interpreted restrictively.

For what concerns artistic interpictoriality, some artists played with the remaking of an already taken photograph. For example, in 2012, Peter Tillessens restaged a photograph previously taken by Andreas Gursky and titled *Ofenpass* (1989). Tillessens emulated the photograph faithfully by using the same camera, film and viewpoint on a day with similar meteorological conditions.[36] Another example is Hubert Becker's photograph *Erich-Ferl-Straße (nach Struth)* (2000), which, as the name suggests, was shot after Thomas Struth's 1991 homonymous picture.[37]

III.III The derivative work (Art. 3 para. 1 CopA)

Second on the line of spatial distance from the work-template are derivative works (also called "unfree utilizations"; in German *unfreie Benutzung*[38]). These are regulated under Art. 3 para. 1 CopA as "intellectual creations with individual character based upon pre-existing works, whereby the individual character of the latter remains identifiable". The first part of the article explicitly repeats the wording of the previously discussed Art. 2 para. 1 CopA: A derivative work is only such if it fulfills the definition at Art. 2 para. 1 CopA for itself, i.e., if it is individual.[39]

What makes a derivative work such is stated in the second part of the paragraph: A derivative work presupposes the use of a work eligible for copyright under Art. 2 para. 1 CopA, that is, of an individual work. The used work's individual character must fade away to leave room for a new individual character, but it must, at the same time, remain identifiable. Individual elements of a previous work are, thus, combined with the newly founded individuality of the derivative work in a way that lets both shine through in the resulting artifact.[40]

The protection of derivative works is the same for works. However, because derivative works invade the scope of protection of the works they use, the protection of the latter remains reserved (Art. 3 para. 4 CopA). One could also imagine that the template used for the creation of a derivative work is used another time to

36 Cf. Irina Vernichenko, Peter Tillessen at Art Genève, April 3, 2017 (<https://artdecision.eu/peter-tillessen-at-art-geneve/>).

37 Cf. Mensger, Déjà-vu, p. 278 et seq.

38 Especially in Germany to differentiate from the free utilization, cf. for example Schulze, Gedanken, p. 506.

39 Egloff, CopA Commentary, N 3 *ad* Art. 3; Züllig, p. 295; however, the Commercial Court of Aargau of January 5, 2015 (*Totenkopf-Tattoo*), sic! 2015, p. 449 et seqq., p. 453 admitted a derivative work according to Art. 3 para. 1 CopA without verifying whether a new individual character had been created.

40 According to some, the derivative use of a non-individual photographic depiction (Art. 2 para. 3bis CopA) cannot serve as a basis for a derivative work and is, therefore, free, Barrelet/Egloff, CopA Commentary, N 13 ad Art. 11; another opinion, Mosimann, N 32.

create another derivative work.[41] In this case, the mix of three individual characters would shine through in one configuration, two still recognizable from the previous works and one new, founded with the creation of the derivative work. The legal treatment of these works is tricky. Because every used work has itself used a work previously, the legal status of the newest work depends not only on how it uses a previous work but also on how this previous work used a previous work.[42]

Whether a work is considered derivative depends on the degree of visual similarity and on the changes that have been made to the template. In art history, it is very common to work derivatively on a previous artwork. This leaves the template recognizable and, at the same time, adds new touches or translates it in a different, contemporary visual language. One example of this is the *Le Déjeuner sur l'herbe* (1863) by Édouard Manet. Although Manet's work is often considered to be completely original, the position of the three people in the foreground is inspired by Marcantonio Raimondi's *Giudizio di Paride* (ca. 1510–1520). *Le Déjeuner* was later returned to in cubist style by Pablo Picasso in his *Le Déjeuner sur l'herbe d'après Manet* (1960); in a postcolonial take by Robert Colescott in *Sunday Afternoon with Joaquin Murietta* (1979) and others; in a performative way by the collective UNTEL in 1975[43] and by many others still.[44] This does not mean that all these subsequent artworks undisputedly have the character of derivative works according to Art. 3 CopA. However, every new variation on this theme forcibly encompasses and enters in interpictorial dialogue with all previous ones, too.[45]

III.IV The free utilization

The free utilization is the third and last step in order of spatial distance from the work-template. Here, the distance from the used work is such that the use becomes free, i.e., it does not interfere with the rights of use of the original's author.[46] For this reason, its dogmatic classification has ranged from its handling as an "unwritten exception to copyright",[47] to an "immanent limitation of the copyright's protection scope".[48] In the first categorization, the accent is put on the fact that the work was used without permission, the unlawful use is then *justified* because the free utilization is seen as creating a fully new individual character. In the second, the accent is put on the fact that the scope of protection of the work was left entirely,

41 Egloff, CopA Commentary, N 5 *ad* Art. 3.

42 Sollfrank, p. 321; lawyer Rolf auf der Maur explains that because Andy Warhol used found images, too, if one intends to use Warhol's artworks "the status of his own reworked images has to be clarified before a case of litigation could even start".

43 Cf. <https://fr.wikipedia.org/wiki/Le_D%C3%A9jeuner_sur_l%27herbe#1975_:_groupe_Untel>.

44 Cf. Isekenmeier, In Richtung, p. 11 and 17 et seq.; Shore, p. 78 et seqq.; the motif was also interpreted from a postcolonial perspective, cf. Childs, p. 103; for a comprehensive account of all the variations, cf. <http://search.it.online.fr/covers/?p=401>.

45 Buskirk, The Contingent Object, p. 104 et seq.

46 DFC 125 III 328 (*Niederhauser*); de Werra/Benhamou, Kultur Kunst Recht, N 33 *ad* § 7.

47 See Dessemontet, L'objet, N 244.

48 Cf. Barrelet/Egloff, CopA Commentary, N 15 *ad* Art. 11.

so the use was not a copyright-relevant in the first place and, thus, no justification was needed.[49]

III.IV.I In Switzerland

In Switzerland, the free utilization was introduced in 1959 with a decision concerning Curt Goetz's theater piece *Dr. med. Hiob Prätorius* (1965).[50] The SFSC borrowed the free utilization from the German copyright law (at the time of the decision § 13 oDE-CopA, then § 24 oDE-CopA) and declared it an unwritten norm of Swiss copyright, concluding that Goetz's use of elements taken from the previous work by Sir Arthur Conan Doyle's *A Study in Scarlet* was admissible as a free utilization.[51]

Forty years later, in DFC 125 III 328 (*Niederhauser*), the free utilization was explained as being a mere inspiration, in which the borrowings from a previous work are so modest that they fade behind the individuality of the new work.[52] In its conclusion, affirming that there was free utilization, the SFSC stated that the architect had – at most – inspired himself from the previous work. If he had taken elements from the previous work at all, these were of a "weak individuality" and had faded into the background of the architect's new project's individual character.[53]

According to this description and to the doctrine, the free utilization in Swiss law seems to fulfill two conditions. First, the use of a previous work in a new work must detach itself from the former in such a way that its important elements (those that made up the individual character of the used work) are elaborated and processed until they fade and are unrecognizable on a sensory level.[54] Second, the elements of the previous work must be incorporated into a completely independent new work. Only if an author merely took inspiration from a protected work, in a way that makes the old work's individual elements disappear in the background of his new work's individual character, there is free utilization.

In other words, the original may have been used at most as a suggestion, but its concrete use must detach itself from all that made the original work eligible for

49 Barrelet/Egloff, CopA Commentary, N 15 *ad* Art. 11.

50 DFC 85 II 120 (*Sherlock Holmes*), c. 8.

51 Egloff, Von der "freien Benutzung", p. 399 et seq, 404.

52 DFC 125 III 328 (*Niederhauser*), p. 332 c. 4.

53 DFC 125 III 328 (*Niederhauser*), p. 333 c. 4.

54 Commercial Court of Aargau of January 5, 2015 (*Totenkopf-Tattoo*), sic! 2015, p. 449 et seqq., p. 453; Zurich Court of Appeal of July 7, 2009 (*Love*), sic! 2010, p. 889 et seqq., c. 2.1; Decision of the Lucerne Court of Appeal of February 5, 2003 (*Knoblauchpresse*), sic! 2003 p. 731 et seqq., p. 740; Decision of the Aargau Court of Appeal of July 31, 1990 (*Swissbase*), SMI 1991, p. 80 et seqq., p. 84: the higher the individuality of the borrowed elements, the more distance the new work has to establish from them. Dessemontet, L'objet, N 243 et seqq., however, does not state in such a decisive manner that the borrowed parts must fade. Rather, he places emphasis on the need for the free utilization to have an independent individual character; cf. Döhl/Hui, p. 861 for the precise expression "fading into the background on a sensory level".

copyright in the first place.[55] If, on the contrary, the new work reaches a level of independent individuality but individual elements of the previous work remain recognizable that use cannot be considered a free utilization but, rather, a derivative work (or "unfree utilization") under Art. 3 para. 1 CopA.[56] What distinguishes a free utilization from an unfree utilization is, thus, that the use of the previous work is less intense, reduced to the mere possibility of having been inspired from it for the creation of a fully new artifact.[57]

This shall only be partially relativized by reminding that the decision is based on the "overall impression" of the work and not a "tessellated examination".[58] The judge will, thus, not look for the individual elements of the previous work in the new creation but, rather, make a global evaluation as to whether they may be considered faded or not in the global configuration of the new work. Another aspect to consider is the existence of the weak individuality (small coin) as it was established in DFC 125 III 328 (*Niederhauser*). In this case, even if elements of the old work remain recognizable, the use might, nonetheless, be considered free, as the small coin only protects against slavish imitation.

III.IV.II In Germany

As mentioned before, the figure of the free utilization has been borrowed by the SFSC from German copyright law. Today, unfree utilizations are regulated at § 3 and § 23 DE-CopA.[59] The latter newly absolves the function of delimitating unfree from free utilizations (i.e., defining the work's scope of protection), which was previously regulated at § 24 para. 1 oDE-CopA.[60]

55 Rehbinder/Haas/Uhlig, OFK CopA, N 5 *ad* Art. 3; on a closer look, the first condition of the free utilization, according to which the elements of the used work must have faded, was not fulfilled in DFC 85 II 120 (*Sherlock Holmes*). The experts' opinion quoted in the decision explicitly stated that the figures of Sherlock Holmes and Dr. Watson did not fade in Curt Goetz's theater piece. Despite this finding, the SFSC stressed that Goetz's work realized the second condition of being a new, independent work. This aspect alone – that the second work globally appeared as an autonomous new work – was given the critical importance for deciding the case. This is criticized by many authors, including Egloff, Von der "freien Benutzung", p. 403 and Handle, p. 164.

56 Cherpillod, SIWR II/1, p. 308; de Werra/Benhamou, Kultur Kunst Recht, N 33 *ad* § 7, explain that the difference between derivative work and free utilization is determined by the recognizability of the individual character of the first work in the secondary work.

57 Cherpillod, L'objet, p. 159.

58 Cf. above at Chapter 3, IV.I.

59 Cf. above at Chapter 3, III.

60 Bullinger, PraxKomm DE-CopA, N 2 *ad* § 23; § 24 para. 1 oDE-CopA used to define free utilizations as "an independent work created *in free utilization* of the work of someone else *may be freely used* without the consent of the author of the used work" (translation is mine, emphasis added), cf. Fischer Veronika, p. 225, describes this formulation as a tautology.

III.IV.II.I THE CONCEPT OF "INNER DISTANCE"

In Germany, too, a free utilization was initially only admitted if the new work was so original and independent[61] that the used work optically faded behind it.[62] The interpretation of § 24 para. 1 oDE-CopA and, particularly, the judicial determination of the required distance from the previous work later slowly evolved toward the concept of "inner distance". This happened as the notion of free utilization was adjusted to the needs of the protection of parodies, something for which German copyright law did not have a specific provision.[63]

- In the decision *Disney-Parody* (1971), the GFCJ recognized the inadequacy of the distance doctrine to judge parodies; explaining that the very "nature" of parodies relies on the possibility of recognizing the work in its parodic rendition,[64] i.e., on the recognizability of the form despite its "shifted" meaning (on parodies more on parodies in Chapter 5, I.II),[65] the court held that the the way in which the individual character had to *visibly fade* in the new work was clearly inadequate. Borrowing had to be permitted insofar as it was necessary for transmitting the parodic message.[66] Even though in the case at stake, the use of the Donald Duck and Mickey Mouse characters was judged by the court to be too extensive and, therefore, infringing, a door had been opened.
- The recognition of the insufficiency of the distance doctrine for the adequate handling of some cases paved the way for the introduction, with two decisions concerning "Asterix", of the concept of the "inner distance". In both cases, at stake was the unlicensed borrowing of the figures of Asterix and Obelix. These characters, originally authored by René Goscinny and Albert Uderzo, had been used for the creation of comics titled *The Hysterical Adventures of Isterix*[67] and *False Game with Alcolix. The Parody*.[68] The GFCJ held that a free utilization was possible even if parts of the previous work had clearly been taken. If the new work managed to be independent in its essence and create an "inner distance" from the previous work, the scope of the work was not entered. This happened, in particular, if the work engaged critically or artistically with the template.[69]

61 In the German wording, *eigentümlich*. See MAASSEN, p. 213.

62 SCHULZE, Gedanken, p. 505; BLUME HUTTENLAUCH, p. 121: in the beginning, in Germany there was no such thing as an "internal distance"; SCHACK, N 340; MAASSEN, p. 213.

63 HAAS, p. 112; BLUME HUTTENLAUCH, p. 116.

64 BLUME HUTTENLAUCH, p. 116 et seq.

65 SCHULZE, Aneignung, p. 52; FISCHER VERONIKA, p. 225.

66 BLUME HUTTENLAUCH, p. 117 et seq.; GFCJ of March 26, 1971 (*Disney-Parodie*), GRUR 1971 p. 588 et seqq., p. 589.

67 In German "Die hysterischen Abenteuer von Isterix. Jubiläums-Persiflagen".

68 In German "Falsches Spiel mit ALCOLIX. Die Parodie".

69 BLUME HUTTENLAUCH, p. 118 et seq.; GFCJ of March 11, 1993 (*Asterix Persiflagen*), GRUR 1994, p. et seqq.; GFCJ of March 11, 1993 (*Alcolix*), GRUR 1994, p. 206 et seqq., p. 208.

- The free utilization was taken two further steps forward in the early 2000s. First in 2000, with the decision *Kalkofes Mattscheibe*, in which the GFCJ withdrew the requirement of "necessity" it had previously established in *Disney-Parody* and admitted that even unchanged borrowings could pass as free utilizations.[70] Second, in 2003, with the decision *Gies Adler*, in which the court held that in a free utilization, the work could be used even for a parody whose message was not directed against the work itself but against the environment of the work, be it society or the state.[71]

Unlike Swiss copyright law,[72] in some cases, German law admitted a free utilization, even if the borrowed traits from the previous work were still clearly recognizable in the downstream work.[73] The required distance from the previous work could be obtained, according to the German doctrine and jurisprudence, not only through the visual fading out of the individual traits of the previous work (in the sense of the distance doctrine exposed above) in the new work,[74] but also by means of an antithematic treatment of the previous work in the new creation, i.e., by subverting the meaning of the work.[75] The distance doctrine, as interpreted in Switzerland, and as presented so far, i.e., the measurement of how much the individuality of the previous work has faded out in the new work, must, therefore, be clearly distinguished from this other version of the free utilization, according to which such distance exists, even if it is not visible in the downstream work but only *intelligible*.[76] To mark this difference, some authors have used the concept of external distance as opposed to the internal distance.[77] In Switzerland, works that create only an internal distance would be considered as unfree utilizations and eventually be subsumed under an exception of copyright.

Even if the concept of internal distance was developed to justify parodies (for which Swiss copyright law provided an explicit exception), according to the GFCJ, an internal distance could be produced, in theory, not only by means of parodic

70 Blume Huttenlauch, p. 120; GFCJ of April 13, 2000 (*Mattscheibe*), GRUR 2000, p. 703 et seqq.

71 Blume Huttenlauch, p. 120; GFCJ of March 20, 2003 (*Gies Adler*), GRUR 2003, p. 956 et seqq.; Jongsma, Parody, p. 662; Pottage, p. 6, underlines that an observation "outside" law could point out at how this evolution shows how law moves "between convention and invention", making up "the tradition which [it] purport[s] only to continue". In the end, it is always the same norm (§ 24 DE-CopA), the same legal concept (the free utilization), but fundamentally changed and expanded.

72 Cherpillod, SIWR II/1, p. 307; another opinion, cf. Handle, p. 155. However, Handle mentions the decision of the Zurich Court of Appeal of July 7, 2009 (*Love*), sic! 2010, pp. 889 et seqq., c. 2.1, in which the criterion of the concept of internal distance was mentioned but applied as a normal distance doctrine. Moreover, Handle quotes only German literature; in detail cf. Haas, p. 113 et seqq.

73 Hilty, Die freie Benutzung, p. 129.

74 Blume Huttenlauch, p. 111.

75 Hilgert, p. 31; Jongsma, Parody, p. 662; GFCJ of March 11, 1993 (*Asterix Persiflagen*), GRUR 1994, p. et seqq., p. 193 and 199; GFCJ of March 11, 1993 (*Alcolix*), GRUR 1994, p. 206 et seqq., p. 207 et seqq.

76 Cf. Haas, p. 112; Rehbinder, N 95.

77 Kreutzer, p. 4.

treatment of the previous work but also in other ways.[78] Central was, thus, not the parodic shift but the creation of an internal distance that parodies, among other things, could create.[79]

In the case of original copies and other interpictorial artworks, such targeted and intensive engagement with the chosen work could be considered lacking in many cases.[80] Indeed, as the Regional Court of Munich stated in an interpictoriality case in which two photographs were used as a template for the creation of a painting: "on no account can free utilization be used as a license for plagiarism".[81]

III.IV.II.II THE FREE UTILIZATION AS AN UNWRITTEN EXCEPTION TO COPYRIGHT

The increasingly large interpretation of the free utilization just described was further enlarged by the 2016 German Federal Constitutional Court's (GFCC) decision on the *Metall auf Metall* case.[82] The proceeding saw the German music producer Moses Pelham, who, in 1997, produced the song "Nur Mir", sung by Sabrina Setlur, against the band Kraftwerk. Pelham had taken a two-second-long sample from Kraftwerk's song "Metall auf Metall" and used it in a loop to create the beat of "Nur Mir". In 1999, the band filed a complaint for the infringement of their right to the sound recording. The first decision on the matter was taken by the Hamburg Regional Court in 2004.[83] At the time of writing, the proceeding is still pending.

In the 2016 decision, the court first applied § 24 oDE-CopA to the phonogram producer's rights under § 85 para. 1 DE-CopA with an analogy.[84] Then, it carried out a specifically artistic interpretation (*kunstspezifische Betrachtung*) of § 24 para. 1 oDE-CopA based on Art. 5 para. 3 of the of the Basic Constitutional Law of the Federal Republic of Germany (in the German Constitution) and held that, when made for artistic purposes in a specific genre (such as hip-hop), the practice of sampling enjoyed a larger freedom, under which it was also possible – if a sufficient distance from the previous work was created – *not* to obtain a license for an

78 Blume Huttenlauch, p. 123; Hilgert, p. 31; GFCJ of March 11, 1993 (*Asterix Persiflagen*), GRUR 1994, p. et seqq., p. 205; GFCJ of March 20, 2003 (*Gies Adler*), GRUR 2003, p. 956 et seqq.

79 For Blume Huttenlauch, p. 133, the free utilization was *de facto* only capable of recognizing the presence of internal distance in parodies or where there was a similar intentional, duly motivated and intense engagement with the work used as template.

80 Blume Huttenlauch, p. 129 et seq.

81 Decision of the regional Court in Munich of November 29, 1985 (*Hubschrauber mit Damen*), GRUR 1988, p. 36 et seqq., p. 37.

82 Decision of the GFCC of May 31, 2016 (*Metall auf Metall*), GRUR 2016, p. 690 et seqq.

83 Cf. decision of the Regional Court of Hamburg of October 8, 2004 (*Metall auf Metall*). For a comprehensive review of the dispute, cf. Haux, p. 5 et seqq., the steps of the proceeding before different instances are reported chronologically at p. 8, fn. 25 (until 2021).

84 Hilty, Die freie Benutzung, p. 133.

occurred use.[85] In this sense, the court used the free utilization as an equivalent to an unwritten exception to copyright.[86]

The court remitted the case to the GFCJ with the explicit instruction to consider the freedom of artistic expression in its judgment. How concretely the GFCJ was to carry out such task was a matter left to its appreciation: For example, it could have obtained such result through a narrow interpretation of the phonogram producer's rights under § 85 para. 1 DE-CopA or through a large application of the quotation right under § 51 DE-CopA.[87]

III.IV.II.III THE END AND A NEW BEGINNING OF THE FREE UTILIZATION

Once confronted with the case, the GFCJ deemed it appropriate to file for a preliminary ruling of the CJEU, which provided a response in July 2019. In the ruling, the CJEU stated that the enumeration of exceptions at Art. 5 para. 3 of Infosoc-Directive, which harmonized copyright exceptions for Member States, is exhaustive.[88] The absence of an equivalent exception in the Infosoc-Directive meant that a user could not rely on § 24 para. 1 oDE-CopA to justify her unauthorized use of a sample if this remained *recognizable to the ear* in the downstream work.[89] A provision of a Member State stipulating a larger scope for exceptions to copyright – for example, based on the freedom of art – would infringe overriding European Union law. The required balancing of the underlying positions, represented by the fundamental rights of artistic freedom and guarantee of ownership, had already been struck by the legislature with the adoption of the Infosoc-Directive.[90] When used as an unwritten exception to copyright beyond those already laid out at Art. 5 para. 3 of Infosoc-Directive, the free utilization infringed overriding EU law.

In the aftermath of the preliminary decision of the CJEU in the *Metall auf Metall* case, some scholars reacted by trying to "save" the free utilization. SCHULZE, one of the main commentators of § 24 oDE-CopA,[91] pointed out that insofar as § 24 oDE-CopA protected parodies, pastiches and caricatures, it could continue to exist,

85 GFCC of May 31, 2016 (*Metall auf Metall*), GRUR 2016, p. 690 et seqq., p. 692 at para. 80 et seq.; WESTKAMP, p. 71.

86 BULLINGER, PraxKomm DE-CopA, N 2 *ad* § 23.

87 GFCC of May 31, 2016 (*Metall auf Metall*), GRUR 2016, p. 690 et seqq., p. 692 at para. 80 et seq., p. 695 at para. 110.

88 CJEU of July 29, 2019 - C-476/17 (*Metall auf Metall*), at para. 58: the exhaustiveness of the enumeration of copyright exceptions is also explicitly enshrined in recital 32 of the Infosoc-Directive's Preamble.

89 CJEU of July 29, 2019 - C-476/17 (*Metall auf Metall*), at para. 22 and 31; FISCHER VERONIKA, p. 238; according to WESTKAMP, p. 73, the court considered the criterion of recognizability as a tool for a proportionality assessment; the same criterion was set out by the CJEU for the possible application of the exception of quotation regulated at Art. 5 para. 3 let. d of Infosoc-Directive. The exception does not extend to situations in which it is not possible to identify the work concerned by the quotation in question, cf. CJEU of July 29, 2019 - C-476/17 (*Metall auf Metall*), at para. 74.

90 SCHULZE, Die freie Benutzung, p. 128; WESTKAMP, p. 72; DÖHL, Systemwechsel, p. 244.

91 HILTY, Die freie Benutzung, p. 127.

since Art. 5 para. 3 let. k of the Infosoc-Directive stipulates these exceptions.[92] Moreover, insofar as § 24 oDE-CopA was interpreted not as a copyright exception but as an immanent limitation of the copyrighted work's protection scope and, thus, as "natural" demarcation to the unfree utilization, EU law would not be in opposition to it, as the protection scope of a work is a matter left to the Member States to determine.[93] Lastly, SCHULZE argued that because the CJEU's preliminary ruling admitted room for an interpretation of the Infosoc-Directive in conformity with the Charter of Fundamental Rights of the European Union, the same should be possible for the balancing of rights operated in Germany, which ultimately enlarged the scope of the free utilization.[94]

Read in this (last) way, however, the concept of internal distance under the free utilization would be a sort of general clause capable of encompassing other artistic forms almost *ad libitum*, especially when applied according to the specifically artistic view in conformity with the constitutional artistic freedom (*kunstspezifische Betrachtung*).[95] However, this was precisely the use of the free utilization that was policed by the CJEU in its ruling for not conforming with EU law. In other words, if § 24 oDE-CopA was deployed as an "open exception", able to include the most diverse types of uses, it ceased to conform with the overriding directive.

The GFCJ considered the preliminary judgment of the CJEU in its 2020 decision on the case. It stated that since the Infosoc-Directive came into force (December 22, 2002,), § 24 oDE-CopA cannot be used anymore. Because the borrowed sound was still "recognizable to the ear" (*Vervielfältigung*, Art. 2 let. c Infosoc-Directive), § 24 oDE-CopA could not pass as an immanent limitation of the copyrighted work's protection scope.[96] Because no general exception of free use was contained in the exception catalogue of the Infosoc-Directive, § 24 oDE-CopA could not be applied as an exception to copyright.[97] The problem was, thus, the recognition of inner distance outside the scope of an exception to copyright.

With effect from June 7, 2021, the German legislature implemented the changes. The provision § 24 oDE-CopA was removed from the DE-CopA because it did not conform with EU law.[98] In its place was introduced the new § 51a DE-CopA, dedicated to the punctual protection of parodies, caricatures and, new for German

92 SCHULZE, Die freie Benutzung, p. 128.

93 SCHULZE, Gedanken, p. 506; cf. DÖHL, Systemwechsel, p. 245.

94 SCHULZE, Gedanken, p. 519; SCHULZE, Die freie Benutzung, p. 130 et seq. also explained that the CJEU left a considerable margin to maneuver for Member States in its decision.

95 SCHULZE, Aneignung, p. 53; critical HILTY, Die freie Benutzung, p. 129 et seq.; cf. also GEIGER/IZYUMENKO, Constitutionalization, p. 27, arguing for an EU-wide general clause. More on this subject in Chapter 7.

96 GFCJ of April 30, 2020 (*Metall auf Metall IV*), GRUR 2020, p. 843 et seqq., p. 846 at para. 31.

97 GFCJ of April 30, 2020 (*Metall auf Metall IV*), GRUR 2020, p. 843 et seqq., p. 846 at para. 38; before this date, instead, § 24 oDE-CopA can be used according to the guidelines sketched out by the GFCC, i.e., such right shall be interpreted accordingly to the Constitutional artistic freedom; the Higher Regional Court of Hamburg confirmed this with its subsequent decision of April 28, 2021 (*Metall auf Metall III*), GRUR 2022, p. 1217 et seqq.

98 Recommendation and Report 19/29894, p. 2.

copyright law, pastiches.[99] The text of § 23 para. 1 DE-CopA was also modified to include, in the second sentence, the function of immanently delimitating the work's scope of protection previously absolved by § 24 oDE-CopA.[100] The jurisprudence about the free utilization will be valid for the interpretation of this new provision.[101] The difference after the revision of the DE-CopA may, thus, only be that if the new work creates only an internal distance from the old work, that is, if the individual traits of the old work remain otherwise recognizable to the senses, an unfree utilization will likely be recognized.[102]

IV.I The work's scope of protection in the United States

IV.II Substantial similarity

In the US, to determine whether there is a relevant use of a work,[103] courts adopt the approach of so-called "substantial similarity".[104] Similarity between two works is substantial when "the ordinary observer, unless he set out to detect the disparities, would be disposed to overlook them, and regard their aesthetic appeal as the same".[105] In order to be infringing, the work and its use must be considered being similar to original expressive elements in the first work which, when viewed in the context of the work as a whole are substantial, both qualitatively and quantitatively.[106] The issue is, thus, one of drawing a line somewhere between one extreme of no similarity at all and another of complete and *verbatim* similarity.[107]

The comparison should happen holistically and consider the artifacts in their entirety and in terms of their overall similarity.[108] Only in instances in which the work merges protectable with unprotectable elements, "[w]hat must be shown is substantial similarity between those elements, and only those elements, that provide copyrightability".[109] Here, the standard of scrutiny shall change into a more discerning, rather than immediate, observation.

99 In GFCJ of April 30, 2020 (*Metall auf Metall IV*), GRUR 2020, p. 843 et seqq., the GFCJ had denied the application of the exception of parody and caricature, stating that the sample was *not* an expression of humor nor of mockery. The applicability of the exception of pastiche had been "suspended", as the German legislature had still not stipulated such exception in the DE-CopA. Such has changed since June 7, 2021. The last decision on the matter of Higher Regional Court of Hamburg of April 28, 2021 (*Metall auf Metall III*), GRUR 2022, p. 1217 et seqq. already considered this legislative change and subsumed the sample under the new exception of "pastiche" (cf. below, Chapter 5, I.2).

100 BULLINGER, PraxKomm DE-CopA, N 2 et seq. *ad* § 23; KREUTZER, p. 18.

101 BULLINGER, PraxKomm DE-CopA, N 3 *ad* § 23.

102 BULLINGER, PraxKomm DE-CopA, N 42 *ad* § 23; DÖHL/HUI, p. 861 and p. 881; KREUTZER, p. 18.

103 BALGANESH, Normativity, p. 206.

104 Cf. STOKES, p. 49.

105 *Boisson vs. American County Quilts and Linens*, 273 F.3d 262 (2d Cir. 2001), p. 272.

106 WALLACE, p. 97.

107 WALLACE, p. 97.

108 BALGANESH, Normativity, p. 224.

109 *Boisson vs. American County Quilts and Linens*, 273 F.3d 262 (2d Cir. 2001), p. 272, this is the so-called "more discerning ordinary observer test", cf. WALLACE, p. 98; BALGANESH, Normativity, p. 222.

The inquiry of substantial similarity is better understood as involving two different elements: "thickness" and "similarity". Determining the former means to assess the scope of the author's entitlement to her work. It, thus, concerns the element of how substantial the similarity needs to be during the following comparison. The similarity analysis, instead, operates as a comparison of the two works.[110]

For example, in the case *Blanch vs. Koons*, in which Jeff Koons had appropriated almost *verbatim* a pair of feet wearing Gucci sandals from a photograph previously taken by Andrea Blanch, the court emphasized that Koons did not copy the aspects of the work that reflected Blanch's "key creative decisions".[111] Blanch had been directed by the magazine to produce a picture that could fulfill the purpose of advertising the sandals. She had provided the idea for the background (hints of an airplane interior and the feet resting on a man's lap), but this had not been precisely used by Koons for his painting *Niagara* (2000). In other words, what Koons copied was similar enough for Blanch to recognize it but not original enough to constitute an infringement of her copyright.[112]

IV.III A brief comparative analysis

If we compare the distance doctrine adopted by Swiss and German courts with the substantial similarity used in the US, we find that the two present many commonalities.

In both the US and Swiss copyright systems, the mark of originality (or individuality) is the standard to judge the scope of the author's entitlement to their work and its limit. For this reason, in both systems, a copyright protection for a not-so original work ("small coin", or "thin copyright" in the US[113]) will only protect against slavish imitation and verbatim similarity, whereas a highly original work will have an accordingly bigger protection scope reaching even against modified borrowings.

Exactly as in civil law systems, the work shall be considered in the US in its overall impression (which, in German, is indicated as *Gesamteindruck*) and may not be dissected into tinier components. Only when the work is composed by protectable and unprotectable elements may the scrutiny become more discerning, as only a similarity between protectable elements will constitute infringement. Finally, in both copyright systems, the method for establishing a relevant use is that of drawing a line – or establishing a distance – between a similarity that is judged entering the protection scope of the work and one that is not anymore. In this sense, the task of today's copyright lawyer consists in the *individuation of the same in the different.*[114]

110 Balganesh, Normativity, p. 208.
111 Buskirk, Creative Intent, p. 246.
112 Buskirk, Creative Intent, p. 246.
113 Balganesh, Normativity, p. 223.
114 Ortland, Bildregime, p. 277.

V.I Interim conclusions: The blind spot of copyright law

In their quest to identify what is valuable, both copyright law and art focus on the search for the new and the unprecedented. Yet this commonality of goals ceases the minute art starts doing something unprecedented precisely by repeating something precedented (we return, here, to the previously described re-entry).[115] The groundbreaking aspect of these interpictorial "original copies" lies precisely in their denial to assert it; thus, theirs is a "meta-novelty" and a "meta-originality".

Yet, we have seen that copyright law considers two artifacts the same artifact mainly based on how strong the similarity between their perceptible forms is.[116] By defining copyrightable works the way it does, this copyright law not only excludes interpictorial original copies from getting autonomous protection – as it does with other forms of conceptual art – but also condemns them to be considered reproductions of previous works or parts thereof.[117] A real discrepancy between art and copyright law in what is meant by originality seems, thus, to arise especially for those artworks that, by inserting themselves into the history of art and referencing their past with the use of something already existing (in short: by being interpictorial), also refuse to assert a creativity of their own.[118]

The problem lies in how copyright law is built and in the fact that it cannot recognize imitation as a form of creation because it is not able to make the difference between the work and the *use* that is made thereof.[119] Indeed, the conceptual possibility of an interpictorial original copy disappears in the writings of copyright scholars who argue, for example, that "the question of whether a (new) original work or a copy exists, *depends on whether changes have been made to the copy and on the extent of these changes*"[120] or that the term "original" means "the *unique*, original work".[121]

This can be explained because of the simultaneous existence of two conceptual dichotomies, which are operated simultaneously within copyright law. On one side, the dichotomy of original/copy. On the other side, that of work/work exemplar.

The concepts of original and copy can be situated on both sides of the difference work/work exemplar[122] (or in systems-theoretical terms: both sides of the

115 Ortland/Schmücker, p. 1764.

116 Cf. Gervais, How Intellectual Property, p. 18.

117 Ortland/Schmücker, p. 1775.

118 E.g., Sherrie Levine's, cf. Römer, p. 88; Hildebrand-Schat, p. 219 et seq.

119 In order to be able to grasp this difference it would be necessary to include the other side of the form, not to see it as a "unity" of form and content anymore but, rather, as a difference that the artwork sets with what it does not include in itself. At the level of the definition of copyrighted work, however, copyright law only sees with the code "work"/"non-work": If the "old" is still recognizable in the new and fulfills the requirement of the definition of work, then its use will be recognized as the use of an already copyrighted work and, thus, as a potential copyright infringement. Cf. Luhmann, Weltkunst, p. 18: because both sides of the form are simultaneously present and, thus, invisible to each other. To do this operation, one would the medium of time.

120 Benhamou, Kultur Kunst Recht, N 170 *ad* § 1 (translation is mine, emphasis added).

121 Benhamou, Kultur Kunst Recht, N 201 *ad* § 1 (translation is mine, emphasis added).

122 Rigamonti, Benjamin, p. 93 et seq.

dichotomy work/work exemplar can be observed through the form original/copy). When we observe the difference work/work exemplar with the side of the "original", we obtain on the side of the work exemplar a material copy (the original exemplar), and on the side of the work, the immaterial concept (the definition of protected work) that precedes it. When we observe the difference work/work exemplar with the side of the "copy", instead, we do not obtain two different things at all. On both sides, the copy coalesces into the author's right of reproduction (Art. 10 para. 2 let. a CopA).

This intellectual exercise explains why, today, copyright law cannot conceive an interpictorial "original copy" as *another* original work. If the "original copy" in question was not realized by the holder of the copyright in the first work, it will fall in its scope of protection. A copy (in the sense of a reproduction) *cannot* be original because it will be classified as a copy (in the sense of the exemplar of an existing work) and, therefore, in the absence of authorization, as an infringement of someone's copyright.[123]

In Chapter 1, Section IV.I, we have seen how, when retaining the modernist difference original/reproduction also used by WALTER BENJAMIN, the interpictorial original copy is in the observation's blind spot. We are now understanding that the same modernist blind spot is at work in copyright law, where the leading difference is defined as work/work exemplar. This blind spot provokes the logical impossibility for copyright law to conceive the artifact-copy as another, different art*work.*

The persistence of the modernist blind spot within copyright law, despite its overcoming in art, seems to be the source of the lack of synchronization between the two. Today, art is comfortable with the instance of interpictorial original copies and conceives them as authentic artworks, which have an existence in their own right. Confronted with the problem posed by plagiarism and not knowing or being able to use the value of authenticity to recognize and protect authentic artworks, copyright law tried to punctually solve instances of interpictoriality and intertextuality within the framework of copyright exceptions. Thanks to these, "not all copying is copyright infringement".[124]

123 RIGAMONTI, Benjamin, p. 94.

124 *Feist Publications, Inc., vs. Rural Telephone Service Co.*, 499 US 340 (1991); Amicus Brief, p. 5 and 11.

Part III

Copyright spaces for interpictoriality

"He started with an old photo, but he created a new new thing."

Justice Elena Kagan (2023), from her dissenting opinion to Andy Warhol Found. for the Visual Arts, Inc. vs. Goldsmith, 598 US ___ (2023)

DOI: 10.4324/9781003598503-8

5 The exceptions to copyright in comparative perspective

I.I The exceptions to copyright

In Switzerland, exceptions and limitations to copyright (in the following just "exceptions")[1] are regulated in Art. 19–28 CopA and in Art. 11 para. 3 CopA.[2] Exceptions to copyright are generally understood to be "islands of freedom in a sea of exclusivity".[3] Their scope is, therefore, interpreted narrowly (on the narrow vs. large interpretation of copyright exceptions, see, however, Chapter 7).[4] While not directly bestowing an independent copyright protection, exceptions to copyright grant artists spheres of precisely regulated freedom within which they are able to make certain uses of copyrighted works without having to ask for permission, often completely free of charge and without risking infringing the rights of an author under copyright.[5] Exceptions aim to prevent exclusive rights to undermine the very creation of new works that copyright law is supposed to promote.[6] Copyright exceptions become a way for artists to "get away" with what could otherwise be a potential copyright infringement.

1 Named differently according to the jurisdiction: in the German speaking countries, they are rather called limitations ("Schranken"); in France exceptions; in the US defense, cf. Brändli-Marmy, p. 13; for the theoretical debates on the difference between the designation as exceptions or limitations to copyright and the dogmatic consequences related to it cf. Geiger, Die Schranken, p. 150 et seqq.

2 In Switzerland and most European continental systems, exceptions are a closed list, cf. Buydens/Dusollier, p. 2.

3 Geiger, Die Schranken, p. 150; Cherpillod, SIWR II/1, p. 258.

4 DFC 125 III 328 (*Niederhauser*), p. 332; critic Geiger, Die Schranken, p. 152 and in detail Brändli-Marmy, p. 82; Gasser/Oertli, SHK CopA, N 15 *ad* Vorbemerkungen Art. 19–28 CopA, remark how the principle of the "narrow interpretation of copyright exceptions", theoretically valid in Germany, did not impede German courts to interpret them extensively, sometimes even by recurring to the fundamental rights of the Constitution. On this topic, see Chapter 7.

5 We use "spheres of freedom" because, on the question whether exceptions constitute "rights" or mere "interests" of the users, there is an ongoing theoretical debate, cf. Geiger, Die Schranken, p. 147 et seqq.; Geiger solves the debate by arguing that because both sides of copyright can be translated into fundamental rights that are, by definition, equivalent, then the debate on whether the author's *rights* are hierarchically higher than users' *interests* virtually decays; in DFC 127 III 26 (*Catalogue*), p. 28 c. 4, the SFSC declared that the dispositions of the CopA are imperative (cf. also Federal Gazette of November 22, 2017 (BBl 2018 591), p. 641.

6 Wielsch, Zugangsregeln, p. 63.

DOI: 10.4324/9781003598503-9

In the following, we expose the four exceptions of parody (Art. 11 para. 3 CopA), quotation (Art. 25 CopA), panorama (Art. 27 CopA) and personal use (Art. 19 para. 1 let. a CopA). We handle them in comparative perspective as well as expose their potential usefulness for justifying instances of interpictoriality in the visual arts. All are comprehensive exceptions (in German: *umfassende Schranken*), meaning that if they apply, the use is free of charge.[7] All four exceptions, despite not being tailored specifically to this end, could also potentially be used as justification for the interpictorial use of copyrighted material in the visual arts.

Each exception is a special case of use of a previous work permitted by the law as an exception to the scope of copyright;[8] for this reason, the delimitation between the exceptions to copyrights and the derivative uses of a work exposed above can sometimes be difficult.[9] The exceptions to copyright primarily limit the exclusive right of the author (or of the copyright holder) to decide whether, when and how her work is used (Art. 10 para. 1 CopA), i.e., the author's economic rights.[10] By allowing certain changes of the work (a cut, an adaptation, the presentation of a portion of the work in another context, etc.) Art. 11 para. 3, Art. 27 CopA and Art. 25 CopA also limit the moral rights of the author without completely deactivating them (Art. 11 para. 2 CopA always remains reserved).[11]

I.II Parodies (Art. 11 para. 3 CopA)

According to Art. 11 para. 3 CopA, it is permissible to use existing works for the creation of parodies. The provision does not contain a legal definition of parodies and, until 2021, no court in Switzerland had ever been confronted with this article in a concrete case. The case *Trittligasse* is the first concrete judicial encounter with this exception.[12] The case concerned the adaptation and modification, by the hand of Christian "Jott" Jenny, of the song lyrics originally written by Werner Wollenberger (1927–1982†) for the musicals *Eusi chlii Stadt* (1959) and *Zürcher Ballade/Trittligasse* (1961). The modified songs were publicly performed in 2017 and 2018 in the framework of theater plays conceived by Jenny. In 2018, Wollenberger's son filed a criminal complaint against Jenny and requested that the latter be found guilty of altering the lyrics of the songs without permission. The Zurich public prosecutor's office opened a criminal investigation, which culminated in a charge and in the subsequent summoning of the parties before the Zurich

7 GASSER/OERTLI, SHK CopA, N 2 *ad* Vorbemerkungen Art. 19 et seqq. CopA.
8 REHBINDER/HAAS/UHLIG, OFK CopA, N 6 *ad* Art. 3; ZÜLLIG, p. 297; HAAS, p. 47; if the requirements are not met, the use of the work amounts to a copyright infringement, RENOLD/CONTEL, CoRo CopA, N 1 *ad* Art. 25; DFC 131 III 480 (*Schweizerzeit*), c. 2.2.
9 VISCHER, Urheberrecht, p. 260.
10 EGLOFF, CopA Commentary, N 7 *ad* Vorbemerkungen Art. 19-28.
11 GASSER/OERTLI, SHK CopA, N 1 *ad* Vorbemerkungen Art. 19-28; RENOLD/CONTEL, CoRo CopA, N 1 *ad* Art. 25; EGLOFF, CopA Commentary, N 7 *ad* Vorbemerkungen Art. 19-28.
12 So too CUENI, p. 695, in 2019; Zurich District Court of May 19, 2021 (*Trittligasse*), sic! 2022, p. 68 et seqq.

district Court in 2021. At stake in the rather uncommon criminal proceeding for copyright infringement was the question whether the modifications of the songs amounted to an unlawful modification of a work for commercial gain according to Art. 67 para. 1 let. c in conjunction with Art. 67 para. 2 CopA, or if the acts were covered by a copyright exception, namely parody. Apart from a couple of "creative" aspects that will be discussed below, the decision largely quotes and confirms the doctrinal concretizations of the provision.

The main characteristic of parodies is the creation of a humoristic effect intended at exercising criticism. This criticism may be directed toward the used work, its author or even situations and people that have no link to the upstream work.[13] To do so, parodies *shift* the meaning of the borrowed work.[14] The original work must remain clearly recognizable in the parody, otherwise the effect of shift in meaning, required for parodies to be recognized as such, cannot be produced.[15]

For this reason, parody has been defined in the doctrine as the change of the content of a work by almost entire preservation of its form.[16] Contrary to what we have seen before regarding the definition of work,[17] here, copyright law goes beyond the surface of the work and considers the intelligible aspects thereof, too.[18]

13 Pfortmüller, SHK CopA, N 10 *ad* Art. 11. In *Rogers vs. Koons*, 960 F 2d 301 (2nd Cir. 1992) and in *Mattel Inc. vs. Walking Mountain Productions*, 353 F.3d 792 (9th Cir. 2003), US courts argued that the copied work must itself be, at least in part, the object of parody (so-called "target parody" as opposed to so-called "weapon parody").

14 Philippin, CoRo CopA, N 30 *ad* Art. 11, argues that most important is the humoristic, satirical side of parody and not so much the criticizing aim. However, the Swiss Federal Council defined parody as "the burlesque representation of an existing work for the purpose of criticism" in the Federal Gazette of June 19, 1989 (BBl 1989 III 477), p. 530.

15 Philippin, CoRo CopA, N 33 *ad* Art. 11; Barrelet/Egloff, CopA Commentary, N 21 *ad* Art. 11; Züllig, p. 297; Dessemontet, Intellectual Property, p. 62; so also the decision of the Zurich District Court of May 19, 2021 (*Trittligasse*), sic! 2022, p. 68 et seqq., c. 6.2.; and Cueni, p. 662, for whom the work shall be recognizable "not by the average reader, but by a well-informed and reasonable addressee" (translation is mine); under UK law similarly, Stokes, p. 174, states that "the parodist has to rely on the audience's awareness of the target work or genre to be successful"; in the US, the Supreme Court stated that "*parody needs to mimic an original to make its point*", cf. *Campbell vs. Acuff-Rose Music, Inc.*, 510 US 569 (1994), p. 580.

16 Federal Gazette of June 19, 1989 (BBl 1989 III 477), p. 530; Barrelet/Egloff, CopA Commentary, N 21 *ad* Art. 11; Cueni, p. 656 and 660 et seq.; Cherpillod, L'objet, p. 147, speaks of "external form". At p. 159 et seq., however, he relativizes his argument that the parodist can borrow the forms and change the content by stating that the parodist will have to modify the forms as well, otherwise the use will be considered as an illicit copy; way more liberal is the position of Mosimann, Kultur Kunst Recht, N 140 *ad* §1; so too the decision Zurich District Court of May 19, 2021 (*Trittligasse*), sic! 2022, p. 68 et seqq., c. 6.1.; cf. also, in Italy, the decision of Tribunale di Milano of July 13, 2011 (*Giacometti Variations*), which states "parodic oeuvres are those that mutate the sense of the parodied oeuvres" (translation is mine).

17 Cf. Chapter 3, especially at IV.

18 The handling of this point by the Zurich district court in *Trittligasse* was explicitly criticized by Rigamonti, Trittligasse, p. 71: the judge supported the defense's claim that the use amounted to a parody and, thus, ultimately absolved Mr. Jenny from the charge of copyright infringement. Yet Wollenberger's musicals were *already* ironic and critical in their content, so, strictly speaking, a "shift" had, therefore, not taken place.

The literature seems to agree on the categorization of parodies as a special type of derivative work (Art. 3 CopA) in which the downstream work has specific features that convey a parodic meaning and make it permissible even without previous authorization of the right holder.[19] RIGAMONTI precises, however, that parodies *can* be derivative works under Art. 3 CopA but *must not* be such. The fact that the district court proved the individual character for Mr. Jenny's adaptations of Wollenberger songs was, thus, superfluous: Provided there is the parodic shift in content, even minor alterations suffice for the exception to be applicable. The parody does not have to fulfill the definition of work for itself, i.e., it must not be individual.[20]

The enjoyment of the exception of parody is subject to the reserve of Art. 11 para. 2 CopA:[21] Parodies should not cause harm or an economical damage to the author of the used work, nor have a malevolent aim whatsoever.[22]

In his comment to the decision, RIGAMONTI discusses whether in the decision *Trittligasse* Jenny's modifications were rightly qualified as parodic and, therefore, justified.[23] RIGAMONTI considers, in this respect, that a considerable enlargement of the scope of the exception of parody was subtly made by the Zurich district court when it held that "the scope of Art. 11 para. 3 CopA is to be described in such a way as encompassing modifications of a work for purposes of criticism *and/or in the interest of politics and art*".[24] To add these interests beside the purpose of criticism makes the parody an open-ended exception, potentially suitable as a sort of general clause.[25] Whereas the emphasized passage is short and incidental, it still has a potential effect of recalibrating the negotiation between the interests of the public and those of the author in preserving control over his work previously found by the legislature with Art. 11 para. 3 CopA.[26] For RIGAMONTI, this was likely the strategy that the district court found to "creatively" justify Jenny's adaptation of Wollenberger's songs. The court considered that a criminal indictment would have been disproportional and found a way to avoid condemning him. To do so, however, the court had to compensate the fact that, on the occasion of the last Copyright

19 CUENI, p. 655; ZÜLLIG, p. 297; interestingly, DESSEMONTET, L'objet, N 244 and 247, explains that, before the entry into force of Art. 11 para. 3 CopA, parodies were subsumed under the unwritten construction of the free utilization (Chapter 4, III.IV.II.I).

20 RIGAMONTI, Trittligasse, p. 71; also in European copyright law, see CJEU of September 3, 2014 - C-201/13 (*Deckmyn vs. Vandersteen*), at para. 33 (in detail, see Chapter 5, I.III.I.).

21 PHILIPPIN, CoRo CopA, N 32 *ad* Art. 11.

22 PHILIPPIN, CoRo CopA, N 32 *ad* Art. 11; BARRELET/EGLOFF, CopA Commentary, N 22 *ad* Art. 11; DESSEMONTET, Le droit d'auteur, N 387 et seq.

23 RIGAMONTI, Trittligasse, p. 71.

24 RIGAMONTI, Trittligasse, p. 71 (translation is mine, emphasis added). The fact that the *Trittligasse* decision is, as already explained, the first and, in the moment of writing, still the only decision on parody to ever be delivered by a Swiss court might amplify its importance.

25 RIGAMONTI, Trittligasse, p. 71

26 CUENI, p. 659; cf. on this EDELMAN, Du mauvais usage, p. 168, who makes a similar argument for the quotation right and states: "the quotation right is a right to information…and combines the right to information with the monopoly of the author" (translation is mine).

Act's revision in 2019, the legislature omitted to address the subject of a possible modernization of the copyright exceptions.[27] Even if agreeing with the result, RIGAMONTI underlines that the exception of parody was not created for encompassing every takeover and modification of previous works in the cultural field.[28]

I.II.I The exception of parody and interpictorial artworks

The exception of parody might justify uses of protected works even if these were barely changed in the process (transformation of content by maintenance of form), provided they convey a parodic, humoristic meaning for the purpose of criticism. This makes the parody exception a potentially suitable instrument for protecting original copies and other interpictorial uses. Like parodies, these artworks rely on maintaining – at least to a certain extent – the appearance of their respective templates to evoke them while they simultaneously create a considerable thematical distance from them. What may be judged as lacking, however, is the parodic component.

Among the artists and artistic movements that have used copying as an artistic strategy, there are some who did it for the purposes of criticizing society, the art market or patriarchy. This decisively critical stance, often with feminist undertones, was typical of the early appropriation art movement.[29] Among these "original copies" there might, indeed, be some that could be subsumed under Art. 11 para. 3 CopA as parodies. We may think of some among the works of Barbara Kruger, for example, *Untitled (It's a Small World, but Not If You Have to Clean It)* (1990), in which she used a photograph previously taken by German photographer Thomas Hoepker (who sued her, but lost, in 2000).[30] For HUTCHEON, Kruger "chooses to appropriate mass-media images and use their formal complicity with capitalist and patriarchal representational strategies to foreground conflictual elements through ironic contradictions".[31] Kruger herself understood her work as parodic and critical.[32]

Other artists' copying practices would, however, encounter difficulties in falling under the exception of parody, as the humoristic or critical element typical of the parody might be judged as lacking or as not sufficiently conveyed by the "form" of the artwork.[33] As we explained, these artworks mostly insert themselves critically

27 RIGAMONTI, Trittligasse, p. 71; RIGAMONTI himself had proposed the introduction of a "subsidiary general clause" in RIGAMONTI, Grundrechte, p. 392.

28 RIGAMONTI, Trittligasse, p. 71; another opinion cf. CUENI, p. 663 et seq., who argues for a case-by-case balancing of interests for modifications of works that do not clearly fit in the exception of parody, for example, because they do not create the necessary inner distance.

29 RÖMER, p. 104 et seq.

30 *Hoepker vs. Kruger*, 200 F.Supp.2d 340 (SDNY 2002).

31 HUTCHEON, p. 102.

32 HUTCHEON, p. 102.

33 BLUME HUTTENLAUCH, p. 123; even if according to some the exception of parody is to interpret "largely", cf. CUENI, p. 656, according to the Federal Council, it only encompasses "comical pres-

in the history of art. Their subject is "the history of representation itself",[34] which is characterized, since the eighteenth century, by a preponderance of artworks constructed as originals – judged positively – over copies – judged negatively. That some artistic endeavors in this recent history of art even tried to ridicule the idea of "the original" by ironically making it small,[35] unimportant[36] or simply untraceable (and, thus, the search for it lost in advance),[37] it could surely be read as parodic when observed through art historical lenses. Whether copyright law's instruments are sharp enough and fine-tuned to grasp the subtle humorous critique to the aesthetical *status quo* operated by postmodern artworks,[38] however, is questionable.

Another obstacle to the admission of some artistic copies as parodies lies in the condition of recognizability of the previous image. A parody lives off the shift in meaning. To grasp this shift, we should be able to recognize or, at least, "contextually situate" the used work.[39] We might recognize the used template because it is particularly famous or because it has recently been in the news. Some post-colonial artworks, in which the artists intentionally use well-known artworks by European artists to create a contrast and subvert the dominant narratives,[40] offer examples. Titus Kaphar referenced Claude Monet's *Woman with a Parasol* (1875) in his *Pushing Back the Light* (2012). With it, he wanted to tell a story that was left unmentioned during the Impressionist artistic "revolution",[41] i.e., that while painters in Europe were capturing idyllic scenes, the African continent was being emptied of its natural and human resources by European powers.[42] Another example might be Hank Willis Thomas's *Icarus* (2016), in which he uses both forms and title of Matisse's *Icarus* (1944) but re-creates the figure by assembling National Basketball Association (NBA) and other sport jerseys.[43] In his work, Thomas often thematizes the exploitation of the black body in agonistic sports. These artworks offer examples in which a regular observer would probably recognize the works used as a template as familiar or, at least, understand that a previously existing

---

entations of an existing work for the purpose of critique", s. Federal Gazette of June 19, 1989 (BBl 1989 III 477), p. 530 (translation is mine), something that forcibly leaves out many other variations.

34 Hutcheon, p. 33.

35 As in the case of Richard Pettibone's "miniature replicas", cf. <http://www.artnet.com/artists/richard-pettibone/>.

36 Prince, Deposition, p. 192.

37 For example, Lippard, p. 32, explains that artists Daniel Buren, Niele Toroni and Olivier Mosset had organized in Paris (and then repeated in Lugano) a collective exhibition in which each artist painted his own "usual" works and, as a provocation, two of the other ones as well. In the accompanying brochure, art critic Michel Claura wrote: "to talk about a forgery, is referring to an original. In the case of Buren, Mosset, Toroni, where is the original?".

38 Sherman, Appropriating, p. 32 et seq.

39 Barrelet/Egloff, CopA Commentary, N 21 *ad* Art. 11.

40 Childs, p. 14.

41 Childs, p. 17, quotes a statement of Titus Kaphar.

42 Nancy McKeon, Virtual Museum: Black Artists and Modernism, July 23, 2020 (<https://mylittlebird.com/2020/07/black-artists-and-modernism/>).

43 Nancy McKeon, Virtual Museum: Black Artists and Modernism, July 23, 2020 (<https://mylittlebird.com/2020/07/black-artists-and-modernism/>).

artwork has been "embedded" in the new one. In these cases, because the original artwork is so well-known, it is likely that the shift in meaning is recognized.

On the contrary, for the works of artists who create copies as art with found imagery, it is more difficult to produce this typical shift, as either the public ignores the work used as a template or has seen it but is unable to connect it to anything that it might recognize as shifted. Estonian artist Katja Novitskova may constitute an exception in this respect. The artist uses imagery she found mostly in scientific databases or on the internet to create upscale installations. The images she includes in her artworks are mostly stock images of animals and microbes that look like photos from *National Geographic* or similar (thus, protected as photographic works according to Art. 2 para. 2 let. g CopA or as non-individual photographic depictions according to Art. 2 para. 3bis CopA). The estranged feeling we get when observing the installations arises not because we recognize the used picture, in particular, but, because we see the animal extrapolated from the natural-scientific context, we are able to see it catapulted into an artificial, quasi-virtual environment.[44] The work of Novitskova pursues a critic of society, climate change, and of social media.[45] Whether this critic and the means the artist uses to achieve her desired effects could be subsumed under the exception of parody if contested before court shall be left open. Novitskova's work surely does not produce the typical parodic effect that we are able to recognize with the help of comic characters, distorted expressions and a satiric-political message. Yet the decontextualization she operates and the criticism arising from it are powerful and equally able to change the *content* of the work by maintenance of its *form*.

I.II.II Other comparable variations on the work (Art. 11 para. 3 CopA)

According to Art. 11 para. 3 CopA, it is permissible to use existing works for the creation of parodies "or other comparable variations on the work". What scholars understand as "comparable variations" can essentially be divided into two categories. The answers depend on whether authors believe that the "internal distance" parodies create (i.e., the maintenance of the form by parallel shift of content[46]) can be stretched well beyond the parodical effect in a sort of general clause or not. In the following, we first expose the more conservative opinion, according to which the second sentence of Art. 11 para. 3 CopA does not open a radically new scope for limiting copyright (1) and then the more liberal opinion, according to which this provision has the potential to serve as a general clause for the justification of artistic endeavors (2).

(1) According to the first opinion, "other comparable variations on the work" subsumes *parodic* variations of other work categories, for example of musical, audio-visual works as well as works of the visual art, as "parody", in the strict

44 Novitskova, p. 5.
45 Vierkant, p. 3.
46 Cf. Chapter 5, I.II.

sense, historically refers to literary works only.[47] For Hilty, "other comparable variations on the work" shall include caricatures and pastiches, in conformity with Art. 5 para. 3 let. k Infosoc-Directive valid in the EU.[48] For authors aligning with this first opinion, the humoristic, comical or even critical effect remains central even for the fulfillment of the second part of the exception stipulated at Art. 11 para. 3 CopA. In this sense, this opinion does not open a substantially new scope for exception under the second part of Art. 11 para. 3 CopA.[49]

(2) For Peter Mosimann, the second part of Art. 11 para. 3 CopA is, instead, a way to overcome the "rigidity" of copyright law that he diagnoses.[50] "Comparable variations on the work" encompasses not only parodies and other variations creating a strictly similar effect but also all sorts of modifications ("Abwandlungen"[51]). The provision would, therefore, contain a sort of general clause, which – building up on the German concept of inner distance and anti-thematic treatment now in disuse (cf. Chapter 4, III.IV.II)[52] – could protect a variety of artistic variations on original works. Mosimann substantiates his view with reference to the German free utilization. As previously discussed, the free utilization becomes an open and flexible clause when interpreted in conformity with the concept of inner distance and a specifically artistic view ("kunstspezifische Betrachtung") flowing from the Constitutional artistic freedom.[53]

However, as previously stated, the Swiss notion of free utilization did not experience an increasingly large interpretation as the German free utilization did. On the contrary, it is to interpret "restrictively".[54] Moreover, the large doctrine of the free utilization in Germany was put to an end with the last amendment of the Copyright Act and the removal of § 24 para. 1 oDE-CopA.[55] Last, it is not clear how far Mosimann intends this exception to reach. First, he understands that parodies and other comparable variations of the work must fulfill the definition of work for themselves.[56] Second, as examples of interpictorial uses of previous artworks that shall be subsumed and, thus, justified under Art. 11 para. 3 CopA, he brings Pablo Picasso's transformation of *Le Déjeuner sur l'herbe selon Edouard Manet* (1961) and Sigmar Polke's *Les Demoiselles d'Avignon* (2006), realized after Picasso's

47 Barrelet/Egloff, CopA Commentary, N 21 *ad* Art. 11; the same thinks Pförtmüller, SHK CopA, N 10 *ad* Art. 11; cf. Cueni, p. 656.

48 Hilty, Urheberrecht, N 525.

49 Cherpillod, Liberté, p. 363; Barrelet/Egloff, CopA Commentary, N 23 *ad* Art. 11; de Werra/Benhamou, Kultur Kunst Recht, N 87 *ad* § 7 quote two decisions from the US to substantiate the fact that the exception of parody must be understood narrowly: *Campbell vs. Acuff-Rose Music, Inc.*, 510 US 569 (1994) and *Mattel Inc. vs. Walking Mountain Productions*, 353 F.3d 792 (9th Cir. 2003).

50 Mosimann, Kultur Kunst Recht, N 125 *ad* § 1.

51 Mosimann, Kultur Kunst Recht, N 125 *ad* § 1.

52 It shall be noted that even Handle, p. 161, who affirms that the inner distance is recognized in Swiss copyright law, does not consider this to be a lawful basis for a copyright exception.

53 Mosimann, Kultur Kunst Recht, N 142 *ad* § 1; Schulze, Aneignung, p. 53;

54 Cherpillod, SIWR II/1, p. 307; also cf. above at Chapter 4, III.IV.I.

55 See Chapter 4, III.IV.II.III.

56 Mosimann, Kultur Kunst Recht, N 141 *ad* § 1 and N 140 *ad* § 4.

original. However, we do not see how these two cases could be deemed remotely unlawful from a copyright perspective. As explained above, motifs (in these cases, people having lunch in a park and a group of semi-naked, lascivious women) are not protected under copyright, and the respective titles are likely not enough individual.[57] Moreover, in both examples, the original has been, formally as well as stylistically, completely abandoned. One could, thus, simply argue with the distance doctrine and unproblematically find, in both cases, two free utilizations of the respective template that are not relevant under copyright law. On the other hand, MOSIMANN seems to deny the application of such open clauses in most cases of appropriation art.[58] As seen in Chapter 5, I.II., however, the individual character is not a condition parodies have to meet to be subsumed under Art. 11 para. 3 CopA.

The second part of Art. 11 para. 3 CopA contains a rather openly formulated provision ("variations on the work"), whose only explicit restriction seems to be the fact that variations must be "comparable" to parodies. According to Art. 35 Const., norms must be interpreted in conformity with the Constitution, i.e., the norm could very well be interpreted in conformity with artistic freedom.[59] For what concerns the interpretation of the Copyright Act's norms, the SFSC repeated this principle in DFC 131 III 480 (*Schweizerzeit*).[60] The question is, thus, not whether this part can be interpreted in conformity with the Swiss Constitution and more specifically with its Art. 21. The question is, rather, how far courts are willing to drag this exception for the justification of other artistic practices beyond parodies, on what theoretical grounds and following which methodology.

I.III Parodies and the concept of "pastiche" in Germany and the European Union

According to German scholars, the new legal *status quo*, after the removal of § 24 oDE-CopA and, thus, the end of the concept of "inner distance", constitutes a huge loss for artistic reuses of copyrighted material.[61] For authors intending to reuse copyrighted material, three exit options remain available under German copyright law: (1) to modify the borrowed work to the point of unrecognizability so that no copyright-relevant use is recognized; (2) the exception of quotation[62] and (3) the new § 51a DE-CopA, which, with a very similar wording to Art. 5 para. 3 let. k Infosoc-Directive, explicitly protects parodies,[63] caricatures and pastiches.[64]

57 ZÜLLIG, p. 296.

58 MOSIMANN, Kultur Kunst Recht, N 152 et seqq. *ad* §1, as uses that would not fall under this open exception, he lists Richard Prince's *New Portraits* (initiated in 2014), Jeff Koons' *String of Puppies* (1988), and Sherrie Levine's *After Walker Evans* (1981), which are all interpictorial original copies.

59 MOSIMANN, Kultur Kunst Recht, N 142 *ad* § 4.

60 BARRELET/EGLOFF, CopA Commentary, N 16 *ad* Art. 11.

61 DÖHL, Systemwechsel, p. 259 et seq.; DÖHL/HUI, p. 886.

62 Cf. Chapter 5, I.IV and I.V.

63 To interpret within the meaning of EU law, see Chapter 5, I.III.I.

64 DÖHL, Systemwechsel, p. 254; for a critique of the insufficiency of these three options, see DÖHL, Systemwechsel, p. 255 et seqq.

I.III.I Parody

With the preliminary ruling *Deckmyn vs. Vandersteen* requested by the Brussels court of appeal in 2014, the CJEU ruled that the parody is an autonomous concept of European Union (EU) law. The facts underlying the case concerned the production, by a Flemish nationalist party, of calendars with a cover largely based on the cover of the 1961 Spike and Suzy comic "The Wild Benefactor" ("*De Wilde Weldoener*"). In the image at stake, a character was replaced with the mayor of Ghent, distributing money to people of dark-colored skin.

According to the harmonized meaning of parody of the CJEU, its three essential characteristics are: (1) to evoke an existing work while (2) being noticeably different from it, and (3) to constitute an expression of humor or mockery.[65] Upon specific request from the Brussels court of appeal, the CJEU also clarified that the concept of parody is not subject to the condition that the parody should display an original character of its own, i.e., be a copyrightable work.[66] Courts of European Member States are now bound by this definition and have to conform their interpretation of parody to the one outlined by the CJEU.[67]

For Döhl/Hui, this indication constitutes an "aesthetically narrow concept of parody" that will represent a huge challenge for the many art forms that reuse existing material neither humorously nor mockingly and that would, therefore, not qualify as parody under the definition outlined in *Deckmyn*.[68] Indeed, French courts ruled out the applicability of the exception of parody as it was described in *Deckmyn* in three cases involving interpictorial original copies.[69] In all three cases, the residual similarity between the works was judged excessive and the humoristic distortion required by the *Deckmyn* definition of parody was judged as lacking, so the verdict fell in favor of the copied, upstream author.

I.III.II Pastiche

In response to the CJEU's narrow understanding of the concept of parody, the German legislature tried to advance a broad interpretation of the concept of pastiche. Such broad interpretation is widely supported by scholarly literature.[70] So interpreted, the concept of pastiche would be a sort of all-purpose-weapon,[71] able to create a continuity with the substance of the repealed § 24 oDE-CopA and,

65 CJEU of September 3, 2014 - C-201/13 (*Deckmyn vs. Vandersteen*), at para. 33; Döhl/Hui, p. 860.

66 CJEU of September 3, 2014 - C-201/13 (*Deckmyn vs. Vandersteen*), at para. 33.

67 CJEU of September 3, 2014 - C-201/13 (*Deckmyn vs. Vandersteen*), at para. 17; Döhl/Hui, p. 860; the GFCJ has adapted its interpretation of parody in the decision of July 28, 2016 (*auf fett getrimmt*), GRUR 2016, p. 1157 et seqq. In the decision, the requirement of the anti-thematic treatment was abandoned.

68 Döhl/Hui, p. 886.

69 Cour d'appel de Versailles of March 16, 2018 (*Malka vs. Klasen*); Cour d'appel de Paris of February 23, 2021, (*Koons vs. Davidovici*); Cour d'appel de Paris of December 17, 2019 (*Bauret vs. Koons*).

70 Döhl/Hui, p. 881 with further references; Kreutzer, p. 4.

71 Peters, p. 1483.

thus, be a functional equivalent of the concepts of "anti-thematic treatment" and "inner distance".[72] In this way, in the words of the German legislature, it could achieve the inclusion of contemporary cultural techniques such as remixes, memes, GIFs, mashups, so-called fan art and fan fiction, covers and sampling.[73] The legislative explanatory memorandum also explicitly recognizes "quoting, imitating and borrowing" as "defining elements of *intertextuality* and contemporary cultural creation".[74] For this reason, at least in the intention of the German legislature, the exception of pastiche could also include interpictorial "original copies".[75] Indeed, in some recent cases handled before German first-instance courts, interpictorial reuses of copyrighted material suspected of being infringing were justified as pastiches.

For example, in a case involving German painter Martin Eder, accused of plagiarism for having included an image found on the internet in his painting *The Unknowable* (2018), a regional court in Berlin dismissed the infringement claim using the new exception of pastiche.[76] The exception was seen as fulfilled in particular because of the change of medium (digital to analog), the fact that the used image appeared in the background, that the painting was more plurivalent than the original and that various elements were added to it.[77] The court ruled that, through the opposition of images, the painter had achieved an "anti-thematic treatment" of the original.[78]

In the already exposed case *Metall auf Metall*,[79] the Higher Regional Court of Hamburg qualified Pelham's sampling of Kraftwerk's song as a pastiche, i.e., justified it for the period from the June 7, 2021 (day of the entry into force of the amended DE-CopA) recurring to the pastiche exception. In its interpretation, a pastiche requires a communicative act with an evaluating reference to the pre-existing work – a confrontation (in German: *Auseinandersetzung*). According to the judges, the pastiche exception goes beyond the sole imitation of style and encompasses the "recognizable borrowing of creative traits of the work". The adding or integration of new formal elements suffices for fulfilling the condition that the previous work must be changed in the process.[80] Following the judgment, Kraftwerk filed again for revision before the GFCJ. As it had done already in 2017, the GFCJ filed for a

72 Cf. Kreutzer, p. 4 et seq.

73 Explanatory Memorandum BT-Drs. 19/27426, p. 91; Peters, p. 1483; Döhl/Hui, p. 881; cf. Loewenheim, DE-CopA Commentary, N 27 et seqq. *ad* § 24; Döhl, Systemwechsel, p. 247; Kreutzer, p. 4.

74 Explanatory Memorandum BT-Drs. 19/27426, p. 91 (translation is mine, emphasis added)

75 Cf. Kreutzer, p. 13 and 17.

76 Regional Court of Berlin of November 2, 2021 (*The Unknowable*), GRUR-RR 2022, p. 216 et seqq.

77 Regional Court of Berlin of November 2, 2021 (*The Unknowable*), GRUR-RR 2022, p. 216 et seqq., p. 221.

78 Peters, p. 1484 et seq.

79 Cf. Chapter 4, III.IV.II.II.

80 Higher Regional Court of Hamburg of April 28, 2021 (*Metall auf Metall III*), GRUR 2022, p. 1217 et seqq.; Peters, p. 1486.

preliminary judgment to the CJEU on the matter for clarification of the concept of "pastiche" under EU law.[81]

What "pastiche" stands for within copyright law is still widely disputed. In its referral, the GFCJ recognized that the musical piece "Nur Mir" does not meet the requirements of a caricature or parody of the musical piece "Metall auf Metall" because it lacks an expression of humor or mockery. It, thus, asked whether the exception for the purpose of pastiche is a catch-all provision that could, at least, cover artistic treatments of a pre-existing work or other subject matter and whether restrictive criteria, such as the requirement of humor, imitation of style or homage, apply to the concept of pastiche.[82] With its preliminary ruling, the CJEU will most likely formulate a definition of pastiche that is harmonized and binding for all Member States.[83]

According to Döhl/Hui, the broad interpretation advanced by the German legislature and courts will encounter problems at the EU level. First, this broad interpretation runs against the legal and aesthetic history of the term.[84] Second, it does not conform to the handling of the pastiche exception in other Member States with a longer pastiche tradition (especially France). Third, it could simply not be the meaning intended under EU copyright law. For example, the fact that the EU legislature deliberately decided not to introduce a free utilization exception through the Directive 2019/790 (DSM-Directive)[85] but, rather, opted for a pastiche exception (in Art. 17 para. 7 let. b DSM-Directive) could mean that pastiche is not deemed to become the equivalent of the free utilization in breadth and scope.[86]

The contrast between the German proposal for a broad interpretation of pastiche and the lack of a unitary European definition creates legal uncertainty and a risk for the involved artists, who could falsely assume that their uses of existing copyrighted material are covered by the exception before discovering that the CJEU is not ready to grant the same treatment as German courts.[87]

81 GFCJ of September 14, 2023 (*Metall auf Metall V*), GRUR-RS 2023, p. 24621 et seqq.

82 Cf. GFCJ of September 14, 2023 (*Metall auf Metall V*), GRUR-RS 2023, p. 24621 et seqq.

83 Cf. Susan Bischoff, The dawn of pastiche: First decision on new German copyright exception, June 7, 2023 (<https://copyrightblog.kluweriplaw.com/2023/06/07/the-dawn-of-pastiche-first-decision-on-new-german-copyright-exception/>).

84 Jameson, p. 114, has defined pastiche as: "like parody, the imitation of a peculiar or unique style, the wearing of a stylistic mask, speech in a dead language: but [pastiche] is a neutral practice of such mimicry, without parody's ulterior motive, without the satirical impulse, without laughter, without that still latent feeling that there exists something normal compared to which what is being imitated is rather comic. *Pastiche is a blank parody, parody that has lost its sense of humour*" (emphasis added); for Kreutzer, p. 14, no "uniform meaning" of pastiche is ascertainable; by adopting a different approach, mainly based on the intentions of the German legislators, Kreutzer, p. 22, arrived at a decisively broader interpretation of pastiche.

85 Directive (EU) 2019/790 of the European Parliament and of the Council of 17 April 2019 on Copyright and Related Rights in the Digital Single Market and amending Directives 96/9/EC and 2001/29/EC.

86 Döhl/Hui, p. 860 and 882.

87 Döhl, Bearbeitungsrechtsregime, p. 745.

I.IV Quotations (Art. 25 CopA)

A "quotation" is usually the identical reproduction of a protected work or of a part of a work in a new work.[88] This unmodified yet fragmented use of a previous work usually differentiates a quotation from the creation of a derivative work in one of the three possible declinations previously discussed (derivative work under Art. 3 CopA, minor alteration and free utilization),[89] as the source work is at least slightly changed in the process. However, boundaries between these categories are blurry and not always easy to establish in the concrete case.

The question whether Art. 25 CopA allows the quotation of images ("Bildzitate") such as photographs and works of visual art was debated for a long time. An attempt at changing the law and explicitly allowing the quotation of images did not make it into the final amendment of the CopA in 1989. The Federal Council justified its choice to exclude quotations of images by explaining that allowing the citing of images would have created an excessive breach in the protection scope for works of visual art and photographs, as the reproduction right of these categories was already managed by collecting societies.[90] With such a rule, the fear at that time was that every publication would have been able to copy images and justify the use by invoking the exception of quotation.[91] This legislative history is held accountable for having suggested an interpretation of the law according to which these work categories could not be quoted,[92] despite the fact that the wording of the law did not provide for such restriction.[93] Notwithstanding this legislative history, scholarship has increasingly argued in favor of the possibility to quote images. The copyright amendment of 2018, entered into force in 2020, ultimately put an end to this debate. In its message to the parliament, the Federal Council clearly stated that

88 Kakies, N 5 and 65; cf. also in art theoretical research Isekenmeier, In Richtung, p. 67: "if an image includes a (partial) reproduction of another image in itself, it is a quotation" and: "an image quotes another image when it refers to it and contains it" (translation is mine).

89 Kakies, N 65 et seqq.; according to Renold/Contel, CoRo CopA, N 4 et seq. *ad* Art. 25, if the "inner correlation" (more on this below) between quoting subject and quoted object is too strong, a derivative work might be created. The demarcation line between quotation and derivative use is, therefore, not so simple to draw.

90 Federal Gazette of June 19, 1989 (BBl 1989 III 477), p. 545.

91 Egloff/Künzi, CopA Commentary, N 3 *ad* Art. 25. Actually, the same reserve is also present in the newest legislative message on the amendment of the Copyright Act, cf. Federal Gazette of November 22, 2017 (BBl 2018 591), p. 610. This time, the fear was reportedly expressed by people active in the cultural sector. The Federal Council does not seem to share it anymore.

92 Federal Gazette of November 22, 2017 (BBl 2018 591), p. 610. For example: Egloff/Künzi, CopA Commentary 2008, N 2 and 8 *ad* Art. 25; Dessemontet, Le droit d'auteur, p. 365 et seqq.

93 As stated by Macciacchini, Wiedergabe, p. 364, the fact that the introduction of an explicit permission to quote images was rejected by the Federal Council did not change anything to the debate, as the article already provided for the quoting of *all published works*. Indeed, the change enforced itself at the level of the interpretation of the law. The Federal Council clearly stated that the text of the law did not need to be changed, see Federal Gazette of November 22, 2017 (BBl 2018 591), p. 610.

the quoting of photographic works and works of visual art shall now be permitted,[94] a fact that makes Art. 25 CopA a relevant provision in this text.

Art. 25 para. 1 CopA allows the quotation of published works if the quotation serves as an explanation, reference or illustration. The extent of the quotation must be justified by such purpose (e.g., commentary, criticism, review, appraisal, illustration). Art. 25 para. 2 CopA establishes that the quotation must be designated as such and the source given. When the source indicates the name of the author, the name must also be cited.

According to the majority opinion, the term quotation ("Zitat") must be understood restrictively. It should not simply mean "extract" or "cutout" but, rather, indicate an "inner correlation" between the quoting and the quoted matter, i.e., a link between the respective contents.[95] The inner correlation must be stronger than a mere thematical connection. The simple fact that the quotation and its context deal with the same subject matter is not enough.[96] There must be a sensible bond between the quoting and the quoted, a conceptual engagement,[97] an association that can, *a posteriori*, be judged as "necessary". Paragraph 1, which states that the quotation must serve the purposes of explanation, reference or illustration, explicitly requires this. Quoting cannot be an end in itself; there must be an extrinsic purpose (the so-called function of documentation, in German *Belegfunktion*).[98] Such correlation can also be achieved by means of artistic – not obligatorily textual – reference to the cited content.[99]

Because the inner correlation between the purpose of the quotation and its concrete or intended use constitutes the foundation for – and simultaneously the limit to – the extent of the quotation,[100] it is decisive for the applicability of the exception that the quotation has a purpose and that the proportion between the own work and

94 Federal Gazette of November 22, 2017 (BBl 2018 591), p. 610; in the EU, the same question was resolved affirmatively with the decision of the CJEU of December 11, 2011 - C 145/10 (*Eva-Maria Painer vs. Standard VerlagsGmbH et al.*); for Egloff/Künzi, CopA Commentary, N 3 *ad* Art. 25, this development was deduced from DFC 131 III 480 (*Schweizerzeit*), "which does not speak of the quotation of images, but explicitly admitted the quotation of entire works" (translation is mine). The Federal Council did not refer to this decision to allow the quotation of images but to the changes in the doctrine.

95 Egloff/Künzi, CopA Commentary, N 4 *ad* Art. 25; Renold/Contel, CoRo CopA, N 3 *ad* Art. 25; Rigamonti, Medienberichterstattung, p. 62.

96 Ruedin, N 446.

97 Rigamonti, Medienberichterstattung, p. 62

98 Canton Basel-City Court of Appeal of October 31, 2018 (*Lichtgestalten*), sic! 2019, p. 367 et seqq., c. 3.2.

99 Egloff/Künzi, CopA Commentary, N 5 *ad* Art. 25, lists as examples the practices of sampling and collage. The question is whether, in such practices, the inner correlation would be strong enough to fulfill the exception of quotation.

100 Ruedin, N 430; Renold/Contel, CoRo CopA, N 4 et seq. *ad* Art. 25, go further and explain that the correlation between the cited and the citing materials cannot be too strong so as to create a derivative work according to Art. 3 CopA, nor too weak so as to make the citing work appear as a mere collection according to Art. 4 CopA.

the quoted material is preserved.[101] This shall not mean that Art. 25 CopA imposes limits to the length or size of the quotation. Unlike Art. 28 CopA, which allows only "short excerpts", Art. 25 CopA does not require the quotation to be short.[102] Under Art. 25 CopA, a work can also be quoted in its entirety, provided that the entire quotation is judged necessary[103] and secondary vis-à-vis their own achievement.[104] If the quoted work stands out too much with respect to the quoting artist's own achievement, in the sense that it gets the main or an independent meaning, it cannot amount to a quotation.[105] In summary, the correlation between citing and cited must always be in relation to (1) subordination, (2) functionality, and (3) proportion.[106] These tensions between quoting and quoted matter delimit the lawful extent of the quotation.

To be quoted, the material must further be published. According to Art. 9 para. 3 CopA, a work is published when it has been made available for the first time by the author, or with his consent, to a large number of persons not constituting a private circle. According to RIGAMONTI, unlawfully published works can also be quoted.[107]

By stipulating formal requirements for the quotation, Art. 25 para. 2 CopA makes sure that recognition of authorship (Art. 9 para. 1 CopA) is not infringed by the assertion of the freedom to quote.[108] The quoted material must be recognizable as such, namely through the use of a different font, of quotation marks for linguistic works, a caption for images and other indications for other works (such as musical works).[109] In other words, it must be made clear that embedded in an own achievement is extraneous material. According to some scholars, the quoting work can indicate the source of the quoted material even outside the body of the work.[110]

I.IV.I Whether the quoting artifact must fulfill the definition of work

Opinions divide on the question of whether only authors of works fulfilling the definition at Art. 2 para. 1 CopA can quote other works or whether all sorts of authors can avail of the exception even if their achievement, considered *without* the

101 DESSEMONTET, Le droit d'auteur, N 484; EGLOFF/KÜNZI, CopA Commentary, N 7 *ad* Art. 25.

102 RIGAMONTI, Medienberichterstattung, p. 64; Cherpillod, Liberté, p. 357 et seq.

103 EGLOFF/KÜNZI, CopA Commentary, N 7 *ad* Art. 25. In DFC 131 III 480 (*Schweizerzeit*), c. 3.2, the quotation of the entire work is "not excluded". However, in DFC 131 III 480 (*Schweizerzeit*), the SFSC explicitly denied the need to cite the article in full and prescribed a citing of extracts of the article for similar cases.

104 MACCIACCHINI/OERTLI, SHK CopA, N 12 *ad* Art. 25.

105 DFC 131 III 480 (*Schweizerzeit*), c. 2.1; Canton Basel-City Court of Appeal of October 31, 2018 (*Lichtgestalten*), sic! 2019, p. 367 et seqq., c. 3.2; MACCIACCHINI, Wiedergabe, p. 365.

106 RENOLD/CONTEL, CoRo CopA, N 5 and 20 et seqq. *ad* Art. 25.

107 RIGAMONTI, Medienberichterstattung, p. 62.

108 EGLOFF, CopA Commentary, N 7 *ad* Vorbemerkungen Art. 19-28.

109 EGLOFF/KÜNZI, CopA Commentary, N 14 *ad* Art. 25.

110 EGLOFF, Von der "freien Benutzung", p. 407, lists as examples the full score for musical works, the booklet for CDs, the title or every other accessory communication medium connected to artworks.

quoted portion, would not qualify for copyright.[111] Whereas German copyright law requires the quoting matter to be an independent work (§ 51 DE-CopA explicitly requires this),[112] the wording of Art. 25 CopA does not require that the quoting be a work according to Art. 2 para. 1 CopA.[113]

Those who plead for the necessity for the citing medium to be a work argue by retracing the history of the quotation exception in different versions of the CopA.[114] This shows that the citing mediums were always mentioned in the wording of the provisions.[115] The historical materials about the adoption of Art. 25 CopA in its current wording do not show any legislative intention to abandon the requirement for the citing medium to be a work. Rather, the legislature seems to have intended keeping the tradition of the older provisions and of German law (§ 51 of the German Copyright Act), which served as a model and requires the citing medium to be a work.[116] Second, they argue, only those who have created works are justified in their punctual borrowing from other works, because only by creating a work of their own are they augmenting the general welfare and providing a benefit for the whole society. According to this opinion, the exception of quotation is interpreted as a sort of reward for the achievement of authors.[117] This last argument is clearly linked to the requirement of proportion between citing and cited material (Art. 25 para. 1 CopA expressed with "the extent of the quotation is justified for such purpose").[118] Put differently, between the citing medium and the cited material, there must be an "inner correlation", as the citing medium must itself be a work with individual character. If it is not, it cannot be a quotation but a mere exploitative – and, thus, infringing – use of another's work.[119]

On the opposite side, scholarship argues that the citing medium does not have to be eligible for copyright.[120] This opinion is substantiated with the simple fact

111 We have seen before that such is not a requirement for parodies.

112 This question was explicitly examined in the decision of the Higher Regional Court of Munich of January 30, 2003 (*Rudolf der Eroberer*), ZUM 2003, p. 571 et seqq., p. 575. Because the *Spiegel* magazine cover was not a work, the exception of quotation was judged as not fulfilled.

113 The SFSC did not mention this condition in DFC 131 III 480 (*Schweizerzeit*).

114 Egloff/Künzi, N 12 *ad* Art. 25; Dessemontet, Le droit d'auteur, N 352.

115 Gasser/Morant, p. 232, expose how Art. 11 of the CopA 1883 spoke of literary-historical works, of works intended for school instruction and of musical works. A later version of the same Act, the CopA 1922, did not speak of works anymore but mentioned various citing mediums. The prevailing opinion on the interpretation of that provision was that the citing medium had to be a work.

116 Maassen, p. 235; Gasser/Morant, p. 233. The authors come to the conclusion that the omission of the term "work" from the wording must be linked with the intention of the legislature to formulate a shorter provision.

117 Gasser/Morant, p. 233 et seq.

118 Renold/Contel, CoRo CopA, N 10 *ad* Art. 25, recognize that Art. 25 CopA does not require the citing material to be a work. However, they express doubts regarding the possibility for the citing artifact to not be a copyrightable work and still fulfill the condition of the proportional correlation with the cited material.

119 Egloff, Von der "freien Benutzung", p. 406.

120 Ruedin, N 420 et seqq.; Macciacchini, Wiedergabe, p. 365; Cherpillod, Liberté, p. 357 s.; Döhl/Hui, p. 869, explain that quotation provisions in Norway, Sweden and the Netherlands do not require the creation of an independent work.

that the wording of the law does not require the citing medium to be a copyrightable work. Moreover, it is noted that Art. 10(1) of the Berne Convention for the Protection of Literary and Artistic Works (Berne Convention), rather than German law, inspired the Swiss legislature when drafting Art. 25 CopA.[121] The quotation provision of the Berne Convention, which makes the exception of quotation mandatory for all contracting parties, does not require the same intensity of interaction between citing and cited materials.[122]

We agree with the latter opinion. Exceptions to copyright concern the use of a copyrighted work and function according to their own logic. Requiring the citing artifact to be a work according to Art. 2 para. 2 CopA is contrary to the law and to the purpose of copyright exceptions.

I.IV.II The exception of quotation and interpictorial artworks

Some commentators see the quotation provision as particularly viable for justifying artistic cross-references and reuses.[123] The fact that the perceptible modification of the template forms is not a requirement for the quotation exception (something which is true, instead, for derivative works and partially for parodies; see Chapter 4, III.III and Chapter 5, I.II) but, rather, the fulfillment of a series of objective requirements is seen as advantageous,[124] as artists who copy as an artistic strategy would not be compelled to change their source material.

The aesthetic neutrality of quotations is also positively regarded.[125] Whereas parodies must fulfill their parodic function (that is, be critical and humorous), quotations adapt to their destination, which could vary and depend on the context of the citing medium. For example, a work could be quoted to be commented on or reviewed but also criticized or praised.

These features of Art. 25 CopA are, indeed, interpictoriality-friendly. Its focus on the interaction between the quoted and quoting artifacts, rather than on the fixed condition of parodic switch of meaning (or visible change, as in the free utilization), is certainly favorable for some interpictorial artworks. An example of a painting that could probably pass as quotation is *Picasso's Studio* (1991) by artist Faith Ringgold. In it, we clearly glimpse Pablo Picasso's *Les demoiselles d'Avignon* (1907), in which he had portrayed some women wearing African masks along with others with uncovered faces. In Faith Ringgold's painting, Picasso himself is portrayed. He is realizing a painting of the artist's naked body, standing in the middle of some unfinished artworks and his collection of African masks.[126]

121 Ruedin, N 422.
122 Döhl, Bearbeitungsrechtsregime, p. 745.
123 Egloff, Von der "freien Benutzung", p. 399 et seqq.
124 Egloff, Von der "freien Benutzung", p. 407.
125 Döhl, Bearbeitungsrechtsregime, p. 745.
126 Childs, p. 99.

With her painting, Ringgold thematizes the nineteenth and early twentieth century Western fascination for the primitive, tribal object and the "exotic body". European avant-gardists, among whom we prominently find Pablo Picasso, admired these artifacts for their simplicity, spirituality and authenticity, often including these in their artworks. Observed from a postcolonial lens, this behavior is judged as problematic because it is inevitably charged with issues of violence and domination as well as misrepresentation. In the occidental discourse, these objects were used in a way that ignored their original meaning.[127] In Ringgold's artwork, the interplay of cross-references is dense. Picasso has (improperly) used African artifacts in his art and is portrayed by Ringgold doing exactly that. The old painter gazes at the artist's naked body, but the public knows that Ringgold is observing back by painting *Picasso's Studio*. In this case, it could well be that the use of Picasso's work is documentative within the scope of Art. 25 CopA. Ringgold includes the artwork of Picasso and enters a dialogue with it. By commenting upon it as she did, she also sheds a new light on the painting.

Art. 25 CopA contains other burdens to a frictionless application to many other artistic copies, which is a reason that other authors categorically exclude its application for the justification of artistic copying.[128] The first obstacle to its application is the necessity of a purpose for the quotation. Some artists included the previous work in a new artwork just because they considered that this was aesthetically right and not out of an intention to particularly engage with it.[129] The lack of an inner correlation with the quoted work also hinders the fulfillment of the condition of proportionality, for if there is no ascertainable purpose dictating the extent of the quotation, the balancing tension sustaining the use of copyrighted material virtually disappears. Imagining a court verifying the necessity of an artistic quotation (and of its extent) in an artwork, however, is rather difficult.

Another burden to the qualification of postmodern original copies as "quotations" is the fact that the cited portion must be secondary in relation to the own achievement.[130] In Andreas Gursky's photographic artwork *Untitled VI* (1997), we clearly recognize Jackson Pollock's *One: Number 31* (1950) as it hangs on the wall of the Museum of Modern Art (MoMA). Gursky does not "add" anything, yet the artwork is a powerful commentary of all that Pollock's art represents. The aura and sacrality we ascribe to paintings of the modern formalist era is, here, made digital, reproducible *ad infinitum*. The "picture within a picture", thus, exposes

127 Childs, p. 26 et seq.

128 Mosimann, Kultur Kunst Recht, N 140 *ad* §1; cf. also De Werra/Benhamou, Kultur Kunst Recht, N 82 et seqq. *ad* § 7.

129 Richard Prince is famous for having (or showing) a careless attitude toward the artworks he appropriates, cf. Prince, Deposition, p. 158 and 192. According to Egloff, Von der "freien Benutzung", p. 407, the correlation between the quoted and the quoting material may simply be indicated by the author himself and must not necessarily arise evidently from the work. However, this is not what the legal text and doctrine say.

130 Disagreeing, Cherpillod, Liberté, p. 358.

the contingence that governs our understanding of art.[131] The photograph does not achieve that through the adding of formal elements but through the sole de- and recontextualization of the painting, the change of medium and subtle technical modifications (such as the digital elimination of people standing and walking in front of the painting).[132]

Even if the proportion between quotation and own achievement was respected, many interpictorial artworks could still face the problem that they do not "designate the quotation as such" explicitly (Art. 25 para. 2 CopA).[133] In this case, the formal requirements are not fulfilled, and the exception risks not applying. Yet, although, for example, Andreas Gursky does not mention the author of the photographed canvas, a public moderately informed about art immediately recognizes it to be "a Jackson Pollock". This is similarly is valid for other artists, whose artworks, even if they have not explicitly indicated their source, use artworks that are easily retraceable, thanks to their fame, to their respective author.[134] Those who *do* mention the sources normally do that in the title of the work or the exhibition (e.g., the aforementioned painting by Ringgold, called *Picasso's Studio*, Elaine Sturtevant's *Warhol's Flowers*, Mike Bidlo's exhibition "Not Leger", Sherrie Levine's *After Walker Evans* and *After Edward Weston*, and many others still). Whether such mentions could, nonetheless, fulfill the formal requirements under Art. 25 para. 2 CopA is not clear.[135]

The question is whether Art. 25 para. 2 CopA has an autonomous meaning or whether it preserves the right of paternity when it would be otherwise infringed. For classics of recent art history that are immediately recognizable to a public relatively informed about art, the formalities at Para. 2 could be redundant. Moreover, images and visual artworks function differently. While text (or a portion thereof) is difficult to relocate after it has been quoted, artworks speak for themselves. A general mention of the name of the artist could, therefore, exceptionally suffice to preserve the paternity right. For other less known works, however, without a proper designation of the source, the public is disoriented with respect to the provenance of the used visual material.

131 Cf. <https://www.sothebys.com/en/auctions/ecatalogue/2012/contemporary-art-evening-n08853/lot.7.html>.

132 For a discussion of the viability of the concept of quotation in the visual arts cf. RÖMER, p. 92 et seq.

133 Cf. RÖMER, p. 92; with found imagery this is also impossible, as the source is often unknown.

134 Cf. RÖMER, p. 89.

135 ZÜLLIG, p. 296 et seq.; MIJATOVIC, Kreativität, p. 104, if the court decides that the citation is not correctly done, the use amounts to a plagiarism. According to Art. 68 CopA, any person who intentionally omits the source used when required by statute (Articles 25 and 28) and when the author is named therein, to provide the name of the author, is liable to a fine on the complaint of the person whose rights have been infringed.

I.V The special case of the "artistic quotation"

I.V.I The artistic quotation in Germany

In Germany, the artistic quotation ("Kunstzitat") is a peculiar form of quotation,[136] defined as the reproduction of works in other works for artistic purposes.[137] The artistic quotation is not explicitly regulated in the DE-CopA, but it is, rather, derived from a specifically artistic view ("kunstspezifische Betrachtung") of the statutory exception of quotation stipulated at § 51 DE-CopA, directly drawn from Art. 5 para. 3 of the German Constitution.[138]

The artistic quotation was introduced by the GFCC in the case *Germania 3*, decided in the year 2000. Playwright and writer Heiner Müller had included in his theater play "Germania 3 – Gespenster am toten Mann" extensive extracts from Bertolt Brecht's *Leben des Galilei* and *Coriolan*. The Munich appellate court had decided that the use of Brecht's works was not a quotation, as they did not fulfill a function of documentation ("Belegfunktion") and, consequently, no "inner correlation" could be found between the two works.[139] The GFCC overturned the judgment of the previous instance by stating that Heiner Müller's artistic freedom, which had not been sufficiently considered, allowed for a quotation to be used as a means for artistic expression beyond the limitations set out at § 51 DE-CopA.[140] The artistic quotation is applicable to all works of art whose authors can invoke the constitutional artistic freedom under Art. 5 para. 3 of the German Constitution.[141]

Three special treatments are granted to the artistic quotation; the first is that the quotation does not forcibly absolve the documentation function ("Belegfunktion") normally prescribed by § 51 DE-CopA;[142] the second is that the source could be not as clearly indicated as § 63 para. 1 DE-CopA would otherwise require;[143] the third is that the prohibition of alterations according to § 62 para. 1 DE-CopA is not to be interpreted as narrowly as with other quotations.[144] The quoted work must, however, maintain a secondary position in relation to the quoting work and not disturb the economical exploitation of the original.[145] The quoted work must insert itself in the artistic configuration of a new work and become an integral part of an autonomous artistic statement.[146]

For DÖHL/HUI, this extensive interpretation of the quotation freedom creates legal uncertainty, failing to provide clear conditions to determine whether reuses

136 MAASSEN, p. 235; SCHACK, N 339, speaks of "exceptional position".
137 KAKIES, N 7.
138 MAASSEN, p. 236; GFCC of June 29, 2000 (*Germania 3*), ZUM 2000, p. 867 et seqq., p. 869.
139 FÖRSTER, p. 105.
140 FÖRSTER, p. 106.
141 SCHULZE, Aneignung, p. 47.
142 GFCC of June 29, 2000 (*Germania 3*), ZUM 2000, p. 867 et seqq., p. 869; MAASSEN, p. 236; KAKIES, N 142 et seqq.; SCHULZE, Aneignung, p. 47.
143 SCHACK, N 339.
144 SCHACK, N 339.
145 SCHACK, N 339; SCHULZE, Aneignung, p. 49.
146 MAASSEN, p. 236; KAKIES, N 138

in the arts are lawful quotations. Ultimately, getting rid of the requirements typical of the copyright exception of quotation (limits to the extent, prohibition to alter, mentioning of the source) causes the quotation to lose its characteristic traits and become a sort of general and unforeseeable exception.[147]

Moreover, as discussed in Chapter 4, III.IV.II, for the case of free utilization in Germany, the possibility of larger interpretations of copyright exceptions derived from the Constitutional artistic freedom operated by the courts of Member States has likely been put to an end by the CJEU.[148] As it had done in previous rulings already, the CJEU stated that the enumeration of exceptions at Art. 5 para. 3 of Infosoc-Directive is exhaustive and argued that derogating from an author's exclusive rights beyond the limits set out by Art. 5 of Infosoc-Directive would "endanger the effectiveness of the harmonisation of copyright and related rights effected by that directive, as well as the objective of legal certainty pursued by it".[149] The exception of quotation is stipulated by Art. 5 para. 3 letter d of Infosoc-Directive and interpreted by the CJEU as requiring an accessory use of the cited material, a narrow correlation between citing and cited material as well as "necessity".[150] The fact that Art. 5 para. 3 let. d Infosoc-Directive does not reach as broadly as the German jurisprudence of the "Kunstzitat" had previously permitted speaks against its compatibility with EU legislation.[151]

I.V.II The "artistic quotation" in Switzerland

In Switzerland, no court has yet had the occasion to express itself on the subject of artworks quoting other artworks and on the lawfulness of their borrowings and their extent. A decision, DFC 131 III 480 (*Schweizerzeit*), concerning a journalistic-political quotation is, nonetheless, informative as to the existence of the "artistic quotation" under Swiss copyright law.

The decision concerned the word-for-word reproduction of two articles in a right-wing Swiss newspaper called *Schweizerzeit*. The two articles were originally published one week apart in the *Tagesanzeiger*; the first article was written by a right-wing politician, who later gave his permission to *Schweizerzeit* to entirely reproduce his article; the second article, a counterstatement to the first, was written by a historian, also president of the "Federal Commission against Racism", who never consented in the republication of his article in the *Schweizerzeit*. The latter, as well as the publisher of the *Tagesanzeiger*, later sued the *Schweizerzeit* for copyright and personality rights infringement.

147 Döhl/Hui, p. 884 et seq.

148 Egloff, Von der "freien Benutzung", p. 401; the CJEU expressly reserves an interpretation of the norms that conform to the fundamental rights but puts an end to the outright opening of new copyright exceptions via fundamental rights, cf. Leistner, Ende gut, p. 1012.

149 CJEU of July 29, 2019 - C-476/17 (*Metall auf Metall*), at para. 63.

150 Leistner, Ende gut, p. 1012.

151 Döhl/Hui, p. 885.

With a broad interpretation of the exception of quotation based on the constitutional right to freedom of expression (Art. 16 of the Federal Constitution) and of the media (Art. 17 Federal Constitution), the Zurich Court of Appeals concluded that neither the copyright nor the personality rights of the historian had been infringed. The historian appealed against this decision; in his appeal to the SFSC, he lamented an infringement of the right to quotation stipulated by Art. 25 CopA and, therefore, of his right of reproduction of Art. 10 para. 2 let. a and b CopA.

In the judgment, the SFSC clarified that, with the statutory exceptions to copyright regulated in Art. 19–28 CopA, the Swiss legislature had exhaustively regulated collisions between fundamental rights (which, in the case of copyright, always collide with the guarantee of ownership anchored at Art. 26 Federal Constitution). In doing so, the legislature strove for an optimal balance between the conflicting interests.[152] The residual tensions between fundamental rights underlying Art. 25 CopA could only be considered in the framework of an "accessory" interpretation in conformity with the Constitution ("verfassungskonforme Auslegung").[153] The previous instance could not simply give the priority to the freedoms of expression and of the media beyond the concessions already set out by Art. 25 CopA.

In the concrete case, the judges of the SFSC concluded that, for the observance of the Constitutional rights of the defendant, a quotation of extracts from the article would have sufficed.[154] The approach of the lower instance was rejected because it had resulted in the creation of a *de facto* new copyright exception that had not been stipulated by the Swiss legislature.[155] The possibility of stretching copyright exceptions beyond their wording by resorting to constitutional rights was, thus, denied by the SFSC in DFC 131 III 480 (*Schweizerzeit*). In conclusion, this decision clarifies that there is no space for an artistic quotation ("Kunstzitat") in Switzerland.[156]

I.VI Other exceptions and their limitations for the justification of interpictorial art

I.VI.I Panorama (Art. 27 CopA)

Art. 27 CopA regulates the so-called freedom of panorama ("Panoramafreiheit"). As Para. 1 of the norm states, a work permanently situated in a place accessible to the public may be depicted, and this depiction may be offered, transferred, broadcast or otherwise distributed. Here, "depiction" means visual reproductions

152 DFC 131 III 480 (*Schweizerzeit*), c. 3.1.; similarly, Opinion of AG Spuznar of December 12, 2018 - C-476/17 (*Metall auf Metall*), at para. 90 and 95: "EU copyright law takes account of various rights and interests which could conflict with the exclusive rights of authors and other rightholders, in particular the freedom of the arts"; "so far as concerns copyright, copyright law itself achieves this through the provision of a number of limitations and exceptions".

153 DFC 131 III 480 (*Schweizerzeit*), c. 3.1 refers to two decisions (DFC 129 II 249, c. 5.4; DFC 128 V 20, c. 3), in which it is stated that an interpretation of the law in conformity with the Constitution can by no means go beyond the wording of the law.

154 DFC 131 III 480 (*Schweizerzeit*), c. 3.2.

155 DFC 131 III 480 (*Schweizerzeit*), c. 3.2 *in fine*.

156 Mosimann, Kultur Kunst Recht, N 139 *ad* §1 and N 140 *ad* § 4.

of the works. It is not permitted to perform the work in other ways, nor to record its sounds (for example, in case of a moving sculpture by Jean Tinguely).[157] The provision primarily concerns works of visual art (Art. 2 para. 2 let. c CopA)[158] but also works of architecture (Art. 2 para. 2 let. e CopA)[159] and photography (Art. 2 para. 2 let. g CopA).[160] The number of visual reproductions is not limited either, and these may be used for commercial purposes as well (meaning that the rights of the author of the work under Art. 10 para. 2 let. a, b, and c CopA are suspended). The right to recognition of authorship is reserved according to Art. 9 para. 1 CopA, as is the right to integrity of the work according to Art. 11 para. 2 CopA. The author has, thus, the enforceable right to be named in the reproductions covered by the freedom of panorama, and he can object to distortions of his work.[161]

Decisive for the admissibility of reproduction is the factual accessibility to the work that has to be located in Switzerland.[162] Works exposed on public grounds that are freely accessible are the primary example of works falling under Art. 27 CopA, but works located on private property that are visible from public ground (for example, the façade of a house visible from the street or a statue in a private garden visible from the adjacent sidewalk)[163] qualify for the freedom of panorama.[164] BARRELET/EGLOFF even include under the freedom of panorama works exhibited in publicly visible vitrines.[165] Only reproductions of the copy of the work that is publicly exposed are permitted, not of other copies of the same work found elsewhere, for example, in a museum.[166]

The works must be located on this accessible position permanently. However, even a temporary exhibition qualifies for the freedom under Art. 27 CopA,[167]

157 BARRELET/EGLOFF, CopA Commentary, N 3 *ad* Art. 27; REHBINDER/HAAS/UHLIG, OFK CopA, N 3 *ad* Art. 27.

158 BARRELET/EGLOFF, CopA Commentary, N 3 *ad* Art. 27.

159 BARRELET/EGLOFF, CopA Commentary, N 3 *ad* Art. 27.

160 REHBINDER/HAAS/UHLIG, OFK CopA, N 2 *ad* Art. 27.

161 BARRELET/EGLOFF, CopA Commentary, N 6 *ad* Art. 27; MACCIACCHINI/OERTLI, SHK CopA, N 13 et seq. *ad* Art. 27 CopA, partially relativizing: as the mentioning of authorship is not regulated in the article – as is the case for Art. 25 CopA – it only applies when it is “customary”.

162 REHBINDER/HAAS/UHLIG, OFK CopA, N 9 *ad* Art. 27.

163 BARRELET/EGLOFF, CopA Commentary, N 4 *ad* Art. 27.

164 MACCIACCHINI/OERTLI, SHK CopA, N 4 *ad* Art. 27.

165 BARRELET/EGLOFF, CopA Commentary, N 4 *ad* Art. 27. This would suggest, however, that even works exposed in an art gallery that are freely visible from the adjacent sidewalk may be depicted by resorting to the freedom of panorama, which we think goes beyond the intention of the legislature; MACCIACCHINI/OERTLI, SHK CopA, N 9 *ad* Art. 27, follow the German interpretation of the article and disagree with the latter affirmation; about this, see DREIER, SHK CopA, p. 364: the German interpretation of the “Panoramafreiheit” is narrower, as it does not encompass works that are, indeed, on public land but that were depicted from a private ground (GFCJ of June 5, 2003 (*Hundertwasser-Haus*), GRUR 2003, p. 1035 et seqq.) and does not consider works as “permanently located” if these are presented within the framework of a temporary exhibition (GFCJ of January 24, 2002 (*Verhüllter Reichstag*), GRUR 2002, p. 605 et seqq.).

166 REHBINDER/HAAS/UHLIG, OFK CopA, N 2 *ad* Art. 27.

167 BARRELET/EGLOFF, CopA Commentary, N 5 *ad* Art. 27; of another opinion are DE WERRA/BENHAMOU, Kultur Kunst Recht, N 91 *ad* § 7 and REHBINDER/UHLIG/HAAS, OFK CopA, N 8 *ad* Art.

provided the works are in their properly assigned location and are not there just randomly.[168] For BARRELET/EGLOFF even works that are normally exhibited indoors and that are just temporarily publicly visible, for example, in the context of a temporary exhibition, are covered by Art. 27 CopA.[169] Moreover, according to MACCIACCHINI/OERTLI, the work may also be depicted alone, i.e., not as part of the panorama where it is inserted.[170]

This very broad scope is restricted at Para. 2, which regulates that the depiction may not be three-dimensional (not even in smaller scale[171]), nor may serve the same purpose as the original. Provided it remains in two-dimensions, the depiction may be realized by means of film and photography (telephoto lenses may be used, too, provided that the work is also recognizable to the naked eye[172]) as well as painting, drawing and so on.[173] For what concerns the purpose, a fresco cannot be realized again as a fresco, and publicly displayed paintings cannot be copied and exposed again in another exhibition.[174]

What will be understood under "same purpose" is not entirely clear. For example, can one realize a painting or a photograph of a publicly visible sculpture and then expose this in an art gallery or a museum? Is the purpose here the exhibition in an artistic context, the artistic medium used or, rather, both cumulatively? The accumulation of exhibition in an artistic context and the artistic medium used seems to be suggested by the examples provided by EGLOFF/BARRELET in their commentary to the provision.[175] In the framework of the US copyright "fair use" defense (more in Chapter 5, II.I), a transformation in purpose does not occur if the artwork is used for another artwork, as, in this case, the court will likely conclude that these share "the same overarching purpose (i.e., to serve as works of visual art)".[176]

27; however, this interpretation is based on the case *wrapped Reichstag* (in German: *Verhüllter Reichstag*) decided by the GFCJ on January 24, 2002 (*Verhüllter Reichstag*), GRUR 2002, p. 605 et seqq.), in which Christo and Jeanne-Claude sued a society that was producing postcards of their oeuvre *wrapped Reichstag* (1995) and won because the German panorama exception is unavailable for works that are only temporary exposed publicly. In Switzerland, however, this does not seem to be the case.

168 BARRELET/EGLOFF, CopA Commentary, N 5 *ad* Art. 27, for example, if they are being transported from one place to another, they are not depictable under Art. 27 CopA.

169 BARRELET/EGLOFF, CopA Commentary, N 4 *ad* Art. 27; MACCIACCHINI/OERTLI, SHK CopA, N 9 *ad* Art. 27, disagree as they follow the German interpretation of the article.

170 MACCIACCHINI/OERTLI, SHK CopA, N 12 *ad* Art. 27.

171 BARRELET/EGLOFF, CopA Commentary, N 7 *ad* Art. 27; Federal Gazette of June 19, 1989 (BBl 1989 III 477), p. 546 explains that it would not be possible to create miniatures of a publicly visible statue and sell it as a souvenir.

172 MACCIACCHINI/OERTLI, SHK CopA, N 5 ad Art. 27.

173 BARRELET/EGLOFF, CopA Commentary, N 6 *ad* Art. 27; MACCIACCHINI/OERTLI, SHK CopA, N 10 *ad* Art. 27 CopA clarify that the application of the norm goes beyond just film and photo reproduction.

174 BARRELET/EGLOFF, CopA Commentary, N 8 *ad* Art. 27.

175 BARRELET/EGLOFF, CopA Commentary, N 8 *ad* Art. 27.

176 Cf. *Andy Warhol Found. for the Visual Arts vs. Goldsmith*, 11 F.4th 26 (2nd Cir. 2021).

Depending on how "purpose" is interpreted, the freedom of panorama could be used to justify interpictorial original copies. If purpose is interpreted as "serving as a work of art", then a publicly exposed artwork cannot be used derivatively to produce a new artwork. Yet, if such purpose is interpreted more narrowly, i.e., as the combination of the used medium and the function as artwork, then the exception becomes broader. Artists could, for example, take a picture of a publicly visible sculpture and include this in their artworks. The Swiss CopA would, thus, allow for a very broad freedom for interpictorial uses of artworks, insofar as these are exposed in a place accessible to the public.

I.VI.II Personal use (Art. 19 para. 1 let. a CopA)

Personal use is regulated in Art. 19 para. 1 let. a CopA as the private use of a published work that is personal or within a circle of persons closely connected to each other, such as relatives or friends (personal sphere). The personal use is available only to natural persons and, for these, free of charge.[177] Within the personal sphere, every use of the work is allowed; the work can be showed, performed, reproduced, distributed and made available (insofar as the person who receives it is part of the circle of closely connected people);[178] and modified, changed and used without authorial credits.[179]

Interpictorial uses, and even the creation of perfect copies of an artwork, are, thus, totally permitted insofar as they occur within the private sphere defined above. An interpictorial use that must remain confined to the personal sphere is, perhaps, useful for the artists' strictly personal practice. Artists may experiment with forms and learn something for their own art, yet, at some point, art will need to be shown. One could go even further and argue that an artwork is only fully realized when it is broadly communicated; exposed in galleries, museums and so on; commented upon; and technically reproduced.[180] The interpictorial artwork may, thus, be created and exist within the framework of a private use. As such, however, it cannot be shown to anyone outside the personal circle. This constitutes a concrete and serious impediment to the fulfillment of its function as artwork.[181]

177 REHBINDER/UHLIG/HAAS, OFK CopA, N 10 *ad* Art. 19; BARRELET/EGLOFF, CopA Commentary, N 11 *ad* Art. 19.

178 REHBINDER/UHLIG/HAAS, OFK CopA, N 12 et seq. *ad* Art. 19.

179 REHBINDER/UHLIG/HAAS, OFK CopA, N 24 *ad* Art. 19.

180 LUHMANN, Art as a Social System, p. 52 et seq. and p. 308: "Today one can even find exhibitions entirely dedicated to paintings that depict exhibitions".

181 MILLET, p. 115

II.I The fair use

The US took a different path compared to Switzerland, EU Member States, Canada, Australia[182] and many more. Whereas all the latter have enacted a closed list of copyright exceptions (we previously exposed those that might be relevant for the protection of artistic copies), the US have – alongside some specific statutory exceptions for libraries, educational and other non-profit uses[183] – an all-purpose general defense called fair use.[184] Fair use provides exceptions to the exclusive rights granted by copyright. By being a dynamic doctrine, it is also relatively open for the creation of new "breathing space",[185] i.e., of a counterbalance to copyright[186] – a legal framework that would otherwise "stifle the very creativity [it] is designed to foster".[187]

II.II A four-factor test

Fair use is codified in the Copyright Act of 1976 at § 107 with a four-factor test that gives courts the discretionary power to decide on a case-by-case basis[188] when the use of a copyrighted work is considered free, i.e., non-infringing,[189] as well as completely free of charge.[190] The introductory clause of § 107 provides an exemplary list of uses that are favored by fair use, such as criticism, comment, news reporting, teaching, scholarship or research.[191] However, it can happen that a use in the list is considered unfair because it fails the four-factor test, as well as a use that does not figure in the list is considered fair.[192] Central are the four steps and their circumstantial evaluation by the judges in each single case.

182 Australia considered introducing an all-purpose fair use defense, but this was ultimately rejected, cf. GINSBURG, Fair use, p. 1414 and NETANEL, Making Sense, p. 717.

183 GINSBURG, Fair use, p. 1386. These exceptions are contained in 17 U.S.C. §108-§122.

184 Notwithstanding the existence of a list of statutory exceptions, fair use still has a central role, cf. KLEINEMENKE, p. 589.

185 "Breathing space" is a concept typical from the field of first amendment (free speech) literature and jurisprudence. It is also found in fair use decisions and literature, something that denotes the connection between copyright discourse and first amendment rationales, cf. NETANEL, Copyright's Paradox, in which he investigates copyright law's conflictual relation to free speech in the United States. According to HUGENHOLTZ/GOLDSTEIN, p. 385, courts in the United States have given constitutional free speech virtually no role in copyright decisions. They explain this by arguing that copyright jurisprudence assimilated from the beginning strong first amendment values: doctrines such as the fair use and the idea-expression distinction make explicit resort to constitutional principles unnecessary, and copyright itself is understood as being "the engine of free expression" in the US.

186 *Campbell vs. Acuff-Rose Music, Inc.*, 510 US 569 (1994), p. 580 et seq.

187 *Campbell vs. Acuff-Rose Music, Inc.*, 510 US 569 (1994), p. 577; cf. TOWSE, p. 15 et seq.

188 LIU, p. 165.

189 NETANEL, Making Sense, p. 719.

190 GINSBURG, Fair use, p. 1385, calling it an "all-or-nothing-choice"; cf. FISCHER VERONIKA, p. 231.

191 NETANEL, Making Sense, p. 720.

192 FISCHER VERONIKA, p. 227; GINSBURG, Copyright, p. 501 and 512; the four factors are not intended as a formula for decision but, rather, as a "checklist", cf. LIU, p. 165.

Under the first factor (1), often concisely called "transformative use",[193] courts look at "the purpose and character of the use, including whether such use is of a commercial nature or is for non-profit educational purposes". The defendant's use of the copyrighted work is considered to be transformative if it adds "something new to the original creation, with a further purpose or a different character, altering the first with new expression, meaning or message".[194] Otherwise it is a merely derivative use.[195]

This definition is susceptible to being interpreted very differently, as courts have developed a variety of definitions of transformation. For example, the work can be transformed by modifying or adding new expression.[196] This happens when the source work is substantially altered in some way, or it is inserted in another context that conveys new and different expression. Transformation can also occur through a change in the purpose or function.[197] A radical change in purpose might tilt the decision in favor of transformativeness, even if the original is not modified and no creative expression is added. Excessive verbatim copying might, however, be a burden to a verdict of fair use, even if the purpose has changed. Scholars signal that where transformation was both purposive as well as with regard to expression, the courts always found the first factor fulfilled.[198]

A change of purpose cannot be affirmed if an artwork (or parts thereof) are used in another artwork, as both share "the same overarching purpose (i.e., to serve as works of visual art)".[199] In this case, according to the court, purpose is not a "useful metric". For interpictorial artworks to fulfill the first factor in this case, they must transform the used visual material more substantially, i.e., through a perceptible change of the artwork's form. Interpictorial uses that do not use a work of visual art but, rather, advertising material have better chances at the first factor even if their use leaves the material relatively unchanged. When a fashion photograph, originally made for a lifestyle magazine, is reproduced in a painting to make a comment about the mass media, the use amounts to a transformation in purpose deemed to fulfill the first factor.[200]

Factor 2 looks at "the nature of the copyrighted work". Under this factor, creative or fictional works are privileged compared to factual or informational works. The same is valid for published works compared to unpublished ones.[201] If the use involves an unpublished, creative work, it is, thus, much less likely to fall into the

193 The "transformative paradigm" was first proposed by justice Pierre N. Leval in his seminal article "Toward a Fair use Standard".

194 *Campbell vs. Acuff-Rose Music, Inc.*, 510 US 569 (1994), p. 579.

195 Cf. *Andy Warhol Found. for the Visual Arts vs. Goldsmith,* 11 F.4th 26 (2nd Cir. 2021), p. 32.

196 Netanel, Making Sense, p. 746 et seq.

197 Netanel, Making Sense, p. 747 et seq.

198 Liu, p. 170, also indicating that purposive transformation is weighed more importantly than physical transformation.

199 *Andy Warhol Found. for the Visual Arts vs. Goldsmith*, 11 F.4th 26 (2nd Cir. 2021).

200 Netanel, Making Sense, p. 748, referring to the *Blanch vs. Koons*, 467 F.3d 244 (2nd Cir. 2006) case.

201 Liu, p. 189.

scope of fair use compared to the use of a published, informational work. However, according to LIU's empirical study, the second factor does not have decisive importance in deciding fair use cases.[202]

The third factor (3) is "the amount or substantiality of the portion used in relation to the copyrighted work as a whole", from both a quantitative as well as a qualitative perspective.[203] On the quantitative side, the third factor determines the amount (meaning volume, extent) of the portion taken from the original work in relation to the rest.[204] On the qualitative side, the factor determines the importance of the portion taken in relation to the whole work. According to LIU's findings, however, the percentage of the portion used did not have a correlation with the outcome of the factor. Copying the entirety of the work was often favorable compared to copying only the work's supposedly most characterizing parts (parts that might be called "the individual traits" of the original work in the Swiss terminology).[205]

The fourth factor (4), i.e., the "effect of the use upon the potential market or value of the work", considers the potential market harm to the original work, i.e., on the primary market as well as the harm to the market of derivative works. Courts look at how opportunities for the original and its derivatives would change on the market if the use of the original, at stake in the proceeding, became widespread.[206] Sometimes courts only assess market harm with respect to "traditional, reasonable or likely to be developed markets".[207] This factor, once called the most important element of fair use in *Harper & Row vs. Nation Enters*, has since then lost importance in favor of the transformative factor.[208] This leads the fair use analysis as its most decisive criterion, often effectively trumping the remaining three.[209] Transformativeness is now used, when fulfilled, as a presumption of no market harm.[210]

202 LIU, p. 190.

203 LIU, p. 193.

204 Cf. *Google LLC vs. Oracle, Inc.*, US 593 (2021), p. 28 et seq., in which the Supreme Court argued that, despite the fact that Google had copied the *per se* substantive amount of 11,500 lines of code, this still represented a mere 0.4% of the total Sun Java API program from which the lines were taken.

205 LIU, p. 193.

206 ASAY/SLOAN/SOBCZAK, p. 916.

207 ASAY/SLOAN/SOBCZAK, p. 916.

208 *Harper & Row Publishers, Inc. vs. Nation Enters.*, 471 US 539, 566 (1985); NETANEL, Making Sense, p. 734 et seqq., since 1994, the year *Campbell vs. Acuff-Rose Music, Inc.*, 510 US 569 (1994) was decided.

209 NETANEL, Making Sense, p. 740; ASAY/SLOAN/SOBCZAK, p. 907 et seq.; LIU, p. 166 and 180, calls it a "shortcut" to fair use.

210 LIU, p. 201.

II.III Interpictoriality under the fair use regime

The use of already existing copyrighted visual material in new artworks does not fall under any statutory exception under the US Copyright Act. Its lawfulness was, thus, always tested under the general defense of fair use.

Artists Jeff Koons,[211] Richard Prince,[212] Barbara Kruger[213] and Andy Warhol[214] have been involved (directly or through the foundations established after their death) in famous fair use disputes concerning artworks they had created, some of them multiple times.[215] It is, therefore, interesting to assess how fair use performed for them and determine to what extent, in general, interpictorial art can be justified under the scope of this defense.

II.III.I Rogers vs. Koons (1992) and Blanch vs. Koons (2006)

The first case involving "star artist" Jeff Koons was decided in 1992. The photographer Art Rogers had portrayed a couple holding eight German shepherd puppies in their arms and staring cheerfully at the camera. The resulting black and white picture was used commercially for greeting cards, one of which was found and bought by Jeff Koons. The artist used the picture as a template for a sculpture (later called *String of Puppies*), the realization of which he outsourced to Italian artisans in 1988 by telling them to use the picture as guidance. The most evident difference between the sculpture and the template picture is that the former is weirdly colored (e.g., the dogs are blue), whereas the picture is black and white. Moreover, the puppies have bigger, cartoonish noses and both man and woman have flowers in their hair and an indecipherable, almost "sedated" look (in the original, they smile at the camera).

The Second Circuit Court found the shifts in medium (from photograph to wooden sculpture), scale, color and even the addition of a dimension (from two- to three-dimensionality) not sufficient for a finding of fair use.[216] The court found that the two artworks were substantially similar and, thus, that *String of Puppies*

211 *Rogers vs. Koons*, 960 F 2d 301 (2nd Cir. 1992), which he lost; *Blanch vs. Koons*, 467 F.3d 244 (2nd Cir. 2006), which he won; the two other cases, *United Feature Syndicate, Inc. vs. Jeff Koons*, 817 F. Supp. 370 (SDNY 1993) and *Campbell vs. Koons*, No. 91-CV-6055, 1993 WL 97381 (SDNY April 1, 1993), were settled out of court after Koons lost at the summary judgment stage.

212 *Donald Graham vs. Richard Prince, et al.*, No. 15-CV-10160 (SDNY July 18, 2017) and *Cariou vs. Prince*, 714 F.3d 694 (2nd Cir. 2013).

213 *Hoepker vs. Kruger*, 200 F.Supp.2d 340 (SDNY 2002).

214 Patricia Caulfield vs. Andy Warhol (1966), the case settled; *Dauman vs. Andy Warhol Found. for Visual Arts, Inc.*, 1997 WL 337488 (SDNY June 19, 1997), *Andy Warhol Found. for the Visual Arts, Inc. vs. Goldsmith*, 598 US ___, 2023. Other suits for copyright infringements filed against Warhol were settled out of court.

215 In another case, *Mattel Inc. vs. Walking Mountain Productions*, 353 F.3d 792 (9th Cir. 2003), photographer Tom Forsythe had used Barbie dolls for the creation of his "Food Chain Barbie" photo series, in which the dolls were portrayed in food processers, ovens and the like. Mattel had argued that Forsythe's use infringed on their copyrights and trademarks. The Ninth Circuit Court ruled that Forsythe's art was fair use because it fulfilled the purpose of criticism and commentary.

216 Buskirk, Creative Intent, p. 247.

was a copy of Rogers's photograph.[217] The court also held that the use could not be parodic, as it did not criticize or comment upon Rogers's photograph but, rather, upon society at large.[218] Moreover, since Koons had sold the sculpture, the use was commercial, which, at that time, strongly implied that it was unfair.[219]

In *Blanch vs. Koons*, decided in 2006, Koons won. As ADLER notes, there are many reasons for this outcome. First, the legal framework had changed slightly. In 1994, *Campbell vs. Acuff-Rose Music* was decided. As explained previously, this decision emphasized the transformative factor and rejected the presumption that a commercial use was prima facie unfair.[220] Second, the disputed *Niagara* (2000) painting, for which Koons had used a picture taken by fashion photographer Andrea Blanch, was a dense assemblage of many visual elements, among which Blanch's picture occupied a relatively marginal position. Decisive for the outcome was also the fact that Koons had not borrowed the "key creative decisions" from Blanch's work but, rather, limited his choice to the element that had been prescribed by the advertising purpose of the photograph.[221] Moreover, according to ADLER, Koons gave the court exactly what it wanted. In stating that he "want[ed] the viewer to think about these images and gain *new insight*", he used the "magic words" that brought the court to conclude for the presence of a transformative use.[222] The Court of Appeals, thus, confirmed the lower instance's summary judgment, stating that Koons's collage used Blanch's photograph not merely by superseding it but by creating a new work of art with different aesthetics and a distinct meaning as well as new information and insights.[223]

II.III.II Cariou vs. Prince (2013)

In 2000, photographer Patrick Cariou published a book of photographs titled *Yes, Rasta*. The book included photographs from a period during which he had done field work in Jamaica, gotten closer to members of the Rastafarian community and portrayed them. In 2008, Richard Prince found and purchased a copy of the book. He then used many images from the book to create his series *Canal Zone* (2008). In Prince's series, the original pictures had been enlarged, their subjects often distorted and, on their surfaces, many collage elements had been added. In 2009, as he

217 In *Rogers vs. Koons*, 751 F. Supp. 474 (SDNY 1990), the first instance had held: "Questions of size and color aside, the sculpture is as exact a copy of the photograph as Koons' hired artisans could fashion, which is precisely what Koons told them to do"; *Rogers vs. Koons*, 960 F 2d 301 (2nd Cir. 1992).

218 *Rogers vs. Koons*, 960 F 2d 301 (2nd Cir. 1992).

219 *Rogers vs. Koons*, 960 F 2d 301 (2nd Cir. 1992). The case was decided before *Campbell vs. Acuff-Rose Music, Inc.*, 510 US 569 (1994), which first put the transformative test at the center of fair use.

220 ADLER, The Future of Art, p. 580 et seq.; BUSKIRK, Creative Intent, p. 246; SPENCE, Rogers v. Koons, p. 217 and 222.

221 BUSKIRK, Creative Intent, p. 246.

222 ADLER, The Future of Art, p. 582.

223 BUSKIRK, Creative Intent, p. 247.

found out about the use, Cariou filed for copyright infringement against Prince and other involved entities, such as the Gagosian Gallery that had exposed the work and published the catalogue. The first instance looking at the case, the Southern District Court of New York found that Prince's works were not transformative under the fair use doctrine and that they were, thus, infringing. It also ordered that Prince's unsold works, along with the printed catalogues, be destroyed.[224]

Upon appeal, the Second Circuit Court reversed the SDNY decision in 2013 and found that 25 of the 30 works at stake were fair use. In the remaining five works, the parties found an extrajudicial agreement. To arrive at this verdict, the appeals court emphasized three aspects. First, it did not consider Prince's statements about his work. The SDNY, on the contrary, had previously emphasized that Prince's statements did not reveal any particular search for meaning, interest in the source work or transformative intent.[225] Second, it rejected the lower court's requirement that Prince's work comment on Cariou's.[226] Third, it focused on a comparison of the aesthetics.

With a judgment based on how the works appear to the "reasonable observer"[227] and "looking at the artworks and the photographs side-by-side",[228] the court concluded that 25 of Prince's 30 artworks "have a *different character,* [and] give Cariou's photographs a *new expression*, and employ *new aesthetics with creative and communicative results distinct from Cariou's*".[229] What the court apparently did, then, was interpret the first factor of the fair use inquiry, i.e., transformativeness, as the necessity of a tangible aesthetical change between the works. The five residual works that were not admitted as fair use "*do not sufficiently differ* from the photographs of Cariou's that they incorporate".[230] In other words, the court argued that "some paintings looked too much like [the borrowed] photographs and others didn't".[231]

In its conclusion, the court also emphasized that there was no evidence of the fact that Prince's alterations usurped the market for Cariou's photographs.[232] With a rather unorthodox argumentation, the judges exposed how certain works from the *Canal Zone* series sold for more than two million US dollars, meaning that Prince's

224 *Cariou vs. Prince*, 784 F. Supp. 2d 337 (SDNY 2011).

225 When asked in his testimony whether he was trying to create a new meaning or a new message, Prince simply answered "No", cf. Adler, The Future of Art, p. 576; we can, thus, conclude that, whereas, Jeff Koons "had given the Court what it wanted", Prince had chosen not to "cooperate". Prince's deposition has been published as Richard Prince (Greg Allen ed.), The Deposition of Richard Prince in the Case of Cariou v. Prince et al, Zurich 2012.

226 *Cariou vs. Prince*, 714 F.3d 694 (2nd Cir. 2013), p. 704.

227 *Cariou vs. Prince*, 714 F.3d 694 (2nd Cir. 2013), p. 707.

228 *Cariou vs. Prince*, 714 F.3d 694 (2nd Cir. 2013), p. 707 et seq.

229 *Cariou vs. Prince*, 714 F.3d 694 (2nd Cir. 2013), p. 708 (emphasis added).

230 *Cariou vs. Prince*, 714 F.3d 694 (2nd Cir. 2013), p. 711 (emphasis added).

231 Adler, The Future of Art, p. 604.

232 *Cariou vs. Prince*, 714 F.3d 694 (2nd Cir. 2013), p. 708 et seq.; Stokes, p. 161; the district court had previously concluded that the fourth factor weighed against fair use and that Prince's artworks damaged the market for Cariou's photographs.

art attracts an entirely different sort of collector than Cariou's. While Prince could boast among his "wealthy and famous" collectors' VIP names (such as musicians Jay-Z and Beyonce Knowles, fellow artists Damien Hirst and Jeff Koons, and actors Robert De Niro, Angelina Jolie, and Brad Pitt), Patrick Cariou remained a relatively unknown photographer who had self-published his photography book.

II.III.III Andy Warhol Foundation for the Visual Arts vs. Goldsmith (2019, 2021, 2023)

In 1984, photographer Lynn Goldsmith licensed one of her photographic portraits of Prince (the singer) to *Vanity Fair* for use as a reference in an illustration, receiving a payment of 400 US dollars and a source credit. The terms of the license included that the use would be for "one time only". *Vanity Fair* passed along the photograph to Andy Warhol, who used his signature silk-screening process to create an illustration to be used in an article about the then rising star in the November 1984 *Vanity Fair* issue. Warhol also created 15 new works from the original photograph.[233] These later became known in the art world as the *Prince Series* (1984). After Prince's death in 2016, Condé Nast (a parent company to *Vanity Fair*) reproduced one of the Warhol versions (the "Orange Prince") for the cover of its memorial issue for the singer. This cover drew the attention of Lynn Goldsmith, who immediately recognized her photograph. In this way, she also became aware of the existence of Warhol's *Prince Series*. Contacted by Goldsmith and threatened with legal action, the Andy Warhol Foundation sued Goldsmith to obtain a declaratory judgment that it had not violated any copyright laws. Goldsmith counterclaimed for infringement.

Perhaps well-instructed by the teachings of *Prince vs. Cariou*, the district court for the SDNY, which first looked at the case, decided in 2019 in favor of the Andy Warhol Foundation, stating that the *Prince Series* were fair use; applying the standards that were set out in *Cariou vs. Prince*, the district court held that "each of the Prince Series work may reasonably be perceived to be transformative of the Goldsmith Prince photograph".[234] That Warhol's work reflects "the opposite" of what Goldsmith's picture communicated was decisive. Instead of a "vulnerable human being", uncomfortable before the camera, Warhol's series made Prince appear as an iconic, larger-than-life figure. Ultimately, then, Warhol's work has an aesthetic and character different from the original. Although commercial in nature, this difference adds value to the broader public interest.[235]

Goldsmith appealed the decision. The Second Circuit Court of appeals, which looked at the case, reversed the judgment in March 2021. The court of appeals

233 Cf. *Andy Warhol Found. for Visual Arts, Inc. vs. Goldsmith*, 382 F. Supp. 3d 312 (SDNY 2019), at para. 319.

234 *Andy Warhol Found. for Visual Arts, Inc. vs. Goldsmith*, 382 F. Supp. 3d 312 (SDNY 2019), at para. 326.

235 *Andy Warhol Found. for Visual Arts, Inc. vs. Goldsmith*, 382 F. Supp. 3d 312 (SDNY 2019), at para. 325.

took the occasion to review all cases in which it had decided on the matter of the transformative nature of works of visual art (*Rogers vs. Koons, Blanch vs. Koons*, and *Cariou vs. Prince*), admitting that they yielded "conflicting guidance". For the court, however, matters become simpler when the works at issue are simply compared against their respective source materials.[236] Based on this substantive comparison, the court of appeals held that a use was transformative when the source work was – as in 25 of 30 works the same court had considered fair in *Cariou vs. Prince* – "obscured and altered to the point that *[the] original was barely recognizable*".[237] On the contrary, the use was not transformative when the source work remained, as it did in *Rogers vs. Koons* and in the remaining five works in *Cariou vs. Prince*, "*a major if not dominant component of the impression* created by the allegedly infringing work".[238] At a bare minimum, the court held, "the secondary work must comprise *something more* than the imposition of another artist's style on the primary work such that the secondary work remains both recognizably deriving from, and retaining the essential elements of, its source material".[239] The sudden recognizability as "a Warhol", which, for the first instance, was evidence of the occurred transformation of the aesthetics, could not be considered because it would create a "celebrity-plagiarist privilege".[240] After carrying out such clarifications – and viewing the works side-by-side – the court concluded that the *Prince Series* was not transformative.

After the judgment of the Second Circuit Court of Appeals, the Andy Warhol Foundation turned to the Supreme Court, which agreed, in March 2022, to hear the case. In May 2023, the Supreme Court delivered its judgment. The question presented before the court was whether the first fair use factor (transformativeness) weighed in favor of the Foundation's licensing to Condé Nast. The legal question was, thus, narrowed down to the first factor of fair use, and the facts at stake were limited to that one challenged use.[241] In particular, the court did not elaborate on the question whether Warhol's use of the photograph for the creation of his *Prince Series* was fair or not.[242]

The Supreme Court affirmed the decision of the previous instance. It held that the question whether a use has a further purpose or a different character is a matter of degree and that the degree of difference must be weighed against other

236 *Andy Warhol Found. for the Visual Arts vs. Goldsmith*, 11 F.4th 26 (2nd Cir. 2021), p. 24 (emphasis added).

237 *Andy Warhol Found. for the Visual Arts vs. Goldsmith*, 11 F.4th 26 (2nd Cir. 2021), p. 25 (emphasis added).

238 *Andy Warhol Found. for the Visual Arts vs. Goldsmith*, 11 F.4th 26 (2nd Cir. 2021), p. 25 (emphasis added).

239 *Andy Warhol Found. for the Visual Arts vs. Goldsmith*, 11 F.4th 26 (2nd Cir. 2021), p. 25 (emphasis added).

240 *Andy Warhol Found. for the Visual Arts vs. Goldsmith*, 11 F.4th 26 (2nd Cir. 2021), p. 31 (emphasis added).

241 *Andy Warhol Found. for the Visual Arts, Inc. vs. Goldsmith*, 598 US ___ (2023), p. 2, 12.

242 *Andy Warhol Found. for the Visual Arts, Inc. vs. Goldsmith*, 598 US ___ (2023), p. 21.

considerations, including commercialism.[243] From this premise, the court found that the use of *Orange Prince* on the cover of Condé Nast and Lynn Goldsmith's photograph of Prince share substantially the same purpose: "both are portraits of Prince used in magazines to illustrate stories about Prince".[244] A use that shares the same purpose of the original is, according to the court, more likely to substitute it, which undermines the goal of copyright.[245] The Andy Warhol Foundation's licensing of the *Orange Prince* "superseded the objects, i.e., shared the objective of Goldsmith's photograph, even if the two were not perfect substitutes".[246] The court went further and held that the more this purpose is similar, the more other justifications are required for copying. It found, however, that the Foundation's 2016 licensing to Condé Nast is of commercial nature and, thus, "both elements [transformativeness and commercial character] point in the same direction".[247] The court also refused the claim of the Andy Warhol Foundation that *Orange Prince* has a new meaning or message, in particular that it conveys the "dehumanizing nature of celebrity". According to the justices, not every use that adds some new expression, meaning or message can be justified as fair lest transformativeness would swallow the copyright owner's right to prepare derivative works.[248]

The change of meaning or message must reasonably be perceived by the observer: the *Orange Prince*, the court considered, merely portrays Prince somewhat differently from Goldsmith's photograph. Given the specific context of use (which shares the same purpose as Goldsmith's original), the degree of difference was not enough for the first factor to favor the Andy Warhol Foundation.[249] Moreover, Warhol's use did not specifically target, comment upon or criticize Goldsmith's photograph, as would be required to be considered a parody, but limited itself to comment on Prince himself, his celebrity status and celebrity culture in general.[250]

Some elements of the decision stand out. First, the Supreme Court gave considerable importance to the commercial character of the use. That, together with the purpose of the use (which the court considered was substantially the same as with Goldsmith's photograph), suggested that the Foundation's use acted as a substitute for the copyrighted work, shrinking its potential market opportunities. These considerations, made (at length) in the framework of deciding the first fair use factor, are surprising, as market substitution is typically an element of the fourth use factor.[251] Still, it can be speculated whether the court did not – *e contrario* – justify

243 *Andy Warhol Found. for the Visual Arts, Inc. vs. Goldsmith*, 598 US ___ (2023), p. 12 and 20 et seq.
244 *Andy Warhol Found. for the Visual Arts, Inc. vs. Goldsmith*, 598 US ___ (2023), p. 22 et seq.
245 *Andy Warhol Found. for the Visual Arts, Inc. vs. Goldsmith*, 598 US ___ (2023), p. 19.
246 *Andy Warhol Found. for the Visual Arts, Inc. vs. Goldsmith*, 598 US ___ (2023), p. 24.
247 *Andy Warhol Found. for the Visual Arts, Inc. vs. Goldsmith*, 598 US ___ (2023), p. 25.
248 *Andy Warhol Found. for the Visual Arts, Inc. vs. Goldsmith*, 598 US ___ (2023), p. 28.
249 *Andy Warhol Found. for the Visual Arts, Inc. vs. Goldsmith*, 598 US ___ (2023), p. 33.
250 *Andy Warhol Found. for the Visual Arts, Inc. vs. Goldsmith*, 598 US ___ (2023), p. 24.
251 This aspect did not go uncriticized. Justice Elena Kagan commented on it in her dissenting opinion to *Andy Warhol Found. for the Visual Arts, Inc. vs. Goldsmith*, 598 US ___ (2023), p. 21: "the majority transplants factor 4 into factor 1".

the mere existence of the *Prince Series* as artwork exemplars, i.e., outside the commercial context of their use, which it held had superseded the original.

Another interesting point is that the court insisted multiple times that justification of a use under the first factor is a matter of degree (among others, the degree of difference, intended as the degree of visible transformation between the two works). It, thus, clarified that decontextualization itself is not recognized as a change of form (as with an on/off switch) but, rather, that the more the purpose of the work remained the same, the more incisive the transformation must be. The fact that the court asked whether the degree of transformation was sufficient, however, already dooms interpictorial artworks at failing the fair use test, as it measures their lawfulness based on a criterion that they willingly do not fulfill. Moreover, the judgment on sufficient transformation is forcibly very subjective. With this criterion, fair use becomes highly unpredictable (which also explains why the case had been pending in court for almost 7 years and that, based on the very same factor, it achieved a completely different outcome in the first instance).

One other point is worth emphasizing, namely that the court underlined the exclusively legal character of the question, dismissing the dissenting opinion, in which Justice Elena Kagan had proceeded with an analysis of Warhol's undertaking informed by art history and the opinion of art experts. The court wrote that "in tracing the history of the Renaissance painting…, the dissent loses sight of the statute and this Court's cases". It then went further and held, not without a tone of sarcasm, that even though "the Lives of the Artists undoubtedly makes for livelier reading, than the US Code or the US Reports, *[the Court] does not have that luxury*".[252] Instead of recognizing the importance of an interdisciplinary approach in handling questions of the lawfulness of visual art in terms of copyright law, the court abruptly shut the door to such an opening.[253]

On one point the US Supreme Court is to be agreed with is that it rightly underlined that the work of Goldsmith was unpublished. Because the picture had not circulated before, Warhol's use targeted and commented on Prince's *persona*, rather than on Prince, as he was portrayed in the work. The element of "mediality", i.e., the quality of the photograph as a means of communication, perceived by the public and used to convey a message, was missing in this case. Because it had still not been communicated, the photograph still had not assumed an existence of its own in society. In other words, one could not recognize the element of interpictoriality (that is, the reference to another artwork) by looking at Warhol's oeuvre.

252 *Andy Warhol Found. for the Visual Arts, Inc. vs. Goldsmith*, 598 US ___ (2023), p. 36 et seq. (emphasis added).

253 Here, too, Justice Elene Kagan expressed her criticism: In the dissenting opinion to *Andy Warhol Found. for the Visual Arts, Inc. vs. Goldsmith*, 598 US ___ (2023), p. 9, 17 et seq., she underlined how the majority of the court simply ignored the opinion of experts.

II.IV A brief comparative analysis[254]

Every copyright regime contains limitations to the rights accruing from the creation of a work. These define spaces of freedom within which the public can exercise creativity.[255] From the point of view of its function, fair use is the way US Copyright law found to counterbalance copyright and prevent it from "stifl[ing] the very creativity [it] is designed to foster".[256] It, therefore, absolves a very similar function to statutory civil law exceptions (as, for example, the exception provisions of parody and quotation).[257] Although the systems are different in many ways, a comparison shows that some characteristics of civil copyright law can be found, perhaps in a slightly varied form, in the US copyright system.

When US courts look at whether the use of copyrighted work is transformative, they are doing something comparable to civil law courts measuring the distance the downstream work creates from the source. The modification of the work or the adding of new expression has a parallel in the classical distance doctrine, in which it is controlled whether and to which extent the work has faded in its use.[258] Transformation under fair use can also comprise instances of wholesale copying.[259] In this case, a parallel can be drawn to the now obsolete German concept of inner distance and to all other statutory exceptions, the fulfillment of which is controlled by ascertaining the content beyond the surface (form) of the work.[260] Indeed, a transformative change is often assumed in cases of parodic use and quoting for making a commentary or criticism, i.e., uses that are typically subsumed under civil law exceptions.[261] Whereas, in the US, a transformative use is judged from a utilitarian-economical perspective, in European copyright systems the protection of moral rights remains reserved, even if the use per se would have fallen in a copyright exception.[262] So, a user could have quoted a source in fulfillment of the requirements set out at Art. 25 CopA, but he could have simultaneously violated the personal rights of the original author (Art. 11 para. 2 CopA).[263] Similarly, a use may be covered by the panorama exception, but if the author has not been named, he maintains the right to sue for infringement of his right to paternity (Art. 9 para. 1 CopA).

254 The comparative analysis is limited to the exceptions and does not cover the rights. In the US, with the "modicum of creativity" doctrine established with *Feist Publications, Inc., vs. Rural Telephone Service Co.*, originality is understood much more comprehensively than in civil law countries, cf. GEIGER, Flexibilising Copyright, p. 188. Such a threshold is equated in Europe only punctually with the "small coin" doctrine.

255 ORTLAND, Bildregime, p. 286; FISCHER VERONIKA, p. 226 and 231.

256 *Campbell vs. Acuff-Rose Music, Inc.*, 510 US 569 (1994), p. 577; cf. TOWSE, p. 15 et seq.

257 Cf. EGLOFF, Commentary CopA, N 1 *ad* Vorbemerkungen Art. 19-28; BLUME HUTTENLAUCH, p. 57.

258 FISCHER VERONIKA, p. 227; JAYME, p. 37.

259 NETANEL, Making Sense, p. 748.

260 FISCHER VERONIKA, p. 227.

261 NETANEL, Making Sense, p. 746.

262 BARRELET/EGLOFF, CopA Commentary, N 18 *ad* 11; FISCHER VERONIKA, p. 230.

263 BARRELET/EGLOFF, CopA Commentary, N 18 *ad* 11.

Elements of the second factor can be found in those considerations of civil law courts measuring the extent and intensity of the first work's individual character. Works of low individuality, so-called small coins, are easier to use with relatively little modification compared to works of considerable individuality.[264] Similarly, this happens in the US with factual-informational work compared to creative or fictional works.[265] Because of the important difference between the two copyright systems with respect to moral rights, in civil law systems, such considerations are entangled with the protection of the personality of the author. Changing a work showcasing a higher degree of individuality is also often coupled to an enhanced risk of infringing the moral rights of its author, even though in Switzerland, the individual character is not associated with the personality of the author anymore.[266] The second factor also looks at whether the work was published or not, favoring the use of published works over unpublished ones. In Switzerland and Germany, only published works can be object of quotations, according to the explicit rule in Art. 25 para. 1 CopA and § 51 DE-CopA. In Germany, the new provision regulating parodies, caricatures and pastiches also provides for this explicit limitation (§ 51a DE-CopA). Despite the lack of an explicit mention in the Swiss parody provision, the effect is virtually the same in its application, as the works parody use must be known, at least to some extent, in order for the parodic effect to happen. Their previous disclosure is an unwritten but *de facto* condition.[267] Again, the important difference of moral rights shall be stressed. Whereas, in European systems, the right to publication is, essentially, a moral right, in the US, it is mainly perceived from an economic perspective.[268]

The third factor considers the amount and importance of the used work. In the US, these aspects are considered in relation to the copied work,[269] i.e., courts look at the ratio between the original work in its entirety and the copied portion. In Switzerland and Germany, the amount and importance of the used work are, instead, put in relation to the new work.[270] However, in both copyright systems, the

264 Fischer Veronika, p. 228; in Switzerland cf. DFC 125 III 328 (*Niederhauser*), p. 333 c. 4, in which the SFSC stated that a weak individuality is more eager to "fade" in the background of a new work's individual character.

265 The analysis of substantial similarity does a similar job in determining the extent of the author's right on her work, cf. Chapter 5, II.1.

266 Egloff, CopA Commentary, N 38 *ad* Art. 2; Barrelet/Egloff, CopA Commentary, N 20 *ad* Art. 11; Oertli, p. 604.

267 See Chapter 5, I.II.

268 Fischer Veronika, p. 229, the moral right to first publication is in force in the Swiss and German systems (respectively at Art. 9 para. 2 CopA and § 12 para. 1 DE-CopA).

269 Paradigmatic are the elucubrations of the Supreme Court in the *Google LLC vs. Oracle, Inc.*, US 593 (2021), p. 28 et seq. case: "If a defendant had copied one sentence in a novel, that copying may well be insubstantial. But if that single sentence set forth one of the world's shortest short stories…the question looks much different, as the copied material constitutes a small part of the novel but the entire short story".

270 Fischer Veronika, p. 228; Dreier/Jehle, S. 229; Decision of the Zurich Court of Appeal of January 24, 2013 (*Bildungssoftware*), sic! 2013, p. 697 et seqq., c. ii.5.2; Decision of the Zurich

more an author takes from the original, the more difficult it becomes not to infringe on the copyright of the previous author. So, even if the focus is set on a different aspect, the effect is similar.[271] A line can also be drawn back to the first fair use factor, as, ultimately, the extent of copying depends on the purpose and on the character of the intended use. Transformative users will have a greater leeway in taking considerable portions of the work if their intended use justifies this taking.[272] This strict necessity, i.e., whether and to what extent the use justifies the taking, is also considered in Switzerland within the exception of quotation.[273]

The only factor that does not have an equivalent in the German and Swiss national legal systems is the fourth factor, which considers potential market harm.[274] A control of how the economical exploitation of the work is impaired by the use was introduced in civil law systems by means of the three-step test included in many international conventions.[275] As the US fair use historical development shows, judges now associate a transformative use to an unlikeliness of market harm, especially because a transformative use is no market substitute for the original.[276] On the contrary, they assume that a non-transformative use will likely compete directly with the original work (i.e., supersede it).[277] A formal or purposive transformation of the original works is, thus, generally used as a proxy to inform whether the use will compete on the market or not.[278]

II.V The reception of the fair use in civil law copyright systems

Fair use has been received by copyright scholarship in Switzerland and in other European countries in essentially two ways. On the one hand, the fair use defense is praised for its enhanced flexibility, which also bring resilience for new developments and adaptability to unforeseen needs. These advantages are considered lacking in the civil law framework, often considered rigid and inflexible.[279] The requirement of the "transformative use" is seen as better suited to encompass

---

Court of Appeal of October 11, 2010 (*Source Code*), sic! 2011, p. 230 et seqq., p. 232, with further references.

271 Asay/Sloan/Sobczak, p. 919; Tushnet, Thousand Words, p. 716.

272 Asay/Sloan/Sobczak, p. 919 et seq.

273 See Chapter 5, I.IV.

274 Fischer Veronika, p. 230.

275 See Chapter 7. However, the three-step test is not verified in *each* decision taken by national courts on the applicability of a copyright exception.

276 *Mattel Inc. vs. Walking Mountain Productions*, 353 F.3d 792 (9th Cir. 2003), p. 805.

277 Liu, p. 171.

278 Fischer Veronika, p. 229 et seq.; Ginsburg, Exceptional Authorship, p. 19; Adler, The Future of Art, p. 622; as in Subotnik, p. 1494, "proxy" is intended in the sense of a means of verifying something by verifying something else; transformation is seen in terms of maximization of societal benefit: "the goal of copyright – to promote science and the arts", so the *Campbell vs. Acuff-Rose Music, Inc.*, 510 US 569 (1994), p. 579, "is generally furthered by the creation of transformative works".

279 In Switzerland: Rigamonti, Grundrechte, p. 392; Brändli-Marmy, p. 328, p 329 and 177 et seq. In Europe, Mendis, p. 32 et seq.; Kleinemenke, p. 585 et seq. It must be pointed out that many of

appropriation art and other similar artistic practices that rely on the use of previous works, as rather than trying to measure the extent of the pre-existing forms visible in the second work, it focuses on the artistic intention and creative power of the second work.[280]

On the other hand, this flexibility is associated with a backlash of criticism for the increase in legal uncertainty supposedly related to it.[281] The fair use doctrine might be too broad and too unpredictable, therefore creating legal uncertainty. This is also the most frequent complaint about fair use voiced by copyright scholars in the US,[282] with some commentators going as far as suggesting that courts welcome the transformative test precisely because of its ambiguity, which is a way to implement their intuitive judgments flexibly and yet maintain the impression of *stare decisis*.[283]

In regard to interpictoriality in the visual arts, we cannot identify any significantly different evolution in the US copyright system that would resolve "the problem" of the unlawfulness of certain artworks. While some artists have achieved positive outcomes for their art (Jeff Koons in *Blanch vs. Koons*, Richard Prince in *Prince vs. Cariou*), there is no clear and uncontested strategy (nor an intention) to de-criminalize appropriation in visual art. Successes are isolated exceptions and denote a general superiority of fair use compared to civil law copyright systems. On the contrary, the most recent decision of the Supreme Court on this very topic showed that the US judiciary has a long way to go to recognize interpictoriality in visual art as a potentially lawful transformation of "original works" (and to clarify, we do not affirm this because of the concrete result achieved in *Andy Warhol Foundation for Visual Arts, Inc. vs. Goldsmith* but, rather, because of its argumentation that did not take into account the subtilities of the interpictorial treating of already existing artworks).

Ultimately, notwithstanding what could appear by reading much of the scholarship in Switzerland and the EU, the grass is not greener (or not much, in any case) on the other side of the Atlantic. European courts have interpreted provisions amply and dynamically, making new unauthorized uses non-infringing even though no exception tailored to this end existed. The result is that, in a variety of controversial

---

the demands for a more flexible framework for the exceptions to copyright refer to the needs of technological developments rather than to the needs of revolutionary artistic movements.

280 EGLOFF, Von der "freien Benutzung", p. 408.

281 HAAS, p. 218 et seqq.: flexibility and economic efficiency but legal uncertainty; BLUME HUTTENLAUCH, p. 84 et seq. seems to fear the insecurity brought about by the fair use; at p. 203, however, she considers the market substitution test to be advantageous; cf. in general RENDAS, p. 3 and 8 et seq.

282 ASAY/SLOAN/SOBCZAK, p. 917; ADLER, The Future of Art, p. 562, 564 (with further references),

283 LIU, p. 172.

topics (e.g., visual art, thumbnails, reuse of code),[284] the outcomes reached in Europe and in the US largely converge, despite the doctrinal differences.[285]

III.I Interim conclusions: Two parameters of copyright exceptions

The handling of visual art interpictoriality under copyright law depends on a variety of aspects, namely on whether the used material is protected by copyright, the scope of protection attributed to the work and how the downstream use is qualified as well as whether the use of the work falls into a copyright exception and, thus, within its own, specific rules. Within the complex mechanisms of copyright protection, the law stipulates spaces of freedom within which artists may be able to use copyrighted works without asking for permission while avoiding being prosecuted for copyright infringement. Ultimately, "not all copying is copyright infringement".[286] We can identify two parameters according to which the decision on whether a use of previously existing and copyrighted material is infringing is taken. On one side, courts look at the content and/or purpose of the work (1). Under this parameter, the copyrighted work does not need to be perceptibly changed in order for its use to be considered lawful. A purposive change, or a transformation of the message of the work, suffice. On the other side, courts verify whether the use is lawful based on the novelty it succeeds in creating. A material distance or a visible transformation is, thus, helpful to substantiate a non-infringing use (2).

III.II The parameter of content or purpose

Given how a copyrighted work is defined, courts do not spontaneously ascertain whether there are individual, protectable elements beyond the surface of the work's form. Consequently, the similarity of two artifacts' perceptible forms prominently signals that a work (or at least some elements thereof) has been used.

Whereas the determination of copyright protection sticks to the visible surface of the artifact, i.e., those that are recognizable to the senses (what we have called "the form"), the underlying, intelligible components of the artifact (what we have

284 On the lawfulness of thumbnails, for example, US and European courts achieved similar results. The US Court of Appeals for the Ninth Circuit found the use to be fair in *Kelly vs. Arriba Soft Corp.*, 336 F.3d 811 (9th Cir. 2003) the GFCJ did so in its three *Vorschaubilder* decisions (cf. the last of September 21, 2017 (*Vorschaubilder III*), GRUR 2018, p. 178 et seqq.). The Cour d'appel de Paris achieved a similar result in Cour d'appel de Paris of January 26, 2011 (*SAIF c. Google*). On caching, a staple in the functioning of web searches, the Nevada District Court ruled in *Field vs. Google, Inc.*, 412 F. Supp. 2d 1106 (D. Nev. 2006) that it was lawful. The CJEU achieved the same result in its decision of June 5, 2014 - C-360/13 (*Public Relations Consultants Association Ltd. vs. Newspaper Licensing Agency Ltd. and Others*). In the decision of the Spanish Tribunal Supremo of April 3, 2012 (*Megakini.com vs. Google Spain*), the Spanish Supreme Court also achieved the same outcome, i.e., considered Google's caching non-infringing.

285 Rendas, p. 3.

286 *Feist Publications, Inc., vs. Rural Telephone Service Co.*, 499 US 340 (1991), p. 361; Amicus Brief, p. 5 and 11; cf. also Ginsburg, Copyright, p. 509.

called "the content") as well as the context and the function (the "purpose") are at the forefront in the ascertainment of a copyright exception's applicability. The used work may (and in some cases must) remain recognizable in the downstream artifact, but the latter could still be deemed an autonomous creation, nonetheless.[287] We call this attention of courts for an invisible change in message, meaning or creative intention the "parameter of content or purpose", i.e., the control of elements that lie underneath (for content) or beside and "around" (for purpose) the form of the work.

Decisive for the applicability of the exception of parody, for example, is the radical switch in meaning that must occur between the original work and its intended use. Courts verify whether the downstream work has changed the content of the previous work into a parodic one. That this ascertainment goes beyond the surface of the work is demonstrated in that both doctrine and court decisions stress how the work shall remain recognizable to fulfill its parodic function.[288]

In a slightly different way, the exception of quotation under Art. 25 CopA also forces courts to make a step beyond the sole appearance of a work. Quotations can leave the original quoted work (or quoted portions from a work) unaltered and intact, provided that the embedding of foreign material is designated as such, e.g., with quotation marks and indication of the source.[289] To verify whether the use of extraneous material is a quotation, courts do not control whether the quoted material has been changed but, rather, whether there is an inner correlation between the quoted and the quoting works that justifies and sustains the taking as well as its extent.[290]

Another door – meanwhile closed by overriding EU copyright law – for the consideration of the content of a work was the concept of inner distance.[291] Introduced in Germany to include parodies within the scope of the free utilization, the inner distance required an anti-thematic treatment of the previous work in the new work. Even if the work's visible characteristics had been largely repeated and no substantial difference was visible, an intelligible distance between the meanings or messages of the original and the downstream work could make the use pass as free utilization.[292] Today, instead, if the work is recognizable in its downstream use, it

287 For parodies, see Zurich District Court of May 19, 2021 (*Trittligasse*), sic! 2022 p. 68 et seqq., c. 6.2. and CUENI, p. 662; for quotations, see KAKIES, N 5 and 65; EGLOFF/KÜNZI, CopA Commentary, N 14 *ad* Art. 25, in which it is explained that the quotation must be identified and identifiable as such; cf. in general Tribunale di Milano of July 13, 2011 (*Giacometti Variations*), in which much of the focus is put on what meaning the oeuvre conveys "notwithstanding the fact that it substantially or partially reproduces an existing oeuvre" (translation is mine).

288 See Chapter 5, I.II.

289 KAKIES, N 5 and 65.

290 RUEDIN, N 447; EGLOFF/KÜNZI, CopA Commentary, N 4 *ad* Art. 25, uses the precise wording of inner correlation, inner tie (in German: *inhaltlicher Zusammenhang, inneres Band*); DFC 131 III 480, c. 2.1 (*Schweizerzeit*).

291 Cf Chapter 4, III.IV.II.III.

292 That the free utilization concerns the dichotomy of form and content is recognized as well by HILTY, Die freie Benutzung, p. 129.

cannot be a free utilization under overriding EU law.[293] Moreover, the definition of parody under *Deckmyn* is based on the "noticeable difference" (read: sensible, perceptible) that must exist between the borrowed work and its parodic use.[294]

Within the US fair use, a change of content or message of the work is considered in cases in which the upstream work is commented upon, criticized in its downstream use[295] or used to deliver a commentary or critique of something else (for example, an advertising picture for shoes was used, as in *Blanch vs. Koons*, to comment upon "the social and aesthetic consequences of mass media"[296]). In these cases, a work might be borrowed entirely or in part and remain relatively unchanged if its message has changed and if it provides a new insight.[297]

Another possibility for a work to remain the same is the purposive change by maintenance of the visible form of a work. In Switzerland, the exception of panorama prescribes that the depiction may not serve the same purpose as the original (Art. 27 para. 2 CopA). According to BARRELET/EGLOFF, a fresco cannot be copied into another fresco, and paintings exposed outdoors cannot serve again as exhibition objects.[298] As it is in the US within the scope of fair use, a visual artwork exposed publicly cannot be used once again in or for another visual artwork, as these would have "the same overarching purpose (i.e., to serve as works of visual art)".[299] This also means, *e contrario*, that when a trademark, commercial logo or advertising is used for aesthetical ends and integrated in an artwork, that could well qualify as repurposed because these were not intended to serve as works of visual art but to serve a commercial end.[300]

293 cf. LOEWENHEIM, DE-CopA Commentary, N 27 et seqq. *ad* § 24.
294 Cf. Chapter 5, I.III.I.
295 CUENI, p. 661.
296 As in *Blanch vs. Koons*, 467 F.3d 244 (2nd Cir. 2006), p. 253.
297 However, this was partially relativized in the decision *Andy Warhol Found. for the Visual Arts vs. Goldsmith*, 11 F.4th 26 (2nd Cir. 2021), p. 25, which explained that "the secondary work itself must reasonably be perceived as embodying an entirely distinct artistic purpose". In our terminology, this means that a change in content must be *perceptible*, i.e., accompanied by a visible transformation of the form.
298 BARRELET/EGLOFF, CopA Commentary, N 8 *ad* Art. 27.
299 As it was stated in *Andy Warhol Found. for the Visual Arts vs. Goldsmith*, 11 F.4th 26 (2nd Cir. 2021), in which the use of an artwork in another artwork was considered having the same overarching purpose of serving as a work of art; cf. also ADLER, The Future of Art, p. 565 fn. 23, with further references; BUSKIRK, Creative Intent, p. 247, questions how the purpose of an artwork might be determined.
300 One example is the case *Mattel Inc. vs. Walking Mountain Productions*, 353 F.3d 792 (9th Cir. 2003), in which Barbie dolls, also protected by trademark law, were repurposed as a parody; another example is the argumentation of the Supreme Court in *Andy Warhol Found. for the Visual Arts, Inc. vs. Goldsmith*, 598 US ___ (2023), p. 26 and 27, in which the court also wrote about Warhol's artwork "Campbell Soup Cans" and held that, while the purpose of Campbell's logo is to advertise soup, Warhol's canvases do not share that same purpose. Rather, the court said, "the Soup Cans series uses Campbell's copyrighted work *for an artistic commentary on consumerism, a purpose that is orthogonal to advertising* soup" (emphasis added).

With the parameter of content and purpose, aspects such as the creative intention, the message of the work, its context and the combination with other elements in the composition that are indications of a changed message, become relevant.[301] By creating room within which artists can engage with others' works irrespectively of how much they visibly change their perceptible form, the parameter of content or purpose envisages ways of appreciating the changes happened within the art system after its passage from modern to postmodern.

Yet the scope within which changes in content and purpose can be considered is relatively narrow. Copyright exceptions were designed for specific cases (*Fallgruppen*[302]) other than interpictoriality in the visual arts, and, therefore, they do not automatically encompass it.[303] Depending on which lens is used to judge the use, a different outcome is possible. If the focus is set on parody, for example, the transformation is considered from this perspective. A different lens (e.g., quotation) could bring it to a completely different outcome.[304]

The exception of quotation, for example, traditionally thought for scientific and literary texts,[305] requires the quotation to fulfill a specific purpose within the quoting artifact, which also establishes the lawful extent of the quotation. Even though the quotation of images is theoretically permitted, it is only with difficulty that we can imagine a judge proving to what extent an artistic quotation is necessary for the artwork.[306]

Similarly, the exception of parody holds. As noted by SOLLFRANK, in the legal context, the notion of what counts as parody seems to be much more limited than in the cultural context.[307] Postmodernism is characterized altogether by a parodic stance with respect to the modernist past.[308] This large understanding of parody

301 DÖHL, Systemwechsel, p. 273, writes for musical works that other parameters such as the text of the song, the context of performance of the musical work, the intermedial combination with visual elements, etc. become relevant; BUSKIRK, Creative Intent, p. 249, individuates a hint, in *Blanch vs. Koons*, 467 F.3d 244 (2nd Cir. 2006), "that transformative use could potentially derive from *a shift in stated purpose rather than a dramatic visual alteration*". For BUSKIRK, this could "converge on an understanding of art based on the paradigm of the Duchampian readymade, where the object's status as art derives from a recontextualisation implemented by the artist's declarative act".

302 DÖHL, Systemwechsel, p. 247.

303 For example, for DÖHL, Systemwechsel, p. 255, the notion of "interaction" required for the fulfillment of the exception of quotation is clearly not tailored to artistic borrowings.

304 ROSATI, Not sufficiently "transformative", p. 525.

305 EGLOFF/KÜNZI, CopA Commentary, N 3 *ad* Art. 25.

306 See Chapter 5, I.IV; the necessity of the quotation is something the judges of the SFSC did prove in DFC 131 III 480 (*Schweizerzeit*); however, according to which criteria shall judges base their examination of the necessity of an aesthetic quotation?

307 SOLLFRANK, p. 87; cf. also the large understanding of parody of HUTCHEON, p. 89.

308 ROSE, Parody, p. 56, explains that "like most new cultural developments postmodernism has found a new target and function for parody[:] the criticism of modernism. The new type of parody found in postmodernism is furthermore not satisfied to simply reflect on the processes or structures of the artwork as was characteristic of parody under modernism – but is concerned to place modernism, and itself, within a self-reflexive history of art".

includes ironic quotation, pastiche, appropriation and intertextuality.[309] Yet the subtle irony of artworks playing with or subverting aesthetical semantics may escape the radar of judges; within the meaning of the law, parodies must be noticeably critical and humorous, in some jurisdictions of the used work itself.[310]

Moreover, even within the scope of copyright exceptions, artifacts are judged with respect to the tangible novelty they succeed in creating. We might call it the parameter of visual transformation (in the US) or of distance (in Germany and in Switzerland).[311] Whereas, under the just-described parameter of content or purpose, visual changes are not decisive (and sometimes they may even prevent an exception to apply), as the parameter of transformation or distance requires the form of the work to be visibly transformed in the downstream artwork.

III.III The parameter of visual transformation or distance

The likelihood for the interpictorial artwork to be justified under copyright tends to increase the less it resembles the used work (and, thus, gets closer to the previously identified blind spot of copyright law).[312] Exactly as the definition of copyrighted work, the copyright regime for interpictoriality is also based on the definition of innovation and creativity as the necessity to produce formal novelty. Copyright exceptions, too, require a visual change on artworks based on previously existing copyrighted material and stick to the principle of the author having to augment reality and create something that is perceptibly, formally new to qualify as one.[313] According to the "parameter of transformation or distance", only uses that visibly transform the protected work, that add something to it, that make it different from what previously was, can be justified.[314]

This idea of having to change the template is very prominent, as exposed, in the so-called distance doctrine. With it, courts compare the upstream and the downstream works, measuring how different the latter has become from the former. The use is only deemed free if the previous work's individual traits virtually disappear in the downstream artifact. Every tangible change in color, style, forms, composition and arrangement might help disguise the used work; the more the reference to the previous work is dissimulated, identifiable only by the expert eye, the better chances the interpictorial artwork must be considered a free utilization and achieve independent protection. Smaller modifications will, instead, be qualified as simple variations of the work and, thus, remain legally dependent from the latter.

309 Hutcheon, p. 89.

310 Sollfrank, p. 139.

311 Buskirk, Creative Intent, p. 247, speaks of "judicially perceived visual distinctions".

312 Balganesh, Normativity, p. 205 et seqq.; cf. Chapter 4, II.I.

313 Ginsburg, Exceptional Authorship, p. 17, explains what she calls "authorship-oriented exceptions".

314 Fischer, Sampling, p. 43.

Copyright exceptions, too, require a certain kind of transformation and the creation of something perceptibly new.[315] In the exception of quotation, for example, we have seen this very clearly in the opinion of those scholars who argue that quoting material must fulfill the definition at Art. 2 para. 1 CopA for itself, because only then the reward of using a work without permission and costs makes sense for society.[316] Even if not considering this minority doctrinal opinion, the presence of a difference is verified by means of the requirement that the quotation fulfills a function of documentation. For a quotation to be within the meaning of the law, it must be strictly necessary and secondary with respect to the artist's own contribution, which must itself be ascertainable. It is, thus, helpful if the copied-quoted material is inserted in a bigger work that can prove that the artist engaged with it. For example, if the new work manages to integrate the quotation in its own composition, e.g., among added forms, various visual elements and an explicit new storytelling. In this way, it is verified that the quotation is not an end in itself but that it was made in the interest of society at large.[317]

For what concerns the exception of parody, we have seen that the used work may remain recognizable in the downstream use thereof as long as a shift in meaning is recognized. The presence of the new meaning, i.e., of a critical or humoristic parodic effect, becomes, however, easier to ascertain if the form of the artifact provides hints for its intended parodic character,[318] for example, distorted characters, comically exaggerated proportions and added elements that hint at a specific new meaning and lead to a certain interpretation.[319] The simultaneous change of the form, thus, becomes a "proxy" for an occurred change in meaning.[320] Within the meaning of parody as interpreted by the CJEU in *Deckmyn*, a change of form is even explicitly required, as the courts will look for a noticeable difference between the evoked original work and its parodic adaptation.[321]

315 However, the question of transformation is not asked explicitly, as it is, instead, with derivative works but is, rather, verified by means of other specific requirements that must be fulfilled if the exception is to be applied. One could say that the question of transformation is verified by means of "proxies", cf. SUBOTNIK, p. 1494.

316 GASSER/MORANT, p. 233 et seq.

317 We see, here, very clearly how copyright exceptions are created on the background of the public interest, cf. EGLOFF, CopA Commentary, N 1 *ad* Vorbemerkungen Art. 19-28.

318 As one Dutch court stated, a parody should keep "sufficient distance from the original so that [it] is not regarded as a simple copy", as quoted in JONGSMA, Parody, p. 659 et seq.

319 Cf. in this respect, the decision Tribunale di Milano of July 13, 2011 (*Giacometti Variations*), in which the court held: "how extensively the imitation of the previous work was, cannot be of decisive importance. This aspect can, however, contribute to the evaluation and constitute an indication of the creative contribution realized by the second author" (translation is mine). For the Milan court, the fact that Baldessari had not based his "Giacometti Variations" (2010) on a concrete sculpture by Giacometti (nor of "La Grande Femme" II, III, and neither IV) but, rather, on the "general image given by the artist to the feminine figure" was an important aspect for the judgment to fall in favor of Baldessari.

320 Cf. SUBOTNIK, p. 1494 for the use of the concept of "proxies".

321 See Chapter 5, I.III.I; this definition was already applied by the GFCJ of April 30, 2020 (*Metall auf Metall IV*), GRUR 2020, p. 843 et seqq., p. 849 at para. 62.

The idea of transformation is also prominent in both the US's substantial similarity standard, which is used to determine whether the work was used (and is, therefore, similar to the distance doctrine adopted in Switzerland), as well as in the fair use test, whose first factor (the transformative test) is, as explained, at the forefront of the determination of fairness since *Campbell vs. Acuff-Rose*. Rather than measuring the extent with which the pre-existing forms are visible in the second work, as is done in Switzerland, the transformative test focuses more on the creative power of the second,[322] but the achieved result is similar. In both legal systems, changing, adding, substantially subtracting or, in short, transforming with visual distinctions the surface of the used work (its form) plays a fundamental role in the determination of whether there is a copyright infringement. The more a work is visibly transformed, the less a creation based upon it will be considered being in its scope of protection and the likelier it will be considered lawful, even without the permission of the first author. On the contrary, the more the subsequent work remains substantially similar to the previous one (i.e., approaching the blind spot), the more probable it becomes that it will qualify as a potential infringement of the first author's copyright, regardless of the change of content or purpose.[323] In this sense, we see how copyright law tends to equate visible, material transformation to a maximization of societal benefit and, thus, to a likelier fulfillment of the goal of copyright.[324]

322 EGLOFF, Von der "freien Benutzung", p. 408; see also Chapter 5, II.II.

323 GINSBURG, Exceptional Authorship, p. 18 et seq.; JAYME, p. 37; as reported by STOKES, p. 160 et seq., courts in the UK similarly require "some element of *material alteration*" and that "in the context of artistic works, such alteration must be *visually significant*"; in another excerpt from a decision, the judges made it clear that it was "although in the process of appropriation *the meaning of the work is changed* by placing it in a new context, *its visual significance* may well not be".

324 So the *Campbell vs. Acuff-Rose Music, Inc.*, 510 US 569 (1994), p. 579: "the goal of copyright, to promote science and the arts is generally furthered by the creation of transformative works".

6 On the relation between art and copyright law

I.I How law irritates art

Copyright law recognizes that works are interpictorial.[1] It provides rules to adjudicate protection for interpictorial works that it judges sufficiently distant from the templates they use and rules to define the protection scope of a work and its similar derivates. With the exception to copyright, it justifies specific uses of previously existing works.

Yet the copyright law we have previously described may declare some interpictorial artworks lawful and others infringing. If an artwork is judged infringing based on copyright law, the artist who created it will, obviously, be directly influenced. Even outside of a proceeding, however, art observes copyright law and reacts to it.[2] Other than concerning individual artists, the regulatory function of copyright has a societal dimension that exerts effects that go beyond the mere coupling of material and procedural law in the form of a subjective right. In this sense, ORTLAND speaks of copyright norms as a "regime of the image" ("Bildregime").[3] By conferring the right to control an image and its derivatives, copyright law *structures the forms of possible uses of images* in both time and intensity, influencing their modes of circulation and attribution and, thus, how it is communicated through images in other spheres of society (in what he calls the "environment of images", or in German *Bilderumwelt*, in which "environment" is understood in system theoretical terms).[4] For this reason, the concrete configuration of the regime, i.e., where and how normative boundaries are drawn, has a decisive effect on the development of the environment of images.[5]

Hereunder, we focus on this societal dimension of copyright law, which, according to WIELSCH, emerges only in the moment the author-owner and his relation to

1 SHERMAN, Appropriating, p. 47.
2 GRÜNBERGER, p. 2.
3 ORTLAND, Bildregime, p. 286; cf. also, although more generally speaking, DOUZINAS, p. 18.
4 ORTLAND, Bildregime, p. 271 and 281; cf. also WIELSCH, Zugangsregeln, p. 4; HOFFMANN-RIEM, p. 437, copyright law creates an inaccessibility of certain forms during a certain time.
5 ORTLAND, Bildregime, p. 272 and 286.

DOI: 10.4324/9781003598503-10

the work are put aside so that the focus can be redirected onto the "multilateral effects" that copyright law may exert in other systems of society.[6]

The systems theoretical concept of irritation helps describe the interactions between art and law more precisely. According to systems theory, an irritation emerges from the confrontation of a system's internal structures with external (environmental, in systems theoretical terms) events.[7] Because of the autopoiesis of societal systems, there is no causal relationship between environment and system. Their operative closure prevents them from being able to directly infiltrate themselves in one another. Rather, their operations will only affect mechanisms of the system itself.[8] For this reason, events happening in other systems determine no automatic action in the system observing them.

Because there is no relationship of causality between environment and system, every time a system reacts to an external event, it is because the system itself observed this event as a potential problem to solve – a nuisance, an obstacle to its normal operativity – and, thus, as something that required a reaction.[9] Irritations must, thus, be understood as internal constructions of the irritated system (in a way, they are "self-irritations").[10] The fact that events happening beyond the system (that is, in the environment of this system, in another system) eventually provoke more, or different, internal communication, which is always determined by the system itself. The investigation of how *this* type of copyright exerts effects on art must be made upon this theoretical premise.

I.II The blurriness of copyright regulations

A first aspect to underline in the relation between copyright law and art is the blurriness of copyright rules, many of which are based on the previously described degree of similarity. As ADLER notes, courts controlling whether an artifact looks too much like another to determine either infringement or fair use (which we summed up under the parameter of transformation, or distance), is "too murky and subjective".[11] Similar critiques, i.e., that the measurement of distance is subjective and unpredictable, have been voiced by Swiss and German copyright scholars.[12]

6 WIELSCH, Zugangsregeln, p. 32 and 269; WIELSCH, Relationales Urheberrecht, p. 61 and 85; with the "multilaterality" of copyright is meant the effects copyright law has on other social systems; cf. also GRÜNBERGER, p. 10.

7 BARALDI/CORSI/ESPOSITO, p. 115 et seq.

8 LUHMANN, Irritationen, p. 61, causal explanations are possible, but they are always attributed to the observer making them.

9 LUHMANN, Law as a Social System, p. 258 et seq.

10 BARALDI/CORSI/ESPOSITO, p. 116; LUHMANN, Law as a Social System, p. 468.

11 ADLER, The Future of Art, p. 604; see also GIBSON, p. 884, who describes the "ambiguity" of the copyright doctrines determining where private entitlement ends and public privilege begins, resulting in the impossibility to make accurate ex-ante judgments regarding the need to secure a license. Cf. also LIU, p. 172 and BALGANESH, Normativity, p. 208.

12 See Chapter 4, II.I.

Indeed, where the line shall be drawn between an infringing interpictorial artwork and a lawful use of previously existing visual material is not clear.

We may take the artwork *Graduation* from Richard Prince's series *Canal Zone* (2008) and its handling by the Second Circuit Court of Appeals as an example. *Graduation* was among the five artworks considered by the court "*not sufficiently differ[ent]* from the photographs of Cariou's that they incorporate to confidently make a determination about their...transformative nature as a matter of law".

The judges in *Cariou vs. Prince* admitted that some changes had been made.[13] Notwithstanding these changes, they concluded that "we cannot say for sure whether *Graduation* constitutes fair use or whether Prince has transformed Cariou's work enough to render it transformative". Because the court expresses the idea that the picture was not transformed "enough", we can speculate on whether the same modifications, but more accentuated, would have caused *Graduation* to be deemed lawful, or whether the court was asking for something else entirely. What seems clear is only that the court wanted *to see* a change and that it considered the changes it saw in *Graduation* insufficient.

This lack of clarity translates into the difficulty for many artists to predict what will be considered infringing and orienting their artistic creations accordingly in order to avoid a lawsuit. Some artists have, thus, recurred to legal counsel before realizing their artworks. In an interview, US American artist Jill Magid explained how she consulted her French lawyer before an exhibition in Paris. When she asked him how to expose the design of the *facistol*, a lectern whose design she had appropriated from the archive of Mexican architect Luis Barragán, he answered, rather puzzlingly: "You can show it, but you can't show it".[14]

In another example, the act of asking legal counsel about an artwork was turned into an artwork. In her video installation *Legal Perspective* (2004),[15] Cornelia Sollfrank presented her work *net.art_generator* to four copyright lawyers (one in Switzerland and three in Germany), asking them to comment on it. The lawyers, who applied their interpretation of the law on the work, "reached very different – sometimes even contradictory – conclusions about its legal status".[16] Even with a profound knowledge of the law, it is very difficult to use the inherent idea of transformation productively, i.e., as a clear guidance to avoid an accusation of copyright infringement.[17] Moreover, asking a lawyer for elucidation is costly, will probably

13 *Cariou vs. Prince*, 714 F.3d 694 (2nd Cir. 2013), p. 711: "*Graduation*, for instance, is tinted blue, and the jungle background is in softer focus...Lozenges painted over the subject's eyes and mouth... make the subject appear anonymous....Along with the enlarged hands and electric guitar...,those alterations create the impression that the subject is not quite human".

14 Cf. Emily Watlington, Copyright Law and Art: Legal Scholar Amy Adler in Conversation with Artist Jill Magid, February 18, 2020 (<https://www.artnews.com/art-in-america/interviews/copyright-law-art-amy-adler-jill-magid-1202678138/>).

15 Sollfrank, p. 314 et seqq.; the artwork can be seen at <https://artwarez.org/projects/legalperspective/>.

16 Sollfrank, p. 326 et seq.

17 As stated by Sollfrank, p. 327, "although the lawyers are experts in their field, all they can do is speculate".

produce a very careful stance (which is not always desirable in the creative field)[18] and is not a guarantee for clarity, either, as the answers as to whether a particular use is permissible or not can vary considerably depending on the question.

Other reactions to the parameters of transformation that are valid in copyright law can be found online in creators' community blogs. In self-help memoranda, for example, artists seem to understand that the mere repurposing in another medium or context of found copyrighted material is not enough to avoid infringement if they have not previously obtained authorization to use that material. They, thus, advise to do *more* and *add new artistic meaning*,[19] which, however, remains a rather abstract piece of advice. In this respect, it is also interesting to point out a diffused internet myth called the "30% rule". According to this rule, a work can be used as a basis for a follow-on work if it is changed at least 30%.[20] Apart from the fact that such an exact rule does not exist in any jurisdiction, we also wonder how a fixed percentage would be of any help: How would the percentage of change be calculated? Would the more individual and original parts of the borrowed work need to be changed more than less original parts? What (and for whom) counts as "changed", really?

Too many variables play a role in determining the legal status of borrowed copyright material in a new artifact, so a quantified rule would not be of great help.[21] Ultimately, the rule points out the fact that artists and other users of copyrighted material received some of the normative aspects of copyright law (indeed, it is true that, in most cases, under the parameter of transformation, one needs to change a work to be able to use it), yet found these unclear or unhelpful. The existence of the "rule" is interesting, as it signals a need to "make sense" of the blurry precepts of copyright law.

Paradigmatic of the lack of clarity surrounding copyright provisions is also the development of the so-called "permission culture", i.e., the assumption, resulting from an exaggerated perception of the risks, that all copyrighted works can be used only with permission, even if, in fact, the intended use would be covered by a copyright exception or would be permissible as substantially transformative.[22] As we have seen, liability under copyright law is difficult to predict, but the consequences of infringement, or even of only a proceeding may, be severe. In order to avoid speculation and finding themselves in gray legal areas, artists may start asking permission and seeking a license for the intended use, even though none would have been needed.

18 Cf. Sollfrank, p. 321; Stalder, p. 46.

19 For example, in the Code of Best Practices in Fair use for the Visual Arts, College Art Association, p. 11, it is advised "Artists should avoid uses of existing copyrighted material that do not generate new artistic meaning, being aware that a change of medium, without more, may not meet this standard".

20 Cf. e.g. Eric Perrott, The 30 Percent Rule in Copyright Law (<https://www.gerbenlaw.com/blog/the-30-percent-rule-in-copyright-law/>).

21 Stalder, p. 46.

22 Aufderheide/Milosevic/Bello, p. 2013; Aufderheide/Jaszi/Bello/Milosevic, p. 7.

This behavior provokes, according to GIBSON, a backlash on the legal system and on the capacity of copyright law to accommodate downstream uses: The lack of clarity of the doctrine, coupled with risk-averse licensing, creates a shrinking effect for downstream users' rights by a parallel expansion of the authors' rights under copyright law.[23] The reasons for this expansion are not to be found in legislative amendments to copyright law that restrict the scope of exceptions but, rather, in the unintended process resulting from the interaction between the legal system and other spheres of society.[24] This lecture of the events is in accordance with legal sociological theories: LUHMANN's differentiation of the legal system in periphery and center, for example, acknowledges the role of peripheries (contracts) in the production of validity and in the juridification of everyday life.[25] Similarly, TEUBNER's theory of legal pluralism states that law will grow from social peripheries, stemming from paralegal rules that are produced "at the margin" of law.[26] The more artists ask for permission for uses that would be unobjectionable from a copyright perspective, the more the line between what is permissible and what is not will move in the direction of the expansion of authors' rights, shrinking users' freedoms.

I.III The risks of a copyright proceeding

After having been notified by Edward Weston's CMO about his reproduction right, Sherrie Levine decided to reorient her work toward the pictures of Walker Evans that were not protected by copyright. From an artistic perspective, such a choice may appear arbitrary, as it was not motivated by anything else other than legal-strategical reasons.[27]

Jeff Koons reportedly started using the technique of collage (as he did in the "Easyfun-Ethereal" series[28]) as a response to his legal losses of the '90s, convinced that this method would offer him some protection against further lawsuits claims.[29] The copyright awareness of Jeff Koons is also demonstrated by his plea to apply US law in the French trial *Jeff Koons vs. Davidovici*, decided by the Cour d'appel de Paris. To enforce the application of US copyright, he explained that the contested sculpture "Fait d'hiver" had been created in the US, was first published in that country and had originally been planned as a traveling exhibition in the US.[30] By trying to enforce the application of US copyright legislation, Koons made clear

23 GIBSON, p. 882 et seqq.; cf. also BUYDENS/DUSOLLIER, p. 8 et seq.

24 GIBSON, p. 882 et seqq.

25 LUHMANN, Law as a Social System, p. 295.

26 TEUBNER, Global Bukowina, p. 7 and 12.

27 RÖMER, p. 88.

28 Cf. <https://gagosian.com/exhibitions/2018/jeff-koons-easyfun-ethereal/>.

29 ADLER, The Future of Art, p. 582; this change of technique did not prevent him from getting sued; as seen in Chapter 5, II.III.I, he was sued by Blanch for the use of one of her pictures in the artwork *Niagara*.

30 SUTTERER, p. 132.

not only that he was aware of the different legal framework in France and that this difference could have affected the lawfulness of his work but also that he had conceived his sculpture on the background of the US copyright framework, thinking that it could have been lawful under it.

In his 1981 work *Myths*, Andy Warhol similarly changed his strategy to prevent possible copyright troubles, as he himself recalled in his personal diary. Rather than using an existing publicity still from the original film, as he would have preferred, the portrait of the witch from *The Wizard of Oz* figuring in the *Myths* series is a picture of the actress realized by Warhol himself. His decision to take the picture himself was, thus, motivated by a will to elude copyright infringement claims and not for aesthetical reasons.[31]

Many other artists, whose opinions on the impact of copyright legislation on their work were anonymously collected in a report in the US, lamented having to change their artworks to circumvent conflicting copyright legislation. Instead of the desired work, artists have chosen public domain versions or "inferior substitutes", or they have abstained from doing certain things altogether (such as collage, pop-culture critiques, digital experiments and multimedia).[32] Artists also reported having performed self-censorship insofar as they have abandoned work or refrained from disclosing it publicly because of copyright concerns.[33]

These examples show that copyright law may represent an obstacle to creativity, which artists have to consider in their creative process and, if necessary, elude in the most varied ways. Artists adapt their techniques (from sculpture to collage, as in the case of Jeff Koons), choose different source material (as in the case of Sherrie Levine) or refrain from using found images altogether (as in the case of Andy Warhol, who chose to take the pictures himself instead). All in all, artists prove to be resourceful and inventive in finding detours. The obstacle represented by copyright is especially problematic when it prevents artists from doing what they would like to do, i.e., when they practice self-censorship or avoid disclosing their work publicly. In that respect, copyright law sensationally fails to fulfill its self-proclaimed function of fostering creativity and the progress of the arts. Such an effect becomes visible when looking at the distribution industry of visual art, i.e., at the effects copyright law exerts at the level of its economic intermediaries (galleries, auction houses and museums).

In an empirical investigation, CUNTZ/SAHLI showed how copyright liability rules and the linked perception of litigation risk negatively affect the incentives of intermediaries to disseminate and curate creative works that build on pre-existing works and that are, thus, perceived as being potentially copyright infringing. Their data shows how following the 2013 *Cariou vs. Prince* decision of the Second Circuit, appropriation artists entered fewer auctions, that there was a decrease in

31 LÜTTICKEN, p. 123.
32 AUFDERHEIDE/JASZI/BELLO/MILOSEVIC, p. 5, 9, 57.
33 AUFDERHEIDE/JASZI/BELLO/MILOSEVIC, p. 5; cf also STALDER, p. 45.

immediate demand for appropriation artworks and that the probability of an appropriation artwork listed in an auction being sold declined by around 2%.[34]

Similarly, in Switzerland, CORNELIA SOLLFRANK reports in her doctoral thesis about one of her exhibitions being preventively cancelled due to copyright concerns. Sollfrank had intended to exhibit her work *net.art_generator,* an internet-based computer program that interactively produces collages at an independent gallery space in Basel, plug.in, which has since closed. A series of prints of reworked versions of Warhol's *Flowers* was also planned to be part of the exhibition under the title of *anonymous-warhol_flowers*. As she reports, "after consultation with the legal advisor of the exhibition space, the board decided to cancel the exhibition, because the risk [of legal action] was too high for such a small art institution".[35] SOLLFRANK later performatively reflected on this experience in the artwork *Legal Perspective* described above.[36] SOLLFRANK also underlined that the censorship was not based on actual legal action but had been an act of "anticipatory obedience" on the part of the institution.[37] This underlines the effect of copyright as a "regime of the image" on creativity and art at large, influencing the way images are distributed, which images are seen and, thus, ultimately, our very communication.

The art world seems to observe the proceedings for copyright infringement that were conducted against artists with concern. In the eyes of artists and other cultural actors, proceedings represent an expensive risk (both financial as well as in terms of time) to be avoided.[38] As a reaction, they may develop behaviors of adaptation or avoidance (in the worst case, self-censorship). Because, in these proceedings, the lawfulness of artworks is (also) judged according to the parameter of distance or transformation, artists will adapt their techniques to avoid the risks, e.g., by visibly changing their sources, even if that might precisely be what they are trying to avoid in their practice.[39] Despite the fact that "not all copying is copyright infringement"[40] and that many interpictorial uses are either irrelevant from a copyright perspective or justifiable under its rules, postmodern forms of copying that include a more wholesale borrowing are penalized by the existing copyright framework more than

34 CUNTZ/SAHLI, p. 3, 25; in AUFDERHEIDE/JASZI/BELLO/MILOSEVIC, p. 57, it can be read how the distribution of a work was limited due to copyright concerns of the television broadcaster.

35 The exhibition is described by SOLLFRANK, p. 257 et seq.

36 Cf. SOLLFRANK, p. 320; this would mean that copyright law would have *de facto* acted as "curator" of the exhibition, deciding which artworks could be exposed and which not.

37 SOLLFRANK, p. 258; the copyright regime also influences the space of the merely possible and not yet realized, cf. ORTLAND, Bildregime, p. 287.

38 How can we disprove them? The proceedings of the case *Metall auf Metall*, as previously discussed, lasted already more than 20 years and underwent two legislative changes, which produced three different outcomes. Moreover, the proceeding did not produce a clear winner–loser situation.

39 FISCHER, Sampling, p. 44; DÖHL, Systemwechsel, p. 255 and 269; ADLER, The Future of Art, p. 563, writes that "the transformative test poses a fundamental threat to art because it evaluates art by the very criteria that contemporary art rejects".

40 *Feist Publications, Inc., vs. Rural Telephone Service Co.*, 499 US 340 (1991), p. 361; Amicus Brief, p. 5 and 11.

other art forms.[41] We have also seen that such a "regime of the image" also concerns the creative space of the "not-yet-realized", influencing the way it is created, communicated and distributed.[42]

I.IV Copyright law as a theme of art

The existence of copyright law does not chill or censor art (as one would think by reading the two previous sections) but, rather, when the normative predications of copyright are sometimes willingly used in the artistic process, copyright law might become a productive medium with which the artwork is materially shaped.[43] We are looking, here, at the "other side" of censorship, that is, not at the part that impedes or suffocates creativity – as a "limit that limits" – but at the part that, if circumvented (and, thus, challenged), becomes a utensil to make new art. As artist and curator Antonio Roberts commented about one of his own works: "the piece is effective only as long as it pushes the boundaries of what is acceptable. *As the laws change, I would need to change the work to reflect this*". For him, "as long as *law can physically alter the appearance of an artwork* [it] is something tangible that can be manipulated and worked with".[44] In this sense, copyright law becomes an artistic medium reflected in the final form of the artwork.[45]

A first example of law used as an artistic medium that becomes visible in the final artwork is Jill Magid's multidisciplinary work *The Barragán Archives* (2013–2018). The work is based – as its title suggests – on the archives of Mexican architect Luis Barragán (1902–1988). Whereas much of his work was built in Mexico, where it still can be seen today, the rights over it and the use of the architect's name, along with his professional archive, were acquired in 1995 by furniture company Vitra under the auspices of the newly founded Barragan Foundation. The archive was then transferred to Birsfelden in Switzerland.[46] By accurately re-creating some of the objects created by Luis Barragán, Magid reflects on the cultural, psychological and juridical repercussions of having the archives displaced – and somehow estranged – far from the architect's birth and workplace.[47] In an interview, Magid explained that when she re-created a lectern previously designed by Barragán (the *facistol*), she had to change it based on the jurisdiction under which the work was exhibited. Whereas, in the US, it is allowed to copy a design object, in Europe, it

41 Buskirk, The Contingent Object, p. 90; Griffiths, p. 350 et seqq.
42 Cf. Chapter 6, I.III; Ortland, Bildregime, p. 287; Coombe, p. 50.
43 Russell Legacy, Amy Adler by Legacy Russell, March 12, 2013 (<https://bombmagazine.org/articles/amy-adler/>); Coombe, p. 50, writes how intellectual property law might "invite critical appropriations".
44 Roberts was interviewed by Burke, p. 272 et seq. (emphasis added).
45 Burke, p. 271; this way of working, however, is not fully free of risks. As previously mentioned, the boundaries between lawful and infringing use are not fully clear and a judge could think differently than the artist.
46 Cf. <https://www.barragan-foundation.org/foundation/activities>.
47 Cf. <http://www.jillmagid.com/projects/the-barragan-archives>.

is forbidden; when the object is exposed in France or in Switzerland, it must be covered with a blanket. Magid, however, does not mind having to work with these limits, as they required her to come up with new forms and ideas, which ultimately made the law visible, adding an interesting layer of meaning to her work.[48]

Another interesting example is *Copy Right* (2006) by Superflex, a Copenhagen based collective.[49] The work included 40 commercially produced knockoffs of Danish designer Arne Jacobsen's iconic Ant Chair. These were constructed with slightly modified curves, just enough to be different from the template, thus diminishing the risk of infringing the intellectual property rights arising from Jacobsen's work. For their artwork-installation, Superflex sawed off the wooden additions of the knockoffs, going back to the original design. By doing so, the lawful replicas were, thus, brought back to the status of unlawful reproductions of Jacobsen's chair. In the final installation, the cut off pieces laid all around each single chair. These made the legal rule materially visible as well as the fact that the lawfulness of the chairs was composed of "mere material fragments, soon to be discarded".[50]

Another example is the video work *The Pure Necessity* (2016) by David Claerbout. In it, Claerbout reused video material from Walt Disney's animated film "The Jungle Book" (1967) but removed from it all anthropomorphic features from the animals, as well as the narration, dancing and dialogues. His purpose was to reflect on the relationship of humans with animals.[51] The result is an uncanny video in which familiar and friendly looking Disney characters behave as if they were in a nature documentary. We expect the animals to start talking from one moment to the other, but they never do.[52] The longer one watches *The Pure Necessity*, the more the radical difference existing between it and the Disney template is revealed. On the contrary, if the spectator only gets short glimpses of the video, the resemblance with the Jungle Book's original characters is in the foreground. When working on the production of the video, Claerbout soon realized that the "copyright issue might be enormous". To minimize risks, he completely changed the colored background to "erase the border between the original and [his] piece".[53] The remarkable aspect of the work is the symbiotic relation it creates with copyright law: The differences between original and copy and between foreground and background and the fact that the duration is pivotal to the understanding of the work are themes that are decisive from a copyright perspective but also at the core of Claerbout's artistic practice.[54]

48 MAGID, p. 1 et seqq.

49 Cf. <https://superflex.net/works/copy_right>.

50 JULIAN MYERS, Superflex, April 15, 2007 (<https://www.frieze.com/article/superflex>).

51 Cf. DAVID CLAERBOUT, Interview, April 23, 2019 (<https://elephant.art/david-claerbout-appropriate-behaviour/>).

52 The video can be watched at <https://vimeo.com/502677017>.

53 DAVID CLAERBOUT, Interview, April 23, 2019 (<https://elephant.art/david-claerbout-appropriate-behaviour/>).

54 DAVID CLAERBOUT, Interview, April 23, 2019 (<https://elephant.art/david-claerbout-appropriate-behaviour/>).

What we have exposed shows that copyright is part of the environment in which artists operate. The art system is *irritated* by copyright law in different ways.[55] The (unclear) parameter of visual transformation makes it more difficult for art to exist in a certain manner. Artists, however, also intentionally reflect these rules in their art, making them visible and part of the intricated meaning of their works. By making copyright a theme of their art, they also tangibly expose how different copyright norms would ultimately create a different environment for art and, therefore, probably different artworks.

II.I How art *irritates* law

The result of conceiving the art system as an autopoietic system of society, as LUHMANN does, is that the societal competence ("Deutungshoheit") to define what counts as art is exclusively the art system's.[56] Law, exactly as every other observer of art external to the system, is put in a position of second-order observation; with its operations, it will limit itself to report what the art system calls art.[57] This corresponds to law's self-description, which wants to see itself as neutral with regard to aesthetic questions.[58] Whenever law encounters artistic facts, as it does in many of its fields, its judgment does not aim to decide whether an artifact is art from an aesthetical perspective; rather, law's judgments depend on a *normative* differentiation between art and non-art,[59] i.e., on a difference that concerns the system's specific operative code legal/illegal.[60]

II.II Copyright law's relation to art

Copyright law's relation to art is slightly different. "Art" is undoubtedly among the objects of copyright protection.[61] Copyright's access to artistic facts, however, is always mediated by the requirement of the individual character (or originality in other legal systems).[62] Copyright applies to artistic facts and artworks, without being able to – as it would be, for example, with the constitutional artistic freedom

55 GRÜNBERGER, p. 10.
56 LUHMANN, Challenge, p. 54; cf. MCCLEAN, p. 318. Or better: Every time the societal operation of deciding what art is according to the code fitting/unfitting is made, it must be attributed to the art system.
57 LUHMANN, Art as a Social System, p. 244; cf. MÜLLER, p. 244, however, states that only a few legal writings of the 1970s in the domain of copyright law managed to resist the suspicion that they were judging what art is and is not.
58 DOUZINAS, p. 19, speaks of law's alleged "aesthetic abstinence", BUSKIRK, Creative Intent, p. 249; TROLLER, Bedeutung, p. 271; MÜLLER, p. 230 et seqq.
59 GRABER, Zwischen Geist und Geld, p. 103.
60 ESPOSITO, Paradoxien, p. 48; DOUZINAS, p. 28, adds that such is dependent on the aesthetic-subjective decision of the judge, as the artistic object at stake will inevitably exert an aesthetic affect on the judge in charge of delivering a decision.
61 In the Swiss CopA, the word "art" is found in the definition of work at Art. 2 para. 1 CopA.
62 BARRON, Claims of Art, p. 378, states that "copyright law knows no concept of art as such".

– perceiving them *qua* art. Because "individual" and "artistic" are not equivalent,[63] copyright law's mode of observation of artworks is not to consider whether they are artistic or not, or aesthetically worthy but, rather, to either bestow copyright protection or not based on the presence or the absence of individual character.[64]

Through the lenses of individuality, judges look for precise characteristics in the artifact. These may, however, differ from art's criteria to judge what art is and, thus, create a potential asynchronization. The discrepancy of copyright law and art only comes to light in those cases in which a court refuses copyright protection to an artwork, but the discrepancy existed before. Copyright law does not protect artworks because they are art but only because they are individual (or original), as the difference with which it operates is individual/non-individual and not artistic/non-artistic. When an artwork is refused copyright protection, such refusal can always be justified by stating that this does not mean that it is not artistic but, simply, that it cannot be protected by copyright law, whose function is not to decide on artistic matters anyway.[65]

Because of copyright law's declared *function* of fostering creativity and innovation to the benefit of society, however, the situation is more nuanced. Even if it does not address the artistic quality of artworks directly, copyright cannot ignore the fact that it applies to artistic facts with the ultimate purpose of fostering their creation. Copyright law cultivates what could be described as a parasitic dependency with art (to speak with Michel Serres).[66] Serres describes the parasite as a "chased entity that always returns".[67] Notwithstanding its self-description as an aesthetically neutral observer of artistic facts and as unbothered by the art system's whereabouts,[68] we have seen that copyright law's mechanisms are permeable to considerations of aesthetic order (e.g., we have seen this when we looked at the oscillations of copyright law protection) and, sometimes, explicitly refers to them by means of external references.[69] Lawyers defending artists in copyright proceedings know this well, that to efficiently defend their clients in their pleas, they may

63 Kearns, p. 63, explains: "the original is broader than the artistic", in the sense that original are also non-artistic, technical works (for example computer programs). At the same time, we add, the artistic is broader than the original: As seen in detail previously, many artworks will not qualify for copyright protection despite their indisputable quality as "art". Cf. also Dreier, p. 208 et seq. at fn. 30: "the concept of originality in the art system changes according to another timetable than the concept of originality in copyright law"; Studer, p. 8.

64 Cf. also Griffiths, p. 348 et seqq.; cf. also Esposito, Paradoxien, p. 38, in which she describes the *tertium non datur* as "the third that is given and which is given as something excluded from the opposition of the two values" (translation is mine).

65 *Andy Warhol Found. for the Visual Arts vs. Goldsmith*, 11 F.4th 26 (2nd Cir. 2021).

66 Kearns, p. 62; cf. also Luhmann, Law as a Social System, p. 459 et seq., describing with similar language the dependency of the law system from its latencies, from the included-excluded that cannot be eliminated.

67 Serres, p. 78.

68 Kearns, p. 66; Griffiths, p. 341.

69 Kearns, p. 61.

need to recur to arguments rooted in art history and art theory,[70] sometimes even stepping away from their clients' true motivations.[71]

Copyright cannot ignore art. For this reason, art, or, rather, copyright law's adherence to it, seems to absolve an existential function for copyright's own subsistence.[72] If an obvious discrepancy between the outputs produced by artists and copyright protection persists, it can legitimately be asked whether copyright law is absolving its societal function to "promote science and the arts" at all[73] and whether artists need copyright in the first place to be incentivized and produce new art.[74] In this sense, SERRES also describes the parasite as a necessity so that "the force that excludes it is immediately overturned to bring it back".[75] In other words, copyright law's inner logic and external, societal justification stands or falls with its capability to accommodate art and its developments. Even if art is excluded from the opposition between individual and non-individual, it is included as "third" in the copyright discourse.[76] The amount of copyright literature dedicated to the whereabouts of the artworld is ineluctable evidence for this necessity of copyright law to be receptive of what happens in its artistic environment.[77]

II.III Copyright law's paradox

Paradoxes are central within systems theory. A paradox arises when two cumulative conditions are fulfilled. First, there must be a situation of *self-reference*, as happens when a statement speaks of itself (e.g., "this sentence is false", or "I am lying"[78]). Second, there must be a situation of oscillation between two poles, or values, that causes *undecidability*. In this situation, one cannot simply exclude one value to come to a clear conclusion, as both are important.[79] In the sentence "I am lying", for example, we cannot believe the liar telling us that he is lying, because that same sentence should not be true.

Copyright's ambiguous and parasitic relation to art, combined with its declared societal function of fostering innovation and creativity for the benefit of all, produces a paradoxical situation. Already described by SOLLFRANK, the paradox arises the moment copyright law declares a *new* artwork infringing of an *old* artwork's

70 MILLET, p. 115 et seq., writes that "On both sides, lawyers engage themselves in demonstrating at what point the creation of their client is veritably a work of art and speak...as art critics would" (translation is mine); SHORE, p. 72.

71 MILLET, p. 115 et seq.

72 GERVAIS, How Intellectual Property, p. 18, writes how copyright needs new works to be created to justify its existence.

73 *Campbell vs. Acuff-Rose Music, Inc.*, 510 US 569 (1994), p. 579; HOFFMANN-RIEM, p. 433.

74 Cf. among many ADLER, Why Art, p. 330 et seqq.; GEIGER, Reconceptualizing, p. 123; GERVAIS, How Intellectual Property, p. 18.

75 SERRES, p. 78.

76 Cf. ESPOSITO, Paradoxien, p. 38.

77 MÜLLER, p. 230 et seqq.

78 This is the so-called Liar Paradox, cf. <https://en.wikipedia.org/wiki/Liar_paradox>.

79 ESPOSITO, Paradoxien, p. 35-38; cf. also LUHMANN, Decision making, p. 91.

copyright: "the paradox of intellectual property is that *the protection of existing works compromises the creation of new ones*".[80]

When confronted with the dilemma of having to declare new art infringing because of the protection of old art, copyright can only take itself, its own rules and categories, as justification. Here lies the paradoxical element of self-reference.[81] New art is infringing because, according to copyright's categories, it amounts not to a new (art)work but to an old work exemplar; not to an original, but to a copy (the previously described blind spot of copyright law).

In the paradoxical element of undecidability we find copyright law's dilemma between protecting the old artwork's author and the new artwork's author. Whereas the former is already included in copyright law and marked with subjective rights, the protection of the individual and of property,[82] the latter could be included at least potentially, as her work represents innovation, creativity and art, i.e., all copyright law is supposed to incentivize.[83]

II.IV Ways of processing the paradox

The legal system has different ways of processing its paradoxical relation to art. The difference concerns how the system receives and reacts to events happening in other social systems, i.e., in the system's environment (to which the art system also belongs). Because of autopoiesis and the fact that there is no causal relationship between the system and its environment, events in the art system determine no automatic action in the system observing them (here, law), only, if any, so-called irritations.[84]

80 SOLLFRANK, p. 327 (emphasis added); cf. also SOLLFRANK, p. 2: "The basic idea of intellectual property is to find a balance between the protection of the economic and moral interests of creators and innovators and, at the same time, to enable cultural, scientific and economic innovation. Where creation and innovation rely on access to and the use of protected works, proprietary rights hamper new creation and innovation. This paradox of intellectual property has always existed, but due to the technological, economic, legal and cultural developments that have taken place since the mid-1990s, it has turned into a central problem of information society".

81 DRAHOS, p. 16; only by reiterating its own categories can the law "proceed". That would also insinuate the doubt of whether the difference "legal/illegal" exists *legally* or *illegally*, cf. LUHMANN, Law as a Social System, p. 460.

82 GRÜNBERGER, p. 10; those authors who, today, insist on copyright protection might have inspired themselves on or used copyrighted material yesterday, as inevitably "among the users of today are the authors of tomorrow"; SENFTLEBEN, Copyright, p. 41.

83 Copyright law fails at eluding the paradox because innovation, creativity and art can potentially be found on both sides of the medal and not only on the side that is already marked (i.e., included) in copyright law; cf. GEIGER, Reconceptualizing, p. 159 et seq.; WIELSCH, Zugangsregeln, p. 25 et seq.; albeit in other terms, the existence of authors on both sides is recognized by MOSIMANN, Kultur Kunst Recht, N 123 and 125 *ad* § 1; cf. also CRAIG, Copyright, p. 19 and 31, who speaks of the "primary-author bias" of copyright law and of "simplifying dichotomies", such as "creation/reproduction" and "author/user".

84 SHERMAN, Appropriating, p. 33 et seq. and BARRON, Claims of Art, p. 399.

Affirmations such as "[appropriation art represents] the most *radical challenge* to the copyright laws to date" and "the most radical *threat* to the copyright law's originality requirement",[85] which imply that new artistic movements could somehow directly challenge and eventually change copyright norms, are oversimplifying. If art could influence copyright directly, it would be inexplicable that it had not succeeded yet after one entire century of avant-gardes, ready-mades, appropriations and other forms of conceptual art.[86]

Instead, the reactions of a system to communication happening in its environment manifest as more, or as different, internal system communication. Statements such as the one reported denote at least something, i.e., that the system has been irritated. Despite the inevitable self-referentiality of its internal legal communication about art,[87] it is receiving the events happening outside itself, and it is reacting to them. In the following, we describe two ways the system of law has found to process its irritation.

II.IV.I A self-referential copyright

The first way to process events happening in its environment is for the law system to close its operations on themselves. Irritated by art, copyright reiterates its habitual mode of functioning, choosing to live with the paradox by only seemingly not addressing it. An example of such a stance can be seen in the following statement by the Second Circuit Court judges in the *Goldsmith v Andy Warhol Foundation* case:

> In reaching this conclusion [that Andy Warhol's artwork is not fair use] we do not mean to discount the artistic value of the Prince Series itself.... But the task before us is not to assess the artistic worth of the Prince Series nor its place within Warhol's oeuvre; that is the domain of art historians, critics, collectors, and the museum-going public. Rather, the question we must answer is simply whether the law permits Warhol to claim it as his own, and AWF to exploit it, without Goldsmith's permission.[88]

Even though with this, apparently, detached stance of the judges, it appears that copyright law is closed in on itself; copyright law has, nonetheless, been irritated. The judges are obviously aware of the artistic value of Warhol's *Prince Series* (as it becomes clear in the quoted passage), and the decision's argumentation is, thus, craftily constructed at explaining why, from a legal point of view, protection cannot be granted *notwithstanding* the artistic status of the artifact at stake.

85 As does, for example, GREENBERG, p. 16 and 33 (emphasis added).

86 SHERMAN, Appropriating, p. 33 et seq.

87 MÜLLER, p. 240.

88 *Andy Warhol Found. for the Visual Arts vs. Goldsmith*, 11 F.4th 26 (2nd Cir. 2021), p. 32. Similar statements were made by the Supreme Court in the same matter. At p. 36 et seq. of the decision, the Supreme Court refused to open its decision-making process to an interdisciplinary approach.

The judges explain that what happens in art is not a matter copyright law should care to address, as the question copyright law must answer is an exclusively legal one and, therefore, concerns legal categories and concepts only. In this way, the judges make an operation that tries to isolate copyright law from the rest of society.[89] This notion of copyright law, conceived and, at the same time, constructed as an ivory tower, sees only itself and, thus, its past. However, it is only an attempt to conceal the fact that a terrible doubt is insinuated. Does the difference applied by copyright law in this case exist legally or illegally, as art – contrary to copyright law's declared function – is, here, not advanced but, rather, curtailed?[90]

With respect to copyright law's declared function of fostering creativity and innovation, we point out an existing contradiction. With this operation of isolation, the legal operations of copyright law are constructed as if they did not have any consequence beyond law itself but also, simultaneously, as if they were automatically able to fulfill copyright's goal of fostering creativity and innovation.[91] Copyright is, thus, sustaining a fiction, which is that only through a recursive confirmation of itself will these objectives be attained. The objectives, however, lie in society, that is, beyond the system of law. The verification of their fulfillment is not a task law can fulfill. The fiction only works insofar as the question of whether it really does is eluded, i.e., only insofar as copyright law does not confront itself with its concrete societal implications.[92]

Asking the question would require openness to an interdisciplinary perspective. Such a perspective would eventually reveal the extent to which the operations of law are short-sighted. Indeed, as described in Chapter 6, I.I, by existing as it does, copyright law happens to exert various effects on the practice of contemporary artists that is not all positive.[93] Art's refusal to comply comes with the heightened exposure to the risk of a proceeding for copyright infringement, which is perceived as a chilling factor for many artists. If copyright law picks out certain innovations among those that are made in the artistic field and declares them infringing, it is certainly not neutral toward what innovation shall entail.[94] Rather, with its understanding of novelty, copyright law enforces an "insularity" of artworks",[95]

89 Grünberger, p. 8.

90 It is in this sense that Edelman, The Law's Eye, p. 91, wrote that "The eye of law has become inward-looking: it only contemplates its own view"; cf. also Grünberger, p. 6 and Luhmann, Law as a Social System, p. 460; this doubt, resulting from the application of the legal code to itself, is irresolvable and represents the paradox at the beginning of the law system.

91 Cf. Peukert, End in Itself, p. 67 et seq.

92 Balganesh, Foreseeability, p. 1577, notes how courts in the US never make references to the mechanism of incentivization in their decisions nor measure copyright's extent with respect to its purpose. Rather, they just assume that "it works".

93 In Chapter 6, we have described the effects of copyright law on interpictorial art. As Grünberger, p. 10, pleads, because of today's complexity of legal relations, the dimension of subjective rights must be investigated beyond the sole centrality of the individuum.

94 Thampapillai, p. 109; Carrier, p. 907 et seqq. and p. 914; Craig, Copyright, p. 31.

95 Fischer, Sampling, p. 48; cf. also Craig, Copyright, p. 20.

an "aesthetic of autonomy"[96] and, thus, automatically, a certain type of authorship finds itself at odds with the artistic reality, especially that of certain movements.[97]

Even if reformulated the other way around (from art's perspective), such a dilemma is unescapable. If art wants to gain legal recognition or otherwise exist undisturbed, it must be a certain way.[98] Art's compliance to the rules, however, will amount to an external influence of the pure aesthetic message, causing an unwanted aesthetical influence of copyright law in the final form of the artwork. This insight shows a picture of copyright law that is at odds with its self-description as being an incentive system in service of the public interest, aesthetically, neutrally configured toward its addressees and equally providing them its rewards in the service of innovation.[99]

By not asking the questions that would reveal its contradictions, copyright risks becoming an end in itself.[100] Fulfilling its function by protecting the already included position of the old author becomes a rhetorical way to reiterate the self-confirming narrative, or, as best expressed by PEUKERT, "teleological statements show a certain tendency towards *a self-sufficient property logic*".[101]

II.IV.II A cognitively open copyright

Many scholars are aware of the fallacies copyright law has collected in various spheres of society, e.g., its incapability to protect new artistic forms but also to keep the pace with technological developments.[102] These scholars have denounced the presence of "dysfunctional conducts" (i.e., of conducts deviating from the declared functions pursued by copyright law).[103] Many have gone even further and diagnosed a "crisis of copyright".[104] On the opposite side, we, thus, observe a more permeable copyright law, preoccupied with the maintenance of its societal function.

Sensitive to the effects its rules exert on its environment, this cognitively open copyright feels responsible for maintaining the best possible conditions for its

96 FISCHER, Sampling, p. 48; CRAIG, Copyright, p. 20 et seq. and p. 234: "the legitimacy of the copyright system is dependent upon the coincidence of the public interest in the maximum generation and exchange of knowledge with the interests of authors in the protection of copyright. Essentially, the copyright system must *stand or fall as an institution that is able to maximise social communication and cultural interaction*" (emphasis added).

97 BARRON, Claims of Art, p. 397; DÖHL, Systemwechsel, p. 269, writing about music sampling, speaks of "open conflicts with the specificities of certain genres" (translation is mine).

98 GRABER, Zwischen Geist und Geld, p. 102.

99 GRÜNBERGER, p. 10.

100 GEIGER, Reconceptualizing, p. 122 et seq.

101 PEUKERT, End in Itself, p. 70 (emphasis added).

102 The two issues are compared from the perspective of copyright law's incapability to protect the "new" by BALGANESH, Foreseeability, p. 1572. This issue, i.e., the interference of copyright law with future creativity, has been called "dynamic inefficiency", cf. BALGANESH, Foreseeability, p. 1578. Static inefficiency, instead, is the situation in which the monopoly on a work lets the rightsholder fix a price that the user is not willing to pay.

103 SGANGA/SCALZINI, p. 408; cf. also HOFFMANN-RIEM, p. 433.

104 Reporting, GEIGER, Access right, p. 74; WIELSCH, Relationales Urheberrecht, p. 61.

environment to thrive unperturbed.[105] The difference to the previously described copyright is, thus, that this copyright is not only irritated by events happening in its environment (the "other copyright", which we called self-referential, is also irritated) but also measures its own rules' goodness based on the reactions they collect beyond the law system.[106]

The diagnosed problem is deep and caused by copyright law itself, i.e., by how it defines protected works, the existence of a blind spot impeding copyright to see interpictorial original copies as autonomous artworks and spaces of freedom within the granted exclusive rights. For these reasons, some authors argue that legislative changes are required and propose solutions in this respect.[107] According to them, only the appeal to the legislature is left to address and solve the fact that, sometimes, innovation constitutes copyright infringement.[108]

For many more copyright scholars, however, a legislative change does not seem like a realistically viable solution. Considering the incremental expansion of authors' rights of the last decades (often implemented not in favor of authors, but of rightsholders and corporations) perpetrated at the national and supranational level alike, these scholars note the legislatures' lack of willingness to change the laws in favor of a more condoning, user-friendly copyright law that is open to learn from other systems to better serve their needs.[109] To accommodate innovations in society without necessarily changing the law, many authors, thus, plead for enhancing the "flexibility" of the copyright regime, thus putting the solution in the hands of judges and courts.[110]

105 LEISTNER, Anforderungen, p. 224; GRÜNBERGER, p. 3; WIELSCH, Relationales Urheberrecht, p. 85; cf. also MÜLLER, p. 231 et seq. for a historical perspective.

106 GRÜNBERGER, p. 21; MÜLLER, p. 258.

107 This was tried, for example, in RIGAMONTI, Grundrechte, p. 392 et seq., with the formulation of a "subsidiary copyright exception" that could be introduced in the then (2017) imminent amendment of the CopA. Five years later, this, mournfully, is used only for ascertaining (cf. RIGAMONTI, Trittligasse, p. 68 et seqq.) that the legislature missed the chance to update the statutory copyright exceptions on the occasion of the copyright revision and that, therefore, the same problem will keep reappearing. Many requests also involve the introduction of an open clause, or of a fair use test in European copyright systems, cf. for example KLEINEMENKE, p. 591 et seq.; GEIGER, A Threat, p. 696; GEIGER, Flexibilizing, p. 196; SENFTLEBEN, Overprotection, p. 157. On the policy side, see for example, Report on the implementation of Directive 2001/29/EC of the European Parliament and of the Council of 22 May 2001 on the harmonization of certain aspects of copyright and related rights in the information society, June 24, 2015, calling for more flexibility in the implementation of the Infosoc-Directive; cf. also the Wittem International Network Project on a European Copyright Code (information available at: <https://www.ivir.nl/copyrightcode/european-copyright-code/>).

108 GRÜNBERGER, p. 11 et seq.; RENDAS, p. 16.

109 Cf. RIGAMONTI, Grundrechte, p. 383; GRÜNBERGER, p. 1, SGANGA/SCALZINI, p. 413; HUGENHOLTZ, p. 281; PEUKERT, Two Cultures, p. 396 et seq.

110 HOFFMANN-RIEM, p. 433; for example, LEISTNER, p. 224; HUGENHOLTZ, p. 290; SUTTERER, p. 138, explicitly arguing that "serving th[e] basic purpose of copyright becomes increasingly difficult when new creations that borrow from pre-existing works can only argue for justification within the existing catalogue of exceptions"; FÖRSTER, p. 211 et seqq.

II.IV.III On copyright law's flexibility

The request for more flexibility is so prevalent and recurring in copyright literature that it has almost taken the dimensions of a "movement". To better understand, we must further differentiate between flexibility, in general, and flexibility as we find it in the copyright literature.

Flexibility, in general (often paraphrased in "adaptability", "changeability", "ability to develop", "sustainability", "dynamicity" and "mobility" of law[111]), is described as law's capacity to adapt to new situations.[112] As such, it is a characteristic that is "oblique" to law itself. It does not characterize the norm per se but, rather, *how* the norm is applied, that is, how strictly a judge is bound by the law as it was conceived by the legislature, or how free she is in proposing new solutions and tailoring them to the case at stake without recourse to the legislature.[113] Tactics to make law inherently more flexible include the inclusion of general principles, open clauses (such as fair use[114]) and indeterminate legal concepts (such as the work)[115] that allow a wide margin of appreciation and accommodate case-by-case tailored solutions.[116]

In this first sense, enhanced flexibility does not allow conclusions as to the consequences of such a flexible approach. On the contrary, the flip side of a more flexible law is the proportional increase in legal uncertainty, i.e., not being able to predict in which direction a judgment will bend. Arguing for more legal flexibility entails a readiness to assume risks, for example, in the form of an unpleasant outcome. In the context of copyright, this means that the judge is given more leeway in interpreting and applying the relevant provisions. She will, thus, be enabled to both *extend* the interpretation of copyright exceptions, favoring derivative uses of protected works, as well as to *restrict* it, thus augmenting the protection scope for authors even more. The same would happen with the protection scope for the work.[117]

The version of flexibility, as we find it in copyright literature, is of another kind. Authors lament that the inherent flexibility of the copyright normative structure only favors a certain set of interests, parallelly disfavoring others.

111 Cf. Brändli-Marmy, p. 39.

112 Brändli-Marmy, p. 40; for Luhmann, Law as a Social System, p. 469 et seq., this is a characteristic of modern law as positive law.

113 Brändli-Marmy, p. 40 et seqq.; see Luhmann, Interesse, p. 1 et seqq., flexibility concerns the (historical) difference between legislation and jurisdiction.

114 Buydens/Dusollier, p. 2; Geiger/Gervais/Senftleben, Revisited, p. 614.

115 Brändli-Marmy, p. 48 et seqq.

116 Hugenholtz, p. 279; Ladeur/Vesting, p. 131, speak of "shifting the certainty of expectations to the promotion of innovation" (translation is mine); Luhmann, Law as a Social System, p. 189 explains that the resorting to hierarchically "higher" principles in law is a strategy to keep invariancy while guaranteeing, on lower instances, to always adapt law and create further differentiations.

117 Geiger, Access right, p. 105.

Whereas the definition of the protection scope flexibility (and, thus, the ability to change) is achieved through the inclusion of general clauses and undefined legal concepts (cf. for example Art. 2 para. 1 CopA, Art. 10 para. 1 CopA), this is not the same at the level of copyright exceptions,[118] which have traditionally been interpreted "strictly".[119] Scholarly opinions aiming at augmenting copyright flexibility are a reflex to this diagnosis and are, thus, not neutral with respect to the interests they advance. Rather, they perceive the need to make copyright flexible as the solution to the problem previously described, that is, copyright's inability to accommodate certain artistic movements and technological developments. A more flexible approach to the application of copyright exceptions is, thus, looked for to counter what is perceived to be an inherently imbalanced copyright, acting within society to the detriment of future creativity and of innovation[120] and to punctually enforce a correction of the outcomes in the interest of users.[121]

The advocacy for more flexibility in this second sense is, thus, only in appearance, a neutral discourse. When courts do not consider certain human rights and apply copyright norms "as they are", the resulting decisions are often criticized for their lack of flexibility. But this always translates in a complaint toward the judges for having opted for a (too) strict interpretation of the exceptions and a (too) strong property protection.[122] This discourse of flexible copyright law is, in fact, always partisan to an interpretation of norms informed by the freedoms of communication; a "fair balancing" is always a vehicle to a larger consideration of users' rights; and an assessment of proportionality is always the proxy for correcting a solution considered too protective of the author's property.[123]

118 Rigamonti, Grundrechte, p. 383; Hugenholtz, p. 280.

119 Cf. Chapter 5.

120 For example, Geiger, Flexibilising Copyright, p. 178; Senftleben, Overprotection, p. 180 et seq.

121 Geiger, Flexibilising Copyright, p. 184 et seq.; Geiger, Reconceptualizing, p. 142 et seqq. and 150 et seqq., pleads for a human rights-informed "reorganization" of copyright law; Geiger/Izyumenko, Constitutionalization, p. 29, where "flexibilization" means the opening of copyright jurisprudence to an external freedom of expression review.

122 E.g., Kaiser/Scheuerer, p. 1160.

123 Luhmann, Interesse, p. 1, writes how legal criticism today is always directed at criticizing the interests advanced by a certain application of the law and at arguing how other interests should have been given priority instead.

Part IV

Displacing the paradox

"It is the disk of Odin," the old man said in a patient voice, as though he were speaking to a child. "It has but one side. There is not another thing on earth that has but one side. (...)" "Is it gold?" I said. "I know not. It is the disk of Odin and it has but one side."

Jorge Luis Borges, The Disk (from The Book of Sand, 1975)

DOI: 10.4324/9781003598503-11

7 Beyond copyright law – external remedies

I.I Introduction

As we have seen, the law of copyright may, at times, be unfavorable toward the interpictorial artwork. A strict application of the law may impose the primary burdens of the copyright regime on interpictoriality – namely, the narrow scope for considering content changes and the requirement for transformation or distance – hindering the successful subsumption of the interpictorial artwork under a copyright exception. If a verdict of copyright infringement is pronounced, both the artwork's undisturbed existence in the world and its relationship with the author are compromised.

As exposed in Chapter 6, II.II, when copyright law declares that new art is infringing, a paradoxical situation within copyright law arises, in which *the protection of old works hampers the creation of new ones, despite copyright law's societal function to foster innovation and creativity*. As seen, lawyers and courts alike – rightfully concerned with maintaining the function of copyright law in society and recognizing the legislatures' failure to provide a regulatory framework that addresses changes in art and technology[1] – try to propose remedies.[2]

The remedies they propose represent an upward shift toward a higher normative level, where hierarchically superior norms justify the abandonment of the copyright framework, whose solutions are perceived as unsatisfactory.[3] The paradoxical situation created within copyright law is, thus, reformulated in other legal terms, which allow for a different rendition of the same situation. When analyzed through systems theory, this transposition of the copyright impasse to a higher normative level represents a strategy known as paradox unfolding. Unfolding a paradox involves

1 Izyumenko, Freedom of Expression, p. 116 et seq.

2 Cf. Rendas, p. 16.

3 Luhmann, Law as a Social System, p. 186: the permission for the self-rejection of the legal code is constructed paradoxically because it claims lawfulness for itself. For this reason, the paradox is unfolded by differentiating "levels of legal validity" (i.e., hierarchically higher norms); cf. also Luhmann, Menschenrechte, p. 229; e.g., Torremans, p. 246 argues that "in normative terms, human rights are fundamental and of higher importance than intellectual property rights"; Geiger, Reconceptualizing, p. 144, speaks of "the nature of fundamental rights as objective principles".

DOI: 10.4324/9781003598503-12

shifting the blind spot[4] – which when uncovered, creates a state of blockage – to another, less disruptive place, rendering it invisible once more.[5]

It would, however, be wrong to assume that the displacement of the paradox to another place would simply dissolve it, paving the way to a paradox-free construction of the world.[6] Rather, to escape a paradox means to enter a different one, as systems of meaning lead to new paradoxes exactly as paradoxes lead to new systems of meaning.[7] In this sense, when observed from a second order perspective, the existence of paradoxes is an agent of evolutionary development, not a problem per se.[8] The question is, therefore, not how to avoid the paradox but, rather, why the law chooses one specific strategy rather than another to unfold and hide the paradox.[9] Another question is whether this newly established stability allows the art system to thrive unperturbed.

In the following chapter, we show some of the strategies lawyers have found to circumvent and surpass the paradoxical situation caused by and within copyright law. We conclude with a methodological critique and an outlook to the conclusive chapter.

II.I The three-step test

The three-step test is contained in the provisions of many international treaties, such as the Berne Convention at Art. 9 para. 2, the TRIPS Agreement at Art. 13, the WIPO Copyright Treaty (WCT) at Art. 10 and the WIPO Performances and Phonograms Treaties (WPPT) at Art. 16 para. 2. The wording of the test is always very similar in all these different provisions. In the Berne Convention, the three-step test is formulated with the following tenor:

> It shall be a matter for legislation in the countries of the Union to permit the reproduction of such works in certain special cases, provided that such reproduction does not conflict with a normal exploitation of the work and does not unreasonably prejudice the legitimate interests of the author.

The three-step test was initially not designed to operate as part of domestic legislation. Rather, it was intended as a guide to national legislatures to measure and maintain the compliance of their copyright laws against an international standard.[10]

4 For copyright law, the blind spot is the impossibility of seeing an interpictorial original copy as an original work. See Chapter 4, V.I.
5 Luhmann, Decision Making, p. 91 et seq.; Luhmann, Law as a Social System, p. 461 et seq.
6 Luhmann, Decision Making, p. 92.
7 Teubner, Umgang mit Rechtsparadoxien, p. 29 et seq.
8 Teubner, Umgang mit Rechtsparadoxien, p. 29 et seq.
9 Luhmann, Decision Making, p. 92; Teubner, Umgang mit Rechtsparadoxien, p. 31; the orientation toward the consequences of a decision and the flexibilization of decision-making through the bias of the balancing of interests, rights or values, is a contemporary phenomenon observable in the legal system, cf. Luhmann, Law as a Social System, p. 448 and 455.
10 Geiger, A Threat, p. 689; Thampapillai, p. 108; Arnold/Rosati, p. 1195; Rendas, p. 4.

However, the test found its way in Art. 5 para. 5 Infosoc-Directive and in the national copyright regimes of many European Union Member States, such as Spain and France.[11] From a test to judge the copyright exception rule, the test, thus, became an additional control for the application of copyright exceptions in judicial decisions.[12] In Switzerland, courts regularly verify whether the application of a certain norm is compatible with the test, even if the test was not transposed in any national provision and even if it is not considered to be directly applicable.[13]

II.II The three steps

The so-called "three steps" outlined in the law, which must be fulfilled cumulatively,[14] are as follows: According to the first criterion, (1) copyright exceptions cannot be overly broad ("certain special cases"). The scope of an acceptable exception must be well defined ("certain") and narrowly limited ("special"). Copyright exceptions of broad and indeterminate general application are, thus, precluded by the three-step test.[15]

Under the second criterion, copyright exceptions (2) cannot rob rightsholders[16] of a real or potential source of income that is substantive ("does not conflict with a normal exploitation of the work"). The question to ask is whether the exempted use would otherwise fall within the range of activities from which the copyright owner would normally expect to receive compensation. The term "normal" denotes any way in which the work is, in fact, exploited but also considers any other potential,

11 ARNOLD/ROSATI, p. 1194 et seqq.; in 2004, SENFTLEBEN, Copyright, p. 43, still describes it as a supranational regulator of the balance between authors' rights and the application of copyright exceptions.

12 GEIGER/GERVAIS/SENFTLEBEN, Understanding, p. 169; SGANGA/SCALZINI, p. 414; RENDAS, p. 5.

13 Decision of the SFAC B-2612/2011 of July 2, 2013, c. 7.5.2 said it is not directly applicable; in DFC 133 III 473 (*Pressespiegel*), c. 6 et seqq., however, the plaintiff argued that the press review activity infringed the three-step test; cf. also DFC 140 III 616 (*ETH Dokumentenlieferdienst*).

14 PAPADOPOULOS/KOUTRAS, p. 633; that the three steps have to be fulfilled cumulatively represents one of the main differences from fair use, cf. FICSOR, p. 282. In the words of the US Supreme Court, fair use is a holistic, context-sensitive inquiry "not to be simplified with bright-line rules[.] All [four statutory factors] are to be explored, and the results weighed together, in light of the purposes of copyright", cf. *Andy Warhol Found. for the Visual Arts, Inc. vs. Goldsmith*, 598 US ___ (2023).

15 PAPADOPOULOS/KOUTRAS, p. 633 et seq.; when considering whether Switzerland's copyright exceptions catalogue is exhaustive or open to a new exception, BRÄNDLI-MARMY, p. 89, also examined whether the three-step test's first step – that the exception shall be limited to certain special cases – limits the idea of a non-exhaustive exceptions catalogue. She concluded that, in the case of the creation of a new exception that was not initially included in the law by the legislator, by means of a narrowly circumscribed analogy, the three-step test does not stand in the way. If the analogy is so circumscribed, the judge creating it sticks to the legislature's guidelines and applies them to a certain special case. We agree with this opinion. Indeed, even copyright exceptions based on an open-ended system such as the US fair use are deemed by the majority to be compatible with the three-step test, cf. GEIGER/GERVAIS/SENFTLEBEN, Revisited, p. 612 et seq. and FICSOR, p. 287.

16 This is an important difference of wording between the Berne Convention and the TRIPS; whereas the Berne Convention speaks only of the legitimate interests of *authors*, TRIPS enlarges the scope to all *rightsholders* and, thus, to all successors in title, cf. JONGSMA, Nature and content, p. 341.

permissible and desirable exploitation of the work.[17] The second step is understood as considering proportionality "in the broad sense".[18]

Under the third and last criterion, copyright exceptions (3) cannot do disproportional harm to the rightsholders[19] ("does not unreasonably prejudice the legitimate interests of the author").[20] Here, a notion of proportionality "in the strict sense" is introduced in the form of a balancing of the right holder's interests against the interests of third parties.[21] A "reasonable damage" to the economic value of a work is a damage that is proportionate to the specific interests of the rightsholder.[22] The prejudices that a copyright exception may cause can even be significant and substantial, provided they satisfy the first two conditions of the test and are within the limits of reason.[23] It shall also be noted that the third step does not speak of "rights" but, rather, of legitimate interests. These comprise those interests provisioned in copyright law.[24] According to the SFSC, the interests addressed by the copyright exceptions align with those balanced in the three-step test, reflecting fundamental rights: On one side, the guarantee of ownership (Art. 26 Const.) and on the other side, the freedoms of communication (i.e., freedom of expression and of information, academic freedom, freedom of artistic expression and freedom of the media).[25]

II.III The interpretations of the three-step test

As a result of a compromise between negotiators from different copyright cultures (most prominently of the civil and common law traditions), the abstract language of the test was intentionally maintained.[26] The test's nature is that of a balancing of interests that introduces the open requirement of "proportionality" into every decision.[27] Stemming from provisions of copyright protection within the framework of trade rules, the test is results-based. The lack of evidence of actual economical damage could prevent a copyright norm from applying or *vice versa*. The thought

17 PAPADOPOULOS/KOUTRAS, p. 637 et seq.
18 DFC 133 III 473 (*Pressespiegel*), p. 485; however, a restrictive approach to what is meant under "normal exploitation" is proposed by some commentators in order to strike a proper balance between copyright protection and competing social, cultural and economic needs, cf. GEIGER/GERVAIS/SENFTLEBEN, Revisited, p. 603.
19 According to the SFSC, the interests of the author and of the rightsholder do not forcibly coincide, and it is unclear which interests are meant in the third step. In DFC 133 III 473 (*Pressespiegel*), p. 487 c. 6.3, the SFSC considered both interests.
20 PAPADOPOULOS/KOUTRAS, p. 632.
21 DFC 133 III 473 (*Pressespiegel*), p. 486.
22 DFC 133 III 473 (*Pressespiegel*), p. 485.
23 PAPADOPOULOS/KOUTRAS, p. 639.
24 PAPADOPOULOS/KOUTRAS, p. 639.
25 DFC 140 III 616 (*ETH Dokumentenlieferdienst*), c. 3.6.3.
26 GEIGER/GERVAIS/SENFTLEBEN, Revisited, p. 591; GEIGER/GERVAIS/SENFTLEBEN, Understanding, p. 173.
27 RIGAMONTI, Medienberichterstattung, p. 52 et seqq.; LADEUR, Recht, p. 27, describes the rise of the principle of proportionality as a methodological tool enabling the harmonization between rights and interests in very different case scenarios.

behind this results-based rationale is that copyright should serve a purpose. The moment the purpose is not fulfilled, copyright should cease to apply or be applied differently to serve this purpose again.[28] This attention on the result allows the "flexibility" of the test to stand in the center of the theoretical discussions about its application,[29] with the consequence that the test accommodates various and even contradicting interpretations.[30]

The introduction of the three-step test has altered the application of exceptions; whereas previously they could be applied *qua* exceptions, it is now necessary to verify whether the exception in question fulfills the open-ended conditions laid out by the three-step test.[31] To the balancing of interests already enshrined in the statutory copyright exception, an additional one is superimposed.[32] If applying the exception results in a disproportionate outcome based on the balancing of interests, the three-step test provides for an *ad hoc* correction of the outcome.[33] In whose interests the correction shall be carried out, however, is an object of debate.

On one side, the three-step test has been interpreted as an exception-exception ("Schrankenschranke"[34]), i.e., a way to externally limit the scope of statutory exceptions and, thus, favor the rightsholders *a fortiori*.[35] If interpreted in this way, the three-step test limits the leeway courts have to apply copyright exceptions, causing a possibly narrower interpretation of existing ones that enhances the scope of exclusive rights of authors and rightsholders.[36]

Many authors have criticized this restrictive application of copyright exceptions based on the three-step test. These authors lament that this application is disruptive of the balance laid down by the law.[37] On the other side, the three-step test is, thus, interpreted as having not only a negative meaning (in the sense of an exception-exception, i.e., of limiting the existing copyright exceptions) but also a positive, enabling one.[38] Provided the solution is applied to only certain special cases, the enabling interpretation of the three-step test makes it possible to set copyright

28 Gervais, How Intellectual Property, p. 6 et seqq.

29 Jongsma, Nature and content, p. 350; Geiger, A Threat, p. 694 et seq.; Geiger/Gervais/Senftleben, Revisited, p. 581 et seqq.

30 Jongsma, Nature and content, p. 341 et seqq.; Geiger/Gervais/Senftleben, Revisited, p. 582.

31 Senftleben, Copyright, p. 43; Wielsch, Relationales Urheberrecht, p. 90.

32 This superimposition is also demonstrated by the addition of the three-step test in the Infosoc-Directive; Geiger, A Threat, p. 690, wonders, if all the limits set out in Art. 5 para. 2 and 3 of InfoSoc-Directive were already supposed to be compatible with this article and the list of the exceptions exhaustive, why was the three-step test introduced at para. 5 of the same Article?

33 Fischer Veronika, p. 231.

34 Rigamonti, Grundrechte, p. 364, fn. 84; Senftleben, Copyright, p. 355.

35 Arnold/Rosati, p. 1199.

36 Förster, p. 99; cf. the interpretation of the three-step test by the Higher Regional Court of Hamburg of April 28, 2021 (*Metall auf Metall III*), GRUR 2022, p. 1217 et seqq., p. 1223 at para. 85.

37 For an account of "suggestions to avoid restrictive outcomes", see Jongsma, Nature and content, p. 342, who also notes that the "balance" has never been immobile but rather constantly changing; see also Geiger, A Threat, p. 688; Geiger/Griffiths/Hilty, p. 707 et seqq.; Buydens/Dusollier, p. 5 et seqq. ; Kaiser/Scheuerer, p. 1156.

38 Geiger/Gervais/Senftleben, Revisited, p. 616.

protection aside,[39] create new exceptions[40] or eventually pair existing copyright exceptions with compensation in order to preserve the economic proportionality of the suffered damage.[41] In this latter "positive" understanding, the three-step test may become an occasional remedy to a verdict of copyright infringement.

II.IV The three-step test as a remedy to copyright infringement

The *Megakini.com/Google Spain* case, decided by the Spanish Supreme Court, is an example in which copyright protection was set aside. Google was sued for copyright infringement for its praxis of reproducing parts of websites in its search results. Although no copyright exceptions were available under Spanish copyright legislation that could justify the unauthorized use of copyrighted material, the court found that, in the absence of a real prejudice, the protection of copyright may not be "misused to harm another party".[42] The Spanish Supreme Court first recognized that the three-step test (also anchored at Art. 40bis of the Spanish Intellectual Property Law) not only has a negative interpretive value but also a positive one. It then interpreted the provision as a copyright-*lex specialis* ("manifestación especial") of the general doctrines of the *ius usus inocui*, the good faith and of the prohibition of abuse of rights.[43] The court further held that the three-step test concretizes the fact that the constitutional right to property is a limited right.[44] In proposing this interpretation and concluding that Google's use of snippets from websites was lawful, the court, thus, created a *de facto* new copyright exception.[45]

According to GEIGER, GERVAIS and SENFTLEBEN, this same positive interpretation of the three-step test enabled the SFSC to "propose *an extensive and liberal interpretation* of the private use exception included in Art. 19 para. 2 CopA" and, thus, to "*legitimize the use* of press articles by specialized commercial services providing electronic press reviews upon demand to enterprises".[46]

In that decision, however, the court had come to this result *before* coming to thematize the test. The SFSC carried out a teleological extension of Art. 19 para. 1 let. c CopA. It held that, even though the wording of the norm only refers to the "*copying* of a work" (and, thus, to the reproduction right of Art. 10 para. 2 let. a CopA), it must be interpreted as also encompassing the right to internally *distribute*

39 GEIGER/GERVAIS/SENFTLEBEN, Understanding, p. 186.

40 GEIGER, Flexibilising Copyright, p. 194 et seq.; GEIGER/GERVAIS/SENFTLEBEN, Understanding, p. 187; GEIGER/GERVAIS/SENFTLEBEN, Revisited, p. 625.

41 FISCHER VERONIKA, p. 231; according to BRÄNDLI-MARMY, p. 96, the introduction of a compensation to re-institute proportionality would be illegal from the perspective of the precept of precision of the law ("Bestimmtheitsgebot"). This precept is unconditional in Switzerland if public levies are to be collected. In other words, the judge cannot introduce a remuneration if the law does not already provide for one.

42 GEIGER/GERVAIS/SENFTLEBEN, Revisited, p. 621 et seq.

43 Tribunal Supremo of April 3, 2012 (*Megakini.com vs. Google Spain*).

44 Tribunal Supremo of April 3, 2012 (*Megakini.com vs. Google Spain*).

45 ALEJANDRE, p. 81 et seqq.

46 GEIGER/GERVAIS/SENFTLEBEN, Revisited, p. 619 et seq. (emphasis added).

those copies (Art. 10 para. 2 let. b CopA) among the circles of institutions, enterprises etc. enumerated in the exception.[47] The test is only mentioned afterward and is used as a control instance to assess the proportionality of the decision taken, which, due to the open-endedness of the test, was affirmed. In its examination, the SFSC rightly considered that "to only take account of the interests of the publisher would fall too short, since the private use exception of Art. 19 CopA aims at striking a balance with third parties' interests".[48]

Applied to interpictorial artworks, the positive interpretation of the three-step test could pave a way to open copyright law's lists of exceptions (or their scope of application). The three-step test could justify the unsanctioned and otherwise infringing use of copyrighted material by an artist on a case-by-case basis, even if a specific exception is lacking or its scope too narrow. Provided it does not interfere with the normal exploitation of the work and does not unreasonably damage its author's interests, the judge could, for example, deem it appropriate to set aside copyright protection for the used material. He could also create a new exception justifying the use for the creation of the artwork (provided it satisfies Step 1 of the test, i.e., that it is confined to "certain special cases") or extend an existing one. Lastly, he could pronounce an obligation for the artist to compensate the damage incurred by the first author for the unsanctioned use.

III.I The role of fundamental rights

Fundamental rights-driven reflections on copyright law, that is, the discussion about the constitutional foundations of copyright and its eventual constitutional-based boundaries, first appeared around the year 2000.[49] In Switzerland, the dogmatic conditions for this reflection was established during the comprehensive revision of the Constitution in 2000, which expanded the scope of fundamental rights.[50] The newly introduced Art. 35 para. 1 Const. declares that fundamental rights must be upheld throughout the entire legal system, while at Para. 3, it stipulates the obligation for authorities to ensure that fundamental rights apply to relationships

47 DFC 133 III 473 (*Pressespiegel*), c. 5.4.; BRÄNDLI-MARMY, p. 96 et seqq., in the same decision, the SFSC also carried out a teleological reduction of Art. 10 para. 2 let. a CopA, holding that the automatically executed act of ephemeral and temporary copying while browsing for results on the internet does not fall under the author's right of producing copies of the work (today, the legislature anchored this exception in Art. 24a CopA). None of these interpretations, which ultimately favored the interests of users, was directly based on the three-step test.

48 DFC 133 III 473 (*Pressespiegel*), c. 6.4. (translation is mine).

49 HELFER, p. 117 et seqq.; cf. the comprehensive literature review by GRABER, Copyright and Access, p. 5 at fn. 20; RIGAMONTI, Grundrechte, p. 365 et seq.; although copyright literature naturally focuses on the interaction between copyright law and human rights, the approach of private law to human rights is observable in the whole legal system. On this cf. LADEUR, Die Beobachtung, p. 493 et seqq., who critically speaks of the "Constitutionalization of the legal system"; uncritical instead cf. PAPAUX-VAN DELDEN, p. 160 et seqq.

50 RIGAMONTI, Grundrechte, p. 365 et seq.; WEBER/BREINING-KAUFMANN, p. 416 et seq.; LADEUR, Kritik der Abwägung, p. 9.

among private persons ("horizontal effect", in German: *Drittwirkung*).[51] The result is an osmosis between legal domains that were traditionally separated. From the negative rights of the individual, vis-à-vis the state ("Abwehrrechte"), fundamental rights have now expanded their function to represent a positive obligation of the state to realize them in the relations among individuals.[52]

Transposed on the constitutional level, the author's pretenses under copyright law regarding control over the fate of his work and its economic exploitation are normally associated to the guarantee of ownership (Art. 26 Const., Art. 1 Protocol No. 1 ECHR, signed but not ratified by Switzerland).[53] On the other side, depending on the case, users appeal themselves to the so-called communication freedoms, i.e., freedom of expression and of information (Art. 16 Const.), academic freedom (Art. 20 Const.), freedom of artistic expression (Art. 21 Const.) and freedom of the media (Art. 17 Const.). If interpictorial artworks are involved, the relevant fundamental right is the freedom of artistic expression enshrined at Art. 21 Const. At the international level, these rights are enshrined at Art. 10 ECHR.[54]

Fundamental rights landed in the doctrine of copyright law, but their role in the practice of judiciary decision-making is not always the same. On the one side, courts have used fundamental rights accessorily and within the boundaries laid out by normal legislation. They have, thus, limited themselves to interpret existing provisions in conformity with the constitution (1).[55] On the other side, courts have used fundamental rights as instruments to open up continental Europe's closed lists of exceptions and achieve a flexibilization of the civil law copyright system (2).[56]

As Rigamonti underlines, the boundaries between these two uses of fundamental rights in copyright case law are sometimes blurry.[57] A possible criterion

51 Papaux-Van Delden, p. 165; Weber/Breining-Kaufmann, p. 416; at EU-level, the question of the horizontal direct effect of the fundamental rights of the Charter among citizens has not yet been confirmed by the CJEU; Geiger/Izyumenko, Shaping, p. 548, argue that the obligation to secure the effective exercise of Convention rights may, however, involve positive obligations of a state even in the relation among individuals between themselves.

52 Papaux-Van Delden, p. 158; Ladeur, Die Beobachtung, p. 493 et seqq.

53 Brändli-Marmy, p. 60; DFC 140 III 616 (*ETH Dokumentenlieferdienst*), c. 3.6.3.; Geiger/Izyumenko, Shaping, p. 572 et seq. point out how sometimes, even if more rarely, authors appeal to communication freedoms to justify their copyright protection and their exercise of "total control over [a] work, as desired".

54 Geiger, Die Schranken, p. 146; Buydens/Dusollier; cf. also DFC 140 III 616 (*ETH Dokumentenlieferdienst*), c. 3.6.3.

55 Papaux-Van Delden, p. 162, explains that a radical application of Art. 190 Const., which admitted absolutely no control of the constitutionality of national norms, has given way to the principle of interpretation of the law in conformity with the Constitution and international law. Judges examine the law and prioritize the interpretation thereof that most conforms to the constitution. This shall prevent conflicts with the Constitution.

56 Buydens/Dusollier, p. 4; Geiger, Die Schranken, p. 152.

57 Rigamonti, Grundrechte, p. 367.

to differentiate these kinds of uses is to ask whether the use of the work would be infringing if it were not for the corrective contribution of a fundamental right.[58]

III.II Interpretation in conformity with the Constitution ("flexibility within")

As previously discussed,[59] the SFSC views the statutory list of exceptions in the CopA as exhaustive. In DFC 120 IV 208 (*Lizentiatsarbeit*), the court held that conflicts between the interests of the author and other potential users are, as a rule, decided exhaustively by the legislature in the CopA.[60] In DFC 131 III 480 (*Schweizerzeit*), the same court similarly clarified that the exceptions of copyright are a matter regulated exhaustively by the legislator.[61] The only residual task of the judge is to interpret law in conformity with the constitution ("verfassungskonforme Auslegung").[62] Such interpretation should help concretize copyright provisions in light of the constitutional rights. It should not, however, open the doors to a balancing of interests that differs from those previously laid out by the legislature.[63]

A very similar approach – fundamental rights as interpretive auxiliaries of a closed list of statutory exceptions – is adopted at the European Union level by the CJEU.[64] As previously discussed,[65] the preliminary ruling in *Metall auf Metall* instructed the courts of the Member States to stick to the exceptions listed at Art. 5 of the Infosoc-Directive. Two further judgments, *Funke Medien* and *Spiegel Online*, decided on the same day as *Metall auf Metall*, have done the same. In all three cases, the court held that fundamental rights anchored in the Charter of the European Union (in the cases at stake: Art. 11, freedom of expression, of information and of the press) are not capable of justifying, *beyond* the exceptions or limitations provided for at Art. 5 of Infosoc-Directive, a derogation from the author's

58 Rigamonti, Grundrechte, p. 368, explains that, as long as the sense of the normal legislation is corrected, it does not make any difference if this happens *ex ante* through an interpretation in conformity with the constitution or *ex post* through an open modification of the interpretation's outcome.

59 See Chapter 5.

60 DFC 120 IV 208 (*Lizentiatsarbeit*), c. 3.

61 If an exception is not contained in the law, it means it was not wanted, cf. Egloff, CopA Commentary, N 4 *ad* Vorbemerkungen Art. 19–28. The same author, however, advances the possibility of an *extra legem* "justification" for some uses of copyrighted works founded for example on the third-party effect of the constitutional artistic freedom (e.g., Art. 21 Const. in conjunction with Art. 35 para. 3 Const.), Barrelet/Egloff, CopA Commentary, N 16 *ad* Art. 11.

62 Egloff, CopA Commentary, N 4 *ad* Vorbemerkungen Art. 19–28.

63 Egloff, CopA Commentary, N 4 *ad* Vorbemerkungen Art. 19–28; DFC 131 III 480 (*Schweizerzeit*), c. 3.

64 The jurisprudence of the CJEU must also be interpreted as a harmonization effort: every open clause or departure from a written rule would remit the protection of authors to the sensitiveness of national courts and constitute a danger for the smooth functioning of the European internal market, cf. Sganga, p. 3, and 13.

65 At Chapter 4, III.IV.II.II.

exclusive rights of reproduction and of communication to the public (stipulated at Art. 2 let. a and Art. 3 para. 1 of Infosoc-Directive).[66]

In the same decisions, the CJEU further held that in striking the balance between the exclusive rights of the author and the rights of the users, a national court must consider the circumstances of the case before it. The court shall rely on an interpretation of the relevant provisions that, "whilst consistent with their wording and safeguarding their effectiveness", fully adheres to the fundamental rights enshrined in the Charter.[67] For example, in its ruling in *Metall auf Metall*, the CJEU held that where users, in exercising the freedom of the arts enshrined at Art. 13 of the Charter, take a sound sample and use it in "a modified form *unrecognisable* to the ear", they do not interfere with the copyright holder's rights within the meaning of Article 2(c) of Infosoc-Directive.[68]

III.III Human-rights-based copyright exceptions ("flexibility without")

In other cases, by interpreting the law in conformity with a constitutional right, courts corrected an outcome judged detrimental for the observance of a fundamental right.[69] Examples thereof are already exposed decisions of the GFCC in the cases *Germania 3* and *Metall auf Metall*. In both decisions, the court substituted the conventional interpretations of § 51 DE-CopA (in *Germania 3*) and of § 24 oDE-CopA (in *Metall auf Metall*) with a larger and more generous interpretation of such articles informed by a specifically artistic interpretation of these exceptions ("kunstspezifische Betrachtung") based on the constitutional artistic freedom (enshrined at Art. 5 para. 3 German Basic Law).[70] In both cases, the copyright exceptions were explicitly enlarged with direct recourse to the constitutional artistic freedom. In a

66 CJEU of July 29, 2019 - C-469/17 (*Funke Medien vs. Bundesrepublik Deutschland*), at para. 56, states that exceptions are exhaustive and, at para. 64, that the freedom of information and of the press cannot create a further exception; same statements in CJEU of July 29, 2019 - C-516/17 (*Spiegel Online vs. Volker Beck*), at para. 41 and 49. Cf. also SNIJDERS/DEURSEN, p. 1182.

67 CJEU of July 29, 2019 - C-516/17 (*Spiegel Online vs. Volker Beck*), at para. 59; CJEU of July 29, 2019 - C-469/17 (*Funke Medien vs. Bundesrepublik Deutschland*), at para. 76; SUTTERER, p. 137; SNIJDERS/DEURSEN, p. 1186, note how especially in Opinion of AG Szpunar of October 25, 2018 - C-469/17 (*Funke Medien vs. Bundesrepublik Deutschland*), at para. 31, 40 and 71, the AG adopted an open stance toward the external reviewing role of fundamental rights in copyright law; SGANGA, p. 10 et seq., relativizes.

68 CJEU of July 29, 2019 - C-476/17 (*Metall auf Metall*), at para. 31 et seqq. (emphasis added); we might ask whether this "restriction" of the author's right of reproduction, informed – in the words of the CJEU – by the artistic freedom, is not merely symbolic: if the sample is "unrecognizable to the ear", how is it even possible for the author to recognize it and sue the user for copyright infringement? Cf. DÖHL, Systemwechsel, p. 258 at fn. 116; on this, DÖHL, Systemwechsel, p. 255, argues that for a real artistic freedom, artists should be free to decide whether the source shall remain recognizable or not, as that is sometimes the very purpose of borrowing from an existing artifact.

69 RIGAMONTI, Grundrechte, p. 367 et seq.; BRÄNDLI-MARMY, p. 52.

70 GFCC of May 31, 2016 (*Metall auf Metall*), GRUR 2016, p. 690 et seqq., p. 693 at para. 86. The court quotes the decision *Germania 3* as reference; RIGAMONTI, Grundrechte, p. 372, criticizes this interpretation calling it "meaningless", regardless of whether one agrees with the outcome or not.

methodological script flip, to circumvent a verdict of copyright infringement, the judges of the GFCC argued that such a verdict would constitute an infringement on the artistic freedom.

A French case, *Fabris vs. France 2*, decided by the Tribunal de Grande Instance de Paris (first instance), in 1999, had a similar effect.[71] On the occasion of an exhibition of paintings by Maurice Utrillo in the Museum of Lodève, the broadcaster France 2 had used 12 reproductions of Utrillo's paintings in a report, with the purpose of informing the public about the exhibition. For its use of the paintings, France 2 neither paid royalties nor asked for permission from the rightsholder, Mr. Fabris. Therefore, after asking for payment and being refused, Mr. Fabris sued the broadcaster. The Tribunal justified France 2 with an exception that it acted based on the public's right to be informed (Art. 10 para. 2 ECHR), thereby opening this option for the very first time in France.[72]

The following instance, the appeal court of Paris, confirmed that copyright law might constitute a restriction of Art. 10 para. 2 ECHR, but, ultimately, it rebutted the decision and pronounced itself in favor of Fabris, stating that the restriction of Art. 10 para. 2 ECHR was legitimate and proportional.[73] The Cour de Cassation, to which France 2 appealed, concluded the same as its previous instance in 2003.[74]

With the method of a fundamental rights-informed balancing of interests, the Austrian Supreme Court of Justice expanded the scope of copyright exceptions multiple times in its jurisprudence.[75] In the *Medienprofessor* case, the court argued that the conflict between the fundamental rights of the guarantee of ownership and the freedom of expression and information must be solved with a balancing of values or goods ("Güter- und Werteabwägung").[76] In the case, the professor had been sued for copyright infringement by the "Neue Kronen Zeitung". To substantiate his claim that a media campaign was being orchestrated against him, the professor had reproduced entire articles that the newspaper had previously published about him. The court concluded that the freedom of expression invoked by the professor "clearly weighed more" than the copyright interests of the plaintiff.[77]

71 Tribunal de Grande Instance de Paris of February 23, 1999 (*Jean Fabris vs. Société France 2*).

72 Kamina, p. 90; Graber, Copyright and Access, p. 16 et seq.; a similar case involved France 2 and the copyright holders of painter Edouard Vuillard. After the condemnation of France 2 for copyright infringement in France, France 2 appealed before the ECommHR (the ECtHR's predecessor) for an infringement of its freedom of expression. In ECommHR of January 15, 1997 (*Société Nationale de Programmes FRANCE 2 v France*), the Commission confirmed the proportionality assessment of the Cour de Cassation.

73 Kamina, p. 93.

74 Kamina, p. 94.

75 A comprehensive review of these cases from 2000 to 2003 can be found in Graber, Access Copyright, p. 24-27.

76 Austrian Supreme Court of Justice of June 12, 2001 (*Medienprofessor*), GRUR Int. 2002, p. 341 et seqq., p. 342.

77 Austrian Supreme Court of Justice of June 12, 2001 (*Medienprofessor*), GRUR Int. 2002, p. 341 et seqq., p. 343.

In another case, this time in the Netherlands, The Hague Court of Appeals held that publishing internal documents of the Church of Scientology on a website for the purposes of criticism, although not qualifying for the exception of quotation, was, nonetheless, covered by the public's right to information, as guaranteed by Art. 10 ECHR.[78]

In early 2013, the European Court of Human Rights (ECtHR) decided two cases involving copyright infringement – *Donald Ashby and Others vs. France*[79] and *Fredrik Neij and Peter Sunde Kolmisoppi vs. Sweden*.[80] In the first case, three fashion photographers were facing considerable criminal penalties and damages for posting pictures of fashion shows on their websites, thereby infringing the copyright of important fashion houses. In the second case, the founders of The Pirate Bay, an online file sharing platform, were convicted in Sweden to prison sentences for their copyright infringements. In both decisions, the ECtHR clearly framed copyright protection as a limitation to freedom of expression for the first time.[81] In this way, copyright law (linked by the court to the protection of property enshrined at Art. 1 of the Protocol No. 1 to the ECHR) automatically became a factor in determining whether a restriction on the freedom of expression, as set out in Art. 10 ECHR, may or may not be justified.[82] The ECtHR ruled that both cases were a conflict between opposed interests that needed to be balanced against each other. Seeing the conspicuous margin of appreciation enjoyed by the contracting states and given the commercial nature of the uses and the lack of contribution to the public debate, the ECtHR found that the convictions for copyright infringements were not disproportionate.[83]

Notwithstanding the verdict in these cases, which ultimately fell in favor of the copyright holders, the ECtHR sent a message to national courts and legislatures across Europe:[84] A freedom of expression-led review of copyright law shall be carried out on a strict case-by-case basis.[85] In copyright infringement cases, it is

78 The Hague Court of Appeals of September 4, 2003 (*Church of Scientology vs. XS4ALL*); GEIGER/IZYUMENKO, Constitutionalization, p. 300.

79 ECtHR of January 10, 2013 (*Donald Ashby and Others vs. France*).

80 ECtHR of February 19, 2013 (*Fredrik Neij and Peter Sunde Kolmisoppi vs. Sweden*).

81 GEIGER/IZYUMENKO, Copyright, p. 318; IZYUMENKO, Freedom of Expression, p. 115 et seq.; GEIGER/IZYUMENKO, Shaping, p. 567 et seq. remind how in its decision of January 15, 1997 (*Société Nationale de Programmes FRANCE 2 vs. France*), the ECommHR had verified, and confirmed, the conformity of copyright law with the freedom of expression. By doing so, it opened the door to an external review of copyright by means of human rights.

82 ECtHR of January 10, 2013 (*Donald Ashby and Others vs. France*), at para. 40; GEIGER, Reconceptualizing, p. 135 et seq.

83 ECtHR of January 10, 2013 (*Donald Ashby and Others vs. France*), at para. 39.

84 Cf. PAPAUX-VAN DELDEN, p. 162 et seqq.; GEIGER/IZYUMENKO, Shaping, p. 535.

85 Or, as held by IZYUMENKO, Freedom of Expression, p. 116, "although in all these cases the applicants lost, the above decisions share one important feature – an approach to *copyright as an exception to the right to freedom of expression*" (emphasis added). As much as this approach is interesting, we cannot but think whether the contrary is not true, too: i.e., that freedom of expression may be an exception to the constitutional guarantee of ownership, which also covers copyright.

required to assess whether copyright's advantages outweigh the encroachment of free speech.[86]

Even if all these cases do not directly concern visual artworks and the freedom of art, the same method of an external review based on fundamental rights superposed to a verdict of copyright infringement could be applied in cases in which interpictorial artworks are prima facie infringing. The artwork, considered to be infringing under copyright, could then be justified based on an exception directly based on the artist's freedom of artistic expression or on the more general freedom of expression.

III.IV Interpictoriality and human rights: has something changed?

Concerning our object of analysis, interpictorial artworks, we may point out some recent French cases. The first case involved painter Peter Klasen, who appropriated pictures of a woman taken by fashion photographer Alix Malka and included them in three paintings. In 2015, when deciding whether Klasen had infringed the copyright of Alix Malka, the French Cour de Cassation followed the approach indicated by the ECtHR. It, thus, quashed the previous decision of the Paris court of appeals that had favored the photographer Malka because the judges had failed to concretely explain why the conviction of Klasen for copyright infringement was proportional under the lens of Art. 10 ECHR to the objective of protecting the rights of Malka.[87] The Cour de Cassation, thus, remitted the decision to the Versailles court of appeals for a new assessment, requiring an explanation of why convicting Klasen for copyright infringement in this case would constitute a "fair balance". In doing so, the Cour de Cassation instructed all French courts to carry out an *ad hoc* balancing of interests between copyright and the relevant fundamental right and, if necessary, to intervene correctively to trump the verdict of copyright infringement.[88] The Cour d'appel de Versailles, nonetheless, found in favor of Malka. It judged that Klasen's use of Malka's pictures did not fulfill the exception of parody, as it had not been distorted enough and was not an expression of humor or mockery.[89] Under the title of "Sur la dérogation du droit d'auteur fondée sur la liberté d'expression", the court further concluded that the unsanctioned use of pictures in Klasen's painting was not *necessary* to the exercise of the freedom of expression.[90]

86 Hugenholtz, p. 289; Geiger, Access right, p. 86; Geiger/Izyumenko, Copyright, p. 322; Helfer, p. 138 et seq.

87 Cour de Cassation of May 15, 2015 (*Malka vs. Klasen*).

88 Rigamonti, Grundrechte, p. 374.

89 Cour d'appel de Versailles of March 16, 2018 (*Malka vs. Klasen*).

90 Cour d'appel de Versailles of March 16, 2018 (*Malka vs. Klasen*). Rosati, Not sufficiently "transformative", p. 525, underlines that for the court "it was rather up to [Klasen] to set a fair balance between the protection of his own freedom of expression and the fact that permission is generally required to use someone else's work, especially if the use is of such works without any substantial alteration". In this way, the freedom of expression is judged not as absolute but, rather, as subject to restrictions that are already typical of copyright law (i.e., the permission of the author or the transformation of the work). It is further interesting to note how the Versailles Court argued that because

The same argument, i.e., that the unsanctioned use of the copyrighted work was not necessary to the exercise of the freedom of expression, was repeated in the 2019 decision of the appeal Court of Paris in the case *Bauret vs. Koons*. Jeff Koons used a photograph of two children previously taken by Jean-François Bauret for one of his sculptures (called *Naked*, created in 1988). The judges ultimately held that Koons's use infringed on Bauret's copyright notwithstanding the former's right to freedom of expression.[91]

In *Davidovici vs. Koons*, taken by the same court 2 years later, the judges followed the same approach to reach the same verdict. At stake was Koons's unsanctioned use of a photograph by Franck Davidovici. The latter had realized the picture for a Naf-Naf advertising campaign. Koons used the picture as a template for the sculpture titled *Fait d'hiver* (1988). Even in this case, notwithstanding their recognition for Koons's freedom of expression in the artistic domain, the judges gave Franck Davidovici's copyright priority.[92]

In all three cases, the commercial character of Koons's and Klasen's artwork, the fact that the used oeuvres were not very well-known and judged by the respective courts to be substitutable, and that the artists had not asked for permission or obtained a license for their use were pivotal in the decisions against them. In all three cases, we point to the subtle circularity of the decision: The court argued that the artists could have asked permission for their uses, implying that there would have been a lawful way to realize their artworks. This ultimately caused the balance to tip in favor of copyright law, as the unsanctioned character of their uses was not "necessary" to the exercise of the freedom of expression.

However, *precisely* because the users had not obtained a permission, they ended up before a court in a proceeding for copyright infringement. To argue that users cannot be justified if a lawful way for doing the same existed is circular insofar as the users only need a justification if they committed an unlawful act.[93] The transposition of the conflict on a higher, fundamental rights level both enables and invisibilizes such circularity. Indeed, if the court had argued with only copyright norms, the use would have simply been unsanctioned and, thus, deemed as infringing because no exception was fulfilled in the cases at stake.[94]

---

not only Klasen is protected by the freedom of expression, but also Malka by Art. 1 of Protocol No. 1 to the ECHR, "it is not for the judge to set himself as arbitrator and decide which right deserves more protection than another" (translation is mine).

91 Cour d'appel de Paris of December 17, 2019 (*Bauret vs. Koons*).

92 Cour d'appel de Paris of February 23, 2021 (*Koons vs. Davidovici*).

93 On the circular use of the argument that if permission was not obtained, the artist may not resort to the court and ask his infringing use to be justified, cf. Noll, p. 61: In DFC 147 IV 297 (*Klimaaktivismus*), the SFSC argued that climate activists may not appeal to a justification for their unlawful acts if there would have been a lawful way to achieve the same result. Yet, of course, a justification is only needed if an unlawful act was committed.

94 In all three cases, the courts proved the applicability of the exception of parody and denied it. A circular argument is only possible if copyright is balanced against another right (and, thus, the level of observation is augmented).

This series of French judgments represents the judicial negotiation between the jurisprudence of the ECtHR, which requires a case-by-case assessment of proportionality using the yardstick of Art. 10 ECHR, and the predicates of the CJEU, which views the list of exceptions contained at Art. 5 Infosoc-Directive as fundamentally closed. Despite the mention of freedom of expression and the discussion about proportionality of the solution achieved under copyright, the verdict of infringement was confirmed in all three cases. In 2004, in the aftermath of the decision *Fabris vs. France 2,* discussed above, KAMINA wrote that, in France, "the exception drawn from Art. 10 para. 2 ECHR has been rejected on the grounds that *copyright law is seen as a legitimate and proportionate restriction in itself*".[95] A legitimate question arises: What is the added value of mentioning Art. 10 ECHR (or any other fundamental right constructed to be in conflict with the guarantee of ownership) in copyright cases if the conclusion is – without exception – that copyright law constitutes a legitimate and proportionate restriction of the freedom of expression?

Before the advent of fundamental rights in the copyright jurisprudence, exceptions used to be the legislatures' solution to the conflict of interests underlying copyright law. In the meantime, a normative layer of "hierarchically higher norms" – that is, fundamental rights – has been added.[96] Under this regime, copyright outcomes are reviewed externally in light of constitutional and conventional legal principles. Yet, if in each case, copyright law is deemed a legitimate and proportionate restriction of the freedom of expression, the obtained result is virtually the same as when copyright law was not open to external human-rights-based reviews. We may, thus, advance the hypothesis that mentioning Art. 10 ECHR is merely symbolic, which, perhaps, augments the overall acceptance of the decision without practically changing anything.

III.V Drawing the line between different uses of human rights in copyright case law

Four further cases – *Scarlet Extended*, *Sabam vs. Netlog*, *Sky Österreich* and *UPC Telekabel* – all decided by the CJEU between 2011 and 2014, are discussed here to draw a line between different uses of an external review of copyright judgments based on human rights. For some scholars, these judgments show an increased sensitivity to fundamental rights, comparable to that of the ECtHR, and make clear that "IP rights are not absolute and that a fair balance has to be struck between copyright and the right to free expression".[97] Yet the stance of the CJEU in these judgments is profoundly different from the ECtHR's in *Ashby Donald* or *The Pirate Bay*.

95 KAMINA, p. 93 (emphasis added); cf. also CHERPILLOD, Liberté, p. 365 et seq.

96 We remind the words of PAPAUX-VAN DELDEN, p. 158, who speaks of an "osmosis" between human rights and civil law as well as between international and national law.

97 GEIGER/IZYUMENKO, Copyright, p. 324.

The *Sky Österreich* case questioned whether the principle of contractual freedom of two private parties could trump the content of Directive 2010/13/EU (Audiovisual Media Services Directive, AVMSD). Specifically, Sky required ORF ("Österreichischer Rundfunk", Austrian Broadcasting Corporation) to pay higher fees than those directly associated with providing access to its broadcasting for the purpose of short news reports of high public interest. The court considered that placing limits on the exclusive broadcasting rights for short news reports of high public interest was valid and justified and that the compensation could not exceed the costs directly incurred in providing access. However, the court based its decision not on "the freedom to receive information"[98] but, rather, on the statutory basis of Art. 15 para. 6 AVMSD and on recital 55 of its preamble. The court mentioned the freedom to receive information (Art. 11 of the Charter) only to further confirm the grounds of the decision as well as the sensibleness of the balancing of interests already laid down by the AVMSD. In other words, Art. 11 of the Charter did not constitute the sole, or even main, reason why the case was decided that way.[99]

In both the *Scarlet Extended* and *Netlog vs. Sabam* cases, at stake was the question whether internet service providers Scarlet Extended SA and Netlog should have been ordered to enforce technical measures (filtering systems) to prevent copyright infringement from happening on their websites. The CJEU held that, indeed, a fair balance between the protection of copyright and the protection of the fundamental rights of individuals who are affected by such measures shall be found. However, a major difference between these and the ECtHR judgments lies in the focus on the proactive enforcement of copyright legislation, specifically the possibility of introducing a filter technology to *prevent* actual (but still abstract) copyright infringements from happening. The ECtHR held, instead, that a balance must be struck even after the infringement and the inapplicability of a copyright exception have been acknowledged.

In the fourth and last case, *UPC Telekabel*, the CJEU was confronted with questions posed by the Austrian Supreme Court in a case involving UPC Telekabel, a major internet service provider as well as an "intermediary" under Art. 8(3) of the Infosoc-Directive and two film production companies, whose movies had unlawfully been uploaded by third parties on a streaming website. The CJEU had to decide whether Member States could use an unspecified court injunction according to Art. 8(3) of the Infosoc-Directive to prohibit internet service providers from allowing its customers (internet users) to access websites containing protected subject-matter online without the agreement of the rightsholders. Alternatively, it had to decide whether fundamental rights precluded such injunction. The CJEU held that a "fair balance"[100] must be struck between the rights involved, i.e., the rights to

98 As argued instead by Geiger/Izyumenko, Copyright, p. 323 et seq.

99 CJEU of January 22, 2013 - C-283/11 (*Sky Österreich vs. Österreichischer Rundfunk*).

100 CJEU of March 27, 2014 - C-314/12 (*UPC Telekabel*), at para. 46, explains that "fair balance" means an interpretation that is consistent with the Directive at stake but also that would not enter into conflict with fundamental rights or other general principles of EU law, such as proportionality.

information of internet users, the freedom to conduct a business of the internet service provider (UPC Telekabel) and the protection of (intellectual) property of the movie production companies (Art. 17(2) of the Charter). Insofar as the injunction of the court was result-oriented, i.e., did not specify by which means exactly the internet service provider was to block the access to the website with the infringing content, it was proportional. The court found the "fair balance" to be in the fact that the provider was free to choose how it would have achieved the result. Its freedom to conduct a business was, thus, not excessively restrained.[101] The chosen means would have had to ensure that internet users would not lose their access to lawful content (so as not to unjustly restrict their freedom of information).[102] The movie production companies would have had to tolerate an imperfect measure because since Art. 17(2) of the Charter is not inviolable ("it is possible that *a means of putting a complete end to the infringements…does not exist or is not in practice achievable…*, some measures taken might be capable of being circumvented in one way or another").[103]

Even if these judgments were interpreted as being very similar to the jurisprudence of the ECtHR, the breadth and "power" given to human rights by the two courts is profoundly different.[104] The fact that the CJEU stated that intellectual property, as enshrined in Art. 17 para. 2 of the Charter, is "not inviolable" and, therefore, must not be absolutely protected,[105] must not be read as the ECtHR did, i.e., that the protection must be submitted to a case-by-case balancing even after the recognition of a copyright infringement. Rather, the CJEU uses fundamental rights as an interpretive auxiliary that concretizes spaces of freedom within the law itself.

Of these decisions, what is striking, however, is the translation – if not plain substitution – of the provisions and rights enshrined in the Directives into fundamental rights language. So, for example, instead of speaking of reproduction and distribution rights according to Art. 2 and 4 of Infosoc-Directive or of the right of making available according to Art. 3 of Infosoc-Directive, the CJEU explained that the addressee of the injunction (UPC Telekabel) did not have to undergo "unbearable sacrifices" in the light of the fact that he was not the author of the infringement of *the fundamental right of intellectual property,* which had led to the adoption of the injunction.[106] Despite not having adopted a radical approach as the ECtHR did, the CJEU has also very well received the advent of the fundamental rights doctrine within its copyright jurisprudence.

101 CJEU of March 27, 2014 - C-314/12 (*UPC Telekabel*), at para. 51 et seqq.

102 CJEU of March 27, 2014 - C-314/12 (*UPC Telekabel*), at para. 55 et seqq. It must further be possible for internet users to assert their rights before the court once the implementing measures taken by the internet service provider are known.

103 CJEU of March 27, 2014 - C-314/12 (*UPC Telekabel*), at para. 58 et seqq. (emphasis added).

104 SNIJDERS/DEURSEN, p. 1180.

105 CJEU of November 24, 2011 - C-70/10 (Scarlet Extended), at para. 43; CJEU of February 16, 2012 - C-360/10 (*SABAM vs. Netlog*), at para. 41.

106 CJEU of March 27, 2014 - C-314/12 (*UPC Telekabel*), at para. 53.

IV.I A methodological critique

In the words of HUGENHOLTZ,

> courts unhappy with the literal application of a precise norm in a given case will sometimes find solace in overriding (and usually vague) norms external to the law of copyright, such as abuse of rights, implied consent, or freedom of expression.[107]

In another text, the application of freedom of expression to copyright cases has been described as a "safety valve" for when the application of the letter of the law would lead to "unjust" results.[108] As the remedies they are, these solutions are thought to be implemented by courts and judges in explicit correction of the law.[109] In this sense, quoting civil disobedience theorist Henry David Thoreau, one author advanced that one has a "right to disobey" an unfair and illegitimate law.[110]

When applied to an interpictorial artwork judged to be infringing on someone's copyright, this judicial approach would mean that its author still has the chance to prevail by invoking his freedom of artistic expression or other general proportionality norms in the process. The success of this *ultima ratio* defense depends on whether the court considers an external review of copyright norms admissible and decides for the second artist's interests or rights to prevail over the original author's interests and rights in the concrete balancing of the case at stake.

As we have previously described, this ad hoc corrective method has been applied on many occasions in several European countries.[111] Although we recognize that the call to a human rights-informed, flexible copyright law is an answer to a normative framework that is perceived as too narrow to accommodate changing (or already changed) societal conditions,[112] we do not forcibly agree with the means used. In the following, we critically analyze these corrective remedies to "unsatisfactory" results achieved under normal copyright legislation from a methodological point of view. By doing so, we also explain why we think that this method, even though it has revealed itself to be punctually favorable for artists (and re-established an *ad*

107 HUGENHOLTZ, p. 282 et seq.

108 GOLDSTEIN/HUGENHOLTZ, p. 383 et seq.

109 GEIGER, Reconceptualizing, p. 147, argues that if legislation does not represent the right values, judges have to interpret the laws in the light of fundamental rights; GEIGER, Flexibilising Copyright, p. 185, writes: "In this option it is essentially the judge applying the rule who will have the task of preventing overprotection. Consequently, the courts will have to resist the multiple requests of some economic players who call for an extension of copyright"; for LADEUR, Die Beobachtung, p. 495, this is an "acceptable form of limiting the power of parliamentary majorities"; RENDAS, p. 16.

110 GEIGER, Reconceptualizing, p. 166 et seq.

111 GEIGER/IZYUMENKO, Constitutionalization, p. 25, in their words "certain cases can arise where even a very liberal interpretation of the norms of copyright law (its subject-matter, scope and exceptions) might not be sufficient to properly safeguard the freedom of expression and information".

112 RIGAMONTI, Grundrechte, p. 382, calls it a "symptomatic reaction" to a copyright exception system perceived as too narrow; RENDAS, p. 16.

interim synchronization between art and law in single cases), can even be detrimental to the objectives advanced by its supporters in the long term.

IV.II Reformulating a "conflict"

When subsumed under interests constructed and understood as existing *before and outside the law*, the interpictorial artwork becomes the emblem of a battlefield.[113] On one side, we find the upstream creators, their artworks plundered without consultation and not wanting to give up the authority over them that the law granted to them. On the other side, we find the downstream artists, who, following the *de facto* accessibility to the cultural assets of society, claim a right to use these creatively on behalf of their position as artists and potential future authors. As seen, these opposed positions are framed as a conflict between the guarantee of ownership (in other legal languages, as e.g., the Protocol No. 1 to the ECHR, "protection of property") and the freedom of artistic expression (or more, in general, the freedom of expression).

The same interests underlie copyright legislation.[114] From the protection scope of the work and the rights of the author,[115] to the formulation of copyright exceptions and their interpretation and the duration of protection, all these norms concern the interests of authors, rightsholders and society alike. At the core of every single normative aspect in copyright is an awareness of the underlying conflict of interests and the willingness to serve the ultimate societal purpose of incentivizing creation. Constructing the societal and economic interests of the author as unrelated and mutually exclusive, therefore, is simplistic. This interpretation fails to consider how deeply interconnected and indivisible these two apparently opposed aspects are in the incentive system for culture and innovation that is copyright law.[116] Moreover, this view does not take into account how art also benefitted from the existence of a copyright system to become an autopoietic system of society.[117]

113 Cf. LUHMANN, Menschenrechte, p. 232 et seq.; LADEUR, Recht, p. 26, argues that conflicts between interests and rights are constructed by the law. From that follows a necessity to "balance" to come to a fair or proportional solution.

114 CUENI, p. 663 et seq.; DFC 140 III 616 (*ETH Dokumentenlieferdienst*), c. 3.6.3.; WIELSCH, Zugangsregeln, p. 67 et seq.; TORREMANS, p. 260 et seq.

115 RAMELLO, p. 132.

116 GINSBURG, Copyright, p. 516, writes that "copyright promotes artistic freedom and free speech by enabling authors to earn a living from their creativity"; COOMBE, p. 50 et seq., for example, speaks of intellectual property laws as depriving us "of possibilities for dialogic interaction" but also, paradoxically, as "inviting critical appropriations" (we have described this irritation between art and law in Chapter 6); for RAMELLO, p. 120, "ambiguously dependent"; GEIGER, Reconceptualizing, p. 134, describes how in the Spanish Constitution intellectual property is protected within the framework of the right to freedom of expression and information; for the same reason, it is possible for the author, whose work was copied without permission, to claim protection under the freedom of art.

117 GRABER, Kunstbegriff, p. 107; WIELSCH, Zugangsregeln, p. 44 et seq., speaks in this sense of the constitutive function of the art system's environment (in systems theoretical terms); at p. 67, he underlines the enabling function of exclusive copyrights for other systems of society.

Indeed, in copyright law, we observe that when provisions provide authors with the possibility of economical rewards, they are simultaneously aiming to promote the creation of new knowledge and are, therefore, thinking about the rest of society.[118] On the other hand, when copyright opens the scope of protection of works, or broadens the scope of exceptions, it is similarly allowing more creators to become authors in the sense of the law. This means that, even when it is favoring authors with exclusive rights, ensuring them control over their outputs and providing them with the possibility of economical rewards, copyright law is pursuing the social function of incentivizing innovation to the benefit of all. However, no formula to balance the interests at stake for the ultimate purpose of maximizing societal profit is perfect: An increase in the supply of new works brought about by the statutory economic incentive will always correspond to a diminution in the supply brought about by the exclusionary effect of copyright.[119] Ultimately, these are the two interconnected faces of the same coin.[120] Formulation such as: "copyright legislation should *protect the interests of the right holder while simultaneously not curtailing those of the user more than necessary* for the protection of the interests of the right holder";[121] or "the intrinsic paradox of copyright law has always been that it *restricts participation* in cultural and social dialogue in order *to encourage cultural production and dissemination*; in other words, it must limit communication in the name of encouraging communicative activities"[122] reveal typical tautologies of copyright law.

This co-dependency can neither be solved if transposed on a constitutional plane, nor with a movement supposedly able to take copyright "back to the roots, i.e., to the basic concepts, [its] function".[123] To think of the problem of copyright law as of one of imbalance (too much of authors' rights, too little users' freedom) inevitably resolves in a mere reformulation of the same old tautology ("too much of this, too little of that"). We, thus, think that copyright law is not "broken" or

118 Perhaps slightly excessively formulated: "copyright is not interested in people making a living, it [is] interested in promoting creativity", quoted in Ginsburg, Exceptional Authorship, p. 15.

119 Bell/Parchomowsky, p. 1056.

120 Coombe, p. 51, writes that intellectual property laws prohibit "the reproduction of vital cultural texts". One could, however, also argue that they *enable* it, by ensuring an economic return and, thus, subsistence to authors who have invested their time and money in producing them; Ramello, p. 121; Wielsch, Relationales Urheberrecht, p. 92, reminds to always think about "the other side of the distinction".

121 Gasser/Oertli, SHK CopA, N 11 *ad* Vorbemerkungen Art. 19-28 (translation is mine, emphasis added). Such formulations are very common in copyright doctrine, cf. also Hilty, Urheberrecht, N 90.

122 Craig, Copyright, p. 232 (emphasis added).

123 Geiger, Flexibilising Copyright, p. 185, writes: "it is sufficient to return to the principles underlying the rule and to apply law in a flexible way that would allow its fundamental purpose to be respected".

"imbalanced" and that it does not need a "re-constitutionalization" (if that were the case, would copyright law, as it is, be unconstitutional?[124]).

Rather, copyright law's problem is that it is excessively self-referential. The fact that, by protecting authors who are already authors and works that are already works (i.e., "included"), copyright prevents *other* authors from becoming authors and new works from becoming works[125] signals a failure to recognize the many ways by which a copyrighted artwork can become "new" once decontextualized and used to convey a radically different message. By being too focused on its already established differences, such as the difference "work/work exemplar", copyright law closes in on itself. For this reason, it provides too little space for the importation of information coming from other societal systems.[126]

IV.III To correct law with law

To correct an outcome reached under copyright law with a legal tool outside copyright law means to *correct law with law*, i.e., to attest that, in a specific case, the use of the law is legally problematic and may have to be punctually declared illegal. Paradigmatic of this situation is the institution known as abuse of rights. When resorting to a legal solution that is declared abusive, the binary distinction between legal/illegal re-enters into itself on the legal side, meaning that the difference is activated twice in a single operation. What can be observed is that – and here lies the paradoxical character of the situation – "illegal" law is law to all effects, even if its application is punctually outlawed.[127]

When judges substitute the verdict found under copyright law with another one based on external tools such as human rights, other proportionality assessments or "copyright misuse"[128] (a form of abuse of right), they are doing something similar: They are using the legal code legal-illegal twice in a single operation. Even though, in the case at stake, the external review of copyright by means of the human right to freedom of expression is constructed as a hierarchically higher norm, which shall naturally prevail over a copyright law producing dysfunctional results, copyright too enjoys constitutional protection. As KAISER/SCHEURER argue, at a constitutional level, it becomes "quite ambiguous *what is the rule and what is the exception*".[129]

124 A few would argue that. Rather, it is argued that copyright is "dysfunctional", "illegitimate" and "unfair". These words signal the presence of the excluded value in the binary code constitutional/unconstitutional (or legal/illegal), cf. LUHMANN, Law as a Social System, p. 339. This is also typical of discourses surrounding civil disobedience.

125 GINSBURG, Exceptional Authorship, p. 15.

126 RAMELLO, p. 135 et seq., writes that knowledge production emerges as being inextricably embedded within social systems. For copyright to recognize it, it must be able to perceive other social system's ways of functioning and of defining meaning.

127 LUHMANN, Law as a Social System, p. 186 and 204.

128 SGANGA/SCALZINI, p. 408.

129 KAISER/SCHEURER, p. 1156 et seq., continue by explaining that "one can start from the fundamental right to intellectual property and consider opposing interests the exceptions. Or alternatively, one can start from the freedom to act as the underlying core of all freedoms".

This insight shows at least one concrete and non-negligible merit of the advent of fundamental rights doctrine into copyright law. Indeed, exactly as the conflicting interests underlying copyright legislation between the rightsholder and the aspiring user, the fundamental rights to which copyright is associated are, by definition, on the same hierarchical level, meaning that no right overrides the other *a priori*.[130] Many authors see here the reason why the dichotomy between "absolute work protection" against "single and limited copyright exceptions" has no tenure.[131] Exceptions should not be interpreted restrictively. Rather, they should be interpreted as broadly as the exclusive rights granted by copyright. Another interpretive rule would fail when transposed on a constitutional level. This principle finds its normative justification not so much in copyright legislation itself, but in the constitutions and human rights conventions that find application on the entire legislation.[132] Moreover, exactly as exclusive rights are enforceable for authors and other rightsholders, so shall exceptions be for users. Exceptions shall not be treated as the statutory anchoring of "interests" but as veritable rights from which a series of concrete entitlements are derived that can be held against parties who do not respect such precepts.[133]

Fundamental rights have a practical value for the interpretation of copyright norms. On the other hand, however, they should not be used as guidance to decide copyright conflicts. As pointed out by RIGAMONTI, to describe the outcome of this balancing exercise as a "fair balance" between opposing rights, or interests, is not self-evident, as the court is deciding – exactly as it would do without the balancing exercise – who wins and who loses in proceeding initiated for copyright infringement.[134] To translate the case into a collision of two hierarchically equal human rights, the outcome of which will eventually suppress the verdict previously achieved under written law, means to try to hide the paradoxical re-entry of the legal code into itself and the existence of a contradiction between different validity claims ("Geltungsansprüche").[135] If the deciding court transposes the conflict at a higher, constitutional or conventional, level, nothing changes except that judges are acting *modo legislatoris*. Indeed, even though the law provides a solution and no legal loophole is attested,[136] the judge trumps the outcome achieved under normal legislation, acting correctively vis-à-vis state legislation and, thus, endangering the principle of separation of powers among institutions of the State.[137]

130 GASSER/OERTLI, SHK CopA, N 6 *ad* Vorbemerkungen Art. 19-28; BLUME HUTTENLAUCH, p. 30; GEIGER, Die Schranken, p. 146; WIELSCH, Relationales Urheberrecht, p. 87.

131 WIELSCH, Zugangsregeln, p. 270; KAISER/SCHEUERER, p. 1156 et seq.

132 WIELSCH, Zugangsregeln, p. 8, 62 and 277 et seq.; CHERPILLOD, Liberté, p. 356.

133 GEIGER, Reconceptualizing, p. 156 et seq.

134 RIGAMONTI, Grundrechte, p. 374.

135 TEUBNER, Umgang mit Rechtsparadoxien, p. 27.

136 BRÄNDLI-MARMY, p. 92.

137 KAISER/SCHEURER, p. 1159; GRABER, Access Copyright, p. 28; RENDAS, p. 16. In countries that have incorporated the three-step test in their copyright legislation (such as Spain and France), this problem has disappeared: To incorporate an open clause such as the three-step test into copyright law means that the legislature delegates power to decide in a single case to the judge; cf. AMSTUTZ,

IV.IV Legal uncertainty

A more flexible copyright can be directly linked to a surge in legal uncertainty.[138] If judges have more leeway in applying the norms and can occasionally reach for legal institutes outside copyright law (e.g., fundamental rights) for correcting undesired outcomes, their decisions become more unpredictable.[139]

Because the normative content of fundamental rights is very abstract,[140] the judge will have a great power of appreciation.[141] Fundamental rights do not allow reliable statements on the extent and limits of copyright protection in the single case. They are, thus, ill-fitted to the purpose of decision-finding in the context of copyright litigation.[142] In regard to the lawfulness of interpictorial artworks, what the judge thinks and knows about art would, thus, have a disproportionate weight on the final decision.[143]

Moreover, because typical methods of balancing interests or assessing proportionality function on a strict case-by-case basis, the outcome achieved in one case will not mean that in another, subsequent case the court will confirm the primacy of the same interests.[144] Decisive for balancing is the holistic assessment of the circumstances of the single case, in which the variables are multiple.[145] Every new case would reset the balancing, providing a solution that is valid for more than a single case would be contrary to the method itself.[146]

From the perspective of art, it should be asked whether it is of any use for artists to work in an environment in which copyright law keeps encouraging the creation of formally new artworks, thereby also discouraging interpictorial uses, but in which courts may punctually intervene, correcting the outcomes in favor of artists. In other words, the question is whether artists can rely on consistent outcomes

Zwischenwelten, p. 227 and 229 and LUHMANN, Law as a Social System, p. 278, the separation of powers regards the self-description of and the structural coupling between the political and the law system. A complete separation of power, however, is impossible, as the "judge-Subsumstionsautomat" does not exist; LADEUR, Recht, p. 25 and 29, argues that there is an observable shift in weight and that the legislative loses ground behind the judicial power.

138 Such is recognized even by those scholars who are otherwise favorable to an external case-by-case review of copyright verdicts, e.g., GEIGER, A Threat, p. 683; HUGENHOLTZ, p. 278; KAISER/SCHEUERER, p. 1159.

139 WEBER/BREINING-KAUFMANN, p. 418; RIGAMONTI, Grundrechte, p. 381.

140 WEBER/BREINING-KAUFMANN, p. 419.

141 RIGAMONTI, Grundrechte, p. 378 et seqq.; WEBER/BREINING-KAUFMANN, p. 418.

142 RIGAMONTI, Grundrechte, p. 378.

143 WESTKAMP, p. 71.

144 For WESTKAMP, p. 71, this is a positive aspect.

145 FISCHER-LESCANO/CHRISTENSEN, p. 171; both the commercial character of *Fait d'hiver* by Jeff Koons and his "first place position" on the art market, for example, have been weighed against him in the balancing of his freedom of expression vs. Davidovici's copyright, cf. Cour d'appel de Paris of February 23, 2021, (*Koons vs. Davidovici*), p. 22. The commercial character of a work and whether his author occupies a good position on the relevant market are not typical arguments of copyright law.

146 Cf. LUHMANN, Law as a Social System, p. 252; see also Ladeur, Kunstfreiheit, p. 447 and FISCHER-LESCANO/CHRISTENSEN, p. 171.

and whether the freedom of (artistic) expression-based correction of a copyright infringement verdict can become, by force of repetition that is currently lacking, the contrafactual expectation that the legal system stabilizes.

The problem seems to lie precisely there. Artists cannot create interpictorial artworks without the worry of potential copyright interferences because copyright law has remained unchanged, unbothered by what might happen on the hierarchically higher normative level of constitutional and conventional human rights. Punctual corrections are certainly favorable for artists in single cases, but because of the instability of outcomes under such an interpretive method, their usefulness to achieve change in the long term is doubtful. Because the balance is always renegotiated, its outcome remains *de facto* unforeseeable, and for the artist, calculating the risk of litigation becomes very cumbersome. For artistic creation, this means that one outcome favoring art (or artistic freedom) over copyright (or the guarantee of ownership) in one single case does not automatically involve the protection of art in subsequent cases.[147]

This characteristic is observable in the whole contemporary law system. The law of postmodern society reflects the societal fragmentation of values, norms and self-descriptions.[148] So, in the art system, the postmodern "overcoming of the author" described above co-exists with ways of functioning that are still decidedly connected to the constitutive figure of the author-as-individual. Because the "aura" of the artwork has been redefined as contextual rather than material, copies can be considered originals, too, as not all artworks have declared themselves as *materially different* from their past. Originality, in other words, has become polyvalent, but its original meaning has not disappeared. Rather, it persists along with other, new forms. For this reason, the expectations directed at the system of (copyright) law are not fruit of a unitary world image anymore but are, rather, expression of fragmented interests, compromises, of partial consensus.[149]

In such a society, the stability of legal concepts and institutes, the interpretation of the "will of the law", does not satisfy anymore.[150] Against this background, law has become a situational "law of balance" in which values are balanced against each other on a strict case-by-case basis.[151] In what LADEUR has called *experimentalist governance*,[152] the focus is not on the necessity to provide solutions that are just in each single case but, rather, to guarantee changeability in a societal environment that requires fast adaptation.[153] Even though one could provocatively advance, as LUHMANN did, that decisions based on the method of the balancing of

147 RIGAMONTI, Grundrechte, p. 385; GERVAIS, How Intellectual Property, p. 28, warns about the dangerous and unwanted effect of human rights potentially strengthening IP rights.
148 LADEUR, Recht, p. 28.
149 LADEUR, Abwägung, p. 66.
150 LADEUR, Abwägung, p. 65.
151 LADEUR, Abwägung, p. 64.
152 LADEUR, Recht, p. 28.
153 LADEUR, Abwägung, p. 65.

interests are taken *ad hoc* and *ad hominem*,[154] they are based on the legal code and are, thus, legal decisions. The legal system can cope with a considerable amount of uncertainty. Unpredictable decisions based on a *modo legislatoris*-approach of the judge, i.e., decisions that could be considered as having neither a history nor a future, do not endanger the maintenance of law's function.[155] Their viability and appropriateness, however, must be judged from the perspective of other systems observing them; in our case: art.

IV.V The deactivation of copyright law or how to dematerialize copyright

In the residual cases in which no statutory exception covers the use of a previous work in an artwork, the resulting illegality of the artwork, its infringing character, stems from the application of copyright norms. When the artwork is made legal again with an external mechanism, copyright law is superseded in two different ways.

First, copyright already provides for law-internal accommodations of the conflicting interests at stake. To state that the solution copyright law provides is dissatisfying, disproportionate or even unconstitutional and to formulate another one that clearly goes beyond the limits laid out by copyright, means to override copyright legislation.[156] Second, because constitutional law and every open-ended balancing of interests does not function according to the same differences that are relevant within copyright law.[157] Rather, the outcome always depends on how heterogenous arguments, coming from completely different societal spheres, are tuned with each other.[158] Applied in a copyright dispute, these arguments disable copyright's "doctrinal str[u]ctures",[159] opening the case to other possible outcomes. We may call this the "punctual deactivation of copyright".

By superseding copyright law in this way, we also note how the difference work/work exemplar, responsible for copyright's blind spot and based, as we have seen, on a material understanding of artworks, is also deactivated. The blind spot of copyright law, that for which copyright law is not able to make the difference between an interpictorial original copy and a work exemplar, disappears temporarily, giving way to a dematerialized notion of art. A solution of a copyright dispute rooted in the constitutional artistic freedom considers and protects the artwork *qua* artistic

154 Luhmann, Law as a Social System, p. 252.

155 Luhmann, Law as a Social System, p. 196.

156 On this point, it is even more surprising that scholars who recognize that the CopA already considers the constitutionally protected interests of communication (information, opinion, art, media) plead for an overlain case-by-case balancing of interests, cf. for example Cueni, p. 663 et seq.

157 The proportionality calculus of the three-step test, which considers the economic damage suffered, or the commercial character of the work, which can affect how the court protects the author under the freedom of expression, are irrelevant aspects under civil copyright law (but they are factors in the US fair use test).

158 Fischer-Lescano/Christensen, p. 170 et seq.; Ladeur, Die Beobachtung, p. 495.

159 Westkamp, p. 72, calls them "strictures" and endorses this as a positive feature of a human-rights-based approach in copyright disputes.

communication, whereas copyright law protects art only if it deems it individual.[160] With a superimposed freedom of art-based correction, the copyright-typical differences between work and work exemplar, author and non-author, protection and exception (or infringement), are supplanted. Although the decision started as a copyright decision, it becomes something else by way of superimposition of fundamental rights values to it.

Yet the differences of copyright that created the necessity of correction remain in force, creating similar situations in the future.[161] The approach, rooted in a fundamental rights-based correction of the law, is always confined to a sort of "emergency solution",[162] in which the undesired result is avoided at the last moment. It is, perhaps, for this reason that LUHMANN described the balancing of interests as the "trojan horse of all juridical reasoning".[163] As the *passepartout* that it is, it can be deployed everywhere to enforce (or correct) whatever solution is deemed dissatisfying.[164] Yet, as exposed, it does not change anything to what was there before, nor is it a reliable and solid base for later cases.

V.I Conclusions

Advocates for reviewing copyright outcomes based on human rights or other broad external legal constructions observe that, when copyright protection becomes overly restrictive, an approach based on fundamental rights (or interests) is the only means of providing creative users with the freedoms they need and deserve to flourish. Their explanation for the deficits of copyright law is that the wrong interests have been privileged for too long and that a counterbalance is now imperative to readjust the distinction between "right" and "exception" provided by copyright statutes.[165] Such enterprise is advanced under titles such as the "humanization",[166] the "constitutionalization"[167] of copyright and the intention of bringing "values back to the system".[168]

160 See Chapters 3 and 6.

161 For a general critique in this direction from a social and economic development perspective cf. OKEDIJI, p. 1 et seqq., arguing at p. 4 that "human rights framework plays a material role in strengthening IP rights" and at p. 66 that human rights protect the IP status quo and are not (always) an agent of change.

162 BRÄNDLI-MARMY, p. 356, describing the effects of the application of the theory of abuse of law in copyright.

163 LUHMANN, Law as a Social System, p. 252.

164 LUHMANN, Law as a Social System, p. 455, writes "doctrinal resources are depleted and replaced with the flexible, if not empty, paradigm of the weighing up of interests and balancing of values".

165 GRABER, Access Copyright, p. 28; GERVAIS, How Intellectual Property, p. 17.

166 Cf. CHRISTOPHE GEIGER, 'Humanising' the Intellectual Property System - Securing a Fair Balance of Interests Through Fundamental Rights at European and International Level, Q. Rev. Corp. L. & Soc'y, 33 (2012), pp. 291 et seqq.

167 GEIGER/IZYUMENKO, Constitutionalization of IP; WIELSCH, Relationales Urheberrecht, p. 86.

168 GERVAIS, How Intellectual Property, p. 18.

Because they are preoccupied with copyright law's syntonization with its environment, these scholars form a *per se* positive movement for more systemic openness and for the augmentation of the legal system's syntonization to its environment.[169] With its supporters, we share the preoccupation of wanting to maintain a copyright law that is fit for purpose and, thus, the need to avoid verdicts of copyright infringement directed at new artworks (and at new technological developments alike).

In Chapter 7, IV.I, however, we have explained why we believe, although we are partisans for a cognitively open legal system that measures its own quality against it and corrects its route if needed, that the strategy of achieving the desired effect by superimposing an external, *ad hoc* correction is flawed. When we describe the problem as exposed, the solution lies within copyright itself – not elsewhere. To recalibrate copyright law externally would mean, on the contrary, to isolate it even more. Every time other external solutions are provided, copyright law misses a chance to evolve and be changed for the better, as the jurisprudence will remember how, at least under copyright, the use was infringing and "dysfunctional" and needed a correction that came from outside.

Punctual and external corrections to undesired outcomes are and should remain "emergency solutions", to be employed parsimoniously – for example, in the case of evident abuse of right – and not methodically as the proposed solution to a (rightfully) diagnosed problem. If we want to stop the same problem from reappearing, the solution must be finely weaved into the normative structure of copyright law itself, that is, implemented internally. This can be achieved through the augmentation of its cognitive openness. To this end, it is imperative to engage more with the domain in question and verify whether aesthetic theories can supply criteria for *making a distinction*.[170]

169 Cf. WIELSCH, Relationales Urheberrecht, p. 85; GRABER, Zwischen Geist und Geld, p. 183 and 189 et seqq. Speaks of "internal imaging of the outer world" (translation is mine) and at p. 199 of the "improvement of law's isomorphy with societal value system" (translation is mine).

170 ORTLAND/SCHMÜCKER, p. 1775; cf. also MÜLLER, p. 257.

Part V

Back to copyright law

> "But if an observer observes what another observer assumes to be identical, he can take the liberty to identify differently, to use other distinctions, to interpret from other counter-concepts, in short: to treat the same as not-the-same."
>
> Niklas Luhmann, Identität – was oder wie? (1990)
> translation is mine

DOI: 10.4324/9781003598503-13

8 Toward a cognitively open copyright law

I.I Introduction

In art writings, it is obvious that an interpictorial original copy, even if it is a faithful reproduction of a previously existing artwork, is not that same artwork anymore. *Everything* has changed about it: The author, the context (of space and time), the meaning or message of the artwork, the technique of realization. Notwithstanding their similar (or same) aspect, a fundamental difference between the two artworks has been created. Arguing any differently would mean to misunderstand the interpictorial artwork completely, reducing its multilayered existence to its form.[1] Within the art world, the interpictorial original copy is, thus, understood to be a proper, autonomous artifact with an independent existence from that of the template. Claims of plagiarism are, thus, refuted.[2]

Programmed as it is, copyright focuses instead on the only part of the artwork that is the same (its appearance, its surface). If copyright law cannot *see* a difference, it lacks a way to make the distinction between the artworks, considering one a derivation of the other. As US Supreme Court justices recently stated in the case *Andy Warhol Found. vs. Goldsmith*, "[The dissenting opinion] offers *no theory of the relationship between transformative uses of original works and derivative works that transforms originals*".[3] In other words, the majority argued, the dissenting opinion did not offer a general and abstract (i.e., juridical) theory to make a distinction between uses that invade the scope of protection of the used work and uses that are to be considered fair. For the majority, the position of Justice Kagan in the dissenting opinion, according to which any use that is creative prevails under the first fair use factor, went too far. What the court needed was a "limiting principle".[4]

While we can agree on the fact that a theory of the relationship between transformative uses of original works is needed in order to not authorize *every* taking of copyrighted material, it also appears difficult to come up with such a theory if the court does not have "the luxury" of engaging with art theoretical and art historical

1 MILLET, L'art d'appropriation, p. 115 et seqq.; HILDEBRAND-SCHAT, p. 220; GRIFFITHS, p. 347 et seq.
2 VAHRSON, p. 31.
3 *Andy Warhol Found. for the Visual Arts, Inc. vs. Goldsmith*, 598 US ___ (2023), p. 36 (emphasis added).
4 *Andy Warhol Found. for the Visual Arts, Inc. vs. Goldsmith*, 598 US ___ (2023), p. 36.

DOI: 10.4324/9781003598503-14

sources.[5] Copyright lawyers should engage with how culture, art and technology are produced, lest they create a cognitive dissonance with the rest of society. In the following, we delve further in the idea of a cognitively open copyright and then propose some interpretive keys to understand the distinction between original artwork and interpictorial variation even without being able to *see it* in the surface of the artworks.

II.I A cognitively open copyright

Copyrighted artworks are not only *intellectual property,* i.e., a coagulation of ownership in the sense of the law. Although they are reformulated into the "form" of ownership, they always remain pieces of communication of the art system, originated in another operative context of society and, thus, inextricably bound with this.[6] Copyright law is, thus, "multilateral": Its rules not only affect the functioning of other systems,[7] they also encompass artifacts that inextricably belong to other communicative and epistemic spheres of society.[8]

Yet copyright law neglects this multilaterality. Instead of reflecting about whether copyright law is still adapted to today's society, copyright lawyers state that artists should take the risks of being sued for copyright infringement into account and behave accordingly.[9] In order to support aesthetic statements made in the context of copyright, lawyers continue to mainly reference other legal sources, even in much-cited articles and other excellent juridical texts.[10] Similarly, LADEUR criticized the use of one sole music-theoretical source by the GFCC in the decision *Metall auf Metall* and the fact that this source was merely quoted once and in an extremely shortened version.[11] And, we repeat, the US Supreme Court recently dismissed the dissenting opinion in the case of the Andy Warhol Foundation against photographer Lynn Goldsmith for having quoted too many art historical sources, having so "lost sight of the statute and th[e] Court's cases". Instead of recognizing the value of an interpretation of the law that considered its object, the justices argued that, "as a court", they did not have that "luxury".[12] In this way, they erected

5 We remind that in *Andy Warhol Found. for the Visual Arts, Inc. vs. Goldsmith*, 598 US ___ (2023), p. 36 et seq., the justices stated that "The Lives of the Artists undoubtedly makes for livelier reading than the US Code or the US Reports, but as a court, we do not have that luxury".

6 WIELSCH, Zugangsregeln, p. 32 and 67; cf. on this GEIGER, Reconceptualizing, p. 126, who underlines the cultural and economic policy character of copyright law.

7 See Chapter 6, I.I.

8 WIELSCH, Zugangsregeln, p. 32.

9 SCHACK, N 359.

10 DÖHL, Systemwechsel, p. 261.

11 LADEUR, Kunstfreiheit, p. 449 et seq.

12 *Andy Warhol Found. for the Visual Arts, Inc. vs. Goldsmith*, 598 US ___ (2023), p. 36 et seq. The subtle sarcasm of the justices is misplaced, to say the least. By stating things such as "The Lives of the Artists undoubtedly makes for livelier reading than the US Code or the US Reports, but as a court, we do not have that luxury", the court creates a sense of superiority of the juridical discipline toward art history. On her side, Justice Kagan criticizes many times the fact that the majority

a hermetical barrier between the law and other sources of knowledge coming from other systems of society.

By continuing to focus only on itself and what it already knows, copyright law falls short of rendering the complexities of the art system. Applying a theory that measures the degree of transformation in order to detect novelty does not align with how novelty is produced in the art system. As long as copyright law functions according to this *status quo*, it cannot fully acknowledge the context of origin of artworks, which, because it is an interpictorial one, will presuppose acts of reproduction.[13] In this way, copyright law gets caught in the fundamental inability to understand that by requiring artists to change their sources, it is asking artists to stop working interpictorially, and this means to impair the autonomy of the art system.[14]

Yet there is a way by which courts can realize and correct this. Instead of applying the statutes unilaterally, courts can take into account the "law in society-element", i.e. how this application is received and the effects it creates when it is applied a certain way.

For example, in a recent decision of the SFSC, the judges admitted that "whether a work is protected by copyright and how far the scope of protection extends can be questionable and often forms the core of a subsequent dispute". Instead of presupposing the existence and the knowledge of copyrights, the SFSC conceded that because the granting of copyright to a work "depends on judgements[,] it can be difficult to predict how the courts will decide",[15] thus concluding that there was no *mala fides* of the defendant who had used the plantiff's protected design.

But the already discussed judgment of the GFCJ in the case *Disney-Parody*, which first introduced the theory of inner distance, is exemplary in this respect:[16]

> In applying the principle that free use can only be said to exist if, in view of the peculiarity of the new work, the borrowed personal features of the protected earlier work "fade away", consideration must be given to the peculiarities inherent in the nature of parody. Since parody is directed against certain peculiarities that are evident in the work of a writer or artist, *parody by its very nature presupposes that these peculiarities are recognizable in it as the object of the artistic examination in the first place.*[17]

In this passage, the GFCJ recognized the fundamental inadequacy of the distance doctrine to judge whether parodies can be considered free uses of existing works or not. Through a careful self-reflection on its rules, the court held that the formula

---

completely ignored the opinions of art experts in their decision, cf. dissenting opinion, *Andy Warhol Found. for the Visual Arts, Inc. vs. Goldsmith*, 598 US ___ (2023), p. 9, 17 and 18.

13 Wielsch, Zugangsregeln, p. 6 et seq. and 31.

14 Cf. Wielsch, Zugangsregeln, p. 69.

15 SFSC 4A_145/2024 of September 11, 2024 (*Feuerring unpublished*), c. 2.2 (translation is mine).

16 Cf. Chapter 4, III.IV.II.II.

17 GFCJ of March 26, 1971 (*Disney-Parodie*), GRUR 1971, p. 588 et seqq., p. 589 (emphasis added).

– according to which, the individual character had to visibly fade in the new work – was clearly inadequate, as parodies depend on the recognizability of the source they choose to use to convey their message. By stating this, the court opened itself cognitively to the functioning of the system of communication that had produced the parody in the first place. It understood that imposing its (inadequate) rules would have jeopardized the existence of parodies, which it implicitly acknowledged as legitimate and worthy of recognition. By recognizing the importance of parodies, it conceded to open a door that was, subsequently, developed into the concept of inner distance.[18]

Like parodies, interpictorial original copies presuppose that the artworks used as templates remain recognizable. Copyright law should, thus, realize that by obstinately applying its rules of transformation, it is ignoring the peculiarities of interpictorial art. To achieve this, it is necessary that copyright observes its own rules from an interdisciplinary perspective, focusing on their multilaterality and, thus, seeing them in the context of the effects they create in other systems of communication.

III.I Understanding the difference without seeing it

It would not be far from reality to argue that the only thing that remained the same in an interpictorial original copy is the external form (the appearance) of the artwork, while *everything else* has changed. Interpictorial original copies underline with their existence the "non-identity of repetition".[19] Insisting on the artwork's form is misleading, as the distinguishing feature of the original copy clearly does not reside in the form it displays but, rather, in the use it makes thereof, i.e., on the relationship of the form with its context.[20]

Such emerges if the perspective on the "work" is changed, i.e., if the work is not thought of exclusively as an object of property anymore but, rather, as a piece of communication coming from the system of art.[21] In this way, other qualities of the work and its context emerge: Authors are not only individual rightsholders but participants to a collective conversation, and the artifact-work gains a three-dimensionality that would otherwise remain invisible. In this way, the doubleness that inhabits original copies, though inevitably not leaping out at first sight, becomes at least intelligible.[22]

III.II Art as process

From a copyright perspective, the interpictorial artwork may appear like the mere result of a "brainless" copying activity, undeserving of any recognition.[23] Instead,

18 Cf. Chapter 4, III.IV.II.II.
19 Luhmann, Art as a Social System, p. 130.
20 Luhmann, The Work of Art, p. 198
21 Craig, Copyright, p. 57.
22 Zuschlag, p. 208.
23 Cf. Craig, Reconstructing, p. 213.

by copying and intending to make art with it, the artist weaves a semantical difference in time, space and context, which changes everything about the artwork. This difference may be grasped when the activity leading to the new artwork is not understood as an effortless act of copying, accomplished in the blink of an eye, but, rather, when it is thought of in terms of a process. By deconstructing the act of copying in the medium of time, different passages, each with its own complexities, become visible.[24]

In her analysis of collage practices (in which "collage" is understood in a very large sense), TAMAR SHAFRIR deconstructs the activity of copying in a process during which the artist assumes three different roles in chronological succession: 1) the surgeon, 2) the seamster and 3) the sorcerer.[25] In a first step, the artist-as-surgeon simply cuts, meaning that she finds and takes extraneous material, removing it from its original context. The "cut" itself, she adds, is a very violent act that insinuates isolation, displacement and decontextualization in the layers of meaning of the found material.[26] We could think of an artist finding an interesting image on a newspaper, cutting it and saving it for later use but also of an artist who does the same thing digitally, that is, by pressing copy and paste.

In a second step, the artist-as-seamster occupies herself with rewriting and recombining the decontextualized and isolated artifacts. In this second step, the various spaces, dimensions, origins and materials of the cuttings are sewn together. Visual material that had lost its original meaning through the cut is used for a different purpose. Once combined, these cuts create a new unity with their own depth and density. The previously existing narratives are, thus, retold by the artist, who invents another meaning for them. Importantly, this passage also raises "the notion of linking, invoking the logic of multiplicity and interconnectivity epitomized by the digital network".[27] Again, we could think about a decontextualized image (for example, an advertising, as we find in *Niagara* by Jeff Koons), which is recombined with other images from other contexts to create a new ensemble.

In the third and last step, a transformation happens. The artist-sorcerer conjures messages and meanings where they did not exist before so that the artwork becomes "more than the sum of its parts".[28] In the new organic combination of

24 Even Justice Kagan in her dissenting opinion to *Andy Warhol Found. for the Visual Arts, Inc. vs. Goldsmith*, 598 US ___ (2023), p. 5 et seq., felt the need of deconstructing Andy Warhol's copying in a "method in action", describing the different passages to make them visible to the unforgiving eyes of the law.

25 SHAFRIR, p. 216.

26 SHAFRIR, p. 217 et seqq.

27 SHAFRIR, p. 220 et seqq.

28 SHAFRIR, p. 223 et seqq.

the artwork, a new order can be found behind the apparent randomness of casual connections,[29] and this is what art does.[30]

Viewed this way, the interpictorial original acquires a temporal dimension. It becomes more than a flat surface; it is a conceptual artifact shaped by context and process that, together, enrich its complex meaning.

III.III A form on another form

The main characteristic of interpictorial original copies is that their immediateness (i.e., what we see by looking at them) is only apparent. Interpictorial original copies actually result from a superposition. Even if what might be visible is only the form of the source work, as in the case of Sturtevant's repeated artworks, they are a sum of heterogenous elements. In her words:

> The employed source works are used only as catalysts. Thus, *any commentary or reference back to them is to confuse and misunderstand the issues at stake.* As catalysts they seek the power to explore the *understructure* of painting and sculpture and function through the dynamics of repetition, reference, opposites as the same, and non-identity through identity. There is both conflict and unity in the work, *a disturbance between surface and under.*[31]

Although her artworks are in some cases virtually indistinguishable from the templates they repeat, in this text, she reinstates the centrality of the duality that is indispensable for understanding her work ("any…reference back to [the source works] is to confuse and misunderstand"). Moreover, she points out the fact that the key to understanding her art does not reside in the "employed source works" but, rather, in the disturbance existing between "surface and under".[32]

29 In an exhibition dedicated to the work of Ukrainian photographer Boris Mikhaïlov at the Maison Européenne de la Photographie (MEP) in Paris, an excerpt of an interview accompanied the display of *Yesterday's Sandwich* (1966–1968), a series of photographic superpositions. Mikhaïlov explained: One day I made a mistake...when I accidentally threw a pile of slides on a bed, two of them stuck together. Fascinated by the accidentally produced image – a new, metaphorical one – I began to superimpose others, like layers of a sandwich...[A]ssembling the images, I obtained new random combinations, reflections of the dualism and contradictions of the Soviet Union. At the time, the regime was broadcasting all kinds of coded messages, and faced with the prevailing disinformation, people were searching for alternative sources, scrutinizing every image for its hidden meaning. Encryption was the only way to deal with taboo subjects such as politics, religion and nudity. Like all dissident works, the Sandwich series was full of allusions and innuendo" (translation is mine).

30 Luhmann, Art as a Social System, p. 148; interestingly, Eduardo Navas, p. 234 et seqq., proposes a similar deconstruction of the copying activity. For him, the process is divided in five different steps: 1) Appropriation, 2) implementation (the moment something is embedded into something else and, thus, repurposed), 3) contextualization, 4) legitimation and 5) finally transformation (which emerges from the relation between the first four steps). These steps are also often accompanied by long periods of research and by the redaction of texts.

31 Sturtevant, p. 143 (emphasis added).

32 Similarly in Elaine Sturtevant, STURTEVANT (Interview by Hans Ulrich Obrist), December 1, 2008 (<https://032c.com/magazine/elaine-sturtevant>) in which she stated: "I realized that, to my

A similar interpretive key is offered by Sherrie Levine in a comment on her own work. As she explained, "[o]ne of [her] main strategies has been *to put one image on top of another*, hopefully creating an interesting gap between the original and the new one".[33] Again, what might seem identical at first sight reveals a "gap", a depth or a dimension when perceived entirely, i.e., not just as a shallow and congruent form. Richard Prince made analogous statements guiding the interpretation of his interpictorial original copies. In slightly different – temporal – terms, he described his work as being about "a delayed density", in which the only immediate aspect in considering the artworks should be that "when you first look at them, you're not exactly sure what hit you".[34]

Similar analyses of interpictorial original copies come from the art theory side. For art critic and curator DOUGLAS CRIMP, one of the major theorists of the so-called "pictures generation", the processes of quotation, framing and staging create "strata of representation" that necessitate uncovering, for "underneath each picture there is always another picture".[35] According to VIOLA VAHRSON, the presence of the template image in Sturtevant's work is merely virtual, i.e., in a way, "present-absent". Although the template images are very present when Sturtevant's artworks are contemplated, they are *de facto* absent, because they are there as something else. The source images insert themselves as a layer that mediates and retards the perception of the repetitions *as* repetitions. The information linked to the template – its authorship and art historical context as well as the visual evidence of their motif – *frustrate* an immediate observation of the work of Sturtevant. In this sense, a pure aesthetic view of the artwork misses the work's meaning.[36]

We can retain the following: Conceiving the form of artworks as mere visual *gestalt* seems not to do justice to interpictorial original copies. Because interpictorial original copies are not "immediate artworks", to conceive them as such is to misunderstand them. As already explained, the novelty of interpictorial copies is a "meta-novelty"[37] that resides not in the surface of the artifacts but in the relation they create with the respective templates, even if what we might see is only the latter.[38] For this reason, LUHMANN wrote that the embedding of other works of art in an artwork "belongs only to the context". The key offered by the artwork to its own understanding, "is not to be found in the quotation, but only in the way this

astonishment, if you took an original source work, and repeated it, you would not only be throwing out resemblance, but you would be dealing with *the understructure of painting*".

33 LEVINE, p. 128 (emphasis added); a similar statement can be found in BUSKIRK, Interviews, p. 100.

34 PRINCE, Interview, p. 86.

35 CRIMP, Pictures, p. 87.

36 VAHRSON, p. 14.

37 SHERMAN, Appropriating, p. 39, uses Sturtevant as example, who, with her "repetition" practice, wanted to explore the "understructure of paintings", i.e., according to SCHAAR, p. 890, its intellectual dimensions.

38 LUHMANN, The Work of Art, p. 198, writes: "style is not to be found in the quotation, but in the way the quotation contributes as quotation to the form of the work of art".

contributes as quotation to the form of the work of art (and not only as an element of the form)".[39]

IV.I A distinction from…plagiarism and forgery

Although forgery and plagiarism are often grouped together as misuses of others' intellectual property, they differ.[40] While both aim to deceive, plagiarism downplays the extensive similarity with an original – even resorting to small or big modifications of the artwork they copy. The forger tries, instead, to conceal the dissimilarity with the real artwork behind a series of similarities.[41]

IV.II Forgery

The *Encyclopedia Britannica* defines forgery in art as "a work of literature, painting, sculpture, or *objet d'art* that purports to be the work of someone other than its true maker".[42] The characterizing element of forgery is, thus, its deceiving purpose.[43] The ultimate finality of the forger is to make people (e.g., potential buyers, the public, a gallerist) believe that the artwork stems from a particular artist in order to sell it at a higher price.[44]

Forgeries are not explicitly addressed under the CopA.[45] Under Art. 67 para. 1 let. a CopA, however, any person who willfully and unlawfully uses a work under a false designation or a designation that differs from that decided by the author is liable on complaint to a custodial sentence not exceeding one year or a monetary penalty. Only if a forger *uses a work* does he become liable under this provision. All those art forgeries (e.g., Wolfgang Beltracchi's[46] or Han van Meegeren's[47]) that simply imitate the style of an author but not a specific existing artwork, would not be punishable under copyright law, as artistic styles per se are not protected by copyright.[48] These forgeries would eventually be punishable under criminal law.

39 LUHMANN, The Work of Art, p. 198.
40 DOLL, p. 35.
41 DOLL, p. 35.
42 Cf. <https://www.britannica.com/art/forgery-art>.
43 SANDMANN, p. 20.
44 Indeed, as HEBBORN, p. 188 – himself a forger – suggests is to sell the fakes at the same price as works "signed with your own name".
45 DREIER, p. 210; however, German copyright law is slightly more attentive with its differentiation between § 106 para. 1 DE-CopA and § 107 para. 1 DE-CopA. Whereas § 106 DE-CopA, just like Art. 67 para. 1 let. a CopA, punishes the forger who uses a copyrighted work made by someone else, § 107 I DE-CopA forbids the application of a signature to a non-original. As explained by SCHACK, N 54 and 58, the application of this article concurs with § 267 of the German Criminal Code about the forgery of documents.
46 HUFNAGEL/CHAPPELL, p. 12.
47 HUFNAGEL/CHAPPELL, p. 1.
48 See the decision about Emil Nolde's watercolors, GFCJ of June 8, 1989 (*Emil Nolde*), NJW 1990, p. 1986 et seqq., p. 1988. Because the two fake watercolor paintings imitating Nolde's style were not copies of existing paintings by Nolde, his copyright was not infringed.

The Swiss Criminal Code ("SCC") does not explicitly mention art forgeries.[49] This brings into question Art. 155 SCC about the counterfeiting of goods[50] and, if the artwork is signed, Art. 251 SCC about the forgery of documents.[51] The trade with forged artworks is also punished as fraud (Art. 146 SCC).

With art forgeries, interpictorial original copies share the characteristic of depicting the work of someone else. The difference between them, however, is easily identifiable, as when creating interpictorial original copies, artists use "forgery" as an artistic technique and not with the intent to deceive (for example, Sherrie Levine described her work as "using the strategy of theft"[52]).[53] For this reason, artists who appropriate and reproduce pre-existing artworks of other artists use their own name and not someone else's: the artwork is exposed, commercialized and distributed under the second artist's name (in case of Sherrie Levine's appropriations, under her name and not, for example, Edward Weston's). The deceitful purpose required to fulfill the criminal provisions of counterfeit, forgery of documents and fraud is, therefore, missing altogether.

Expressed with a dichotomy of terms, the forgery's opposite would be the "authentic artwork".[54] The interpictorial original copy, instead, is itself an authentic repetition of an original, authored by the artist who copied. The "layering" of different authorships, the duality inhabiting the interpictorial original copy (or in systems theoretical terms, the "re-entry") is crucial for its succeeding as art.[55] For this same reason, artists using copies of previously existing material have the least intent to make people believe that the work shall be attributed to another author's name.

IV.III Plagiarism

Plagiarism is the appropriation of someone else's visual content but not of the name.[56] Or as the *Encyclopedia Britannica* states, it is the act of taking the writings

49 BANDLE, Kultur Kunst Recht, N 488 *ad* § 6
50 BANDLE, Kultur Kunst Recht, N 488 et seqq. *ad* § 6.
51 BANDLE, Kultur Kunst Recht, N 491 et seqq. *ad* § 6.
52 LEVINE, p. 126, describes her work as "using the strategy of theft".
53 RÖMER, p. 6; as also stated by the *Encyclopedia Britannica*, "forgery must be distinguished from copies produced with no intent to deceive".
54 Even though this claim might be inaccurate from an art theoretical perspective, cf. LENAIN, p. 311, who states that "ideologues of connoisseurship and other enforcers of authenticity…maintain that fakes are in fact authentic works of a certain kind, and that there is no such thing as art forgery"; moreover, some forgeries were long deemed to be authentic originals by experts; sometimes, they were even considered to be the "masterpiece" of the respectively imitated artist, cf. GOPNIK, p. 21; cf. also BLUNCK, p. 19, stating that van Megeerens are now sold as "authentic van Megeerens". How and when exactly this "switch" happens is a topic that goes beyond the scope of this work.
55 Cf. Chapter 1, III.I.
56 ADLER, Why Art, p. 330.

(but it could be any other creative output as well) of another person and passing them off as one's own.[57]

Even though we do not find the noun "plagiarism" in any provision of the CopA,[58] in copyright literature, it is defined as the "altered or unaltered takeover of a copyrighted work or part of a copyrighted work by implying authorship thereof".[59] Under Swiss copyright law, an act of plagiarism constitutes a possible infringement of the author's moral rights under Art. 9 and 11 CopA for what concerns the "usurpation of authorship"[60] and the eventual derogatory treatment of the used artwork (when the copy is not a perfect reproduction but has been changed). The author's economic rights under Art. 10 CopA are also infringed by the unauthorized use of another author's work. These acts can be punished under Art. 67 CopA and 68 CopA.[61]

The distinction between plagiarism and an interpictorial original copy is subtler than that between the latter and forgeries, as both display someone else's work under the name of the person who used it, not the original creator. Moreover, as with plagiarism, many interpictorial original copies do not indicate the original source.[62] However, the fact that the artifact has another origin than the one disclosed is actively dissimulated by plagiarists with different stratagems. For example, the plagiarist will recur to small or big modifications of the original to break the link to the original work.[63] Interpictorial original copies, however, do not actively conceal the work's different origin. Yet, by failing to properly credit the source (or omitting it entirely), the artist risks violating copyright laws on quotation, effectively appearing as a plagiarist in the eyes of the law.

The difference between plagiarism and an interpictorial original copy is, thus, not visible from the outside. Rather, it lies somewhere in the relationship that the final artifact constructs with its source material. Whereas plagiarism is tacit on the duality of the two authors and tries to make it disappear behind a simulated authorial and stylistic uniformity, the interpictorial original is – as a typical postmodernist

57 Cf. <https://www.britannica.com/topic/plagiarism>.

58 SCHACK, N 346; for Switzerland see MOSIMANN, Kultur Kunst Recht, N 112 *ad* § 1; BUNG/GRUBER/KÜHN, p. 15; nonetheless, used in DFC 88 IV 123 (*Lehrbuch*), DFC 113 II 190 (*Le Corbusier*), c. II.1, and DFC 125 III 328 (*Niederhauser*), c. 4.

59 SCHACK, N 346.

60 BARRELET/EGLOFF, CopA Commentary, N 14 *ad* Art. 9.

61 MOSIMANN, Kultur Kunst Recht, N 117 *ad* § 1, fn. 206, states that unconscious copying does not amount to plagiarism.

62 BLUME HUTTENLAUCH, p. 28, writes that in the frequent case in which the copied artwork is recognizable and well-known, a plagiarism effect is "objectively not possible", as the public will recognize the work as being from someone else. A false attribution will, thus, be impossible.

63 DOLL, p. 35; the website <https://plagiarismcheck.org/blog/top-3-manipulations/> indicates common text manipulation strategies used to conceive the similarity between the plagiarized text and the original. These include word rearrangements, changes in the structure of a sentence and change of the sentence from active to passive voice.

artifact – inhabited by multiplicity and comfortable with the resulting aesthetics of incoherence.[64]

IV.IV What is different about interpictorial original copies

Forgeries and plagiarisms do not present or reference anything; instead, they suppress their respective "original" and try to pass as their substitute. In this sense, they free-ride on the original work, almost "cannibalizing" it.[65] The perils of free riding are what historically and politically justifies the existence of copyright law.[66] As a consequence, its instruments are adjusted to identifying uses of works that supplant the original, sabotaging the positive incentivizing of creativity that copyright is supposed to support. With interpictorial original copies, however, copyright law's instruments reach too far, seeing a mere copy where there is also an original, authentic artwork.

Interpictorial original copies are the postmodern translation of a phenomenon – interpictoriality – that characterizes the whole art system. In Chapter 1, we described, in detail, how the interpictorial original copy constitutes a new artwork even if – or precisely because – it makes use of an old artwork. In this sense, the artistic copy does not supersede the original. It leaves the original intact and multiplies it (or *amplifies* it) for aesthetic reasons.[67] Whereas plagiarism remains stuck in its condition as plagiarism (at least as soon as it is unveiled), original copies have the capability to *oscillate* between their double and simultaneous status as copies and as original, autonomous artworks. As it is typical with oscillations, the moment one considers only one side, it becomes impossible to forget the other side and resist its attraction: The original copy is more than just an original just as it is more than a copy.[68]

Indeed, artists who realize interpictorial original copies are not trying to get away with it or to deceive anyone. They are often open and vocal about the fact that they included extraneous material in their artworks, as, in many cases, it is precisely the marking of this very difference, its accentuation, that completely realizes the artwork.[69] The title of their artworks, their artistic statements, the artistic movement to which they belong or the critical analysis of their work often allow recognizing that there are parts of their artwork that are not fully their own.[70]

64 Doll, p. 36; Pochat, p. 129.
65 Doll, p. 36; Pochat, p. 125.
66 As the Supreme Court in *Andy Warhol Found. for the Visual Arts, Inc. vs. Goldsmith*, 598 US ___ (2023), p. 15, put it, "[fair use's] first factor relates to the problem of substitution – copyright's bête noire".
67 Vahrson, p. 104; Pochat, p. 125.
68 On the figure of oscillation cf. Chapter 3, V.IV; this characteristic of interpictorial original copies induces a sense of disorientation in the viewers, see: <http://societeberlin.com/exhibitions/sturtevant/>; for Luhmann, cf. Huber/Luhmann, p. 129, this sense of disorientation and marvel (in ancient Greek θαυμάζω, thaumázō) is at the beginning of art itself.
69 Pochat, p. 125.
70 Zuschlag, p. 208.

Of the double, oscillating existence of the interpictorial original copy, copyright law is only capable of focusing on the repetition of a copyrighted work, failing to see its polyhedric existence. This results from the placement of the previously described blind spot of copyright law.[71] Whereas similarity between works may rightly signal the presence of plagiarism in many cases, to rely exclusively on this metric would be short-sighted. If copyright law wants to avoid creating a disconnect from the social reality it is inserted in, it needs to follow an interdisciplinary approach to ensure it stays aligned with societal changes and values. With regard to interpictorial art, copyright law needs a strategy to counter the overbroad application of its rules and re-establish its societal purpose of fostering creativity and innovation.

71 Cf. Chapter 4, V.I.

Conclusions

The interpictorial original copy is a paradoxical object: New because it showcases the old and original because it denies originality. We have described it as the new use of the old, that is, the re-entry, on the side of the new, of the difference old/new in itself. This passage allowed us to deconstruct the operation that the interpictorial original copy does "all at once" and, thus, grasps what is radically different and new about an artifact that just looks like the copy of another one.

When faced with this paradoxical object, copyright law is obliged to confront its own blind spot: A place in which it is logically impossible to conceive the interpictorial artifact-copy as another art*work* that is different from its template, notwithstanding the striking formal similarities. Because of how copyright law defines its object of protection – the work – it simply cannot qualify an equal-looking artifact as a new, different one. This blind spot, which is similar to the blind spot of modernism as epitomized by Walter Benjamin in "The Work of Art in the Age of its Technological Reproducibility", is the source of the lack of synchronization between the two systems. While the history of art has produced, since the 1960s, dematerialized, conceptual artworks, copyright law has largely stuck to the material qualities of artworks to determine their protection. Put differently, what matters to copyright law is still how the artifact looks (and, of course, by whom it was made).

Luckily, copyright law has exceptions. Within the framework of the freedom of quotation, panorama, or parody, some interpictorial artistic instances are, indeed, accommodated. This allows visual artists to work interpictorially, i.e., to use existing artworks and other copyrighted visual material to create new artworks, which placates and contains the asynchronization between art and law. Yet exceptions were not conceived to justify interpictorial visual artworks. If their rules and requirements can be stretched to justify an interpictorial original copy, it is only by analogy and, thus, uncomfortable. Moreover, exceptions are also attached – even if to a lesser extent compared to the definition of work – to the material qualities of artifacts. So, for example, the exception of quotation will only allow quotations that are "secondary" to the quoting artist's own creation. This means that if the artist wants to appeal to this exception, she will have to demonstrate that she also created something new, something of her own. Only this evident novelty justifies quoting extraneous material.

DOI: 10.4324/9781003598503-15

The result is that while some interpictorial artworks could be justified under an existing copyright exception, many fail to fulfill the requirements. Yet, when copyright law declares new art infringing, an uneasy situation arises, as the protection of old works hampers the creation of new ones despite copyright law's societal function to foster innovation and creativity. Rightfully concerned with the maintenance of copyright law's function, lawyers and courts alike flee the normative framework of copyright to find refuge in the hierarchically higher sphere of fundamental rights. From there, they reformulate verdicts of copyright infringements as a conflict between a communication freedom – in the case of interpictorial artworks, the freedom of (artistic) expression – and the guarantee of ownership. Alternatively, they submit the result obtained with copyright law to an external review based on freedom of expression rationales.

While transposing this conflict on a Constitutional or Conventional level has at least the (important) advantage of lifting the theoretical basis underlying the inequality between the right of authors (considered, in copyright theory, as the rule) and the exceptions to this right (considered, as the choice of words says, as narrowly scoped exceptions), the outcomes obtained with this method are sometimes in favor of artists (or users) and other times not. Rather, the result is often that copyright rules are confirmed to be, indeed, legitimate, proportionate and constitutional. Restrictions of the freedom of expression based on copyright law must, therefore, be tolerated. One way or another, the method is highly case-specific: With every new case, the balancing must be reset, as its "relevant circumstances" are forcibly different. Resolving conflicts this way cannot be the final solution to a problem rooted in copyright law. This approach does not create legal certainty for the parties involved and is methodologically problematic.

Rather, copyright lawyers should confront themselves with what we think is an unavoidable decision: In front of new art that is declared infringing on copyright grounds, they can either choose to stick to their conventional standards and confirm the verdict of infringement, or they can start working interdisciplinarily, opening themselves up to information coming from other systems of society. This would allow them to understand interpictorial original copies and grasp the novelty they bring into the world. The latter is the approach we plead for.

Interpictorial original copies have the capability to oscillate between their double and parallel status as copies and as original, autonomous artworks. They are simultaneously more than just copies and not perfectly accomplished originals: Describing them as one or the other would be insufficient and is where the oscillation starts its inexorable movement. This characteristic elevates them to art objects and distinguishes them from plagiarism. Since the 1960s, comparing artworks in search of (visual) differences has not been a viable criterion to distinguish authenticity from plagiarism. The challenge is to develop criteria that allow drawing a line and only justify uses that are artistically and not fraudulently motivated. In the last part of this book, we have outlined possible approaches. A focus on the process of creation and context in which the artwork is communicated (e.g., the title of the artwork, which often contains an interpretive key to the understanding of the artwork, the texts accompanying the exhibition, the exhibition itself) could bring to light the doubleness that inhabits interpictorial original copies and from which they – contrary to plagiarism – do not shy away from.

In general, our hope is for a more cognitively open copyright law, curious toward knowledge produced in other systems of our society. With this book, we hope to have shown what can be learned in the process of not looking at art from a detached, legal perspective but also from listening attentively to what art has to say about itself.

Bibliography

Adler Amy, Against Moral Rights, California Law Review (97) 2009, pp. 263–300 (cit. Adler, Against Moral Rights, p. …).

Adler Amy, Fair Use and The Future of Art, New York University Law Review (91) 2016, pp. 559–626 (cit. Adler, The Future of Art, p. …).

Adler Amy, Why Art Does Not Need Copyright, The George Washington Law Review (86) 2018, pp. 313–375 (cit. Adler, Why Art, p …).

Alejandre Gemma Minero, Google Cache Is Legal in Spain – Spanish Supreme Court, 3 April 2012, The Megakini.com v Google Spain case (N. 172/2012), Queen Mary Journal of Intellectual Property (3) 2013, pp. 81–89.

Amstutz Marc, Zwischenwelten: Zur Emergenz einer interlegalen Rechtsmethodik im europäischen Privatrecht, in: Joerges Christian/Teubner Gunther (eds.), Rechtsverfassungsrecht: Rechtfertigung zwischen Privatrechtsdogmatik und Gesellschaftstheorie, Baden-Baden 2003, pp. 213–237 (cit. Amstutz, Zwischenwelten, p. …).

Amstutz Marc, Der zweite Text. Für eine Kritische Systemtheorie des Rechts, in: Amstutz Marc (ed.), Kritische Systemtheorie. Zur Evolution einer normativen Theorie, Bielefeld 2013, pp. 365–401 (cit. Amstutz, Der zweite Text, p. …).

Amstutz Marc/Fischer-Lescano Andreas, Einleitung, in: Amstutz Marc (ed.), Kritische Systemtheorie. Zur Evolution einer normativen Theorie, Bielefeld 2013, pp. 7–12.

Arnold Richard/Rosati Eleonora, Are National Courts the Addressees of the InfoSoc Three-Step Test?, GRUR Int 2015, pp. 1193–1200.

Art & Language, Roma Reason. Luhmann's Art as a Social System, Radical Philosophy (109) 2001, pp. 14–21.

Asay Clark D./Sloan Arielle/Sobczak Dean, Is Transformative Use Eating the World?, Boston College Law Review (61) 2020, pp. 905–970.

Athanassopoulos Vangelis, Paradoxes et contradictions du Postmoderne, La voix du regard (17) 2004–2005, pp. 284–290.

Aufderheide Patricia/Jaszi Peter/Bello Bryan/Milosevic Tijana, Copyright, Permissions, and Fair Use among Visual Artists and the Academic and Museum Visual Arts Communities – An Issues Report, 2014 (available at: <https://www.collegeart.org/pdf/FairUseIssuesReport.pdf>).

Aufderheide Patricia/Milosevic Tijana/Bello Bryan, The Impact of Copyright Permissions Culture on the US Visual Arts Community: The Consequences of Fear of Fair Use, New Media & Society (18) 2016, pp. 2012–2027.

Baecker Dirk, The Unique Appearance of Distance, in: Gumbrecht Hans Ulrich/Marrinan Michael (eds.), Mapping Benjamin. The Work of Art in the Digital Age, Stanford 2003, pp. 9–23 (cit. Baecker, Appearance, p. …).

Baer Susanne, Verfassungsvergleichung und reflexive Methode: Interkulturelle und intersubjektive Kompetenz, ZaöRV (64) 2004, pp. 735–758.

Balganesh Shyamkrishna, Causing Copyright, Columbia Law Review (117) 2017, pp. 1–78 (cit. Balganesh, Causing Copyright, p. …).

Balganesh Shyamkrishna, Foreseeability and Copyright Incentives, Harvard Law Review (122) 2009, pp. 1569–1633 (cit. Balganesh, Foreseeability, p. …).

Balganesh Shyamkrishna, The Normativity of Copying in Copyright Law, Duke Law Journal (62) 2012, pp. 203–284 (cit. Balganesh, Normativity, p. …).

Bantleon Katharina, From Readymade to 'Meta^2' Metareference in Appropriation Art, in: Werner Wolf (ed.), The Metareferential Turn in Contemporary Arts and Media, Amsterdam 2011, pp. 305–337.

Baraldi Claudio/Corsi Giancarlo/Esposito Elena, Unlocking Luhmann. A Keyword Introduction to Systems Theory (transl. by Katherine Walker), Bielefeld 2021 (1999) (cit. Baraldi/Corsi/Esposito, p. …).

Barrelet Denis/Egloff Willi (eds.), Das neue Urheberrecht. Kommentar zum Bundesgesetz über das Urheberrecht und verwandte Schutzrechte, 4th Ed., Bern 2020 (cit. Author(s), CopA Commentary, N … *ad* Art. …).

Barron Anne, Copyright Infringement, 'Free-Riding' and the Lifeworld, in: Bently Lionel/Davis Jennifer/Ginsburg Jane C. (eds.), Copyright and Piracy. An Interdisciplinary Critique, Cambridge 2010, pp. 93–127 (cit. Barron, Copyright Infringement, p. …).

Barron Anne, Copyright Law and the Claims of Art, Intellectual Property Q (4) 2002, pp. 368–401 (cit. Barron, Claims of Art, p. …).

Barthes Roland, The Death of the Author, Aspen, 5+6/1967 (available at: <https://www.ubu.com/aspen/aspen5and6/threeEssays.html#barthes>).

Bauer Eva-Maria, Die Aneignung von Bildern. Eine urheberrechtliche Betrachtung von der Appropriation Art bis hin zu Memes, PhD Thesis, Baden-Baden 2020.

Bell Abraham/Parchomovsky Gideon, The Dual-Grant Theory of Fair Use, The University of Chicago Law Review (83) 2016, pp. 1051–1118.

Bellido Jose, Experimenting with Law: Brecht on Copyright, Law and Critique (31) 2020, pp. 127–143.

Benjamin Walter, The Work of Art in the Age of Its Technological Reproducibility (1935), in: Jennings Michael W./Doherty Brigid/Levin Thomas Y. (eds.), The Work of Art in the Age of Its Technological Reproducibility and Other Writings on Media. Walter Benjamin, Cambridge (MA)/London 2008, pp. 19–55.

Benkler Yochai, Law, Innovation, and Collaboration in Networked Economy and Society, Annual Review of Law and Social Science (13) 2017, pp. 231–250.

Berger John, Understanding a Photograph (ed. by Geoff Dyer), London 2013.

Berger Mathis, Irrtum: Das Urheberrecht regelt den Schutz von Urheberinnen und Urhebern von Werken der Literatur und Kunst, in: Berger Mathis/Macciacchini Sandro (eds.), Populäre Irrtümer im Urheberrecht – Festschrift für Reto M. Hilty, Zurich 2008, pp. 3–24.

Berger Mathis/Macciacchini Sandro (eds.), Populäre Irrtümer im Urheberrecht – Festschrift für Reto M. Hilty, Zurich 2008 (cit. Author, Populäre Irrtümer, p. …).

Beyer Andreas, Interpikturalität oder: Kunst kommt vor Kunst. Die Aneignung als Konstante und Prinzip, in: Mosimann Peter/Schönenberger Beat (eds.), Kunst & Recht 2016/Art & Law 2016. Referate zur gleichnamigen Veranstaltung der Juristischen Fakultät der Universität Basel vom 17. Juni, Bern 2016, pp. 59–74.

Bidlo Mike, Mike Bidlo Talks to Robert Rosenblum, Artforum (48) 2003, pp. 192–193 and 248–252.

Blume Huttenlauch Anna, Appropriation Art – Kunst an den Grenzen des Urheberrechts, PhD Thesis, Baden-Baden 2010.

Blunck Lars, Wann ist ein Original, in: Nida-Rümelin Julian/Steinbrenner Jakob (eds.), Original und Fälschung, Ostfildern 2011, pp. 9–30.

Bogdan Michael, Concise Introduction to Comparative Law, Groningen 2013.

Bohn Cornelia, Autonomien in Zusammenhängen. Formenkombinatorik und die Verzeitlichung des Bildlichen, Paderborn 2017 (cit. Bohn, Autonomien, p. …).

Bohn Cornelia, Gegenwarten der Kunst. Ereignisse, Grossereignisse, Morphogenesen, in: Buckermann Paul (ed.), Die Welten der documenta. Wissen und Geltung eines Grossereignisses der Kunst, Weilerswist 2022, pp. 64–82 (cit. Bohn, Gegenwarten, p. …).

Bourriaud Nicolas, Postproduction, Milan 2004.

Brändli-Marmy Sandra, Die Flexibilität urheberrechtlicher Schrankensysteme, PhD Thesis, Bern 2017.

Brinkmann Franziska, Formen der Kopie von der Fälschung bis zur Hommage – Eine Begriffsbestimmung und ihre Grenzen, in: Dreier Thomas/Jehle Olivier (eds.), Original – Kopie – Fälschung, Baden-Baden 2020, pp. 57–104.

Brunet François, The Birth of the Idea of Photography, Toronto 2019.

Buccafusco Christopher J., How Conceptual Art Challenges Copyright's Notions of Authorial Control and Creativity, Columbia Journal of Law & the Arts (43) 2020, pp. 375–379.

Bung Jochen/Gruber Malte-Christian/Kühn Sebastian, Einleitung, in: Bung Jochen/Gruber Malte-Christian/Kühn Sebastian (eds.), Plagiate. Fälschungen, Imitate und andere Strategien aus zweiter Hand, Berlin 2011, pp. 11–20.

Burke Shane, Intellectual Property Law as Artistic Medium, in: McCutcheon Jani/ McGaughey Fiona (eds.), Research Handbook on Art and Law, Northampton 2020, pp. 259–277.

Buskirk Martha, Interviews with Sherrie Levine, Louise Lawler, and Fred Wilson, October (70) 1994, pp. 98–112 (cit. Buskirk, Interviews, p. …).

Buskirk Martha, The Contingent Object of Contemporary Art, Cambridge (MA) 2003 (cit. Buskirk, The Contingent Object, p. …).

Buskirk Martha, Creative Intent: The Recent Fortunes of Appropriation in the United States, in: McClean Daniel (ed.), The Trials of Art, London 2007, pp. 235–251 (cit. Buskirk, Creative Intent, p. …).

Buss Esther/Graw Isabelle/Krümmel Clemens, Vorwort, October (46) 2002, p. 2.

Buydens Mireille, La protection de la quasi-création: information, publicité, mode, photographies documentaires et esthétique industrielle... : droit belge, droit allemand, droit français, Brussels 1993.

Buydens Mireille/Dusollier Séverine, Les exceptions au droit d'auteur: évolutions dangereuses, Communication Commerce Electronique (9) 2001, pp. 10–16.

Camenisch Livia, Innovationsoffenheit als Verfassungsgrundsatz, PhD Thesis, Zurich/ St.Gallen 2021.

Carlut Christiane, Copyright/Copywrong. Les enjeux des pratiques contemporaines d'appropriation, in: Carlut Christiane (ed.), Copyright/Copywrong: acte du colloque, Le Mans, Nantes, Saint-Nazaire, février 2000, Nantes 2003, pp. 11–18.

Carrier Michael A., Copyright and Innovation: The Untold Story, Wisconsin Law Review (4) 2012, pp. 891–962.

Cherpillod Ivan, L'objet du droit d'auteur: étude critique de la distinction entre forme et idée, PhD Thesis, Lausanne 1985 (cit. Cherpillod, L'objet, p. …).

Cherpillod Ivan, Le droit d'auteur en Suisse: précis et guide pratique, Lausanne 1986 (cit. Cherpillod, Le droit d'auteur, p. …).

Cherpillod Ivan, Droit d'auteur et liberté de l'art, sic! 2024, pp. 355–373 (cit. Cherpillod, Liberté, p. …).

Cherpillod Ivan/Berger Mathis, "Mummenschanz". Kantonsgericht St. Gallen vom 19. Juni 2002 Urheberrechtsschutz für Körpermasken; Strafbarkeit des Auftraggebers eines das Urheber- und Lauterkeitsrecht verletzenden Werks Strafkammer; Teilabweisung der Berufung; Akten-Nr. ST.2002.8-SK3, mit Anmerkung von Cherpillod Ivan/Berger Mathis, sic! 2003, pp. 116–125.

Childs Adrienne L. (ed.), Riffs and relations: African American Artists and the European Modernist Tradition, New York/Washington 2020.

Clair Jean, Elogio del falso in una bassa epoca, in: Cavina Ottani Anna/Natale Mauro (eds.), Il falso specchio della realtà, Torino 2017, pp. 11–35.

Cohen Julie E., Creativity and Culture in Copyright Theory, University of California Davis Law Review (40) 2007, pp. 1151–1205.

College Art Association, Code of Best Practices in Fair Use for the Visual Arts, 2015 (available at: <https://www.collegeart.org/pdf/fair-use/best-practices-fair-use-visual-arts.pdf>).

Coombe Rosemary J., The Cultural Life of Intellectual Properties: Authorship, Appropriation, and the Law, Durham (NC) 1998.

Craig Carys J., Copyright, Communication and Culture. Towards a Relational Theory of Copyright Law, Cheltenham 2011 (cit. Craig, Copyright, p. …).

Craig Carys J., Reconstructing the Author-Self: Some Feminist Lessons for Copyright Law, American University Journal of Gender, Social Policy & the Law (15) 2007, pp. 207–268 (cit. Craig, Reconstructing, p. …).

Cras Sophie, Robert Filliou face à l'économie du multiple dans les années 1960. Standardisation, démocratisation et marchandisation, in: Beyer Andreas/Jollet Étienne/Rath Markus (eds.), Wiederholung. Répétition. Wiederkehr, Variation und Übersetzung in der Kunst, Paris/Berlin 2017, pp. 183–198.

Crimp Douglas, Appropriating Appropriation (1982), in: Douglas Crimp (ed.), On the Museum's Ruins, Cambridge (MA) 1993, pp. 126–137 (cit. Crimp, Appropriating, p. …).

Crimp Douglas, Pictures, October (8) 1979, pp. 75–88 (cit. Crimp, Pictures, p. …).

Crow Thomas, The Return of Hank Herron, in: Bois Yve-Alain et al. (eds.), Endgame. Reference and Simulation in Recent Painting and Sculpture, Boston (MA) 1986, pp. 11–27.

Cueni Raphaela, Schutz von Satire im Rahmen der Meinungsfreiheit, PhD Thesis, Zurich 2019.

Cuntz Alexander/Sahli Matthias, Intermediary Liability and Trade in Follow-on Innovation, WIPO Economic Research Working Paper No. 66, October 2021 (available at: <https://www.wipo.int/edocs/pubdocs/en/wipo_pub_econstat_wp_66.pdf>).

Derrida Jacques, De la grammatologie, Paris 1967 (available at: <http://dhspriory.org/kenny/PhilTexts/Derrida/De%20la%20grammatologie.pdf>) (cit. Derrida, Grammatologie, p. …).

Derrida Jacques, The Law of Genre (transl. by Avital Ronell), Critical Inquiry (7) 1980, pp. 55–81 (cit. Derrida, Genre, p. …).

Derrida Jacques, Margins of Philosophy (transl. by Alan Bass), Chicago (IL) 1984 (1972) (cit. Derrida, Margins, p. …).

Dessemontet François, L'objet du droit d'auteur et les droits d'auteur, in: Dessemontet François et al. (eds.), La nouvelle loi fédérale sur le droit d'auteur: travaux de la Journée d'étude organisée par le Centre du droit de l'entreprise le 3 mars 1993 à l'Université de Lausanne, Publication CEDIDAC, Lausanne 1994 (cit. Dessemontet, L'objet, p. …).

Dessemontet François, Le droit d'auteur, Lausanne 1999 (cit. Dessemontet, Le droit d'auteur, p. …).

Dessemontet François, Intellectual Property Law in Switzerland, 4th Ed., Alphen aan den Rijn, 2019 (cit. Dessemontet, Intellectual Property, p. …).

de Werra Jacques/Gilliéron Philippe (eds.), Commentaire Romand de Propriété intellectuelle, Basel 2013 (cit. Author(s), CoRo CopA, N … *ad* Art …).

Döhl Frédéric, Mashup in der Musik: Fremdreferenzielles Komponieren, Sound Sampling und Urheberrecht, Bielefeld 2016 (cit. Döhl, Mashup, p. …).

Döhl Frédéric, Nach § 24 Abs. 1 UrhG: Zum Pastichebegriff im Kontext der anstehenden Neuaufstellung der Spielregeln freier Benutzung, UFITA 2019, pp. 19–41 (cit. Döhl, Pastichebegriff, p. …).

Döhl Frédéric, Das neue Bearbeitungsrechtsregime, kunstspezifisch betrachtet, ZUM 2020, pp. 740–749.

Döhl Frédéric, Systemwechsel – Vom Gebot des Verblassens zum Gebot der Interaktion. Kunstspezifische Betrachtung des Bearbeitungsrechts nach den Urteilen von EuGH (C-476/17) und BGH (I ZR 115/16) in Sachen Metall auf Metall, UFITA 2020, pp. 236–283 (cit. Döhl, Systemwechsel, p. …).

Döhl Frédéric/Hui Alan, Collateral Damage: Reuse in the Arts and the New Role of Quotation Provisions in Countries with Free Use Provisions After the ECJ's Pelham, Funke Medien and Spiegel Online Judgments, International Review of Intellectual Property and Competition Law (52) 2021, pp. 852–892.

Döhl Frédéric/Wöhrer Renate, Einleitung, in: Döhl Frédéric/Wöhrer Renate (eds.), Zitieren, appropriieren, sampeln. Referenzielle Verfahren in den Gegenwartskünsten, Bielefeld 2014, pp. 7–19.

Doll Martin, Plagiat und Fälschung: Filiationen von Originalität und Autorschaft, in: Bung Jochen/Gruber Malte-Christian/Kühn Sebastian (eds.): Plagiate. Fälschungen, Imitate und andere Strategien aus zweiter Hand, Berlin 2011, pp. 35–51.

Douzinas Costas, Sublime Law: On Legal and Aesthetic Judgements, parallax (14) 2008, pp. 18–29.

Drahos Peter, The Universality of Intellectual Property Rights: Origins and Developments, in: Intellectual Property and Human Rights, WIPO Publication No. 762(E), 1999, pp. 13–41.

Dreier Thomas, Original, Kopie und Fälschung im Recht, in: Dreier Thomas/Jehle Olivier (eds.), Original – Kopie – Fälschung, Baden-Baden 2020, pp. 195–218.

Dreier Thomas/Jehle Olivier (eds.), Original – Kopie – Fälschung, Baden-Baden 2020.

Edelman Bernard, The Law's Eye: Nature and Copyright, in: Sherman Brad/Strowel Alain (eds.), Of Authors and Origins. Essays on Copyright Law, Oxford 1994, pp. 79–91 (cit. Edelman, The Law's Eye, p. …).

Edelman Bernard, De l'urinoir comme un des beaux-arts: de la signature de Duchamp au geste de Pinoncelly, in: Edelman Bernard/Heinich Nathalie (eds.), L'art en conflits. L'oeuvre de l'esprit entre droit et sociologie, Paris 2002, pp. 83–95 (cit. Edelman, De l'urinoir, p. …).

Edelman Bernard, Du mauvais usage des droits de l'homme (À propos du jugement du tribunal de grande instance de Paris du 23 février 1999), in: Edelman Bernard/Heinich Nathalie (eds.), L'art en conflits. L'oeuvre de l'esprit entre droit et sociologie, Paris 2002, pp. 162–173 (cit. Edelman, Du mauvais usage, p. …).

Egloff Willi, Neues im neuen URG, Anwaltsrevue 2020, pp. 273–277 (cit. Egloff, Neues, p. …).

Egloff Willi, Von der "freien Benutzung" zum "künstlerischen Zitat", sic! 2020, pp. 399–411 (cit. Egloff, Von der "freien Benutzung", p. …).

Eliot T.S., Tradition and the Individual Talent (1919), Perspecta: The Yale Journal of Architecture (19) 1982, pp. 36–42.

Ernst Wolfgang, (In)Differenz: Zur Extase der Originalität im Zeitalter der Fotokopie, in: Gumbrecht Hans Ulrich/Pfeiffer K. Ludwig (eds.), Materialität der Kommunikation, Frankfurt a.M. 1988, pp. 498–518.

Esposito Elena, Paradoxien als Unterscheidungen von Unterscheidungen, in: Gumbrecht Hans Ulrich/Pfeiffer Ludwig K. (eds.), Paradoxien, Dissonanzen, Zusammenbrüche: Situationen offener Epistemologie, Frankfurt am Main 1991, pp. 35–57 (cit. Esposito, Paradoxien, p. …).

Esposito Elena, Wieviel Altes braucht das Neue, in: Fischer Hans Rudi (ed.), Wie kommt Neues in die Welt?, Phantasie, Intuition und der Ursprung von Kreativität, Weilerwist 2013, pp. 133–147 (cit. Esposito, Altes, p. …).

Esposito Elena, Die Konstruktion der Unberechenbarkeit, in: Avanessian Armen/Malik Suhail (eds.), Der Zeitkomplex: postcontemporary, Berlin 2016, pp. 37–42 (cit. Esposito, Unberechenbarkeit, p. …).

Esposito Elena, Predicting Innovation. Artistic Novelty and Digital Forecast, in: Lijster Thijs (ed.), The Future of the New. Artistic Innovation in Times of Social Acceleration, Amsterdam 2018, pp. 235–242 (cit. Esposito, Predicting Innovation, p. …).

Evans David, Introduction/Seven Types of Appropriation, in: Evans David (ed.), Appropriation, London/Cambridge (MA) 2009, pp. 12–23.
Feireiss Lukas, Radical Cut-Up: Nothing is Original, in: Feireiss Lukas (ed.), Radical Cut-Up: Nothing is Original, London 2019, pp. 7–25.
Ficsor Mihály, Fair use versus triple test. La promotion agressive d'un droit d'auteur a minima, in: Bernault Carine et al. (eds.), Mélanges en l'honneur du professeur André Lucas, Paris 2014, pp. 277–290.
Filk Christian/Holger Simon, Wie ist Kunst möglich? Zur Konstitution von Kunstkommunikation, in: Filk Christian/Holger Simon (eds.), Kunstkommunikation: "Wie ist Kunst möglich?" Beiträge zu einer systemischen Medien- und Kunstwissenschaft, Berlin 2010, pp. 17–36.
Fischer Georg, Sampling in der Musikproduktion: das Spannungsfeld zwischen Urheberrecht und Kreativität, Marburg 2020 (cit. Fischer, Sampling, p. …).
Fischer-Lescano Andreas, Systemtheorie als kritische Gesellschaftstheorie, in: Amstutz Marc (ed.), Kritische Systemtheorie. Zur Evolution einer normativen Theorie, Bielefeld 2013, pp. 13–38.
Fischer-Lescano Andreas/Christensen Ralph, Das Ganze des Rechts, Vom hierarchischen zum reflexiven Verständnis deutscher und europäischer Grundrechte, Berlin 2007.
Fischer Veronika, Digitale Kunst und freie Benutzung, PhD Thesis, Baden-Baden 2018.
Fleck Robert, Qu'est-ce que l'appropriationisme, in: Carlut Christiane (ed.), Copyright/ Copywrong: acte du colloque, Le Mans, Nantes, Saint-Nazaire, février 2000, Nantes 2003, pp. 92–93.
Focillon Henri, Vie des formes, Paris 1934.
Förster Achim, Fair Use. Ein Systemvergleich der Schrankengeneralklausel des US-amerikanischen Copyright Act mit dem Schrankenkatalog des deutschen Urheberrechtsgesetzes, PhD Thesis, Tübingen 2008.
Foucault Michel, What is an Author? (1967), in: Faubion James D. (ed.), Michel Foucault, Aesthetics, Method, and Epistemology. Essential works of Foucault 1954–1984, Vol. 2, New York 1998, pp. 205–222.
Fuchs Christine, Avantgarde und erweiterter Kunstbegriff. Eine Aktualisierung des Kunst- und Werkbegriffs im Verfassungs- und Urheberrecht, PhD Thesis, Baden-Baden 2000 (cit. Fuchs Christine, Avantgarde, p. …).
Fuchs Peter, Die Unbeeindruckbarkeit der Gesellschaft – Ein Essay zur Kritikabilität sozialer Systeme, in: Amstutz Marc (ed.), Kritische Systemtheorie. Zur Evolution einer normativen Theorie, Bielefeld 2013, pp. 99–110.
Fuchs Stephan, Kinds of Observers and Types of Distinctions, in: John René/Henkel Anna/ Rückert-John Jana (eds.), Die Methodologien des Systems: Wie kommt man zum Fall und wie dahinter?, Wiesbaden 2010, pp. 81–96.
Gamer Elisabeth-Christine, Die Intertextualität der Bilder: Methodendiskussionen zwischen Kunstgeschichte und Literaturtheorie, Berlin 2020.
Gasser Christoph/Morant Marc O., Das Zitatrecht im Lichte von "Kreis vs. Schweizerzeit", sic! 2006, pp. 229–241.
Geiger Christophe, Copyright as an Access Right: Securing Cultural Participation Through the Protection of Creators' Interests, in: Giblin Rebecca/Weatherall Kimberlee (eds.), What If We Could Reimagine Copyright?, Acton 2017, pp. 73–109 (cit. Geiger, Access right, p. …).
Geiger Christophe, Die Schranken des Urheberrechts im Lichte der Grundrechte – Zur Rechtsnatur der Beschränkungen des Urheberrechts, in: Hilty Reto M./Peukert Alexander (eds.), Interessenausgleich im Urheberrecht, Baden-Baden 2004, pp. 143–158 (cit. Geiger, Die Schranken, p. ...).
Geiger Christophe, Flexibilising Copyright – Remedies to the Privatisation of Information by Copyright Law, International Review of Intellectual Property and Competition Law (178) 2008 (cit. Geiger, Flexibilizing, p. …).

Geiger Christophe, Reconceptualizing the Constitutional Dimension of Intellectual Property: An Update, in: Torremans Paul L.C. (ed.), Intellectual Property and Human Rights, 4th Ed., Alphen aan den Rijn 2020, pp. 117–167 (cit. Geiger, Reconceptualizing, p. …).

Geiger Christophe, The Three-Step Test, a Threat to a Balanced Copyright Law?, International Review of Intellectual Property and Competition Law (37) 2006, pp. 683–699 (cit. Geiger, A Threat, p. …).

Geiger Christophe/Gervais Daniel/Senftleben Martin, The Three-Step Test Revisited: How to Use the Test's Flexibility in National Copyright Law, Amsterdam University International Law Review (29) 2014, pp. 581–626 (cit. Geiger/Gervais/Senftleben, Revisited, p. …).

Geiger Christophe/Gervais Daniel/Senftleben Martin, Understanding the "Three-Step Test", in: Gervais Daniel J. (ed.), International Intellectual Property. A Handbook of Contemporary Research, Cheltenham/Northampton 2015, pp. 167–189 (cit. Geiger/Gervais/Senftleben, Understanding, p. …).

Geiger Christophe/Griffiths Jonathan/Hilty Reto M., Declaration on a Balanced Interpretation of the "Three-Step Test" in Copyright Law, International Review of Intellectual Property and Competition Law (39) 2008, pp. 707–713.

Geiger Christophe/Izyumenko Elena, The Constitutionalization of Intellectual Property Law in the EU and the Funke Medien, Pelham and Spiegel Online Decisions of the CJEU: Progress, But Still Some Way to Go!, Center for International Intellectual Property Studies (CEIPI), Research Paper No. 2019-09 (available at: <https://papers.ssrn.com/sol3/papers.cfm?abstract_id=3472852>) (cit. Geiger/Izyumenko, Constitutionalization, p. …).

Geiger Christophe/Izyumenko Elena, Copyright on the Human Rights' Trial: Redefining the Boundaries of Exclusivity Through Freedom of Expression, International Review of Intellectual Property and Competition Law (45) 2014, pp. 316–342 (cit. Geiger/Izyumenko, Copyright, p. …).

Geiger Christophe/Izyumenko Elena, Shaping Intellectual Property Rights Through Human Rights Adjudication: The Example of the European Court of Human Rights, Mitchell Hamline Law Review (46) 2020, pp. 527–612 (cit. Geiger/Izyumenko, Shaping, p. …).

Gelshorn Julia, Aneignung und Wiederholung: Bilddiskurse im Werk von Gerhard Richter und Sigmar Polke, Paderborn 2012.

Gervais Daniel, Feist Goes Global: A Comparative Analysis of the Notion of Originality in Copyright Law, Journal of the Copyright Society of the U.S.A. (49) 2002, p. 949–981 (cit. Gervais, Feist, p. …).

Gervais Daniel, How Intellectual Property and Human Rights Can Live Together: An Updated Perspective, in: Torremans Paul L.C. (ed.), Intellectual Property and Human Rights, 4th Ed., Alphen aan den Rijn 2020, pp. 3–28 (cit. Gervais, How Intellectual Property, p. …).

Gervais Daniel, Originalité(s), in: Bernault Carine/Clavier Jean-Pierre/Lucas-Schloetter Agnès (eds.), Mélanges en l'honneur du professeur André Lucas, Paris 2014, pp. 389–400 (cit. Gervais, Originalité(s), p. …).

Gibson James, Risk Aversion and Rights Accretion in Intellectual Property Law, The Yale Law Journal, (116) 2007, pp. 882–951.

Ginsburg Jane C., Copyright, in: Dreyfuss Rochelle/Pila Justine (eds.), The Oxford Handbook for Intellectual Property Law, Oxford 2017, pp. 487–516 (cit. Ginsburg, Copyright, p. …).

Ginsburg Jane C., Exceptional Authorship: The Role of Copyright Exceptions in Promoting Creativity, in: Frankel Susy/Gervais Daniel (eds.), The Evolution and Equilibrium of Copyright in the Digital Age, Cambridge 2014, pp. 15–28 (cit. Ginsburg, Exceptional Authorship, p. ….).

Ginsburg Jane C., Fair Use for Free, or Permitted-But-Paid?, Berkeley Technology Law Journal (29) 2015, pp. 1383–1446 (cit. Ginsburg, Fair Use, p. …).

Glaus Bruno/Studer Peter, Kunstrecht: ein Ratgeber für Künstler, Sammler, Galeristen, Kuratoren, Architekten, Designer, Medienschaffende und Juristen, Zurich 2003.
Goldstein Paul, What Is a Copyrighted Work? Why Does it Matter?, UCLA Law Review (58) 2011, pp. 1175–1187.
Goldstein Paul/Hugenholtz Bernt P., International Copyright. Principles, Law, and Practice, 4th Ed., New York 2019.
Gopnik Blake, On "In Praise of Art Forgeries", in: Charney Noah (ed.), Art Crime: Terrorists, Tomb Raiders, Forgers and Thieves, Basingstoke 2016, pp. 21–26.
Graber Christoph Beat, Zwischen Geist und Geld: Interferenzen von Kunst und Wirtschaft aus rechtlicher Sicht: interdisziplinäre und rechtsvergleichende Untersuchung unter besonderer Berücksichtigung des schweizerischen Rechts, PhD Thesis, Baden-Baden 1994 (cit. Graber, Zwischen Geist und Geld, p. …).
Graber Christoph Beat, Der Kunstbegriff des Rechts im Kontext der Gesellschaft, in: Institut suisse de droit comparé, Lausanne/Centre du droit de l'art, Genève, Liberté de l'art et indépendance de l'artiste = Kunstfreiheit und Unabhängigkeit der Kunstschaffendem: actes du colloque international des 27 et 28 novembre 2003 à Lausanne, Lausanne 2004, pp. 91–112 (cit. Graber, Kunstbegriff, p. …).
Graber Christoph Beat, Can Modern Law Safeguard Archaic Cultural Expressions? Observations from a Legal Sociology Perspective, in: Antons Chistoph (ed.), Traditional Knowledge, Traditional Cultural Expressions and Intellectual Property Law in the Asia-Pacific Region, Alphen aan den Rijn 2009, pp. 159–176 (cit. Graber, Archaic Cultural Expressions, p. …).
Graber Christoph Beat, Copyright and Access. A Human Rights Perspective, in: Graber Christoph Beat et al. (eds.), Digital Rights Management – The End of Collecting Societies?, Bern/New York/Brussels/Athens 2005, pp. 71–110 (cit. Graber, Copyright and Access, p. …).
Graber Christoph Beat, Copyright Insight Out: A Legal Sociologist's Perspective, in: Hanns Ullrich et al. (eds), Kritika: Essays on Intellectual Property, Vol. 6, Cheltenham 2024, pp. 120–139 (cit. Graber, Copyright, p. …).
Graber Christoph Beat, Kulturverfassung, in: Diggelmann Oliver/Hertig Maya/Schindler Benjamin (eds.), Verfassungsrecht der Schweiz, 2nd Ed., Zurich 2020, pp. 649–666 (cit. Graber, Kulturverfassung, p. …).
Graber Christoph Beat, Using Human Rights to Tackle Fragmentation in the Field of Traditional Cultural Expressions: An Institutional Approach, in: Graber Christoph Beat/Burri-Nenova Mira (eds.), Intellectual Property and Traditional Cultural Expressions in a Digital Environment, Cheltenham 2008, pp. 96–120 (cit. Graber, Using Human Rights, p. …).
Grammel Søren, Grusswort, in: Kunstmuseum Basel/Museum für Gegenwartskunst (eds.), Manual No. 4. Von Bildern. Strategien der Aneignung, Basel 2015 (available at: <https://kunstmuseumbasel.ch/de/file/2288/f4b1c0c0/manual04_von_bildern_2015.pdf>).
Graw Isabelle/Kleefeld Stefanie/Rottmann André, Preface, Texte zur Kunst (71) 2008, p. 6.
Greaney Patrick, Essentially the Same: Eduardo Costa's Minimal Differences and Latin American Conceptualism, Art History (4) 2014, pp. 648–665.
Greenberg Lynne A., The Art of Appropriation: Puppies, Piracy, and Post-Modernism, Cardozo Arts & Ent Law Journal (11) 1992, pp. 1–33.
Griffiths Jonathan, Copyright's Imperfect Republic and the Artistic Commonwealth, in: Bently Lionel/Davis Jennifer/Ginsburg Jane C. (eds.), Copyright and Piracy. An Interdisciplinary Critique, Cambridge 2010, pp. 340–354.
Groys Boris, Logic of the Collection, Berlin 2021.
Grünberger Michael, Aspekte eines umweltsensiblen Urheberrechts: Eine Einleitung, in: Grünberger Michael/Leible Stefan (eds.), Die Kollision von Urheberrecht und Nutzerverhalten, Tübingen 2014, pp. 1–22.

Gumbrecht Hans Ulrich, Our Broad Present. Time and Contemporary Culture, New York 2014 (cit. Gumbrecht, Broad Present, p. …).

Gumbrecht Hans Ulrich, Prose of the World: Denis Diderot and the Periphery of Enlightenment, Stanford 2021 (cit. Gumbrecht, Prose, p. …).

Gumbrecht Hans Ulrich, Über den Stil der "Forschungsgruppe Poetik und Hermeneutik", in: Geulen Eva/Haas Claude (ed.): Der Stil der Literaturwissenschaft, Sonderheft der Zeitschrift für deutsche Philologie, Berlin 2021, pp. 289–303 (cit. Gumbrecht, Über den Stil, p. ...).

Haas Eliane, Die Verwendung von Bearbeitungen urheberrechtlich geschützter Werke, PhD Thesis, Baden-Baden 2019.

Habermas Jürgen, Modernity – An Incomplete Project (1980), in: Foster Hal (ed.), The Anti-Aesthetic: Essays on Postmodern Culture, Port Townsend (WA) 1983, pp. 3–15.

Halsall Francis, Systems of Art. Art, History and Systems Theory, Bern 2008.

Handle Marco, Der urheberrechtliche Schutz der Idee, PhD Thesis, Bern 2013.

Haug Walter, Innovation und Originalität. Kategoriale und literarhistorische Vorüberlegungen, in: Haug Walter/Wachinger Burghart (eds.), Innovation und Originalität, Tübingen 2012, pp. 1–13.

Haux Dario Henri, Die digitale Allmende: zur Frage des nachhaltigen Umgangs mit Kultur im digitalen Lebensraum, PhD Thesis, Zurich/Baden-Baden 2021.

Hebborn Eric, The Art Forger's Handbook, London 1997.

Heidenreich Stefan, Form und Filter – Algorithmen der Bilderverarbeitung und Stilanalyse, zeitenblicke (2) 2003 (available at: <https://www.zeitenblicke.de/2003/01/heidenreich/index.html>).

Helfer Laurence R., Intellectual Property and Human Rights: Mapping an Evolving and Contested Relationship, in: Dreyfuss Rochelle C./Pila Justine (eds.), The Oxford Handbook of Intellectual Property, Oxford/New York 2018, pp. 117–143.

Helstosky Carol, Giovanni Bastianini, Art Forgery, and the Market in Nineteenth century Italy, The Journal of Modern History (81) 2009, pp. 793–823.

Hildebrand-Schat Viola, Appropriation oder Simulacrum? Zur Funktion und Absicht interpiktorialer Bezüge in der zeitgenössischen russischen Kunst, in: Isekenmeier Guido (ed.), Interpiktorialität. Theorie und Geschichte der Bild-Bild-Bezüge, Bielefeld 2013, pp. 219–236.

Hilgert Felix, Urheberrechtlicher Schutz neuer Kunstformen, in: Hoeren Thomas/Holznagel Bernd/Ernstschneider (eds.), Handbuch Kunst und Recht, Frankfurt a.M. 2008, pp. 9–34.

Hilty Reto M., Anmerkung zum Urteil vom 19. August 2002 (Hobby Kalender), sic! 2003, pp. 28–31 (cit. Hilty, Hobby Kalender, p. …).

Hilty Reto M., Bildungssoftware – Obergericht Zürich vom 24. Januar 2013, sic! 2013, pp. 697–707 (cit. Hilty, Bildungssoftware, p. …).

Hilty Reto M., Die freie Benutzung nach § 24 UrhG – Grenzen und Potential, in: Dreier Thomas/Peifer Karl-Nikolaus/Specht Louisa (eds.), Anwalt des Urheberrechts. Festschrift für Gernot Schulze zum 70. Geburtstag, Munich 2017, pp. 127–136 (cit. Hilty, Die freie Benutzung, p. ….).

Hilty Reto M., Urheberrecht, 2nd Ed., Bern 2020 (cit. Hilty, Urheberrecht, p. …).

Hoffmann-Riem Wolfgang, Innovation und Recht – Recht und Innovation: Recht im Ensemble seiner Kontexte, Tübingen 2016.

Huber Hans-Dieter/Luhmann Niklas, Interview mit Niklas Luhmann, Texte zur Kunst (1) 1991, Nr. 4, pp. 121–133.

Hufnagel Saskia/Chappel Duncan, The Beltracchi Affair: A Comment and Further Reflections on the "Most Spectacular" German Art Forgery Case in Recent Times, in: Charney Noah (ed.), Art Crime. Terrorists, Tomb Raiders, Forgers and Thieves, Basingstoke 2016, pp. 9–20.

Hug Gitti, Bob Marley vs Christoph Meili: ein Schnappschuss, sic! 2005, pp. 57–63 (cit. Hug, Bob Marley, p. …).

Hug Gitti, Switzerland, in: Gendreau Ysolde/Nordemann Axel/Oesch Rainer (eds.), Copyright and Photographs: An International Survey, London 1999, pp. 255–282 (cit. Hug, Switzerland, p. …).
Hugenholtz Bernt P., Flexible Copyright. Can EU Author's Right Accommodate Fair Use?, in: Stamatoudi Irini A. (ed.), New Developments in EU and International Copyright Law, Alphen aan den Rijn 2016, pp. 417–433.
Hutcheon Linda, The Politics of Postmodernism, 2nd Ed., London/New York 2002.
Ickowicz Judith, Le Droit après la dématérialisation de l'œuvre d'art, Dijon 2013.
Isekenmeier Guido, In Richtung einer Theorie der Interpiktorialität, in: Isekenmeier Guido (ed.), Interpiktorialität. Theorie und Geschichte der Bild-Bild-Bezüge, Bielefeld 2013, pp. 11–86 (cit. Isekenmeier, In Richtung, p. …).
Isekenmeier Guido, Zur Einführung, in: Isekenmeier Guido (ed.), Interpiktorialität. Theorie und Geschichte der Bild-Bild-Bezüge, Bielefeld 2013, pp. 7–10 (cit. Isekenmeier, Einführung, p. …).
Izyumenko Elena, The Freedom of Expression Contours of Copyright in the Digital Era: A European Perspective, Journal of World Intellectual Property (19) 2016, pp. 115–130.
Jameson Frederic, Postmodernism and Consumer Society, in: Foster Hal (ed.), The Anti-Aesthetic: Essays on Postmodern Culture, Port Townsend (WA) 1983, pp. 111–125.
Jayme Erik, Nachahmung oder Transformation: Zweitkunst im Zwielicht des Rechts, in: Mosimann Peter/Schönenberger Beat (eds.), Kunst & Recht 2016/Art & Law 2016. Referate zur gleichnamigen Veranstaltung der Juristischen Fakultät der Universität Basel vom 17. Juni, Bern 2016, pp. 13–38.
Jones Caroline A., Machine in the Studio: Constructing the Post War American Artist, Chicago/London 1996.
Jongsma Daniël, The Nature and Content of the Three-Step Test in EU Copyright Law: A Reappraisal, in: Rosati Eleonora (ed.), The Routledge Handbook of EU Copyright Law, Abingdon 2021, pp. 338–353 (cit. Jongsma, Nature and content, p. …).
Jongsma Daniël, Parody After *Deckmyn* – A Comparative Overview of the Approach to Parody Under Copyright Law in Belgium, France, Germany and The Netherlands, International Review of Intellectual Property and Competition Law (48) 2017, pp. 652–682 (cit. Jongsma, Parody, p. …).
Kaiser Ansgar/Scheurer Stefan, The Impact of Fundamental Rights on European Copyright Law – Opinion on the CJEU Decisions C-516/17 – Spiegel Online and C-469/17 – Funke Medien, GRUR Int 2019, pp. 1153–1160.
Kakies Celia, Kunstzitate in Malerei und Fotografie, PhD Thesis, Cologne 2007.
Kamina Pascal, Un point sur le droit d'auteur et l'article 10 de la Conv. EDH, Légicom (30) 2004, pp. 88–94.
Karnow Curtis E.A., Data Morphing: Ownership, Copyright and Creation, Leonardo (27) 1994, pp. 117–122.
Kearns Paul, The Legal Concept of Art, Oxford 1998.
Keuper Ulrike, Reproduktion als Übersetzung: eine Metapher und ihre Folgen – vom Salonbericht bis zur frühen Fotokritik, Paderborn 2018.
Kleinemenke Manuel, Fair Use im deutschen und europäischen Urheberrecht? Eine rechtsvergleichende Untersuchung zur Flexibilisierung des urheberrechtlichen Schrankenkataloges nach dem Vorbild der US-amerikanischen Fair Use-Doktrin, PhD Thesis, Bern 2013.
Koller Markus, Die Grenzen der Kunst. Luhmanns gelehrte Poesie, Wiesbaden 2007.
Kost Lynn, Always Different, Always the Same. An Essay on Art and Systems, in: Kost Lynn (ed.), Always Different, Always the Same. An Essay on Art and Systems, Cologne 2018, pp. 118–132.
Krauss Rosalind, The Originality of the Avant-Garde: A Postmodernist Repetition, October (18) 1981, pp. 47–66.

Kreutzer Till, The Pastiche in Copyright Law: Expert Opinion on a Copyright-specific Definition of Pastiche According to Sec. 51a German Copyright Act (UrhG), September 5, 2022, Gesellschaft für Freiheitsrechte (available at: <https://freiheitsrechte.org/en/themen/demokratie/expert-opinion-on-pastiche>).

Kruger Barbara, "Taking" Pictures: Photo-Texts by Barbara Kruger, Screen (23) 1982, pp. 90–96.

Kucsko Guido, Concept Art und Urheberrecht, in: v. Lewinski Silke/Wittmann Heinz (eds.), Urheberrecht! Festschrift für Michel M. Walter zum 80. Geburtstag, Vienna 2018, pp. 325–330.

Kummer Max, Das urheberrechtlich geschützte Werk, Bern 1968 (cit. Kummer, Werk, p. …).

Kummer Max, Die privatrechtliche Rechtsprechung des BGer im Jahr 1980: Handels- und Immaterialgüterrecht, ZBJV (118) 1982, pp. 197–203 (cit. Kummer, Rechtsprechung 1980, p. …).

Kummer Max, Der Werkbegriff und das Urheberrecht als subjektives Privatrecht, in: Schweizerischen Vereinigung für Urheberrecht (ed.), 100 Jahre URG. Festschrift zum einhundertjährigen Bestehen eines eidgenössischen Urheberrechtsgesetzes, Bern 1983, pp. 123–144 (cit. Kummer, Werkbegriff, p. …).

Ladeur Karl-Heinz, Kritik der Abwägung in der Grundrechtsdogmatik: Plädoyer für eine Erneuerung der liberalen Grundrechtstheorie, Tübingen 2004 (cit. Ladeur, Kritik der Abwägung, p. …).

Ladeur Karl-Heinz, Die Beobachtung der kollektiven Dimension der Grundrechte durch eine liberale Grundrechtstheorie: Zur Verteidigung der Dominanz der abwehrrechtlichen Dimension der Grundrechte, Der Staat (50) 2011, pp. 493–531 (cit. Ladeur, Die Beobachtung, p. …).

Ladeur Karl-Heinz, "Abwägung" – ein neues Rechtsparadigma? Von der Einheit der Rechtsordnung zur Pluralität der Rechtsdiskurse, in: Vesting Thomas/Augsberg Ino (eds.), Das Recht der Netzwerkgesellschaft: Ausgewählte Aufsätze, Tübingen 2013, pp. 55–76 (cit. Ladeur, Abwägung, p. …).

Ladeur Karl-Heinz, Kunstfreiheit und geistiges Eigentum in digitalen Netzwerken. Zur Entscheidung des BVerfG v. 31.5.2016, 1 BvR 1585/13, ZGE/IPJ (8) 2016, pp. 447–461 (cit. Ladeur, Kunstfreiheit, p. …).

Ladeur Karl-Heinz, Recht – Wissen – Kultur: Die fragmentierte Ordnung, Berlin 2016 (cit. Ladeur, Recht, p. …).

Ladeur Karl-Heinz/Vesting Thomas, Geistiges Eigentum im Netzwerk – Anforderungen und Entwicklungslinien, in: Eifert Martin/Hoffmann-Riem Wolfgang (eds.), Innovationsrecht: Geistiges Eigentum und Innovation. Innovation und Recht I, Berlin 2008, pp. 123–144.

Latour Bruno/Antoine Hennion, How to Make Mistakes on So Many Things at Once – And Become Famous for It, in: Gumbrecht Hans-Ulrich/Marrinan Michael (eds.), Mapping Benjamin. The Work of Art in the Digital Age, Stanford 2003, pp. 91–97.

Latour Bruno/Lowe Adam, La migration de l'aura ou comment explorer un original par le biais de ses fac-similés, Intermédialités/Intermediality (17) 2011, pp. 173–191.

Lawson Thomas, Last Exit: Painting, in: Hertz Richard (ed.), Theories of Contemporary Art, Englewood Cliffs (NJ) 1985, pp. 143–155.

Leach Neil, The Culture of the Copy, Architectural Design – Special Issue: Digital Property: Open-Source Architecture (86) 2016, pp. 126–133.

Leistner Matthias, Anforderungen an ein umweltsensibles Urheberrecht, in: Grünberger Michael/Leible Stefan (eds.), Die Kollision von Urheberrecht und Nutzerverhalten, Tübingen 2014, pp. 211–226 (cit. Leistner, Anforderungen, p. …).

Leistner Matthias, "Ende gut, alles gut"…oder "Vorhang zu und alle Fragen offen"?, GRUR 2019, pp. 1008–1015 (cit. Leistner, Ende, p. …).

Lenain Thierry, Art Forgery: The History of a Modern Obsession, London 2011.

Lenski Sophie-Charlotte, Öffentliches Kulturrecht und Urheberrecht als wechselseitige Auffangordnungen, in: Goldhammer Michael/Grünberger Michael/Klippel Diethelm (eds.), Geistiges Eigentum im Verfassungsstaat: Geschichte und Theorie, Tübingen 2016, pp. 141–158.
Lethem Jonathan, The Ecstasy of Influence. A Plagiarism, Harper's Magazine, February 2007, pp. 59–71.
Leval Pierre N., Toward a Fair Use Standard, Harvard Law Review (103) 1990, pp. 1105–1136.
Levine Sherrie, Born Again, in: Salzburger Kunstverein (ed.), Original. Symposium Salzburger Kunstverein 15.10.–16.10.1993, Ostfildern 1995, pp. 126–129.
Lewitt Sol, Paragraphs on Conceptual Art, Artforum (5) 1967, pp. 79–83.
Lijster Thijs, Harder, Better, Stronger, Faster. Introduction, in: Lijster Thijs (ed.), The Future of the New. Artistic Innovation in Times of Social Acceleration, Amsterdam 2018, pp. 9–19.
Lipman Jean/Marshall Richard, Art about Art, New York 1978.
Lippard Lucy R., Six Years: The Dematerialization of the Art Object from 1966 to 1972, London 1973.
Liu Jiarui, An Empirical Study of Transformative Use in Copyright Law, Stanford Technology and Law Review (22) 2019, pp. 163–241.
Looser Martin E., Art. 190 BV, in: Ehrenzeller Bernhard/Egli Patricia/Hettich Peter/Hongler Peter/Schindler Benjamin/Schmid Stefan G./Schweizer Rainer J. (eds.), Die schweizerische Bundesverfassung, St. Galler Kommentar, 4th Ed., St. Gallen 2023.
Lüdemann Susanne, Beobachtungsverhältnisse. Zur (Kunst-)Geschichte der Beobachtung zweiter Ordnung, in: Koschorke Albert/Vismann Cornelia (eds.), Widerstände der Systemtheorie: Kulturtheoretische Analyse der Werke von Luhmann, Berlin 1999, pp. 63–75.
Luhmann Niklas, Soziale Systeme: Grundriss einer allgemeinen Theorie, Frankfurt a.M. 1984 (cit. Luhmann, Soziale Systeme, p. …).
Luhmann Niklas, Darum Liebe, in: Baecker Dirk/Stanitzek Georg (eds.), Niklas Luhmann, Archimedes und wir: Interviews, Berlin 1987, pp. 61–73 (cit. Luhmann, Darum Liebe, p. …).
Luhmann Niklas, Individuum, Individualität, Individualismus, in: Niklas Luhmann (ed.), Gesellschaftsstruktur und Semantik. Studien zur Wissenssoziologie der modernen Gesellschaft, Band 3, Frankfurt a.M. 1989, pp. 149–258 (cit. Luhmann, Individuum, p. …).
Luhmann Niklas, Essays on Self-Reference, New York/Oxford 1990.
Luhmann Niklas, Identität – was oder wie?, in: Niklas Luhmann (ed.), Soziologische Aufklärung 5. Konstruktivistische Perspektiven, Opladen 1990, pp. 14–30 (cit. Luhmann, Identität, p. …).
Luhmann Niklas, Interesse und Interessenjurisprudenz im Spannungsfeld von Gesetzgebung und Rechtsprechung, Zeitschrift für Neuere Rechtsgeschichte (12) 1990, pp. 1–13 (cit. Luhmann, Interesse, p. …).
Luhmann Niklas, The Self-Reproduction of Law and Its Limits (1984), in: Niklas Luhmann (ed.), Essays on Self-Reference, New York 1990, pp. 227–245 (cit. Luhmann, The Self-Reproduction, p. …).
Luhmann Niklas, The Work of Art and the Self-Reproduction of Art (1985), in: Niklas Luhmann (ed.), Essays on Self-Reference, New York 1990, pp. 191–214 (cit. Luhmann, The Work of Art, p. …).
Luhmann Niklas, Weltkunst, in: Luhmann Niklas/Bunsen Frederick D./Baecker Dirk (eds.), Unbeobachtbare Welt. Über Kunst und Architektur, Bielefeld 1990, pp. 7–45 (cit. Luhmann, Weltkunst, p. …).
Luhmann Niklas, Die Welt der Kunst (1991), in: Niklas Luhmann (ed.), Schriften zu Kunst und Literatur (ed. Niels Werber), Frankfurt am Main 2008, pp. 299–315 (cit. Luhmann, Die Welt, p. …).

Luhmann Niklas, Die Wissenschaft der Gesellschaft, Frankfurt a.M. 1992 (cit. Luhmann, Wissenschaft, p. …).

Luhmann Niklas, Das Paradox der Menschenrechte und drei Formen seiner Entfaltung (1993), in: Niklas Luhmann (ed.), Soziologische Aufklärung. 6. Die Soziologie und der Mensch, Opladen 1995, pp. 229–236 (cit. Luhmann, Menschenrechte, p. …).

Luhmann Niklas, Law as a Social System (1993) (transl. by Klaus A. Ziegert), New York 2004 (cit. Luhmann, Law as a Social System, p. …).

Luhmann Niklas, Risk: A Sociological Theory (1993) (transl. by Rhodes Barrett), New Brunswick (NJ) 2005 (cit. Luhmann, Risk, p. …).

Luhmann Niklas, The Paradox of Decision Making (1993) (transl. by David Seidl and Karen Finney-Kellerhoff), in: Seidl David/Helge Becker Kai (eds.), Niklas Luhmann and Organization Studies, Kristianstad 2005, pp. 85–107 (cit. Luhmann, Decision Making, p. …).

Luhmann Niklas, Die Behandlung von Irritationen. Abweichung oder Neuheit? (1995), in: Luhmann Niklas (ed.), Gesellschaftsstruktur und Semantik. Studien zur Wissenssoziologie der modernen Gesellschaft, Bd. 4, Frankfurt am Main 2005, pp. 55–100 (cit. Luhmann, Irritationen, p. …).

Luhmann Niklas, Art as a Social System (1997) (transl. by Eva M. Knodt), Stanford 2000 (cit. Luhmann, Art as a Social System, p. …).

Luhmann Niklas, The Challenge of Being New, in: Salzburger Kunstverein (ed.), Original. Symposium Salzburger Kunstverein 15.10.–16.10.1993, Ostfildern 1995, pp. 51–55 (cit. Luhmann, Challenge, p. …).

Luhmann Niklas, Ausdifferenzierung der Kunst, in: Institut für soziale Gegenwartsfragen, Freiburg i. Br./Kunstraum Wien (eds.), Art & Language & Luhmann, Vienna 1997, pp. 133–148 (cit. Luhmann, Ausdifferenzierung Kunst, p. …).

Luhmann Niklas, The Medium of Art (1987), in: Niklas Luhmann (ed.), Essays on Self-Reference, New York 1990, pp. 215–226 (cit. Luhmann, Medium, p. …).

Luhmann Niklas, Theory of Society (1997) (transl. by Rhodes Barrett), Vol. 1, Stanford (CA) 2012 (cit. Luhmann, Theory of Society I, p. …).

Luhmann Niklas, Theory of Society (1997) (transl. by Rhodes Barrett), Vol. 2, Stanford (CA) 2013 (cit. Luhmann, Theory of Society II, p. …).

Luhmann Niklas, Die Ausdifferenzierung des Kunstsystems (1998), in: Niklas Luhmann (ed.), Schriften zu Kunst und Literatur (ed. Niels Werber), Frankfurt am Main 2008, pp. 316–352 (cit. Luhmann, Ausdifferenzierung Kunstsystem, p. …).

Lüthi Vital, Die Berücksichtigung sogenannt technischer Merkmale im sogenannt nicht technischen Immaterialgüterrecht, sic! 2020, pp. 63–70.

Lütticken Sven, The Feathers of the Eagle, New Left Review (36) 2005, pp. 109–125.

Maassen Wolfgang, Plagiat, freie Benutzung oder Kunstzitat? Erscheinungsform der urheberrechtlichen Leistungsübernahme in Fotografie und Kunst, in: Weller Matthias/Kemle Nicolai/Dreier Thomas (eds.), Raum – Beute – Diebstahl. Tagungsband des Sechsten Heidelberger Kunstrechtstags am 28. und 29. September 2012, Zurich 2013, pp. 191–246.

Macciacchini Sandro, Die unautorisierte Wiedergabe von urheberrechtlich geschützten Werken in Massenmedien, sic! 1997, pp. 361–371 (cit. Macciacchini, Wiedergabe, p. …).

Macciacchini Sandro, Konflikt? Welcher Konflikt?, Medialex 2002, p. 167 (cit. Macciacchini, Konflikt, p. …).

Macciacchini Sandro, Die urheberrechtlich schützbare Doppelschöpfung: Ein populärer Irrtum. Bemerkung zu Gregor Wild, Von der statistischen Einmaligkeit zum soziologischen Werkbegriff, sic! 2004, pp. 61 ff., sic! 2004, pp. 351–354 (cit. Macciacchini, Doppelschöpfung, p. …).

Macciacchini Sandro, Irrtum: Die Doppelschöpfung ist urheberrechtlich schützbar, in: Berger Mathis/Macciacchini Sandro (eds.), Populäre Irrtümer im Urheberrecht – Festschrift für Reto M. Hilty, Schulthess, Zurich 2008, pp. 25–38 (cit. Macciacchini, Irrtum, p. …).
Magerski Christine, Theorien der Avantgarde. Gehlen – Bürger – Bourdieu – Luhmann, Wiesbaden 2011.
Magid Jill, Locating Legacy. Jill Magid in Conversation with Nikolaus Hirsch and Hesse McGraw, in: Hirsch Nikolaus et al. (eds.), Jill Magid – The Proposal, Berlin 2016, pp. 1–28.
Malraux André, Le musée imaginaire, 3rd Ed., Paris 1965.
Marcoci Roxana/Taylor Phil (eds.), Wolfgang Tillmans. A Reader, New York 2021.
Maset Pierangelo, Die "Kunst der Gesellschaft" in Gesellschaft der Kunst, in: Runkel Gunter/Burkart Günther (eds.). Funktionssysteme der Gesellschaft, Wiesbaden 2005, pp. 89–100.
McClean Daniel, Piracy and Authorship in Contemporary Art and the Artistic Commonwealth, in: Bently Lionel/Davis Jennifer/Ginsburg Jane C. (eds.), Copyright and Piracy. An Interdisciplinary Critique, Cambridge 2010, pp. 311–339.
Mendis Sunimal, Copyright, the Freedom of Expression and the Right to Information. Exploring a Potential Public Interest Exception to Copyright in Europe, PhD Thesis, Baden-Baden 2011.
Menocal Maria Rosa, The Flip Side, in: Gumbrecht Hans Ulrich/Marrinan Michael (eds.), Mapping Benjamin. The Work of Art in the Digital Age, Stanford 2003, pp. 291–300.
Mensger Ariane (ed.), Déjà-vu?: die Kunst der Wiederholung von Dürer bis YouTube, Bielefeld 2012.
Mersch Christian, Die Welt der Patente. Soziologische Perspektiven auf eine zentrale Institution der globalen Wissensgesellschaft, Bielefeld 2013.
Metzger Rainer, Work, Original and the Demise of the Author. Some Strategies of Art in the Sixties, in: Salzburger Kunstverein (ed.), Original. Symposium Salzburger Kunstverein 15.10.–16.10.1993, Ostfildern 1995, pp. 20–27.
Mijatovic Ivan, Kreativität als Voraussetzung für den urheberrechtlichen Schutz von Geisteserzeugnissen, PhD Thesis, Bern 2005 (cit. Mijatovic, Kreativität, p. …).
Mijatovic Ivan, Ein Werk erfüllt die Schutzvoraussetzungen wenn es vogelig genug ist, sic! 2006, pp. 435–439 (cit. Mijatovic, Werk, p. …).
Millet Catherine, L'art d'appropriation devant les tribunaux, in: Christiane Carlut (ed.), Copyright/Copywrong: acte du colloque, Le Mans, Nantes, Saint-Nazaire, février 2000, Nantes 2003, pp. 115–123.
Mortier Roland, L'originalité: une nouvelle catégorie esthétique au siècle des Lumières, Genève 1982.
Mosimann Peter, Das revidierte Urheberrecht. Die wesentlichen Neuerungen – Eine Standortbestimmung, Basel 2020.
Mosimann Peter/Herzog Peter, Zur Fotografie als urheberrechtliches Werk – Bemerkungen zum Bundesgerichtsentscheid vom 5. September 2003, "Bob Marley", in sic! 2004, pp. 705–708.
Mosimann Peter/Hostettler Yannick, Zur Revision des Urheberrechtsgesetzes, recht 2018, pp. 123–141.
Mosimann Peter/Renold Marc-André/Raschèr Andrea (eds.), Kultur Kunst Recht. Schweizerisches und internationales Recht, 2nd Ed., Basel 2020 (cit. Author(s), Kultur Kunst Recht, N … *ad* § …).
Moskowitz Anita F., The Case of Giovanni Bastianini: A Fair and Balanced View, Artibus et Historiae, (59) 2004, pp. 157–185.
Müller Barbara K./Oertli Reinhard (eds.), Stämpflis Handkommentar zum Urheberrechtsgesetz (URG). Bundesgesetz über das Urheberrecht und verwandte Schutzrechte, 2nd Ed., Bern 2012 (cit. Author, SHK URG, N … *ad* Art. …).

Müller Marius, Kunstbegriffe zwischen Recht und Praxis: Historische Wechselwirkungen zwischen Ästhetik, Kunsttheorie und Rechtswissenschaft, Bielefeld 2022.

Mulvey Laura, A Phantasmagoria of the Female Body: The Work of Cindy Sherman, The New Left Review (188) 1991, pp. 137–150.

Natale Mauro, I falsi e la storia dell'arte, in: Cavina Ottani Anna/Natale Mauro (eds.), Il falso specchio della realtà, Torino 2017, pp. 49–88.

Navas Eduardo, Re-versioning the Elements of Selectivity: Transformation and Originality after Remix, in: Feireiss Lukas (ed.), Radical Cut-Up. Nothing is Original, London 2019, pp. 227–244.

Netanel Weinstock Neil, Copyright's Paradox, Oxford 2008 (cit. Netanel, Copyright's Paradox, p. …).

Netanel Weinstock Neil, Making Sense of Fair Use, Lewis & Clark Review (15) 2011, pp. 715–771 (cit. Netanel, Making Sense, p. …).

Noll Andreas, Protestaktionen und klimaspezifische Rechtfertigungsgründe: der Klimawandel ist im Strafrecht angekommen: gleichzeitig eine Kommentierung des bundesgerichtlichen Leitentscheids BGE 147 IV 297, Berne 2022.

Novitskova Katja, Pattern of Activation, in: Steinbrügge Bettina/Kunstverein in Hamburg (eds.), Dawn Mission, Hamburg 2016, pp. 4–8.

Oertli Reinhard, Neues Urheberrecht für Fotografien, sic! 2020, pp. 599–607.

Ohly ansgar, Urheberrecht zwischen Innovationsstimulierung und -verhinderung, in: Eifert Martin/Hoffmann-Riem Wolfgang (eds.), Geistiges Eigentum und Innovation, Berlin 2008, pp. 279–298.

Okediji Ruth L., Does Intellectual Property Need Human Rights?, New York University Journal of International Law & Politics (51) 2018, pp. 1–68.

Ortland Eberhard, The Aesthetics of Copyright, WCP 2008 Proceedings, Vol. 1: Aesthetics and Philosophy of Arts (cit. Ortland, Aesthetics, p. …).

Ortland Eberhard, Urheberrecht als Bildregime, in: Joly Jean-Baptiste/Vismann Cornelia/ Weitin Thomas (eds.), Bildregime des Rechts, Stuttgart 2007, pp. 268–288 (cit. Ortland, Bildregime, p. …).

Ortland Eberhard/Schmücker Reinold, Copyright and Art, German Law Journal (12) 2005, pp. 1762–1776.

Ortmann Günther, Neues, das uns zufällt. Über Regeln, Routinen, Irritationen, Serendipity und Abduktion, in: Fischer Hans Rudi (ed.), Wie kommt Neues in die Welt?, Phantasie, Intuition und der Ursprung von Kreativität, Weilerwist 2013, pp. 171–185.

Pahud Eric, Die Sozialbindung des Urheberrechts, PhD Thesis, Bern 2000.

Papadopoulos Marinos/Koutras Nikos, Openness Through the Lenses of the Three-Step Test: International Perspectives on Copyright Protection, Publishing Research Quarterly (37) 2021, pp. 626–641.

Papaux Van Delden Marie-Laure, L'influence de la CEDH en droit civil: aspects choisis du droit des personnes physiques et de la famille, ZSR (141) 2022, pp. 155–274.

Peters Nils, Das Pastiche – erste Gehschritte zur neuen Freiheit?, GRUR 2022, pp. 1482–1489.

Peukert Alexander, Copyright and the Two Cultures of Online Communication, in: Torremans Paul L.C. (ed.), Intellectual Property and Human Rights, 4th Ed., Alphen aan den Rijn 2020, pp. 387–413 (cit. Peukert, Two Cultures, p. …).

Peukert Alexander, A Critique of the Ontology of Intellectual Property Law (2018) (transl. by Gill Mertens), Cambridge (MA) 2021 (cit. Peukert, A Critique, p. …).

Peukert Alexander, Ein möglichst hohes Schutzniveau des Urheberrechts fördert Kreativität und dynamischen Wettbewerb: Ein Irrtum?! in: Berger Mathis/Macciacchini Sandro (eds.), Populäre Irrtümer im Urheberrecht – Festschrift für Reto M. Hilty, Schulthess, Zurich 2008, pp. 39–60 (cit. Peukert, Irrtum, p. …).

Peukert Alexander, Intellectual Property as an End in Itself?, European Intellectual Property Review (33) 2010, pp. 67–71 (cit. Peukert, End in Itself, p. …).

Peukert Alexander, Drei Entstehungsbedingungen des Urheberrechts und seines Schutzgegenstands, in: Meder Stephan (ed.), Geschichte und Zukunft des Urheberrechts, Göttingen 2018, pp. 127–146 (cit. Peukert, Drei Entstehungsbedingungen, p. …).

Philippopoulos-Mihalopoulos Andreas, Beauty and the Beast: Art and Law in the Hall of Mirrors, Entertainment Law (3) 2003 (available at: <https://papers.ssrn.com/sol3/papers.cfm?abstract_id=1334670>).

Plumpe Gerhard, Eigentum – Eigentümlichkeit: Über den Zusammenhang ästhetischer und juristischer Begriffe im 18. Jahrhundert, Archiv für Begriffsgeschichte (23) 1979, pp. 175–196.

Pochat Götz, Die Kunst der Fälschung – die geraubte Aura, in: Goltschnigg Dietmar/Grollegg-Edler Charlotte/Gruber Patrizia (eds.), Plagiat, Fälschung, Urheberrecht, Berlin 2013, pp. 125–146.

Pottage Alain, Introduction, in: Pottage Alain/Mundy Martha (eds.), Law, Anthropology, and the Constitution of the Social. Making Persons and Things, Cambridge 2004, pp. 1–39.

Prince Richard, The Deposition of Richard Prince in the Case of Cariou v. Prince et al. (Allen Greg ed.), Zurich 2012 (cit. Prince, The Deposition, p. …).

Prince Richard, Richard Prince Interviewed by Peter Halley, ZG Magazine (10) 1984, in: Evans David (ed.), Appropriation, London/Cambridge (MA) 2009, pp. 83–86 (cit. Prince, Interview, p. …).

Ramello Giovanni B., Private Appropriability and Sharing of Knowledge: Convergence or Contradiction? The Opposite Tragedy of the Creative Commons, in: Takeyama Lisa N./Gordon Wendy G./Towse Ruth (eds.), Developments in the Economics of Copyright. Research and Analysis, Cheltenham/Nothampton 2005, pp. 120–141.

Rau Gerhard, Antikunst und Urheberrecht: Überlegungen zum urheberrechtlichen Werkbegriff, Berlin/Boston (MA) 1978.

Rehbinder Manfred, Schweizerisches Urheberrecht, 3rd Ed., Bern 2000.

Reinhart Beat, Die Einordnung der Bearbeitung ins schweizerische Urheberrecht, in: Schweizerischen Vereinigung für Urheberrecht (ed.), 100 Jahre URG. Festschrift zum einhundertjährigen Bestehen eines eidgenössischen Urheberrechtsgesetzes, Bern 1983, pp. 221–238.

Rendas Tito, Destereotyping the Copyright Wars: The "Fair Use vs. Closed List" Debate in the EU, 2015 (available at: <https://papers.ssrn.com/sol3/papers.cfm?abstract_id=2657482>).

Ribettes Jean-Michel, Portrait de l'artiste en plagiaire proclamé. De l'invention de son nom à son abolition, in: Christiane Carlut (ed.), Copyright/Copywrong: acte du colloque, Le Mans, Nantes, Saint-Nazaire, février 2000, Nantes 2003, pp. 157–175.

Rigamonti Cyrill P., Geistiges Eigentum als Begriff und Theorie des Urheberrechts, PhD Thesis, Baden-Baden 2001 (cit. Rigamonti, Geistiges Eigentum, p. …).

Rigamonti Cyrill P., Deconstructing Moral Rights, Harvard International Law Journal (47) 2006, pp. 353–412 (cit. Rigamonti, Deconstructing, p. …).

Rigamonti Cyrill P., Urheberrecht und Grundrechte, ZBJV (153) 2017, pp. 365–394 (cit. Rigamonti, Grundrechte, p. …).

Rigamonti Cyrill P., Medienberichterstattung im Internet mit Sendungen Dritter, sic! 2019, pp. 57–76 (cit. Rigamonti, Medienberichterstattung, p. …).

Rigamonti Cyrill P., Walter Benjamin und das Urheberrecht. Zur Unterscheidung zwischen Original und Kopie, Kulturwissenschaftliche Zeitschrift (3) 2019, pp. 91–99 (cit. Rigamonti, Benjamin, p. …).

Rigamonti Cyrill P., Anmerkung zu "Trittligasse" Bezirksgericht Zürich vom 19. Mai 2021, sic! 2022, pp. 68–73.

Rigamonti Cyrill P./Bernasconi Antonio, La fotografia non originale nel diritto d'autore svizzero e comparato, Annali italiani del diritto d'autore, della cultura e dello spettacolo (AIDA), Vol. XXX–2021, Milan 2022, pp. 329–345.

Roberts John, Art after Deskilling, Historical Materialism (18) 2010, pp. 77–96.
Römer Stefan, Künstlerische Strategien des Fakes. Kritik von Original und Fälschung, Cologne 2001.
Rosati Eleonora, Not Sufficiently "Transformative" Appropriation of a Photograph Held Infringing by French Court, Journal of Intellectual Property Law & Practice (13) 2018, pp. 525–526 (cit. Rosati, Not sufficiently "transformative", p. …).
Rosati Eleonora, Why Originality in Copyright Is Not and Should Not be a Meaningless Requirement, Journal of Intellectual Property Law & Practice (13) 2018, pp. 597–598 (cit. Rosati, Why originality, p. …).
Rösch Perdita, Aby Warburg, Paderborn 2010.
Rose Margaret A., Parody/Post-Modernism, Poetics (17) 1988, pp. 49–56 (cit. Rose, Parody, p. …).
Rose Margaret A., Pictorial Irony, Parody and Pastiche. Comic Interpictoriality in the Arts of the 19th and 20th Centuries, Bielefeld 2011 (cit. Rose, Pictorial irony, p. …).
Ruedin Pierre-Emmanuel, La citation en droit d'auteur. Etude de l'art. 25 LDA dans son contexte constitutionnel et international, PhD Thesis, Basel 2020.
Sandmann Melanie, Die Strafbarkeit der Kunstfälschung, PhD Thesis, Augsburg 2003.
Said K. Zahr, Copyright's Illogical Exclusion of Conceptual Art, Columbia Journal of Law & the Arts (39) 2016, pp. 335–354.
Saunders David, Dropping the Subject: An Argument for a Positive History of Authorship and the Law of Copyright, in: Sherman Brad/Strowel Alain (eds.), Of Authors and Origins. Essays on Copyright law, Oxford 1994, pp. 94–110.
Schaar Elisa, Spinoza in Vegas, Sturtevant Everywhere, Art History (33) 2010–2012, pp. 886–909.
Schack Haimo, Kunst und Recht. Bildende Kunst, Architektur, Design und Fotografie im deutschen und internationalen Recht, 3rd Ed., Heidelberg 2017.
Schlüter Claudia, Die urheber- und persönlichkeitsrechtliche Beurteilung der Erstveröffentlichung persönlicher Aufzeichnungen, PhD Thesis, Baden-Baden 2014.
Schmidt-Gabain Florian, Recht der bildenden Kunst, in: Raschèr Andrea F.G./Senn Mischa (eds.), Kulturrecht – Kulturmarkt, Zurich 2012, pp. 131–136.
Schricker Gerhard/Loewenheim Ulrich et al. (eds.), Urheberrecht: UrhG, KUG, VGG: Kommentar, 6th Ed., Munich 2020 (cit. Author(s), UrhG Kommentar, N … *ad* § …).
Schulze Gernot, Die Aneignung fremder Werke für eigenes Werkschaffen, in: Mosimann Peter/Schönenberger Beat (eds.), Kunst & Recht 2016/Art & Law 2016. Referate zur gleichnamigen Veranstaltung der Juristischen Fakultät der Universität Basel vom 17. Juni, Bern 2016, pp. 39–58 (cit. Schulze, Aneignung, p. …).
Schulze Gernot, Gedanken zur freien Benutzung und zu einer allgemeinen Grundrechtsschranke am Beispiel Metall auf Metall, in: v. Lewinski Silke/Wittmann Heinz (eds.), Urheberrecht! Festschrift für Michel M. Walter zum 80. Geburtstag, Vienna 2018, pp. 504–519 (cit. Schulze, Gedanken, p. …).
Schulze Gernot, Die freie Benutzung im Lichte des EuGH-Urteils "Pelham", GRUR 2020 (cit. Schulze, Die freie Benutzung, p. …).
Senftleben Martin, Copyright, Limitations and the Three-Step Test. An Analysis of the Three-Step Test in International and EC Copyright Law, PhD Thesis, The Hague 2004 (cit. Senftleben, Copyright, p. …).
Senftleben Martin, Overprotection and Protection Overlaps in IP Law – The Need for Horizontal Fair Use Defences, in: Kur Annette/Mizaras Vytautas (eds.), The Structure of Intellectual Propery Law: Can One Size Fit All?, Cheltenham 2011, pp. 136–180 (cit. Senftleben, Overprotection, p. …).
Senn Mischa, Innovation als Schutzobjekt im Immaterialgüterrecht, KUR 2014, pp. 73–80 (cit. Senn, Innovation, p. …).
Senn Mischa, Wie aus einer Fotografie ein Bild wird, sic! 2015, pp. 137–154 (cit. Senn, Fotografie, p. …).

Senn Mischa, Die urheberrechtliche Individualität – eine methodische Annäherung, sic! 2017, pp. 521–537 (cit. Senn, Individualität, p. …).

Senn Mischa, Die Zweckänderung bei einer Grundform als Individualitätskriterium? Diskussionsbeitrag zum BGer vom 17. Juni 2022, 4A_482/2021 (sic! 2023, 44 ff., "Feuerring"), sic! 2023, pp. 211–219 (cit. Senn, Zweckänderung, p. …).

Serres Michel, The Parasite (1980) (transl. by Lawrence R. Schehr), Baltimore (MD)/ London 1982.

Sganga Caterina, A Decade of Fair Balance Doctrine, and How to Fix It, European Intellectual Property Review (11) 2019 (available at: <https://papers.ssrn.com/sol3/papers.cfm?abstract_id=3414642>).

Sganga Caterina/Scalzini Silvia, From Abuse of Right to European Copyright Misuse: A New Doctrine for EU Copyright Law, International Review of Intellectual Property and Competition Law (48) 2017, pp. 405–435.

Shafrir Tamar, Surgeon, Seamster, Sorcerer: The Embodied Practice of Collage, in: Feireiss Lukas (ed.), Radical Cut-Up. Nothing is Original, London 2019, pp. 211–226.

Sherman Brad, Appropriating the Postmodern: Copyright and the Challenge of the New, Social & Legal Studies (1) 1995, pp. 31–54 (cit. Sherman, Appropriating, p. …).

Sherman Brad, What is a Copyright Work?, Theoretical Inquiries in Law (1) 2011, pp. 99–121 (cit. Sherman, What is a Copyright Work, p. …).

Shore Robert, Beg, Steal and Borrow. Artists against Originality, London 2017.

Siri Jasmin/Möller Kolja, Systemtheorie und Kritik. Ein Interview mit Armin Nassehi, in: Möller Kolja/Siri Jasmin (eds.), Systemtheorie und Gesellschaftskritik. Perspektiven einer kritischen Systemtheorie, Bielefeld 2016, pp. 207–222.

Snijders Thom/van Deursen Stijn, The Road Not Taken – the CJEU Sheds Light on the Role of Fundamental Rights in the European Copyright Framework – A Case Note on the Pelham, Spiegel Online and Funke Medien Decisions, International Review of Intellectual Property and Competition Law (50) 2019, pp. 1176–1190.

Soentgen Beate, Am Rande des Ereignisses: Das Nachleben des 19. Jahrhunderts in Andreas Gurskys Serie "F1 Boxenstopp", in: Kunstmuseum Basel (ed.), Andreas Gursky: Kunstmuseum Basel, 20. Oktober 2007 bis 24. Februar 2008, Ostfildern 2007, pp. 49–68.

Sollfrank Cornelia, Performing the Paradoxes of Intellectual Property. A Practice-Led Investigation into the Increasingly Conflicting Relationship Between Copyright and Art, PhD Thesis, Dundee 2012 (copy available on request).

Sommer Brigitte I./Gordon Clara-Ann, Individualität im Urheberrecht – einheitlicher Begriff oder Rechtsunsicherheit?, sic! 2001, pp. 287–303.

Spence Michael, Rogers v. Koons: Copyright and the Problem of Artistic Appropriation, in: McClean Daniel (ed.), The Trials of Art, London 2007, pp. 213–233.

Stalder Felix, Urheberrecht – Wenn das Recht kunstfeindlich wird, Kunstbullettin (1–2) 2014, pp. 44–49.

Stokes Simon, Art and Copyright, 3rd Ed., Oxford/New York 2021.

Strowel Alan, Le droit d'auteur et le copyright entre histoire et nature, in: Gérard Philippe/ Ost François/Van de Kerchove Michel (eds.), Images et usages de la nature en droit, Bruxelles 1993, pp. 289–339.

Studer Peter, Zum (Kunst-)Werkbegriff im Urheberrechtsgesetz (URG), in: AXA Versicherung AG (ed.), Kunst & Recht, Schwerpunktthemen für den Kunstsammler, pp. 6–13.

Sturtevant Elaine, Sliding parameters of Originality, in: Salzburger Kunstverein (ed.), Original. Symposium Salzburger Kunstverein 15.10.–16.10.1993, Ostfildern 1995, pp. 140–145.

Stutz Robert Mirko, Das originelle Design: eigenartig genug, um individuell zu sein? in sic! 2004, pp. 3–13.

Subotnik Eva, Originality Proxies: Toward a Theory of Copyright and Creativity, Brooklyn Law Review (774) 2011, pp. 1487–1552.

Sutterer Moritz, Paris Embraces Modern Art – But Not in Court: Opinion on the Cour d'Appel de Paris Decision – *Jeff Koons v Frank Davidovici*, GRUR Int (71) 2022, pp. 131–138.

Teilmann-Lock Stina, The Object of Copyright: A Conceptual History of Originals and Copies in Literature, Art and Design, New York 2016.

Terzidis Kostas, Hybrid Form, Design Issues (19) 2003, pp. 57–61.

Teubner Gunther, "Global Bukowina": Legal Pluralism in the World Society, in: Teubner Gunther (ed.), Global Law Without a State, Dartmouth 1997, pp. 3–28 (cit. Teubner, Global Bukowina, p. …).

Teubner Gunther, Der Umgang mit Rechtsparadoxien: Derrida, Luhmann, Wiethölter, in: Joerges Christian/Teubner Gunther (eds.), Rechtsverfassungsrecht, Baden-Baden 2003, pp. 25–46 (cit. Teubner, Umgang mit Rechtsparadoxien, p. …).

Teubner Gunther, Selbstsubversive Gerechtigkeit: Kontingenz- oder Transzendenzformel des Rechts?, Zeitschrift für Rechtssoziologie (29) 2008, pp. 9–36 (cit. Teubner, Selbstsubversive Gerechtigkeit, p. …).

Teubner Gunther, Kritik der staatszentrierten Drittwirkung der Grundrechte am Beispiel des Publication Bias, Kritische Justiz (47) 2014, pp. 152–170.

Teubner Gunther/Fischer-Lescano Andreas, Cannibalizing Epistemes: Will Modern Law Protect Traditional Cultural Expressions?, in: Graber Christoph Beat/Burri-Nenova Mira (eds.), Intellectual Property and Traditional Cultural Expressions in a Digital Environment, Cheltenham 2008, pp. 17–46.

Thalmair Franz, Copying as Performative Research – Toward an Artistic Working Model, in: Kargl Michael/Thalmair Franz (eds.), Originalcopy. Post-Digital Strategies of Appropriation, Berlin 2019, pp. 348–353 (cit. Thalmair, Copying, p. …).

Thalmair Franz, Thinking in the Exhibition Format – Postproduction Notes on Originalcopy, in: Kargl Michael/Thalmair Franz (eds.), Originalcopy. Post-Digital Strategies of Appropriation, Berlin 2019, pp. 24–36 (cit. Thalmair, Exhibition Format, p. …).

Thampapillai Dilan, Creating an Innovation Exception? Copyright as the Infrastructure of Innovation, SCRIPTed (7) 2010, pp. 104–134.

Thouvenin Florent, Irrtum: Je kleiner der Gestaltungsspielraum, desto eher sind die Schutzvoraussetzungen erfüllt, in: Berger Mathis/Macciacchini Sandro (eds.), Populäre Irrtümer im Urheberrecht. Festschrift für Reto M. Hilty, Zurich 2008, pp. 61–73 (cit. Thouvenin, Irrtum, p. …).

Thouvenin Florent, "Love", Obergericht Zürich vom 7. Juli 2009 – Urheberrechtliche Schutzfähigkeit des Werkes "Love" und dessen Verletzung durch Verwendung auf Uhren, sic! 2010, pp. 889–900 (cit. Thouvenin, Love, p. …).

Torremans Paul L.C., Copyright (and Other Intellectual Property Rights) as a Human Right, in: Torremans Paul L.C. (ed.), Intellectual Property and Human Rights, 4th Ed., Alphen aan den Rijn 2020, pp. 245–280.

Towse Ruth, Creativity, Incentive, and Reward: An Economic Analysis of Copyright and Culture in the Information Age, Cheltenham/Northampton 2001.

Troller Alois, Immaterialgüterrecht, Basel 1968 (cit. Troller, Immaterialgüterrecht, p. …).

Troller Alois, Die Bedeutung der statistischen Einmaligkeit im urheberrechtlichen Denken, in: Merz Hans/Schluep Walter R. (eds.), Recht und Wirtschaft heute: Festgabe zum 65. Geburtstag von Max Kummer, Bern 1980, pp. 265–276 (cit. Troller, Bedeutung, p. …).

Tushnet Rebecca, Worth a Thousand Words: The Images of Copyright, Harvard Law Review (125) 2012, pp. 683–759.

Ullrich Wolfgang, "Gurskyesque". Das Web 2.0, das Ende des Originalitätszwangs und die Rückkehr des nachahmenden Künstlers, in: Nida-Rümelin Julian/Steinbrenner Jakob (eds.), Kunst und Philosophie. Original und Fälschung, Ostfildern 2011, pp. 93–113 (cit. Ullrich, "Gurskyesque", p. …).

Ullrich Wolfgang, Rituale der Wiederholung. Zum wiedererwachten Interesse zeitgenössischer Künstler an Formen der Kopie, in: Mensger Ariane (ed.), Déjà-vu?:

die Kunst der Wiederholung von Dürer bis YouTube, Bielefeld 2012, pp. 136–145 (cit. Ullrich, Rituale, p. …).

Vahrson Viola, Die Radikalität der Wiederholung: Interferenzen und Paradoxien im Werk Sturtevants, Paderborn 2006.

Verwoert Jan, Living with Ghosts: From Appropriation to Invocation in Contemporary Art, in: Feireiss Lukas (ed.), Radical Cut-Up. Nothing is Original, London 2019, pp. 139–159.

Vierkant Artie, The Image Object Post-Internet, 2010 (available at: <https://jstchillin.org/artie/pdf/The_Image_Object_Post-Internet_us.pdf>).

Vischer Frank, Neue Tendenzen in der Kunst und im Urheberrecht, in: Merz Hans/Schluep Walter R. (eds.), Recht und Wirtschaft heute: Festgabe zum 65. Geburtstag von Max Kummer, Bern 1980, pp. 277–289 (cit. Vischer, Neue Tendenzen, p. …).

Vischer Frank, Urheberrecht und bildende Kunst, in: Schweizerischen Vereinigung für Urheberrecht (ed.), 100 Jahre URG. Festschrift zum einhundertjährigen Bestehen eines eidgenössischen Urheberrechtsgesetzes, Bern 1983, pp. 251–262 (cit. Vischer, Urheberrecht, p. …).

von Büren Roland, Gedanken zum Werkbegriff in der Praxis des Bundesgerichts und im Entwurf für eine Totalrevision des schweizerischen Urheberrechtsgesetzes, GRUR Int 1985, pp. 385–392.

von Büren Roland et al. (eds.), Schweizerisches Immaterialgüter- und Wettbewerbsrecht – Urheberrecht und verwandte Schutzrechte, 3rd Ed., Basel 2014 (cit. Author(s), SIWR II/1, p. …).

Von Rosen Valeska, Interpikturialität, in: Pfisterer Ulrich (ed.), Metzler Lexikon Kunstwissenschaft, 2nd Ed., Stuttgart 2011, pp. 208–211.

Wallace Rachel, Framing the Issue: Avoiding a Substantial Similarity Finding, Washington Journal of Law, Technology & Arts (10) 2014, pp. 89–108.

Walravens Nadia, L'oeuvre d'art en droit d'auteur. Forme et originalité des oauvres d'art contemporaines, Paris 2005.

Walter Giulia, Der neue Art. 2 Abs. 3bis URG – Die Umkehrung des Urheberrechts?, sic! 2021, pp. 377–383.

Wandtke Artur-Axel/Bullinger Winfried, Praxiskommentar zum Urheberrecht, 5th Ed., Munich 2019 (cit. Author(s), PraxKomm UrhG, N … *ad* § …).

Weber Rolf H./Breining-Kaufmann Christine, Grundrechtsdimensionen im Urheberrecht? Zugleich Besprechung von: Christophe Geiger, Droit d'auteur et droit du public à l'information, Paris 2004, sic! 2005, pp. 415–420.

Wenzel Horst, The Reverent Gaze, in: Gumbrecht Hans Ulrich/Marrinan Michael (eds.), Mapping Benjamin. The Work of Art in the Digital Age, Stanford (CA) 2003, pp. 204–220.

Westkamp Guido, Two Constitutional Cultures, Technological Enforcement and User Creativity: The Impending Collapse of the EU Copyright Regime?, International Review of Intellectual Property and Competition Law (53) 2022, pp. 62–93.

Wielsch Dan, Zugangsregeln: Die Rechtsverfassung der Wissensteilung, Tübingen 2008 (cit. Wielsch, Zugangsregeln, p. …).

Wielsch Dan, Grundrechte als Rechtfertigungsgebote im Privatrecht, in: Vesting Thomas/Korioth Stefan/Augsberg Ino (eds.), Grundrechte als Phänomene kollektiver Ordnung, Tübingen 2014, pp. 119–157 (cit. Wielsch, Grundrechte, p. …).

Wielsch Dan, Relationales Urheberrecht: Die vielen Umwelten des Urheberrechts, in: Grünberger Michael/Leible Stefan (eds.), Die Kollision von Urheberrecht und Nutzerverhalten, Tübingen 2014, pp. 61–100 (cit. Wielsch, Relationales Urheberrecht, p. …).

Wild Gregor, Die künstlerische Darbietung und ihre Abgrenzung zum urheberrechtlichen Werkschaffen, PhD Thesis, Fribourg 2001 (cit. Wild, künstlerische Darbietung, p. …).

Wild Gregor, Von der statistischen Einmaligkeit zum soziologischen Werkbegriff. Zum 35-jährigen Publikationsjubiläum von Max Kummers "Das urheberrechtlich schützbare Werk", in sic! 2004, pp. 61–66 (cit. Wild, Soziologischer Werkbegriff, p. …).

Wild Gregor, Urheberrechtsschutz der Fotografie, sic! 2005, pp. 87–95 (cit. Wild, Urheberrechtsschutz, p. …).
Woodmansee Martha, On the Author Effect: Recovering Collectivity, Cardozo Arts & Entertainment Law Journal (10) 1997, pp. 279–292.
Zeller Christoph, Language of Immediacy: Authenticity as a Premise in Benjamin's "The Work of Art in the Age of Its Technological Reproducibility", Monatshefte (104) 2012, pp. 70–85.
Ziegert Klaus A., Soziologische Rechtsvergleichung als Vermittlung zwischen normativer und empirischer Rechtswissenschaft: eine Fallstudie, in: Becchi Paolo/Graber Christoph Beat/Luminati Michele (eds.), Interdisziplinäre Wege in der juristischen Grundlagenforschung, Luzerner Beiträge zur Rechtswisseschaft (LBR), Zurich 2007, pp. 31–61.
Zijlmans Kitty, Foreword, in: Francis Halsall (ed.), Systems of Art. Art, History and Systems Theory, Bern 2008, pp. 1–12.
Züllig Riccarda B., Die Behandlung von Plagiaten in der bildenden Kunst, AJP 2008, pp. 293–300.
Zumthor Paul, Concerning Two "Encounters" with Benjamin. The Reproducibility of Art, in: Gumbrecht Hans Ulrich/Marrinan Michael (eds.), Mapping Benjamin. The Work of Art in the Digital Age, Stanford (CA) 2003, pp. 142–146.
Zuschlag Christoph, Appropriation Art aus China und Japan? Song nan Zhang und Hiroyuki Masuyama, in: Isekenmeier Guido (ed.), Interpiktorialität: Theorie und Geschichte der Bild-Bild-Bezüge, Bielefeld 2013, pp. 205–217.

Annex

Annex 1

Swiss Federal Court decisions

The rulings of the SFSC can be found on the court's website (www.bger.ch). The decisions are divided into published decisions, which are the most important decisions of the SFSC (so-called "A-publications" or "DFC"; in German "BGE", in French "ATF" and in Italian "DTF"), and unpublished decisions. In the book, published decisions are cited as follows:

DFC 131 III 480 (*Schweizerzeit*), c. 2.1

The abbreviation DFC means that the decision is published in the official collection of SFSC decisions. The first number (here, "131") is the year of the decision. The year of the decision is calculated by subtracting 26 from the year of the decision (e.g. 131, 131 − 26 = 5: The decision was made in 2005). The Roman numeral indicates the legal field of the decision. The number "III" indicates decisions in civil law; before 1994, the number "II" indicated civil law decisions. The last number, in the example "480", corresponds to the first page of the decision in the official paper publication.

In the book, unpublished decisions are cited as follows:

SFSC 4A_78/2011 of May 2, 2011 (*Le Corbusier 2*), c. 1

The first number indicates the division of the SFSC that made the decision ("4" corresponds to the civil law division). The letter (here, "A") corresponds to the type of proceeding; in the example, it was an appeal in civil law. The letter "C" (also cited quite often in the book) refers to public law appeals to the SFSC.

To help the reader, the decisions are also given a name (e.g. *Schweizerzeit*). These decisions are mostly known under this name in Switzerland, but this does not apply to every decision. Finally, the paragraph is cited as "c. 2.1" or "c. 1". SFSC decisions are divided in considerations (in German: *Erwägungen*), numbered "1", "1.1", "1.1.1" and so on. When a consideration is too long, sometimes the page number is given, too.

Published (in chronological order)

DFC 85 II 120 (*Sherlock Holmes*)
DFC 88 IV 123 (*Lehrbuch*)
DFC 100 II 167 (*Späti Laden*)
DFC 101 II 102 (*Annabelle*)
DFC 105 II 297 (*Montre "Monsieur Pierre"*)
DFC 106 II 71 (*Kasperlifiguren*)
DFC 110 IV 102 (*Zierpuppen*)
DFC 113 II 190 (*Le Corbusier*)
DFC 113 II 306 (*Psychologie Dissertation*)
DFC 116 II 351 (*Medium*)
DFC 117 II 466 (*Sekundarschulanlage*)
DFC 120 IV 208 (*Lizentiatsarbeit*)
DFC 125 III 328 (*Niederhauser*)
DFC 127 III 26 (*Catalogue*)
DFC 130 III 168 (*Marley*)
DFC 130 III 714 (*Meili*)
DFC 131 III 480 (*Schweizerzeit*)
DFC 133 III 473 (*Pressespiegel*)
DFC 134 III 166 (*Arzneimittelkompendium*)
DFC 136 III 225 (*Guide Orange*)
DFC 140 III 616 (*ETH Dokumentenlieferdienst*)
DFC 142 III 387 (*Terrasse*)
DFC 143 III 373 (*Max Bill*)
DFC 147 IV 297 (*Klimaaktivismus*)
DFC 148 III 305 (*Feuerring*)

Unpublished (in chronological order)

SFSC 4C_448/1997 of August 15, 1998 (*Clown*)
SFSC 4C_86/2000 of June 13, 2000 (*Vaca lechera*)
SFSC 4C_120/2002 of August 19, 2002 (*Hobby Kalender*)
SFSC 4A_78/2011 of May 2, 2011 (*Le Corbusier 2*)
SFSC 4A_472/2021 of June 17, 2022 (*Feuerring unpublished*)
SFSC 4A_145/2024 of September 11, 2024 (*Feuerring 2*)

Annex 2

Cantonal Courts decisions

Switzerland has 26 cantons, with each its first instance and second instance courts. The administration of cantonal courts is competence of the cantons, so every canton has different nomenclatures for its courts and different classification methods for its decisions. Whether cantonal decisions are publicly available depends on the canton and on the type of proceeding. As a rule, these decisions are not publicly available but are published and discussed in specialized reviews, e.g. the sic! Zeitschrift für

Immaterialgüter-, Informations- und Wettbewerbsrecht (https://www.sic-online.ch/de/). In the following, we list the cited cantonal decisions to give a chronological overview to the readers.

Zurich Court of Appeal of June 30, 1983 (*Managertyp*)
Aargau Court of Appeal of July 31, 1990 (*Swissbase*)
Cantonal Court of Vaud of March 2, 1993 (*Zeitungsartikel*)
Civil Court of Canton Basel-City of January 24, 1995 (*Postkarte*)
Lucerne Court of Appeal of June 24, 1998 (*Watch Flemming I*)
Cantonal Court of St. Gallen of June 19, 2002 (*Mummenschanz*)
Lucerne Court of Appeal of February 5, 2003 (*Knoblauchpresse*)
Zurich Court of Appeal of July 7, 2009 (*Love*)
Zurich Court of Appeal of October 11, 2010 (*Source Code*)
Zurich Court of Appeal of May 24, 2012 (*Tunnels d'Arrissoules*)
Aargau Commercial Court of August 29, 2012 (*Nicolas Hayek*)
Zurich Court of Appeal of January 24, 2013 (*Bildungssoftware*)
Commercial Court of Aargau of January 5, 2015 (*Totenkopf-Tattoo*)
Basel-City Court of Appeal of May 20, 2016 (*Panoramabild*)
Basel-City Court of Appeal of October 31, 2018 (*Lichtgestalten*)
Zurich District Court of May 19, 2021 (*Trittligasse*)
Commercial Court of Zurich of January 25, 2022 (*Hotelrevue*)

Index